Karl Dändliker, E. Salisbury

A short History of Switzerland

Karl Dändliker, E. Salisbury

A short History of Switzerland

ISBN/EAN: 9783337173005

Printed in Europe, USA, Canada, Australia, Japan

Cover: Foto ©ninafisch / pixelio.de

More available books at **www.hansebooks.com**

A
SHORT HISTORY
OF
SWITZERLAND

BY

Dr. KARL DÄNDLIKER

INSTRUCTOR AT THE TRAINING COLLEGE
AND PROFESSOR AT THE UNIVERSITY OF ZURICH

TRANSLATED BY

E. SALISBURY

WITH TWO COLOURED MAPS

LONDON
SWAN SONNENSCHEIN & CO., LIM.
NEW YORK: THE MACMILLAN COMPANY
1899

CONTENTS.

	PAGE
TRANSLATOR'S PREFACE	ix
AUTHOR'S PREFACE	xi
INTRODUCTION	xiv
Literature and Books of Reference	xvi

FIRST PERIOD.

The Early History of Switzerland
(BEFORE 1218).

PART I.
THE MOST ANCIENT RACES AND THEIR STATE OF CIVILIZATION (DOWN TO 750).

1. The Celtic Population 1
2. The Roman Civilization 5
3. The Alamanni, Burgundians and Rhæto-Romans . . . 11

PART II.
UNION OF THE CONSTITUTION UNDER THE CARLOVINGIAN AND GERMAN RULE (750–1057).

1. Introduction of the Franco-Carlovingian Empire . 17
2. New Union under the Rule of the German Emperors . 21

PART III.
TERRITORIAL DIVISIONS (1057–1218)   25

SECOND PERIOD.

Rise and Development of the Swiss Confederation.

PART I.
ORIGIN OF THE CONFEDERATION (1218–1315).

1. The First Leagues (1218–1291) 37
2. Beginning of the Wars of Freedom (1291–1315) . . . 44

Part II.
GROWTH OF THE CONFEDERATION. EMANCIPATION FROM AUSTRIA AND FROM THE NOBILITY (1315-1400).

1. Commencement of the Federation of Eight States . . . 55
2. The War of Liberation between Austria and the Eight Original States 62
3. Nature of the Federal League 69

Part III.
SWITZERLAND AT THE HEIGHT OF HER POWER (1400-1516).

1. First Alliance with Adjacent Communities 74
2. The Strengthening of the Confederation during and after the old Zurich War (1436-1468) 84
3. Switzerland as a European Power 94
4. Internal Conditions 116

THIRD PERIOD.
Intellectual Progress and Political Stagnation of the Confederation
(1516-1798).

Part I.
THE ERA OF THE REFORMATION (1516-1600).

1. The Reformation in the East of Switzerland 126
2. The Reformation in Western Switzerland and its connection with Eastern Switzerland 146
3. The Growth of Civil and Intellectual Life . . . 150
4. The Counter-Reformation and its Effects . . . 157

Part II.
THE ERA OF RELIGIOUS WARS AND OF THE FORMATION OF ARISTOCRATIC CONSTITUTIONS (1600-1712).

1. Switzerland during the Thirty Years' War . . . 163
2. The Aristocracy and the Peasants' War . . . 169
3. Period of the Vilmergen Wars and of the Dominating Influence of Louis XIV. (1656-1712) 180

Part III.
PRESAGES OF MODERN TIMES (1712-1798).

1. Intellectual Regeneration 192
2. Political Ferments and Revolts 204

Contents.

FOURTH PERIOD.
Phases of the New Development
(1798-1874).

PART I.
THE REVOLUTION AND ATTEMPTED REORGANIZATION UNDER FOREIGN INFLUENCE (1798-1830).

1. The Invasion of the French, and the Helvetic Republic (1798-1800) . 211
2. The End of the Helvetic Constitution, and Peaceable Development under the Constitution of Mediation (1800-1813) . . . 229
3. The Period of Restoration (1813-1830) 237

PART II.
INTERNAL REORGANIZATION OR REGENERATION OF THE CANTONS AND OF THE LEAGUE (1830-1848).

1. The Remodelling of the Cantons 246
2. The Struggles between Radicals and Conservatives. Establishment of the Modern Federal State (1839-1848) 259

PART III.
THE CONSOLIDATION OF THE FEDERAL STATE AND PROGRESS OF MODERN TIMES (1848-1874) . . . 274

SYNOPTICAL TABLE OF THE HISTORY OF FEDERAL AFFAIRS . 295

CHRONOLOGICAL TABLE 298

INDEX 305

TRANSLATOR'S PREFACE.

HAVING been for some years engaged upon the Swiss State Papers preserved among the archives of the Public Record Office, it occurred to me that it would be of great interest to me in connection with that work, and possibly of some general use, to make an English translation of a thoroughly good and trustworthy history of Switzerland. Finding that Dr. Dändliker had published a short history of that country, as well as the larger one in three volumes, I decided (with the author's consent) to use the smaller work for the purpose, and have now completed the translation of the second edition, especially revised and annotated by Dr. Dändliker. I trust that it may help to arouse more interest among English readers in the past of the little land whose beauties are a never-failing source of pleasure to English travellers. The translation has been made in the spare moments of a busy life, and my only regret is that my knowledge of the subject has, I fear, been too limited to admit of my doing full justice to Dr. Dändliker's very excellent work.

My warmest thanks are due to the author for his hearty co-operation and helpful suggestions, especially in the matter of the Chronological Table (an abridged translation of that appended to the earlier edition), to M. Charles D. Bourcart, the Swiss Minister in London, for much valuable assistance in explaining knotty points, and to Mr. Hubert Hall of the

Translator's Preface.

Public Record Office, Secretary of the Royal Historical Society, through whose introduction I first undertook the work I have been doing for the Swiss Government, and without whose kindly counsel and encouragement the present translation would never have been attempted.

E. SALISBURY.

STREATHAM.

AUTHOR'S PREFACE.

FOR some time past my *Manual of the History of the Swiss People* has been practically out of print. But the completion of a greater undertaking, a history of Switzerland in three volumes, prevented both author and publisher from taking in hand the publication of a new edition. Meanwhile, the experience and practical observations necessary for the elaboration of this extensive work furnished welcome suggestions and new lights for a useful remodelling of the smaller book.

Author and publisher were agreed that certain radical alterations must be made. As a matter of fact, it has been in many parts entirely re-written. Many portions of less importance or less interest have been abridged to make room for the fuller treatment of the more valuable sections. The description of the conditions and constitutional position of the Middle Ages, in particular (§ 13), the tradition of the origin of the Confederation (§ 17), where the stories in the Chronicle of the White Book are given in full, the description of constitutional conditions in the fourteenth century (§ 23), and the history of the fifteenth century, have been essentially enlarged. The last-mentioned portion, in accordance with the larger work, is so arranged that the section containing the "First Advances beyond the Alps" is separated from the history of the Milanese expeditions at the commencement of the sixteenth century, and treated in a separate section (§ 27) in chronological sequence; the conquest of the Aargau is described in a special paragraph (§ 28), and the political movements in the interior at the time of the Covenant of Stans and of Hans Waldmann are similarly placed in chronological order (§ 33). Moreover, the causes of the old Zurich War (§ 29), and those of the Burgundian Wars (§ 32), are described in more detail according to the latest researches. The history of the fifteenth, and also that of the seventeenth and nineteenth centuries have been almost re-cast on the model of the larger work, and the last section (§ 78) in particular has been completely remodelled.

Moreover, it was desired to make the representation more life-like and vivid than was the case with the first edition, and this without losing the original character of the little book, which depended upon its concise form, a strict adherence to leading ideas and scientific arrangement of material, as well as a close interweaving of the history of politics with that of civilization. For this reason, for instance, care has been taken to describe our great battles of freedom, and also the struggles of the old Zurich War and of Milan, and the events of political wars in modern history, in detail. Here and there, especially in the history of the nineteenth century, one-sided judgments are modified and calmer consideration applied than in the larger work. Further, we aimed as far as possible at simplicity. Many useless quotations are therefore omitted, as well as the former tables,[1] and also the table of contents, unnecessary in a book of so small compass. The chronology seemed to us superfluous for the use of the work as a school-book; it is of more value if the pupil construct such a table for himself. On the other hand, a review of Federal affairs is given which may serve to illustrate these matters considerably. The references given in foot-notes to specially important or popular literature seemed to us desirable for the teacher and those desiring to pursue the subject; hence these are not shortened,

[1] An abridged chronological table has been added to the English translation.

but on the contrary increased in number where possible. Finally, the publisher has endeavoured to give the little book a better setting, and has fulfilled modern requirements by the use of Roman type and the new orthography.

Thus, although the framework as a whole remains the same, in detail the book is to a great extent new, and so justifies the new title desired by the publisher.

My special thanks are due to Professor Dr. Gerold Meyer, of Knonau, who has been kind enough to allow me the use of his own copy of the first edition, corrected by himself for educational purposes. Although I only received it after my manuscript had gone to press, and when some sheets were already in print, I was nevertheless able to utilize many of the corrections.

Let this little book, then, in its new garment, go forth among our schools and the public, and throw in its mite towards bringing home the history of the Fatherland to the hearts of both children and older folk!

THE AUTHOR.

INTRODUCTION.

SWITZERLAND unites within a limited area such a multitude of different natural forms, that it might be called the "Land of Contrasts." This is equally true of the Swiss people. The German, French and Italian nationalities occupy the territory between the Alps, the Jura and the Rhine; and among the Alpine valleys of the Grisons the last remains of the Rhæto-Romance race has survived. The astonished traveller often meets with German villages in the midst of Romance districts, or places which are half German and half Romance in origin. Every valley, almost every place, differs in dialect, character, customs and mode of life. Moreover, there are great contrasts between the states—the untrammelled native of the Alps side by side with the accomplished citizen, the artisan by the refined merchant, the toil-worn peasant by the thoughtful man of letters!

But the peculiarity of Switzerland lies not only in these contrasts, not only in this manifold diversity of country and people; these are, after all, not so very much greater or more marked than we find in other mountainous countries. Rather is it the unity which binds these contrasts together which forms the distinctive character of Switzerland. The Romance people live peaceably with their German brother-confederates, who, as pioneers of freedom, preponderating in numbers, more easily susceptible to the elements of foreign culture, form the connecting link which binds the nationalities of Switzerland into one harmonious whole. The citizens of all the states, too, labour unanimously towards the solution of problems affecting the Fatherland.

It is the common possession of quite peculiar political and

social institutions which forms the indissoluble cement uniting these otherwise heterogeneous elements. The French of western Switzerland, the Germans of eastern Switzerland, the Italians and the Romance people of Rhætia, all these hold in common the principles of the democratic state, which are nowhere else in Europe carried so perfectly and so uniformly into execution: the sovereignty of the people, popular legislation (in one form or another), a free communal system, political equality, the liberty of the press, of trade and manufacture, and of religious creed. Hence a common national feeling inspires and unites the Swiss of every state and of every nationality. The Frenchman of the Vaud, who was under the dominion of Berne until the beginning of the present century, feels himself no less a "*Suisse*" than the inhabitant of the original cantons feels himself a "*Schweizer*"; and oppressed as the dweller in Ticino formerly was under the bailiffs of the original cantons and of the Confederation, since 1798 he, nevertheless, as a good "*Svizzeri*," utters a hearty "*Evviva*" (hurrah!) to the "*Confederazione*" (Confederation).[1]

This unity of the Swiss people, amidst striking differences, is the product of centuries of living together and learning mutual toleration—the result of a common development; hence the deep significance which Swiss history has for the Swiss people. For that history shows the conditions which created this harmonious unity out of plurality, and the events which led first to the budding of liberty, then to the formation of the political league, and finally to the development of the Federal State, whose institutions make Switzerland the envy of many, by nature, richly endowed nations. For this reason Swiss history strengthens Swiss feeling; it not only has, like every other history, a scientific interest from the fact that it explains what already exists, but it warms every Swiss heart with enthusiasm for the interests and rights of the people, for the tasks and concerns of the whole Confederation.

[1] BERLEPSCH, *Schweizerkunde*, p. 524.

LITERATURE AND BOOKS OF REFERENCE.

For fuller information reference may be had throughout to the author's *Geschichte der Schweiz*, 3 vols., Zurich, F. Schulthess, 1884-1888. Further to the following works: Dierauer, *Geschichte der schweizerischen Eidgenossenschaft*, vol. i. (down to 1415), Gotha, Perthes, 1887. Vulliemin, *Histoire de la Confédération Suisse*, 2 vols., 1877; also in two German editions by J. Keller, 1882. Daguet, A., *Histoire de la Confédération Suisse*, 2 vols., 7th edition, 1879-1880; also in German by Hagnauer after the 6th edition of 1867. O. Henne-Amrhyn, *Geschichte des Schweizervolkes*, 3 vols., Leipzig, 1865. Of older works the following may still be partially used: Müscheler, *Geschichte des Schweizerlandes*, 1842, 2 vols. (down to 1516). L. Meyer von Knonau, *Handbuch der Geschichte der schweizerischen Eidgenossenschaft*, 2 vols., 1829; and Vögelin and Escher, *Geschichte der schweizerischen Eidgenossenschaft*, 4 vols.; as also Joh. v. Müller's *Schweizergeschichte mit ihren Fortsetzungen*. Shorter epitomes: Stiefel, *Pragmatische Geschichte der schweizerischen Eidgenossenschaft*, 1858; and Sal. Vögelin, *Lehrbuch der Schweizergeschichte*, 1872. Dr. Strickler, *Lehrbuch der Schweizergeschichte für höhere Schulen*, Zurich, Orell, Füssli & Co., 1874. Dr. W. Oechsli, *Lehrbuch für den Geschichtsunterricht (Vaterländische Geschichte mit 8 Karten)*, Zurich, 1885. Dr. B. Hibder, *Schweizergeschichte für Schule und Volk*, and many others. Of separate narratives and biographies containing Swiss history we have Geilfuss, *Helvetia*, and the excellent modern works, *Galérie Suisse, Biographies Nationales*, published by E. Secrétan, Lausanne, 1874. For a clear description of remarkable events based upon original sources, the following are to be recommended: Dr. W. Oechsli, *Quellenbuch zur Schweizergeschichte, für Haus und Schule*, Zurich, F. Schulthess, 1886. For geographical illustration the Historical Geographical Atlas of Switzerland, by J. C. Vögelin, G. v. Wyss and G. Meyer von Knonau (F. Schulthess), is indispensable. An excellent chronological aid is found in the *Chronologische Übersicht der Schweizergeschichte*, by J. K. Zellweger, in four editions, newly elaborated by Dr. J. Strickler, Zurich, Meyer & Zeller, 1887.

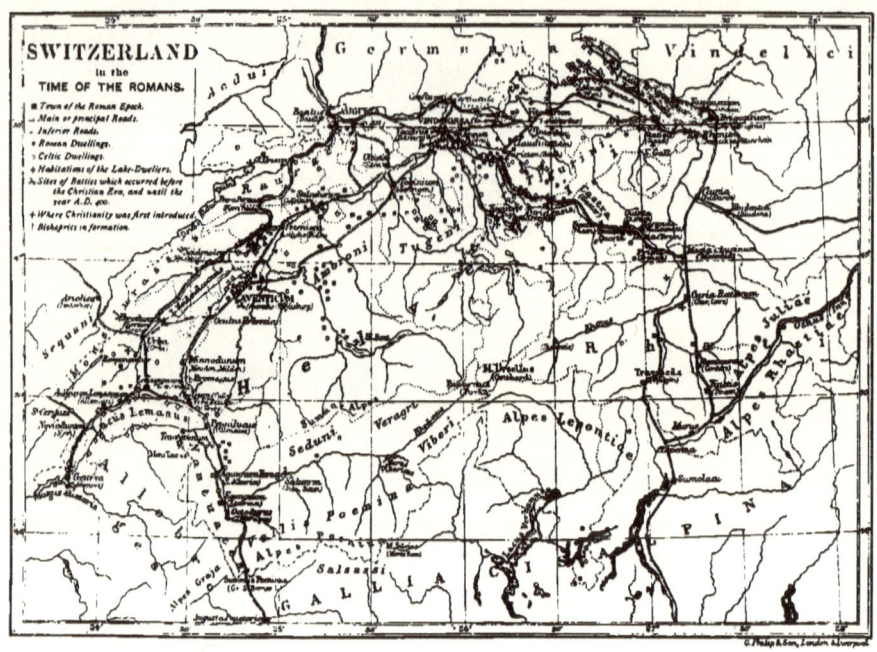

HISTORY OF SWITZERLAND.

First Period.
THE EARLY HISTORY OF SWITZERLAND.
(From the Earliest Times to the Commencement of the Wars of Freedom after the Extinction of the Zäringens, in 1218.)

PART I.
THE MOST ANCIENT RACES AND THEIR STATE OF CIVILIZATION.
(Down to the Beginning of the Carlovingian Period, about 750.)

1. THE CELTIC POPULATION.[1]

§ 1. **Primeval Period and Lake-Dwellings.** We have no information, nor even any tradition, to tell us when and how Switzerland was first peopled. But monuments and remains of hoary antiquity teach us that it was inhabited at the earliest time when mankind appears at all in Europe. Here, as in France and Belgium, human implements made of flint, together with the bones of mammalia long since extinct, such as the mammoth, reindeer, cave bear, &c., have been found in caves in many places, notably at Thäyngen, in Canton Schaffhausen. The nature of the country and the

---

[1] Ferdinand Keller, *Pfahlbauten* (*Mitteilungen der antiquarischen Gesellschaft in Zurich*). Abridged accounts in: Staub, *Die Pfahlbauten der Schweizerseen.* Gross, *Les Proto-helvètes.* Wartmann, *aus der Urzeit des Schweizerlandes* (*Neujahrsblatt von St. Gallen*, 1861). W. Gisi, *Quellenbuch zur Schweizergeschichte*, 1869. Troyon, *Les habitations lacustres.*

climate must in those days have been rude and inhospitable, as they now are in the extreme north, and men lived like the savages of to-day, dwelling probably mostly in caves ("Cave-Dwellers" or "Troglodytes"). But their origin, their fate, and their disappearance are wrapt in obscurity. Many centuries, possibly hundreds of thousands of years, must have elapsed after this before Nature assumed her present form. The first settlements, of the period when men took to fixed dwellings and began to seek a higher civilization, were the lake (or pile) dwellings, discovered about forty years ago.[1] Their existence is traced to the first thousand years before Christ. These dwellings were made of wicker-work, clay, and straw, and stood upon a row of piles driven firmly into the bed of the lake, and joined together by wooden planks. It is not quite clear whether these remarkable habitations were chosen by the inhabitants for the sake of fishing, or from the necessity of defending themselves against wild beasts and savage tribes. But a distinct picture of the mode of life of the inhabitants is handed down to us by the numberless utensils, implements, and animal and vegetable remains which have been found on the sites of such lake-dwellings deeply embedded under layers of peat or in the beds of lakes. Judging by these articles, the pile-builders had already taken the first step towards a higher civilization; they were no longer in the primitive condition of mere hunters and fishers, but already engaged in cattle-farming and agriculture; they kept oxen, sheep, goats and pigs; they planted barley, wheat and flax, and were at least acquainted with fruit-trees, if they did not cultivate them. For these purposes they used implements skilfully fashioned out of stone, bone, wood, and horn, such as knives, hatchets, chisels, awls, needles, &c. When they later, probably by means of barter, became acquainted with the metals, bronze and iron, they employed these more pliable and more durable materials, and could then make their implements much more perfect. By the

---

[1] The first discoveries of importance were made at Overmeilen, on the lake of Zurich, during the winter of 1853–54.

The Celtic Population. 3

pile-dwellings of the lakes of Neuchâtel and Bienne we find that this progress was first made in western Switzerland, which lay nearer to the advanced civilization of the Rhone district. In very early times, too, the lake-dwellers knew how to make excellent thread and cord, cloth and clothing out of flax and linen, and could mould cooking utensils, plates and dishes out of clay. Time perfected their skill; their household utensils became more numerous and more artistic, and soon ornaments and trinkets, such as rings and bracelets, brooches, hairpins, &c., came into use, which show that the necessaries of life and its customs were growing gradually more refined. Little by little men forsook these lake-dwellings (few of which seem to have been preserved even as late as the time of the Romans), and settled themselves on the mainland in the vicinity. Most of the pile-buildings were destroyed by fire, and many were forsaken in very early times, even before the discovery of metals.

§ 2. **The Celtic Tribes—The Helvetians.** We know no more of the name and descent of the population than we do of the period of the lake-dwellings. It seems to have belonged to the Indo-European race; and as the objects that have been found belonging to the epoch of the lake-dwellers bear a close resemblance to those discovered on the mainland in the tombs and ruins of a later period, which are undoubtedly Celtic (Gallic) in origin, it is thought that those older settlements may also be ascribed to that race. The Celts originally inhabited almost the whole of Middle and Western Europe, and also Switzerland, before they were driven out by the Romans and the Teutonic tribes; but the first certain information we have of those in Switzerland comes to us through Romans and Greeks of the two last centuries before Christ. A number of different tribes then occupied this land, by nature so varied in aspect: the Allobroges (around Geneva), the Sequani (around the lakes of Neuchâtel and Bienne, chiefly beyond the Jura), the Raurici (around Basle), the Rhætians, a mingled race of Celts and Etruscans, throughout the Alpine district of the south-east, as far as the lake of Zug, the upper lake of Zurich and the lake of Constance, the Veragri and Seduin in Valais. The most noteworthy are the Helvetians, who originally occupied southern Germany as far as the Main, besides central Switzerland, and whose power surpassed that of any other Celtic tribe. They were divided into almost independent tribes or counties (*Gaue*), such as those of the Tigorini, Verbigeni, &c., the county assemblies managing common affairs. In the possession of many elements of a higher civilization, such as gold coinage and the Greek alphabet, they were also, as Cæsar (later their conqueror) says, "the bravest people of the Gauls." At the commencement of the great German migration (with the invasion of the Cimbri and Teutons) they followed the general course towards the sunny south, and in the year B.C. 107, under their youthful leader, Divico, totally defeated the Romans at Aginnum (now Agen) on the Garonne,[1] and forced them to pass under the yoke. But failing to follow up their victory, they were forced to retreat, after the greater part of them had been defeated (B.C. 101), together with the Cimbri, by Marius in the plains of Lombardy.

The Celts did not remain independent much longer after this: the brilliant victory obtained by the Romans over the Cimbri and Teutons, and the gradual advance of the Roman eagles across the Alps, menaced their freedom; divided, scattered, and incapable of founding any durable state, they became an easy prey to the warlike conquerors of the world. The Romans had already found a footing at Geneva by conquering the country of the Allobroges, when the Helvetians, remembering the sunny lands of southern Gaul, wishing to avoid the continual aggressions made upon them by Teutonic hordes from the north, and also incited by their ambitious chief, Orgetorix, migrated afresh, under the leadership of Divico, on 28th March, B.C. 58, after having set fire to all their twelve towns and four hundred villages. Notwithstanding

[1] Not on the lake of Geneva, as has been hitherto accepted, owing to an erroneous reading.

their valiant resistance, they were defeated by Cæsar, then engaged in the conquest of Gaul, at Bibracte (Mount Beuvrais, west of Autun). The survivors were sent back home by him, as Roman subjects, to defend the Rhine frontier against the Teutons. In the following year Valais was brought into subjection by one of Cæsar's generals, and about forty years later the wild Rhætian tribes, who had frequently ravaged the valley of the Po, succumbed to the might of the Roman legions, and to the persistence of Drusus and Tiberius, the stepsons of the Emperor Augustus (B.C. 15).

The Celts of our land were thus subjected to the Romans, and their own national development was entirely arrested. They have left a durable heritage behind them, inasmuch as a number of places, which have now grown into flourishing towns, owe their origin to them, as for instance, Geneva, Lausanne, Avenches, Soleure, Zurich, Basle and Coire; many mountains and rivers also received their present names from them, as the Jura, Albis, Kamor and Sentis; the Rhine, Töss, Thur, Rhone and Reuss.

2. THE ROMAN CIVILIZATION.[1]

§ 3. **The Organization of the Country.** The Celts did not attain to any high or lasting degree of civilization; the neighbouring tribes of the Helvetians in especial eked out a miserable and unquiet existence, the Rhætians and Allobroges led a wild life of war and pillage; moreover, the country was as yet only partially cultivated, the valley of the Rhine towards the lake of Constance still consisting of wild and impenetrable forest and marsh land.

The Romans brought with them a more refined civilization, the product of southern soil. In the course of the conquest

---

[1] MOMMSEN, *Die Schweiz in römischer zeit* (*Mitteilungen der antiquarischen Gesellschaft*, voL ix., 1854). FERD. KELLER, *Römische Ansiedlungen* (*Mitteilungen der antiquarischen Gesellschaft*, vols. xii. and xv.). WARTMANN, *Die Schweiz unter den Römern*, im *St. Galler Neujahrsblatt*, 1862. G. V. WYSS, *Uber das römische Helvetien*, *Archiv fur Schweizergeschichte*, vol. vii.

the political and military organizations were formed as follows. The territory conquered by Cæsar and before his time formed a part of Gaul, while the country of the Allobroges was united to the province of Narbonne (Provence), that of the Sequani, Raurici and Helvetians to Belgian Gaul; the south-east, however, formed a part of the province of Rhætia, including what are now Bavaria and the Tyrol; the "Valais" (meaning "valley") was at first considered part of Rhætia, but afterwards formed a separate province on account of its isolated position. Every several territory had its own provincial governor; various subordinate officials came into the country to collect taxes and tolls and to command the garrisons. Custom-houses were established at all places of commercial importance on the frontiers, at Zurich (Turicum), St. Maurice, and other places. The conquered people were not, on the whole, oppressed, and the Romans did their utmost to accommodate their arrangements to existing conditions. The Helvetians, for instance, still, as hitherto, formed a separate community, as did the Allobroges and others, and the division into counties was preserved. Aventicum (Avenches) and Augusta Rauricorum (Basel-augst) both became towns after the Italian style; they had their own mayor and their municipal council; both were, like Nyon (Noviodunum), colonies with Roman rights; Octodurum (Martigny) had a purely civic constitution. Aventicum was still the chief town of the Helvetians, and its senate formed the central Helvetic authority.

The Helvetians soon took an active part in the development of the empire, but amid the disorders of the civil war after Nero's death (A.D. 68-69) they drew upon themselves a total defeat by embracing the cause of Galba: Alienus Cäcina, lieutenant-general of Galba's rival Vitellius, routed them at the Bözberg (near Baden), took Aventicum the capital, and put Julius Alpinus,[1] the leader of the revolt, to death; further chastisement was only averted by the persuasive eloquence

---

[1] The story of Julia Alpinula, his supposed daughter, rests upon a gross falsification of an inscription.

of Cossus, the Helvetic envoy. With this exception the vanquished peoples of the land seem to have enjoyed a peaceful quietude. The Romans were more concerned about military precautions towards the north than about the enjoyment of their supremacy. To this end a line of fortresses was constructed along the course of the Rhine (Arbon, Stein, Zurzach, Basel-augst, and others). The military centre was at Windisch (Vindonissa), which, situated at the junction of the Aar and the Reuss in the vicinity of the Rhine, formed a natural defence, and an excellent strategic centre. Out of the three legions which served to protect the frontier of the Upper Rhine of Gaul against the Teutons, one had their camp at Windisch. Military roads were made for military communication. Two of these led from Italy northwards, one over the great St. Bernard through Lower Valais, by Aventicum and Soleure to Basel-augst; the other over the passes of the Grisons to Coire, and through the Rheintal along the lake of Constance to Bregenz. They were united in the north by a road leading from Basel-augst through Windisch, over Winterthur (Vitudurum), Pfin (Ad fines) to Arbon and Bregenz. The garrisons and fortresses were mostly occupied by foreign troops.

This military organization soon underwent a change, as in the time of the Emperor Domitian or Trajan (about A.D. 100), when the adjacent territory beyond the Rhine nearly as far as the Danube was united to the Roman empire, and the frontier troops were also pushed forward. The land of the Helvetians was now free from troops for 150 years, and seems to have remained undisturbed by any war, a condition of things particularly favourable to the development of Roman civilization.

§ 4. **Roman Influence.** To meet the military requirements, workshops, inns and towns were established. The veterans (discharged soldiers) built themselves many villas or country houses after the Roman style, with splendid mosaics and frescoes, baths, &c. In Baden or Aquæ (Canton Aargau) public baths were established of great size and magnificence, which became much frequented. Romans betook themselves thither in numbers. The miserable conditions of the Celtic period vanished by degrees before Roman civilization; roads were made across the Alps, over the Julier, Splügen, Septimer, and St. Bernard; even across the wild forest and marsh land of the Rheintal and around the lake of Constance a passable and broad road was constructed by the energy of Rome. Commerce developed rapidly; various products found their way from the north of France and Germany through Switzerland to Italy, and the products of the country most esteemed by the Romans, such as cheese, wax, honey, pinewood, resin, &c., were likewise exported. The wares of the south were in return brought into the country, such as oil, oysters, and wine; and vineyards were planted around the lake of Geneva and in the Pays de Vaud. With Roman civilization their pompous state religion was also introduced, and the rude rites of the Celtic worship almost disappeared. Roman culture exercised a salutary influence even over the dispositions and habits of the people: the Allobroges now exchanged the sword for the plough, the predatory Rhætians adopted gentler habits, and conducted the traveller and his sumpter mule (whom they formerly would have robbed) peaceably across the mountains, or employed themselves in agriculture and Alpine farming. In the larger towns, such as Aventicum and Augusta, the Celts learned divers arts and crafts from their Roman masters.

Thus was the foundation laid of an entirely new development. Roman civilization took much deeper and more lasting root in what is now western Switzerland than it did further eastwards. The former lying in close proximity to the southern part of Gaul, which had become altogether Roman, Roman colonies sprang up, forming centres of culture. Here the manners of Rome were adopted, as also her arts and learning. Aventicum, about ten times as large as the modern Avenches, surrounded by walls, protected by between eighty and ninety towers, had an amphitheatre for gladiatorial contests, a theatre, a temple, a triumphal arch, a public gymnasium, trade guilds, and even an academy with Roman professors. The magnificent capitals of columns, friezes and ornaments which have been found there prove that they had attained to great perfection in Italian art. The Celtic language and customs, which the few colonists in eastern Switzerland were insufficient to expel, vanished in the west before those of Rome, and the Latin tongue took such firm root, that it withstood the storms of migration, and is still preserved, though in a modified form, in western Switzerland and Lower Valais, while the Roman culture of the eastern parts being but little disseminated and little developed, crumbled like a rotten edifice under the blows of the German conquerors.

§ 5. **The Fall of the Roman Power—Introduction of Christianity.** But the golden age of Roman civilization lasted barely a century and a half in Switzerland. As early as the third century the Roman empire began to totter before the advance of the hardy Teuton. Amid the universal ruin under Gallienus, about 260, the Alamanni, a Teutonic tribe, overran Switzerland, and burnt beautiful Aventicum to the ground, to lie thenceforth almost in ashes. The Romans were forced to cede the frontier of the Danube, and to withdraw behind the Rhine, and the old fortresses along the Rhine from Basel-augst to Arbon became once more Roman points of defence. Repeatedly destroyed, they were always rebuilt and fortified afresh (notably Oberwinterthur and Stein under Diocletian and Maximian about 300); several emperors (Constantine Chlorus, Julian, Valentinian I., and Gratian) achieved passing successes in their advances through northern Switzerland; public buildings, bridges and roads were from time to time repaired, and in 374 Basle, the "royal city,"[1] arose at the great bend of the Rhine. But no imperial hand could long protect the empire from the youthful daring of the Alamanni; the latter had already established themselves in Alsace and on the lake of Constance, and were striving for the possession of

[1] "*Königsburg.*"

Switzerland; the inhabitants fled in terror from their property, buried their most treasured possessions, hoping to enjoy them again in better days, or migrated to the south; the empire, meanwhile, divided and enfeebled, was sinking fast.

This period of the decline of the Roman empire was not without beneficent effects in other ways. As early as the second century Christianity, with its world-regenerating moral and religious principles, began to develop into the religion of the world; amid the universal decay, when all things seemed to totter, it became the anchor of hope to which thousands joyfully clung. By the many roads made by the Romans the trade of Gaul and Italy reached Swiss territory, beginning (A.D. 200-300) at Geneva, Valais, and Rhætia; an official Christian inscription has been found in Valais, dating from the year 377. From these districts Christianity penetrated into the interior, being chiefly propagated by legionaries, by whose instrumentality it probably reached Zurich from Italy by way of Rhætia. Bishoprics were soon established in the larger Roman towns, Geneva, Aventicum, Basel-augst, Windisch (afterwards Constance), Octodurum (Martigny), and Coire. But Christianity only gained the victory after many hardships and struggles, the natural clinging to an ancient faith and the power and might of the religion of the Romans forming obstacles hard to overcome. The Roman emperors necessarily looked upon Christianity as hostile to the state; their governors were enjoined to hinder its progress, and in the third century violent persecutions began. The most severe and extensive—that under Diocletian (303-304)—seems to have extended to what is now Switzerland, for Christian tradition tells of several martyrs of that time, mostly Christian legionaries, such as the "Thebans" St. Maurice and his fellows at St. Maurice, Ursus and Victor at Soleure, Felix and Regula at Zurich, all of whom firmly refused to sacrifice to idols, and were put to death amid excruciating tortures. The fame of these Christian martyrs surrounded the Christian churches of these places with a halo of sanctity, and gave a great impetus to the Christian church; without the lustre shed by the honoured martyrs, the ideal seeds of religious life sown by Christianity would hardly have survived the wild storms of this and the following periods.[1]

3. THE ALAMANNI, BURGUNDIANS AND RHÆTO-ROMANS.

§ 6. The Immigration and Settlement of the Teutonic Tribes. In the beginning of the fifth century the obstinate struggle between the Roman and the Teuton was finally decided entirely in favour of the latter. In order to defend the heart of the distressed empire, garrisons were withdrawn from the Rhine to Italy, and the Rhine frontier was thus left exposed. Consequently, when the great migration of tribes set in at the end of the year 406, pouring from Germany towards the south-west, the Alamanni crossed the Rhine on the night of New Year's Eve, as is said, and the wild storm of devastation ruthlessly swept away the last vestiges of Roman culture. In the succeeding years the Alamanni advanced nearly to the Rhætian Alps (Grisons), and by the middle of the century Roman supremacy was at an end in the north-east of Switzerland. Besides this territory, the Alamanni, like the Helvetians of former times, held the country between the Rhine and the Main, as also Alsace. Roman manners and the Roman tongue continued only in the rocky districts of Rhætia and in the south-west of Switzerland, being protected in the former by the mountains, and having taken deep root in the latter. But in neither of these parts was the Roman speech preserved in its purity; for while in Rhætia it mingled with the Celtic (Rhætian) tongue, in the south-west a Teutonic element was introduced by the Burgundians. These latter had followed in the wake of the Alamanni; in vain they had sought a new home on the banks of the Rhine, around Worms: their realm was laid waste by the Romans and the Huns; they sub-

[1] GELPKE, *Kirchengeschichte der Schweiz*, vol. i., 1856. *Die christliche Sagengeschichte der Schweiz*, 1862. LÜTOLF, *die Glaubensboten der Schweiz*, 1871. O. HUNZIKER, *zur Regierung und Christenverfolgung des Kaisers Diocletian*, 1868.

sequently pushed southwards, and in 443 received "Sabaudia" from the hands of Ætius the Roman, *i.e.*, Savoy as far as the lake of Geneva, Lower Valais and the south-eastern part of Vaud; they extended their territory considerably to the west and south, embracing Provence, Besançon and Langres; the Saane probably formed their eastern boundary. The Burgundians drove the Alamanni out of west Switzerland eastwards. The kingdom flourished under King Gundobad, who in the year 500 thrust out his brother and ruled alone, and who sought by wise laws to civilize his people and to amalgamate them with the Romans.

The Alamanni and Burgundians met with very different conditions in their new land, and established themselves in quite different ways. During their fierce struggles of almost two centuries, the Alamanni had conceived a deep hatred of the Romans. At the time of their conquest the population was thin, and civilization at a low ebb; thus they were free from all Roman influence, and might settle down in their own fashion. They therefore took possession of the already Christianized land as pagans, sword in hand, effaced almost every trace of Roman civilization which still existed, and killed or enslaved the former inhabitants. They thus fully established a purely German mode of life, which has continued to this day. Their settlements were made altogether in old German style: relatives, families, and individuals settled wherever they pleased, attracted by some spring, field, or forest. They scorned to live like Romans in towns and attached houses, preferring open villages and hamlets, or better still scattered farmsteads, where each man surrounded his dwelling with a court-yard and a hedge (then called an "*etter*"), such as may yet be seen in Appenzell and Toggenburg. The name of the first founder of the farmstead was afterwards transferred to the place itself, hence the many place-names derived from the names of persons or families ending in *wiler*, *wil*, *hofen*, *hausen*, &c.[1]

---

[1] From *weiler*, a hamlet, *hof*, a farm, and *haus*, a house: *e.g.*, *Bärentswil* (from *Berolteswilare*), *i.e.*, "Berolt's hamlet"; *Wädenswil* (from *Wadineswilare*),

With the Burgundians it was quite different. These latter stood in more friendly relations to the Romans than did the Alamanni; they obtained their land by a formal treaty, and shared it also peaceably with a number of Romans, the Burgundians receiving two-thirds of every house or farm, and of all arable lands and servants. In west Switzerland they were confronted by a far more fully developed civilization, respected and esteemed Roman ways, lived together in Roman fashion in enclosed towns or boroughs, and were soon merged into one nation with the Romans, as had been the case with the Franks, thus forming the basis of the Romance or French character.

But in spite of these important differences, the two races had certain political and social principles and institutions in common, such as the systematical division of "districts" and "hundreds" (*centenæ*), the legal constitution (Wergeld),[1] popular assemblies, and the divisions of rank, viz., **freemen**, subdivided into nobles (*primi*), landowners (*medii*), and freemen without land (*minoflidi*); **freedmen** (*liti*), and **serfs** or **bondmen**; as well as affairs relating to the community in general, the **Almend,**[2] **Mark,**[3] and the **Markgenossenschaft.**[4]

§ 7. The Supremacy of the Franks, and the Spread of Christian Culture.

The development of this new state was by no means free and unrestrained, the Teutonic peoples soon

"Wadin's hamlet"; *Volketswil*, "Volkart's hamlet," &c. As also, *Dänikon*, originally *Tanninghofen*, "at the farms of Tanno's descendants"; *Ellikon* (from *Ellinghofen*), "the farms of the descendants of 'Allo' or 'Ello'"; *Ottikon* (from *Ottinghofen*), *i.e.*, "the farms of the Ottingers"; *Uerikon* (from *Uringhofen*) *i.e.*, "farms of the Uringers"; *Gütikhausen* (from *Guotinghusen*), "at the houses of the Guotings"; *Irgenhusen* (from *Iringeshusa*), *i.e.*, "at the house of Iring."— S. MEYER, *die Ortsnamen des Kantons Zürich ;* MEYER VON KNONAU, *Alamannische Denkmäler* (*Mitteilungen der antiquarischen Gesellschaft in Zürich*).

[1] *i.e.*, the fine which a murderer was obliged to pay to the kindred of his victim. This was regulated according to the rank of the person injured; a higher "Wergeld" was set upon freemen than upon serfs, and the clergy and nobles were more highly valued than ordinary freemen.

[2] Undivided land surrounding a settlement.

[3] The boundary between two settlements.

[4] The "Association of the Mark."—E. S.

turned their arms against one another, and another Teutonic race, the Franks, succeeded, by their own energy and by a skilful use of their opportunities, in gaining the supremacy over the others. The Alamanni were first overthrown by Clovis, in 496, in a battle on the Upper Rhine.

Internal dissensions soon brought about the fall of the Burgundians.[1] Notwithstanding the zealous efforts of the Roman Catholic clergy, the Burgundians obstinately adhered to their Arian faith, Gundobad declaring emphatically that he "would not have two gods."[2] The dispute became keener, when after the conversion of the Frankish king Clovis to Catholic Christianity, after the battle against the Alamanni, the Roman Catholics fixed their hopes upon this enterprising prince; and Gundobad's own son Sigismund went over to the Catholics. Clovis made encroachments even in Gundobad's time, and after the death of the latter in 516 the confusion increased, and in 532 the sons of Clovis completely routed the Burgundians in the battle of Autun. Some years later, in 536, Coire-Rhætia was ceded to the Franks by the Ostro-Goths, to whose empire it had belonged, and the Merovingians now reigned supreme throughout Switzerland.

The Franks encouraged the continuance of native institutions. Coire-Rhætia remained as before subject to a *präses* chosen by the people as chief magistrate and administrator, and from the end of the sixth century for a period of almost two hundred years this office remained hereditary in the hands of the family of the so-called Victorides, who even acquired the bishopric of Coire; and the customs of Coire-Rhætia remained undisturbed. Burgundy, too, had its own organization and administration. The Alamanni likewise retained their dukes and their national rights; these were, however, renewed and extended, in accordance with Christianity, at the beginning of the eighth century under Clotaire IV., king of the Franks,

---

[1] Binding, *Das burgundisch-romanische Königreich.* Jahn, *Geschichte der Burgundionen.*

[2] Because according to Catholic teaching Christ was a Divine Being, who had existed from everlasting, equal with God the Father, while according to Arianism he was dependent upon God the Father and subject unto Him.

and were greatly expanded in favour of the church. The Franks also introduced the county system and royalties.

At this period of the supremacy of the Franks, the propagation of Christian culture divides itself naturally among the three races. In this respect western Switzerland once more had the advantage over the eastern parts, as had been the case in the time of the Celts and Romans. For by its position Burgundy was naturally the first to feel the impulse given to Catholic Christianity in Gaul. Soon after St. Martin had introduced a great revival into the monastic life of Gaul, about the year 500, the two brothers Romanus and Lupicinus arrived in the wooded mountains of the Jura, and led there a life full of strict self-denial and earnest meditation. Romanus probably gave rise to the foundation of the famous monastery of Romainmotier (Canton Vaud). The sister foundation of Condat in the French Jura (St. Claude) was a nursery of cultured life; from it, "as from a beehive," says the biographer of Romanus, "sped hosts of missionaries and teachers in all directions," brought the land under cultivation, founded monasteries and schools, and encouraged learning. Beside Condat and Romainmotier there flourished the monastery of St. Maurice in the Valais, founded by a bishop in honour of the "Thebans," and enlarged in 515 by the Burgundian king Sigismund. Octodurum (Martigny) and Aventicum had hitherto formed the centre of church life; when, however, Aventicum fell into decay, the seat of the bishopric was removed to beautiful Lausanne (about 580), and that of Martigny to Sion. Bishop Marius, who conferred this favour upon Lausanne, encouraged Roman education, and found time in the midst of other labours to write a chronicle; it was he, too, who laid the foundation of the town of Payerne.

The Frankish kings and their clergy did their utmost to spread Christianity among the Alamanni. According to a somewhat doubtful tradition, St. Fridolin is said to have gone as a missionary to Alamannia, under the protection of Clovis himself; he founded Säckingen, and the Tal Glarus, which was soon united to Säckingen, honours him as its patron saint.

The greatest influence over the Alamanni was exercised by Irish monks, who devoted themselves to their missionary labours with youthful enthusiasm and heroic self-sacrifice. Columban and his fellows, driven out of Gaul, came to the lake of Zurich about 610. With fervent zeal he disturbed the pagans at Tuggen in the midst of their sacrifice, barely escaped being stoned to death, and proceeded to Arbon and Bregenz, Roman stations on the lake of Constance, where he found Christians already, and a Christian minister in the midst of the heathen. Here, too, excess of zeal against pagan rites brought him and his companions into great peril; Columban escaped into Italy; Gallus, one of his disciples, remained behind on account of sickness, built himself a cell, in 614, on the wilds of Steinach, regardless of danger, gathered disciples, and thus formed an oasis in the desert. Afterwards, in 720, Othmar founded on the spot the Benedictine monastery of St. Gall, destined to become a beacon of Christian culture illuminating the land. The activity of Columban and his companions had a far-reaching effect, extending as far as western Switzerland and Rhætia; disciples and followers from both those parts founded the monasteries of Granval in the Bernese Jura, St. Ursanne on the Doubs and Dissentis in the valley of the Upper Rhine. Pirminius, a native of the Grisons mountains, founded Pfäffers (720), Reichenau, &c. And such foundations were everywhere followed by cultivation of land, clearing of forests, and encouragement of learning. The ecclesiastical organization of Alamannia had also by this time become more settled. After the decay of Vindonissa, Constance became the ecclesiastical centre of north-eastern and central Switzerland. And the more Christianity was favoured by those in authority, so much the more the ground gave way under the feet of paganism.

PART II.

UNION OF THE CONSTITUTION UNDER THE CARLOVINGIAN AND GERMAN RULE.
(750-1057.)

1. INTRODUCTION OF THE FRANCO-CARLOVINGIAN EMPIRE.

§ 8. **The Carlovingian Rule.**—The Merovingians soon proved unequal to the great task of governing their realm; they were mostly incapable weaklings, and the kingdom fell to pieces. The German family of Carlovingians, which originally held only the rank of mayors of the palace, thereupon rose more and more into power, and in 751 dispossessed the Merovingians. The new dynasty abolished the dukedom of Alamannia, and took the country under their immediate control. The same alteration took place with regard to Burgundy and Coire-Rhætia, and thus about 800 our whole land became a province and an integral part of the empire of Charles the Great (Charlemagne).

The uniform organization which was now introduced into every one of the different parts furthered a general development and cohesion. The whole land was still divided into counties according to older local institutions. The most important counties were: Thurgau (comprising north-eastern Switzerland), Zürichgau, Aargau, Augstgau, Vaud, Valais, Coire and Geneva. The counts were royal governors, who administered justice and mustered troops in the king's name. The feudal system also now came into existence. In Rhætia, too, bishops and counts gathered around themselves a following of liegemen, to whom they granted lands, privileges and offices, and who in their turn had their own servants and vassals. Charles alone was able to avert the fatal results of this system. It is chiefly after his time that the influential position of the church becomes noticeable. The clergy gradually acquired great temporal riches by donations and enfeoffments;

Charles assigned them tithes as a source of regular income. He specially favoured bishops; the bishops of Coire and Basle were befriended by him; by the help of Charles, the bishop of Constance was enabled to maintain his claims against the monastery of St. Gall, which had been obliged to resist the pretensions of the bishops even in the time of Pepin: St. Gall was now forced to pay a yearly tribute to Constance, in token of dependence. Charles also encouraged the clergy in their custom of living together (canons); the management of the Institute of Canons (*Chorherrenstift*) of Zurich seems to have been settled by his orders, and the canons of the Grossmünster always thenceforth honoured him as their patron, and even (erroneously) as their founder. Zurich tradition, however, rightly reveres him as the first founder of the cathedral school or *Carolinum*, and has kept his unbounded administrative activity in well-deserved remembrance. Tradition speaks of a house called the "House of the Hole" ("*Zum Loch*"), where a snake begged for his aid against a toad, and to this day the statue of the incomparable emperor adorns the Grossmünster, with the sword of justice on his knees, like a patron protecting the town. His grandson, Louis the German, afterwards, in 853, founded the abbey in Zurich called the "Fraumünster," and bestowed upon it his estates in the little canton of Uri, and many other possessions.

At Charles's instigation a life of learning was roused into activity in the religious houses and everywhere among the clergy. Bishop Hatto, of Basle, issued orders commanding priests to collect books; the monastery of Reichenau had already a considerable library, and was in a very flourishing condition. At this time agriculture, trade and commerce also made great progress under the splendid legislation and excellent administration of the emperor. The position of freemen was protected, and the nobility were kept in check.

§ 9. Political Dissolution after Charles the Great. Revival of Learning.

Thus Switzerland also benefited by the many-sided creative and organizing activity of the emperor. But after his death in 814 the uniform administration collapsed, and manifold differences arose.

The county system was dissolved. The counties became hereditary fiefs in the hands of powerful families; numerous episcopal and monastic churches received "immunity" or freedom from the jurisdiction of courts, and established their own courts of justice, as St. Gall, Pfäffers, the "Fraumünster" of Zurich, Coire, &c. A reaction against enforced uniformity also set in on the part of the various races and divisions of the empire. The immediate result of this reaction was the division of the empire by the Treaty of Verdun in 843; the present German or Alamannian Switzerland, with Coire-Rhætia, went to Louis the German and his empire of the East Franks; western Switzerland and Valais to Lothaire and his "Middle Empire," and afterwards to the empire of the West Franks. Thus Burgundy and Alamannia remained for a long time separate, and soon formed themselves into separate states. In the confusion caused by the fall of the Carlovingian dynasty, Burgundian Switzerland came into the Guelf family, and Rudolf I. succeeded in establishing himself as an almost independent prince in the country between the Jura, the lake of Geneva and the Alps. In January, 888, he was made king at St. Maurice of a realm extending as far as Basle. Fierce struggles in Alamannia were followed by a like result. Count Burkhard of Rhætia, aspiring to become a duke, was prevented by two ambitious officers of the Thurgau exchequer, Erchanger and Berchtold, and by Salomon III., the crafty bishop of Constance and abbot of St. Gall, and was slain at a diet in 911. His young son of the same name profited by a dispute between the bishop and the officers of the exchequer to make a faction for himself, and finally obtained the ducal rank in 917, the officers having been overthrown by the bishop. Thus arose the dukedom of Alamannia or Suabia, which lasted till the thirteenth century.

The people suffered much at this time. Not only did the neighbouring predatory peoples of the Hungarians and Saracens (the latter from the south of France) begin to make raids upon the land, to penetrate into towns, villages and monasteries, to devastate the fields and interrupt traffic, but among themselves feuds and civil wars raged. The haughty nobles strove one against another, and the peasants were unprotected. The condition of the freemen became worse and worse; they either yielded themselves as vassals or copyhold tenants to some temporal or spiritual lord, or else became bondmen and freedmen of the nobility. A powerful aristocracy was gradually developed.

During this dissolution of political conditions, about the end of the ninth and the beginning of the tenth century, ecclesiastical learning developed greatly. The more wealthy monasteries of Reichenau, Rheinau, St. Gall and Zurich, which had become independent domains, cultivated the intellectual life which had been awakened in the time of Charles the Great. The monastery of St. Gall specially distinguished itself. It set itself free from all dependence upon the bishops of Constance, and the monastery itself was rebuilt in magnificent style (830 to 835).[1] It included about forty buildings, for besides the actual monastic accommodation it contained wide-stretching domestic buildings, bakehouses, breweries, mills, various workshops, &c., and so formed a small town in itself. From thence the abbots zealously cultivated intellectual life. There were two schools, an inner school for monks and an outer for the laity. The discipline is said to have been so exemplary, that when King Conrad I. visited the monastery, and tempted the young scholars during their exercises with gold pieces and apples, they would not even glance at them. Eminent teachers, such as the famous singer and composer, Notker the Stammerer or the Saint, Ratbert of Zurich, the historian of the monastery, and Tutilo, the great master-sculptor, laboured here. The ancient classics were read; boys learnt to make

---

[1] F. KELLER, *Bauriss des Klosters St. Gallen*, Zurich, 1844. RAHN, *Geschichte der bildenden Künste in der Schweiz*, vol i., pp. 88-96. GELPKE, *Kirchengeschichte der Schweiz*. WARTMANN, *St. Gallen unter den ersten Karolingern* (*St. Galler Neujahrsblätter*).

extempore Latin hexameters and pentameters, and were taught to play stringed instruments. All the arts and sciences were taught and cultivated; here the study of the German language received a powerful stimulus, and here the first German celestial globe was finished. St. Gall was also the school of music and song of that age; it produced numerous compositions for the service of the mass, and a contemporary historian writes that St. Gall had filled the church of God with brightness and joy, not only in Alamannia, but in all lands from one sea to another, by his hymns, songs and melodies. Writing and painting became high arts at St. Gall. These arts were cultivated quite like manufactures—some made parchment, others drew lines; some wrote, while others again illuminated and painted the titles and initial letters with magnificent ornament; others bound the books in covers, which were often adorned with beautiful carved work in ivory, silver and gold. Such perfection was attained nowhere else in all these arts and sciences, and the influence of St. Gall in this respect extended to the monasteries of Rheinau, Reichenau and Pfäffers.

In striking contrast to Alamannia, Burgundy remained for centuries later intellectually dead; the rude and warlike nobility reduced the kingdom to a state of confusion, which has enveloped the history of that land in a profound obscurity. Alamannia and the German element, therefore, took the lead in the development of our land. The influence of this German element was considerably increased by the rule of the German emperors, which now also united Burgundy with Alamannia and Coire-Rhætia.

2. NEW UNION UNDER THE RULE OF THE GERMAN EMPERORS.[1]

§ 10. **Incorporation into the German Empire.** From the time when Henry I. united the German races into one permanent empire, in 919, the whole of the present Switzer-

[1] G. v. WYSS, *Geschichte der Abtei Zürich* (*Mitteilungen der antiquarischen Gesellschaft*, vol. viii.). STÄLIN, *Würtembergische Geschichte*, vols. i. and ii. (new edition).

land and Burgundy, as also Alamannia and Rhætia, became closely united to Germany; and at the same time the several parts were more firmly attached to one another. Burkhard I. of Alamannia, count of Zurich and of Coire-Rhætia, was the first to yield voluntarily to the success in arms of Henry I. (920); he surrendered himself and his land to the German monarch; Henry, however, contented himself with the position of chief feudal lord, and allowed Burkhard to keep his dukedom. From that time the dukedom of Suabia became an integral part of the German empire. The emperor Otto I. afterwards (948) made his son Liudolf duke of Alamannia and count of Coire-Rhætia. Liudolf's successor, Burkhard II., was related to Otto, and that emperor often visited the present Swiss territories.[1] The succeeding dukes remained in close friendship or relationship with the imperial house, and the emperor in return often stayed in German Switzerland, especially in Zurich. Henry II. held imperial diets at Zurich in 1004 and 1018, and tradition (probably with truth) attributes the foundation of the cathedral of Basle and the golden altar-piece to the liberality of Henry II. and his consort Kunigunde.[2]

Burgundy, too, came under German influence. Rudolf II. pressed his conquests beyond the lake of Zurich, but was there encountered by Burkhard I., and defeated at Winterthur in 919. They made terms of peace, however, and Burkhard's daughter Bertha gave her hand to King Rudolf. This marriage formed a bond of union between east and west Switzerland; with Bertha the German territory in upper Aargau was annexed to Burgundy. The alliance must have become still more effective when Burgundy shortly afterwards came under the dominion of Germany. For Conrad, the young and feeble son of Rudolf II., was placed in 940 by the nobles of Burgundy under the protection and guardianship of Otto I.; and ten years later Otto married Conrad's sister,

---

[1] *Mitteilungen der antiquarischen Gesellschaft in Zürich*, iv., 1840.

[2] WACKERNAGEL, *Mitteilungen der Gesellschaft für vaterländische Altertümer zu Basel*, No. 7, 1857.

the beautiful and famous Adelaide, Bertha's daughter, queen of Italy. These two women, Adelaide and Bertha, are held in lasting remembrance in Burgundy; the former strove to restore the peace af Burgundy, disturbed by intestine troubles, and Bertha was the "Guardian Angel" of the people at a time when internal feuds were raging, and the enemies already alluded to were making predatory inroads; she is said to have founded the religious house at Payerne (962). Tradition represents her as spinning (like the goddess Freya), and all that was beautiful and good in antiquity is ascribed to her, the honoured mother of her country, the promoter of good works and holiness.[1] Later generations lamented bitterly "the times are no more when Bertha span." Succeeding kings of Burgundy undertook nothing without the advice and consent of the German emperor.

It now only remained to incorporate Alamannia and Burgundy entirely into the German empire. Rudolf III. of Burgundy (993-1032) was a feeble, bigoted prince, who relied upon the church for support against the encroachments of the nobles, and bestowed lands and privileges upon it with so liberal a hand, that he was forced at last to look to the alms of the bishops for his own maintenance. Being more and more oppressed by the nobles, who wished to depose him, the government became a burden to him, and he took refuge with his sister's son, the German emperor Henry II., who already had designs upon Burgundy, and appointed him as his heir and successor. Henry, however, could only establish his authority by force of arms; what he was unable himself to achieve was completed by his successor, Conrad II. ("*der Salier*," or the "Salic"), who advanced with his victorious army as far as Morat and Neuchâtel, had himself made king and crowned at Payerne in 1033 after the death of Rudolf III., and received general recognition in the cathedral at Geneva. In 1038, at Soleure, he conferred Burgundy upon his son Henry amid the rejoicings of the people. In the same year he also ceded to this son Alamannia and Rhætia, and thus

[1] G. v. Wyss, *über die Quellen zur älteren geschichte der Schweiz.*

almost the whole of the present Switzerland came under German rule. Henry III. (1039-1056) managed his affairs personally as far as possible; he visited Basle and Zurich, staying in the latter town at six different times; he took these opportunities to hold diets, and to settle important national matters. By provisions made at diets held at Soleure, he subdued Burgundy with a strong hand, where, owing to the avarice and arrogance of the nobles, club law (*Faustrecht*) had prevailed.

§ 11. **Intellectual Progress in the Monastery of St. Gall.** The attention which the German emperor paid to this country was of no little benefit to the religious foundations, which became centres of intellectual life. At this time our land possessed a number of master minds, and was in the forefront of learning among German lands. St. Gall formed an educational school for the whole of Germany. Ekkehard I. (*ob.* 973), from Toggenburg, the head of the inner monastic school, cultivated German poetry (*Walthari-Lied*) under the patronage of Otto I. Ekkehard II., his nephew (*ob.* 990), was the most renowned scholar of his time; he instructed Hedwig, Duchess of Alamannia, in the classics at the castle of Hohentwiel, and Otto appointed him as tutor to his son. Notker III. (or Labeo the "Thick-lipped," *ob.* 1022) distinguished himself in almost every branch of learning, especially in the knowledge of languages and philosophy; he interested himself in German, wrote both poetry and prose in that language, and translated the most notable works of classic literature and portions of the Bible into German. His pupil, Ekkehard IV. (*ob.* 1056), at one time the head of the school of St. Gall, then of the cathedral school in Mayence, and the historian of St. Gall, was likewise master of all the knowledge of his time, and was held in high honour by the imperial court; the emperor's sister-in-law was once so charmed with his song that she placed her own ring upon his finger. St. Gall, however, did not long continue the only educational centre; it was eagerly followed by Reichenau and Constance, and more notably by the monastery of Einsiedeln, which, built in the tenth century upon the spot hallowed by the sufferings of St. Meinrad, and raised to eminence by the favour of the ducal family of Alamannia and of the German imperial court, cultivated the arts and sciences in its famous school.

An important event of this period was the advance of the German population. From the eleventh century we find Germans in great numbers in Romance territory; the Rhætian aristocracy, the ruling class, was chiefly formed of Germans (German names of castles and German records have been found even in completely Romance valleys of the Rhine district.[1]) In like manner the German population advanced to the south-west; the Bernese Oberland, Engelberg, &c., were now eagerly colonized from Alamannia, and later on Upper Valais was also peopled and settled by those of the Bernese Oberland; Germans advanced even to the valley of the Saane. According to tradition, Romance shepherds, passing up the river through the woods with their flocks, met with shepherds of another tongue, which was German.[2] Thus the predominant character of Switzerland became gradually German.

PART III.

TERRITORIAL DIVISIONS.

(1057-1218.)

§ 12. **Rudolph of Rheinfeld and the Supremacy of the Zäringens.** After the death of Henry III., the feeble Empress Agnes, in 1057, bestowed the dukedom of Alamannia upon her favourite, Rudolf of Rheinfeld. Rudolf had likewise great possessions in Burgundy, between the Saane, the great St. Bernard, Geneva and the Jura. Thus the Swiss territories were again united, and came under the rule of a native prince. Rudolf, in whom the empress had hoped to find a

[1] VON PLANTA, *das alte Rätien*, 1873.
[2] BURKHARDT, *Untersuchungen über die erste Bevölkerung der schweizerischen Urkantone* (*Archiv für schweizergeschichte*, vol. iv. pp. 99-101).

supporter of the court, soon ranged himself on the side of the opposition against the youthful Henry IV.; and when the latter was excommunicated by the Pope, he caused himself to be made a rival king by the princes in 1077, chiefly by the help of Duke Guelf of Bavaria and Berchthold of Zäringen. But in Switzerland Rudolf met with an energetic resistance at Constance, St. Gall and Zurich; the bishops of Lausanne and Basle raised an army and devastated his estates. After Rudolf's death in 1080 the Zäringen and Guelf faction took up the cause; but there arose against them the Staufen faction, with Frederick of Staufen, to whom Henry IV. had ceded Alamannia, at their head. A devastating war broke out, and many monasteries, towns, castles and churches were destroyed.

The struggle was also carried on with spiritual weapons; the monks of Cluny, eager for the revival of ecclesiastical discipline and for the development of the papal power, disseminated the idea of the independence and omnipotence of the church. Romainmotier and Payerne had become dependent upon Cluny as early as the tenth century, and now other Cluniac foundations were erected (Rougemont and Rüeggisberg). The example of Cluny was followed by the monasteries of Einsiedeln, Muri, Allerheiligen (Schaffhausen), and Rheinau; the monks, in concert with the Zäringen-Guelf party, preached war to the death against the excommunicated emperor and his followers. The Zäringens meanwhile had taken the place of the house of Rheinfeld; when the last of the Rheinfelds died in 1090, Berchthold II. of Zäringen inherited all the estates of that house, and was made Duke of Suabia in opposition to Frederick of Staufen. It was one continual party strife, until by the peace of 1097 Berchthold II. of Zäringen renounced the dukedom of Alamannia, and received in its stead the imperial bailiwick of Zurich with the title of Duke. In the decay of all authority under the Staufens and Zäringens, and the division of the dukedom of Alamannia, the first step was made towards the independent development of Switzerland.

Through the acquisition of Zurich by the peace of 1097

the Zäringens became the largest landowners of Switzerland; since the tenth century they had possessed the county of Thurgau; from the house of Rheinfeld they received an extensive property between the Reuss and the Aar. Zurich itself was so flourishing in the twelfth century, that a German writer calls it the chief town of Suabia; an inscription over the gate of the town[1]—" Zurich the noble with abundance of many things "—is supposed to have denoted its wealth and prosperity. Supported by these possessions the Zäringens might well conceive the idea of occupying once more the position of Henry III. and Rudolf of Rheinfeld. The powers and rights inherited by them from the house of Rheinfeld were, however, called in question by the counts of Upper Burgundy, till in 1127 William IV. of Upper Burgundy was killed, and Conrad III. of Zäringen, a relative of William, was declared " Rector " (*Reichsvicar*), and made Duke of Burgundy, by the Emperor Lothaire, in opposition to a Burgundian kinsman. But the Burgundian lords of Geneva, Ottingen, Grandson, Gruyeres, &c., and the bishops, in all of whom the dislike to German supremacy was once more aroused, rose against the Zäringens as one man, and a succession of passionate struggles and terrible feuds raged as long as the Zäringens lived. The latter sought to find in the towns and boroughs a counter-balance against the haughty nobles. They erected castles and fortresses, around which larger places gradually arose, or they fortified the settlements already standing, manned them with forces capable of resistance, and bestowed upon them estates (*Burglehen*)[2] and privileges. Thus Berchthold IV., about 1177, founded the fortress of Fribourg. To him or to his son Berchthold V. the fortifications and first municipal laws of Burgdorf, Moudon, Yverdon, Laupen, Gümminen, Thun, &c., also owe their origin. Berchthold V. had to maintain a hard struggle. The whole nobility of Burgundy conspired against him. Berchthold, however, defeated some at Avenches, others in the valley of Grindelwald, and afterwards, in 1191,

[1] " *Das edle Zürich mit Uberfluss an vielen Dingen.*
[2] *i.e.*, the tenure of a feudal castle and the land attached to it.—E. S.

established the town of Berne[1] on an island in the Aar (which was imperial soil), as a strong bulwark, whence he could easily dominate the surrounding country, as from a castle. But all these efforts had no lasting result. The Burgundians and the house of Savoy revolted afresh, and Berchthold V., driven back from the Vaud and Valais, was obliged in his last days to look upon the wreck of all his plans; his race died with him in 1218, having attained celebrity by the foundation of many towns.

§ 13. INTERNAL CONDITIONS IN THE STATE, THE CHURCH, AND SOCIETY DOWN TO THE BEGINNING OF THE THIRTEENTH CENTURY. (*a*) **Constitution and Classes of Society, Spiritual and Temporal Supremacies.** The German empire, under whose rule Switzerland had come in the eleventh century, and to whom it practically belonged until the end of the fifteenth century, was advancing from the twelfth century towards an internal dissolution. The strong and uniform imperial authority, which Otto I. and the "Salic" rulers had established, was gradually relaxed. The authority of the empire became more and more limited, partly by the ambition of powerful and bold vassals and nobles, partly by the heavy blows which were inflicted on the empire by the popes and the church. The imperial estates were wasted; the representatives of the empire, the emperors themselves, undermined their own power by the remission of royalties (coinage, customs, rights of hunting and fishing, and feudal sovereignty), and by the granting of numerous privileges and liberties, being forced thereto by political circumstances; and under either feeble rulers, or despots who wasted their time and strength upon the foundation of a dominion in Italy, numberless petty states were formed, which rendered useless the empire and the imperial authority.

---

[1] This name has nothing whatever to do with "bears," but is simply derived from the name "Verona," which was in the possession of the Züringens, and was in German called "Bern." The fact that Bern was founded upon imperial soil constitutes an essential difference between that town and Fribourg: it had therefore afterwards the character of an imperial town.

The all-absorbing feudal system formed an important factor in this process of disorganization. Not only were estates and lands bestowed in fee, but even offices and rights of lordship, and when in the eleventh century fiefs became generally hereditary, the bond between vassals and their lords became lax; the former became more independent, and finally cared nothing for their feudal lords. Thus dukedoms and earldoms became the hereditary property of powerful families. But the division went further. These great lords or crown-vassals, forming the high nobility, also distributed fiefs, and bestowed portions of their principalities, smaller counties, or the dominion over separate villages, upon vassals, dependents of the lower nobility, who in their turn contrived to make themselves more free. Thus the county system, which had formed the solid basis of imperial government under the Franks, was dissolved.

This dissolution of the county system and the development of the feudal system were essentially furthered by the "Immunity," or the right of exemption from the county jurisdiction, which was first granted to monastic houses and bishops, and later to royal vassals also. The foundation was thereby laid for the formation of smaller states within each county. The bishops and abbots, not being allowed to exercise criminal jurisdiction themselves, appointed either for themselves or by the king, a deputy or advocate to administer for them, called a bailiff or governor (*Vogt*), who entirely managed their temporal and agricultural affairs (*Kastvogtei*). Even the office of governor was afterwards converted into a hereditary possession, and temporal lords also appointed similar governors.

This localization of authority was very closely connected with a change of another kind. From the eighth century families of the nobility had increasingly succeeded, either by purchase or by craft and force, favoured by the growing need and impoverishment of the small peasants, in uniting enormous landed possessions in their own hands. Thus large estates became the rule everywhere, and the small holding of the freeman an ever rarer exception. Part of these estates was bestowed upon vassals (*ministeriales*, or retainers), under obligation of military or knight's service; and part upon dependents, bondmen, or free peasants, as copyhold tenants. These great landed proprietors in counties or villages sought to acquire political power, and abrogated to themselves everywhere rights of dominion and jurisdiction. They received a manorial jurisdiction, that is, the right of punishing offences in wood and field, and the control over affairs of the soil. Many lords of manors then contrived to obtain the office of under-governor or bailiff, that is, the jurisdiction over smaller misdemeanours not punishable by death. The office of the higher bailiff, or criminal jurisdiction, was quite separate, being the right of punishing more serious offences, such as theft, robbery, arson, murder, &c., but even this might chance to come to the hands of the lower jurisdiction or lord of the manor. These feudal relations were altogether different in different places, and were but little regulated by law and rule. On the other hand, the rights of the different lords and those of their subjects were everywhere definitely limited and fixed. Handed down at first from generation to generation by oral tradition, they were fixed in writing in the fourteenth and fifteenth centuries by publication (*Offnungen*) of legal sentences, rules of court, &c. Every time that the lords held their courts, in spring and autumn, these rights and customs were read aloud before the people, as a continual reminder. These spring and autumn courts, at which all those who were under any sort of obligation to the lord had to appear, were either held by the lord himself or by his manorial officers, the steward or cellarer (*Keller*), who received rents and made inspection. The constitution of these courts tended more than anything else to dispossess the old uniform constitution, which had rested upon the county system.

The political conditions of the people were very various, according to their rank. All power was in the hands of the higher and lower nobility, who lived upon their freeholds or their feudal estates. The offices of house bailiff, or imperial bailiff, &c., had their dwellings in strong towers and castles, dressed in handsome armour, and found their pleasure in hunting, in feuds and tournaments, and also here and there practised minstrelsy (*Minnegesang*). The worst position was that of the bondmen (*Leibeigenen*), who, being far removed from their lord, and not attached to the estate, could be sold at any time, and in their miserable wooden huts had scarcely means of subsistence. The freedmen (*Hörigen*) were in rather better circumstances, and could only be exchanged with the estate upon which they lived. Freedmen and bondmen had other feudal obligations to discharge, besides their rents and feudal duties, such as death-dues or "*Besthaupt*,"[1] socage, &c. The dependents of a religious house or of a church (*Gotteshausleute*) enjoyed special advantages over these servile folk; they were not under any hereditary lordship, and could claim the immunity above alluded to. Outside the nobility, the best position, at least in social respects, was that of the freemen, who possessed either freehold or copyhold estates; but even they found but a very scanty livelihood. For a copyhold tenement a ground-rent had to be paid in kind to the lord of the manor. These customary free tenants, however, lived in continual danger of being robbed of their freedom, for the lords sought perpetually to extend and complete their own authority, to efface the rights of the various classes, and to depress all into a similar subjection. On the other hand, the lower classes in their despair struggled upwards more and more, and strove to obtain a better position either by force or by attaining to the freedom of the empire.

Under such forms the conditions of mediæval government progressed. The spiritual territories were first formed by means of the Immunity, and by the grants to bishops of royalties and county rights, which became very frequent after the tenth century. Thus the bishops of Lausanne, Sion, Basle, Constance and Coire, the abbots of St. Gall, Einsiedeln, Muri, Engelberg, &c., the abbess of the Fraumünsterstift, &c., became powerful manorial lords and possessors of princely rights. Among the most notable of the secular

[1] Probably the same as the Anglo-Saxon *wergild*.

lords were the counts of Savoy, of Geneva, Gruyères and Neuchâtel in west Switzerland, the counts of Lenzburg, Kiburg, Hapsburg, Rapperswil and Toggenburg, the barons of Regensberg, and others in east Switzerland. The Hapsburgs were the most fortunate in the extension of their territory; in addition to their hereditary estates in Alsace and Aargau, they inherited in 1172 and 1173 the possessions of the Lenzburgs in Aargau and in the Forest States; and later, in the thirteenth century, those of the families of Rapperswil and Kiburg. They seemed to have taken the place of the houses of Rheinfeld and Zäringen.

(*b*) **The Development of Village, Town and Country Communities.** A counterbalance to the overweening power of the nobility was formed by the communes. A large number of houses and farmsteads lying near together formed sooner or later a domestic and political society, called a "commune" (*Gemeinde*) or peasantry (*Pursame*). Such a fellowship related especially to the possession of a common portion of wood and pasture, undivided and enjoyed by the whole community, called the "Mark" or "Allmend." This "Markgenossenschaft," or association of the Mark, also looked after other agricultural concerns, and fixed the time for vintage, harvest and such-like. Some communes succeeded in extending these rights, and in obtaining their freedom by increasing limitations of the rights of their lords, by purchase or by force, and in the formation of these free communes we find the germ of Swiss liberty.

The communes in towns were of special importance. They were formed in places surrounded by walls, with houses adjoining one another. This method of colonization, once so detested by the Alamanni, came more and more into favour as an excellent means of defence during the time of the Hungarian inroads and intestine feuds. Such walled towns gradually received considerable privileges beyond those of the villages: the right of holding fairs, privileges of jurisdiction and tolls, rights of coinage, and the right to elect municipal officers, &c. The development of these towns differed according to their origin. Some—and those by far the greater part —rose around some religious institution, or around the court of a spiritual lord, such as the episcopal towns of Geneva, Lausanne, Basle, Coire and Sion, or towns dependent upon monasteries and religious foundations, such as Soleure, St. Gall, Lucerne, &c. These from their commencement enjoyed the privilege of Immunity, and had the earliest municipal councils. But with the decline of ecclesiastical power in the thirteenth century, these towns were enfranchised little by little, and acquired the right of electing their own town councils. Moreover, being under no hereditary rule, and the bailiffs being nominated by the empire, most of them preserved a certain connection with the empire, and managed to raise themselves to the rank of imperial towns and to shake off the spiritual yoke. Other towns were founded by temporal lords for military purposes or in the interests of trade, such as Fribourg, Berne, and others built by the house of Zäringen; Winterthur, Diessenhofen and Frauenfeld by that of Kiburg. Some of these, such as the towns of the Zäringens, enjoyed special privileges from the first; others acquired them when their lords were in difficulties and required their service; they, too, gradually succeeded in obtaining their freedom. Lastly, there were towns towards whose foundation and development various circumstances had contributed, such as Zurich, which was partly a royal town, and partly ecclesiastical.

All the towns, however, rose to distinction in the twelfth and thirteenth centuries chiefly by their trade and manufactures, and in this way they became the seats of a new civilization. The population within the walls was a very mixed one in point of rank: side by side with the freedmen and bondmen of the lords of the town dwelt the vassals or officers of the crown and numerous freemen; the former lived by their handicrafts, the latter by knight's service, agriculture and commerce. Only knights and freemen originally took part in the civic administration, and the bondmen or handicraftsmen first obtained political rights in the fourteenth century. Thus the towns became of the greatest importance in social and political development. A free political spirit ruled within them. Bondmen and freedmen who settled in a town became free if they were not fetched back by their lords within a year. ("The air of towns sets one free.") So the class of freemen whose very existence had been so seriously threatened by the feudal system gradually increased.

The valley communes developed like the towns. The people in the mountain valleys of Uri, Schwyz, Unterwalden, Glarus, Hasle, &c., followed the example of the towns. They were protected by their mountains, as were the towns by their walls. The freemen everywhere formed a nucleus, to which the bondmen attached themselves, in order to avail themselves of favourable circumstances for their emancipation; for the dwellers in the valleys were mostly united (as in Uri and Schwyz) by the possession of a common or *Allmend*. Uri was first settled by subjects of the empire; then in 853 it came under the mild ecclesiastical rule of the *Fraumünster* of Zurich, and acquired the right of Immunity. The higher administration of justice was exercised by the bailiffs of the convent, and in the twelfth century and the beginning of the thirteenth by the Zäringens. But the *Gotteshausleute* of Uri[1] gradually acquired many precious liberties. There was in Schwyz a whole commune of freemen, over whom the counts of the district exercised sovereignty. Hence Schwyz also early became unusually powerful and independent. It had a quarrel with the monastery of Einsiedeln about the wood and pasture land on its borders; and although Henry V., in 1114, and Conrad III., in 1144, decided in favour of Einsiedeln, and in spite of the spiritual weapon of excommunication directed against them, they adhered immovably to their claims. Compared to the two valleys already named, Unterwalden was politically backward. It is true that here, too, there existed a fair number of freemen in and about Sarnen and Stanz; but they were scattered, and the land was divided

---

[1] "People of God's house," a name applied to certain inhabitants of Uri in partial subjection to the abbey of Zurich.—E. S.

among divers spiritual and temporal lords. But in the thirteenth century they also were struggling for freedom with other valley communities.

(c) **Ecclesiastical Conditions.** Since the ninth and tenth centuries the power of the church had increased mightily. She amassed enormous riches by gifts, donations, festivals, masses, &c. The bishops and higher clergy supported the imperial government, and received royalties and princely powers. The popes, the highest bishops, acquired an ever increasing ascendency, and made successful use of the religious agitations of the eleventh and twelfth centuries to their own advantage and that of the church. They interfered in all ecclesiastical concerns, organized crusades, and deposed emperors and kings.

Ecclesiastical institutions and orders multiplied incredibly. The oldest order was that of the Benedictines, to which belonged numbers of the famous monasteries of the land— St. Gall, Einsiedeln, Dissentis, Pfäffers, Rheinau, Muri, Engelberg, &c. In the tenth century, when this order languished somewhat, that of Cluny arose to a fresh struggle in the cause of the papacy, the church, and asceticism. (*See* p. 26.) When the strength of this order also began to flag (about 1100) the Cistercian, Premonstratensian and Carthusian orders were founded. To the first of these orders belonged Lützel near Soleure, Hauterêt in Vaud, Hauterive near Fribourg, St. Urban, Kappel, Wettingen, and others. The second included Bellelay, Rüti in canton Zurich, and others; the third, La Lance, Ittingen, &c. Together with asceticism, these orders attached great importance to manual labour and solitude as the principal methods of strict discipline. The new monasteries carried on the cultivation of the land, cleared the forests, drained marshes, and planted vineyards. But in the thirteenth century, when it became needful to prevent the downfall of the church, and to re-assert the principle of renunciation of the world, the monasteries of mendicant friars arose in every town: the Dominicans or preaching friars, and the Franciscans or barefooted friars. A number of nunneries were likewise founded, and the religious orders of knights also established themselves in Switzerland. By means of these orders and ecclesiastical societies the church became a stupendous power, to which magnificent cathedrals and minsters, beautiful churches and splendid ecclesiastical monuments still testify.[1] But the more wealth the church amassed, and the more she mingled in worldly concerns, so much the more her inner life waned. She neglected her holy calling, and the cultivation of intellectual life. Monasteries which had formerly been distinguished by their literary and artistic performances, were remarkable in the thirteenth century for their ignorance. Opposition to the church grew apace, sectarian tendencies increased, and in all parts recourse was had to the authorities of the state to restrain the power of the church.

[1] Of ancient churches in the Romanesque (or round-arch) style, we may name Payerne, the *Grossmünster* in Zurich, Neuchâtel, Ufenau, Coire, Katzis, Dissentis, Sion, &c. Later ones in the Gothic (or pointed-arch) style: Geneva, Lausanne, Berne, Kappel, and the churches of the mendicant friars everywhere.

Second Period.
RISE AND DEVELOPMENT OF THE SWISS CONFEDERATION.
(1218-1516.)

PART I.

ORIGIN OF THE CONFEDERATION.

(1218-1315.)

1. THE FIRST LEAGUES.

(1218-1291.)[1]

§ 14. **Struggles for Liberty.** The death of Berchthold V. and the extinction of the house of Züringen preserved Switzerland from the fate of many other parts of the empire, that of becoming permanently a royal possession. The estates of the Züringens in west Switzerland (such as Herzogenbuchsee, Thun, Burgdorf and Fribourg) fell, it is true, to the house of Kiburg; the rectorate of Burgundy, however, reverted to the emperor, and became extinct; the dynasties, which had been dependent upon the rector as such, and the towns which had been conferred upon the Züringens as imperial estates, likewise reverted to the empire, and so obtained a sort of independence or freedom of the empire (*Reichsfreiheit*). This was the case with the counts of Buchegg Neuchâtel, &c., and the towns of Zurich, Berne, Soleure, Laupen, Gümminen and Morat. By

---

[1] KOPP, *Geschichte der eidgenössischen Bünde*, 4 vols. *Urkunden zur Geschichte der eidgenössischen Bünde*, 2 vols. E. v. WATTENWYL-DIESBACH, *Geschichte der Stadt und Landschaft Bern*, 2 vols. G. v. WYSS, *über die Geschichte der drei Länder Uri, Schwyz und Unterwalden* (*Rathausvortrag*). BLUMER, *Geschichte der schweiz. Demokratien*. DIERAUER and others. (See p. xvi.)

these means their free development was greatly advanced, but could not make much progress without hard struggles.

The house of Kiburg united powerful possessions in eastern Switzerland (the county of Thurgau and Baden) to the hereditary estates of the house of Zäringen in west Switzerland; and thus, like that house, conceived the idea of forming a united principality in Switzerland. In the south-west (Valais and Geneva) a menacing attitude was adopted by the house of Savoy; the bitterest enemy of which house being removed by the extinction of the Zäringens, it was now at liberty to attack the northern territories of western Switzerland. The house of Hapsburg had at last obtained a firm footing in central Switzerland and in the east; it occupied the left bank of the Reuss in Aargau, the counties of Zurich and Aargau, and extensive though scattered possessions in Zug, Schwyz, Unterwalden and Lucerne. Thus the free communes were straitened and threatened on all sides.

These antagonists first came into collision with the outbreak of the struggle between the papacy and the empire in the time of Frederick II. The towns and free communes of Switzerland then openly espoused the cause of the emperor, looking to him to protect them against the overwhelming power of the aristocracy; only by his help could they hope to save their imperial freedom. The counts and lords, however, like the Guelfs and Zäringens of former days, inclined rather to the side of the papacy.

The Forest States commenced the attack. The jurisdiction of the Zäringens over Uri had been transferred to Count Rudolf the Old of Hapsburg[1] in 1218 as an imperial fee. The

---

[1] The following genealogical table will serve as explanation.

RUDOLF THE OLD, *ob.* 1232.

Albrecht (the elder line), *ob.* 1239; *married* Heilwig von Kiburg.

    Rudolf III., became king 1273; *ob.* 1291.

        Albert of Austria, king 1298–1308.

Rudolf II., the "Silent," of Hapsburg-Laufenburg (the younger line).

    Godfrey; *married* Elizabeth von Rapperwil.

    Everhard; *married* Anna von Kiburg.

The First Leagues.

imperial bailiwicks and fees being at this time gradually converted into hereditary sovereignties and provinces, the people of Uri began to fear they would come under the dominion of the house of Hapsburg, and lose their Immunity. They therefore had recourse to King Henry, the son of Frederick, who managed the affairs of the empire in his father's absence, and who granted them a charter on the 26th May, 1231, placing them under the protection and sovereignty of the empire. The bailiwick seems to have been acquired by the Hapsburgs by purchase. Uri had thus lawfully secured her freedom, and from that time the valley takes its place as a free and independent commune. In 1243 it had its own seal, like the towns. The freemen of Schwyz were not less hampered by the Hapsburgs; here also the authority of the counts seems to have been converted into a hereditary sovereignty, as was the case with the imperial bailiwick in Uri.[1] When in 1232 the power of the house of Hapsburg was shattered by its division between the younger (or Laufenburg)[2] and the elder line, the people of Schwyz also determined to avail themselves of the help of the emperor in order to obtain the freedom of the empire like their neighbours. In 1240 they sent delegates to Frederick II., when the latter, then under papal excommunication, was besieging Faenza in Italy; and the emperor, in December, 1240, probably out of gratitude for help rendered, acknowledged the people of Schwyz as subjects of the empire by a charter under his own hand.

Hitherto circumstances had been extremely favourable to these progressive movements, but the situation was completely altered when Frederick II. was excommunicated in 1245 at the Council of Lyons by Pope Innocent IV., the adherents of the church increased in number, and the wars of the time of Henry IV. were renewed. All towns and states which

---

[1] *Cf.* F. v. WYSS, *die friein Bauern,* &c., *Zeitschrift für schweiz. Recht,* vol. vii., 1872.

[2] The younger line kept (roughly speaking) the possessions in the Forest States, the elder those in Alsace and Aargau.

adhered to the emperor were threatened with excommunication, and Zurich, which had most zealously taken Frederick's part, was laid under an interdict. The whole empire was divided into two hostile camps, those of the Ghibellines and the Guelfs, and a tempest raged throughout the land, the effects of which extended even to the remote Alpine valleys. The free communes, however, nothing daunted, took energetic measures to secure their liberties. Zurich expelled the Dominican monks from her walls for inciting against Frederick, and also the clergy who refused to hold divine service; Lucerne revolted against the rule of the Abbot of Murbach and the Count of Hapsburg, as did also the Forest States.

In order to advance more safely upon the beaten track both town and country communes followed the example of the Lombardic and a few North German towns, and entered into alliances with one another for the maintenance of peace and for the protection of traffic in troublous times. Thus in 1243 Berne concluded an offensive and defensive alliance with Fribourg to secure herself against the attacks of the Kiburgs; for the same cause Fribourg and Morat combined, as did also Berne and Lucerne. Following the example of the towns, Schwyz also made a league with Unterwalden and Uri, and about 1245-1247 they entered into an alliance with Lucerne and Zurich. This was the first mutual alliance of town and country communes, a prelude to the founding of the Confederation! The Forest States then took up arms bravely, and the Count of Hapsburg was obliged to form an advantageous military outpost by building the castle of New Hapsburg on the lake. Strife arose around the lake of the Four Cantons. Then at last were the hostile officials of the haughty retainers of the Hapsburg nobility expelled, and their strongholds destroyed. In vain did Rudolf II. of Hapsburg implore the aid of Pope Innocent IV.; the latter threatened Schwyz, Sarnen and Lucerne with an interdict, but the struggle went on for many years, and only came to an end when the commencement of the "Interregnum" in 1256 effaced all party strife. The people of Uri, whose liberty rested on a firm foundation, remained free, but Schwyz and Unterwalden appear to have been forced to submit once more to the Hapsburgs. About 1250 began that troublous time without an emperor, that period of confusion, when unbridled passion made all parts unsafe, and "club-law" prevailed. The encroachments of the nobility upon the towns recommenced everywhere. In western Switzerland Hartmann von Kiburg tried to extend his rights, and to possess himself of the estates of the empire; but the imperial states of Berne, Morat and Basle found an able protector in his chief opponent, the bold Count of Savoy, Peter II. This powerful champion of the house of Savoy had exchanged his spiritual calling for the sword, and now (1230-1260) extended his dominion by inheritance, purchase and conquest over the greater part of the Romance territory; little by little he gained the whole of the Pays de Vaud, and repulsed the encroachments of the Kiburgs. He endeavoured to attach the Vaud to himself by securing the constitution, and made himself famous by his laws and statutes ("*le petit Charlemagne*"). In eastern Switzerland also feuds raged. Zurich was attacked by the Barons of Regensberg and other nobles of the neighbourhood, but afterwards joined Rudolf III. of Hapsburg, the opponent of the Regensbergs,[1] and destroyed many of the enemy's castles. The towns enjoying the freedom of the empire were now practically free, since the empire had no generally recognised head. The imperial castles of Lindenhof in Zurich and Nidegg in Berne were either left to decay or destroyed.[2] Other towns, too, were struggling for freedom; Winterthur destroyed the citadel of the counts of Kiburg, Lucerne broke into a castle belonging to its ecclesiastical lord of Murbach, and Zug withstood the surrounding nobility.

In those times of the surging of party strife the towns formed a quiet refuge for the cultivation of intellectual life. Chivalrous poetry flourished in the castles of knights of

---

[1] The Regensbergs laid claim to the county of Kiburg, which Rudolf had inherited in 1264.
[2] G. v. Wyss, &c.

Thurgau, Aargau and Zurich (Klingenberg, Toggenburg, Wart, Teufen, Regensberg, Sax and Montfort), and also within the walls of the town of Zurich the sweet notes of the minnesingers resounded in love songs collected by a knight of Zurich (the *Manessische Liedersammlung*, or "Songs of Manegg"). In Zurich we find, side by side with the poet John Hadlaub, the famous poet, singer and writer, Conrad von Mure.

§ 15. **The Menacing Power of Rudolf of Hapsburg, and the Perpetual League of the Forest States.** At the very moment when the house of Hapsburg seemed to tremble, a man placed himself at its head who devoted his whole life to strengthen and consolidate its power: this was Count Rudolf III. of Hapsburg (one of the elder line). By a clever use of various opportunities, by the support of divers boroughs (*e.g.*, Zurich, Basle and Winterthur), and also by force, he gradually attained on this side of the Rhine to such power as approached that of the Zäringens.

When in 1263 and 1264 the male representatives of the house of Kiburg expired with Hartmann the Younger and his uncle Hartmann the Elder,[1] Rudolf, not content with the portion of the Kiburg inheritance which he inherited in his mother's right,[2] laid claim to the whole of the possessions of that house in eastern and western Switzerland; disregarding the equally legitimate claims of the house of Savoy,[3] he defeated Peter II., and in 1267 acquired the dominions of the Kiburgs by the peace of Morat. He next made war upon the Bishop of Basle, in consequence of some territorial disputes in Alsace, and in 1273 he obtained the estates of the younger Hapsburg-Laufenburg line in the Forest States for a very trifling sum. His election as King of Germany followed speedily in the same year. He availed himself of his royal

[1] Anna, the daughter of the younger Count Hartmann of Kiburg, afterwards (1273) married Count Eberhard of Hapsburg-Laufenburg, and thence sprang the new house of Kiburg. (*See* p. 57.)

[2] *See* p. 38, note.

[3] The wife of the last of the Kiburgs was Margaret of Savoy, sister of Peter II.

The First Leagues.

dignity to restore and extend the power of his house; he secured for it the Duchy of Austria, and now openly strove to tread in the footsteps of the Zäringens, and to re-establish the kingdom of Burgundy. He pushed his way over the Aar by force of arms and besieged Berne, which opposed his schemes, in concert with Savoy and the Burgundian dynasties (1288). The Bernese withstood him manfully, and Rudolf was obliged to raise the siege. It was not until the spring of 1289 that a band of Bernese was defeated by an ambuscade of Rudolf's troops at Schoosshalde. By purchase and intrigue Rudolf gradually acquired Fribourg, Neuchâtel, Lenzburg, Einsiedeln, Pfäffers, Seckingen, the stewardship of Glarus, and the bailiwick of Urseren; even the monastery of St. Gall, whose rich landed possessions he coveted, was frequently threatened and driven to great straits. By these acquisitions Rudolf made enemies of many towns, and harassed them, moreover, by heavy taxes. He recognised, it is true, the imperial freedom of Uri, but his double powers as king and claimant of the title of Landgrave must have filled them with alarm. The people of Schwyz fared the worst. He strenuously asserted the rights of his house, appointing vassals of the Hapsburgs as judges in the valleys; and shortly before his death he obtained Lucerne by purchase from the Abbey of Murbach.

The whole of Switzerland seemed to be caught in the net of the powerful Hapsburgs: little was wanting to make the whole land between the Alps, the Rhine and the Jura one united principality under that house. But Rudolf died suddenly on 15th July, 1291; and it may well be imagined that on this side of the Rhine all breathed more freely, towns, communes and dynasties feeling relieved from oppression. Hopes of freedom revived once more, and the formerly free communes now boldly pursued the course they had taken under Frederick II., and during the Interregnum, until arrested by Rudolf. While in eastern and western Switzerland leagues were formed directed against the Hapsburgs (in the east under the Bishop of Constance, and in the west under the house of Savoy), the three states of Uri, Schwyz and Unterwalden met together a fortnight after Rudolf's death, on 1st August, 1291, and swore to adhere for ever to their old alliance made in the time of the struggle between Frederick II. and the Pope. They pledged themselves to faithful aid in every need and danger, against all aggression; to acknowledge none but natives of the soil as judges in the valleys, to punish impartially all disturbers of the peace, and thus to preserve the peace of the country; in all other respects everyone should serve his lord dutifully as hitherto.[1] Disputes among the Confederates themselves were to be peaceably settled by the "Wise men."

This **first Perpetual League** became the historical basis of the Confederation. Like the earlier and contemporary alliances of towns, it was not directed against the emperor or his realm, the Confederates having but one aim—that of providing for themselves by their own united strength the protection which the imperial power could not offer them. But in this case the allies were not wealthy towns, such as those of Italy and Germany, but simple, homely country-folk, who, with a full perception of the political situation, had the courage to strike out a path for themselves. The league was to be "for ever," and it has endured without interruption. While the leagues of the towns died out in the course of time, the Swiss Federation developed, steeled by necessity in the after days into an irresistible power, before which the house of Hapsburg in Switzerland, and finally the nobility itself, sank, as stars vanish before the rising sun.

2. BEGINNING OF THE WARS OF FREEDOM.
(1291-1315.)

§ 16. The First War with Austria. Battle of Morgarten. For further support, the Forest States of Uri and Schwyz, shortly after the formation of the Perpetual League, attached themselves to Zurich, and joined the alliance formed in eastern

---

[1] Schiller has represented this last point absolutely accurately in "William Tell" (Act II. Scene II., towards the end: the proceedings on the Rütli.)

Switzerland against the Hapsburgs. The house of Austria, descended from the Hapsburgs, was at that time represented by Rudolf's son Albert, who entertained hopes of the crown. When Adolf of Nassau, his rival, was elected King of Germany, every enemy of the house of Hapsburg took his part, and war broke out. But the men of Zurich, who had marched against the Austrian town of Winterthur, were defeated there in April, 1292, with much slaughter; Albert thereupon advanced swiftly upon Zurich. "He was unable to swallow it" (*Sage von den Frauen*[1]), but induced the town to make peace in August, and to promise military service. Thus the league formed against the Hapsburgs was broken; and even the Forest States and Lucerne were finally obliged to give up the struggle. King Adolf secured imperial freedom to Uri and Schwyz in 1297.

In the west the cause of Austria underwent a defeat in 1298 by the victory of the Bernese at the battle of Dornbühl. Albert, however, being made king by the electors in opposition to Adolf, and remaining sole monarch after the fall of his adversary, refused to acknowledge the liberties of the Forest States and Berne, and did all he could to place the Austrian power on a firm basis in the whole of eastern and central Switzerland, and to extend the Austro-Hapsburg patrimony, first established by Rudolf. Once more, as under Rudolf, the desires of the Forest States for freedom seemed about to be stifled in subjection to the Hapsburgs, when suddenly, in May 1308, Albert was murdered at Brugg by his own nephew, John of Austria (whose claims to Bohemia he had refused to recognise), and some discontented knights (Rudolf von Wart, Walter von Eschenbach, Conrad von Tegerfeld, and Rudolf von Balm).

The Forest States took the opportunity to wring fresh charters from the new king, Henry VII. of Luxembourg. At that time Werner von Attinghausen took the lead in Uri, and one of the Stauffach family in Schwyz; Unterwalden also

[1] Or "Tradition of the Women"; this tradition will be found in full in Dr. Dändliker's larger history.—E. S.

was now for the first time admitted to the imperial freedom (1309), and so stood on an equal footing with the other Forest States. Henry by his deed formed the Forest States into a separate jurisdiction, and appointed one of his knights, Werner von Homberg, imperial bailiff there. The dukes of Austria vainly tried to re-establish their rights, and proceeded to take vengeance on the regicides. Shortly after Henry VII. had become reconciled to them, and had effected a treaty of arbitration, settling the rights of the Hapsburgs and those of the empire in the Forest States, he was snatched away by death in 1313, in Italy.

A disputed election to the throne in 1314 (Louis the Bavarian against Frederick of Austria) gave fresh occasion to the Forest States to array themselves against Austria; the people of Schwyz even went so far as to attack the monastery of Einsiedeln (then under the protection of Austria[1]), with which they had been for two centuries at strife, and to possess themselves of the Austrian town of Art. Frederick then determined to subdue the Forest States by force of arms, and commissioned his brother Leopold to carry out his project. On November 14th, 1315, the latter assembled his contingent in Zug, in order to attack Schwyz; another portion of his army was to advance over the Brunig pass against Obwalden; and lastly the men of Lucerne were to engage Nidwalden and Uri by the lake. But as soon as the inhabitants of Schwyz grasped the intention of the main army, they occupied the heights and the narrow pass of Morgarten, the natural defence of the land on the north-west, and as it were the gate of the little state of Schwyz. On the morning of the 15th November, the cavalry advanced along the lake of Egeri, the infantry following, full of thoughtless gaiety. Suddenly, from the heights, the men of Schwyz rolled down trunks of trees and blocks of stone, and wrought terrible confusion among their enemies;[2] then, swift and sure-footed as the chamois, they

---

[1] *See* p. 34.

[2] In JUSTINGER's Bernese Chronicle, 1420, tradition ascribes this deed to some exiles, who endeavoured in this way to win their pardon. John of Winterthur

rushed boldly and fearlessly from their hiding-places, and Leopold's army fell under the battle-axes of Swiss peasants, like a flock led to the slaughter. Many were drowned in the adjacent lake. Half dead with terror and excitement, Leopold's hasty flight brought him to Winterthur, and the Austrian power seemed shattered at a blow by a handful of peasants. The troops which had crossed the Brunig pass turned back upon the news of Leopold's defeat.

This first great victory had decisive results. It not only freed the three states from the dominion of Austria, but it also tightened the old alliance. United more firmly by a common danger, the three states renewed the league of 1291 at Brunnen on December 9th, 1315. The unity of the allied states was declared yet more emphatically; no single state was to accept any lord, or to conclude any negotiations or treaties without the knowledge and consent of the others; whoever should either assail or betray any one of the states should be hated and outlawed by all. In the following year Louis ratified the charter of the Forest States; Austria, however, concluded a truce with them in 1318, by which the enjoyment of the rents and revenues of estates was confirmed to Austria, but the sovereign rights of the counts were declared void.

§ 17. **The Development of the Tradition of the Enfranchisement of the Forest States.** The memory of these glorious events in the struggle for freedom long remained in the minds of the people, and since there was at first no chronicler found, it was handed down by word of mouth from generation to generation. The father told the son, the latter the grandson, the grandson the great-grandson, with fervour and enthusiasm, of the joys and sorrows of the Confederates, of actors and scenes in the past. It was inevitable that here and there the colouring became rather vivid, and that occasionally a fresh and fragrant flower sprang of itself out

(about 1330), who describes the battle in more detail from the accounts of eye-witnesses, says nothing of such exiles, and it is also more probable that the feat was accomplished by the army of Schwyz itself.

of the ever fresh gardens of tradition. Many things were obliterated from the minds of later generations; others became unduly prominent; others, again, became confused in the various narratives, as always happens when the popular imagination transmits and elaborates history. In this way events were misplaced, and the whole course of development was gradually quite differently conceived, rather as it was imagined to have been, than as things had actually occurred.[1] Little by little people forgot that Swiss liberty first arose on the basis of the original legal conditions of the population, by slow birth and growth, in the same way and at the same time that the towns were attaining their rights and liberties step by step. The different revolts against the Hapsburgs (1245-1273 and 1291-1315) became confused in the mind of the people, and were combined into one single and sudden revolution. In order to justify the latter, the condition of imperial freedom, to which states had in reality attained gradually, was erroneously referred to the most ancient times, that the dispute might assume the character of a struggle for ancient and holy rights against impious oppression. In the fifteenth and sixteenth centuries popular and learned authors did their part towards the formation of more decided opinions, by adding personal conjectures, their own combinations and arrangements, and sometimes even their own errors as historical truth. At the beginning of the fifteenth century the Bernese chronicler Conrad Justinger (about 1420) knew with certainty from records that Schwyz and Unterwalden had been under the Hapsburgs, but that Uri had maintained an exceptional position as belonging to the Fraumünster of Zurich. He likewise knew that the Austrian Hapsburgs had purchased their rights in the Forest States of

---

[1] The best works on the tradition of the origin of the Swiss Federation are:—G. v. WYSS, *Die Waldstätte*. RILLIET, *Les origines de la confédération suisse; histoire et legende*, translated by Brunner, 1870. HUBER, *Die Waldstätte, Uri, Schwiz, Unterwalden*. W. VISCHER, *Die Sage von der Befreiung der Waldstätte*. HAUSSER, *die Tellsage*. GEILFUSS, *Zur Entstehung der eidgenössischen Bünde*; three editions, 1872. G. MEYER VON KNONAU, *Die Sage von der Befreiung der Waldstätte*, 1873.

the earlier or younger line of Hapsburg, and that two rebellions had taken place (against the Hapsburgs and the Austrian Hapsburgs). According to tales, which he probably gathered from the people, he then proceeds to relate that the bailiffs and officials of the Hapsburgs had indulged in wicked actions against "pious folk."

Twenty or thirty years later we meet with isolated episodes out of these traditions. Hämmerlin, canon of Zurich, in a lampoon upon the people of Schwyz, in 1450, relates that a bailiff of Schwyz, appointed by the Hapsburgs, was murdered by two of the inhabitants at the castle of Lowerz, because he had insulted their sister. When the Count of Hapsburg would have interfered with punishment, these men of Schwyz were said to have joined with others, and finally all combined, and to have destroyed the said castle. When the people of Unterwalden, neighbours of Schwyz, heard it, they had possessed themselves of the castle of Sarnen and destroyed it while their lord, a noble of Landenberg, was at mass on Christmas-day, and had afterwards allied themselves with the men of Schwyz.

The whole wealth of the rich cycle of tradition of the liberation of the Forest States is first produced in the *Chronik des weissen Buches* ("Chronicle of the White Book"), about 1470, now in the archives of Sarnen. After Rudolf's time, so runs this record, the bailiffs and officers of the house of Hapsburg proceeded with great arrogance in the Forest States; one "Gesler" in Uri and Schwyz, and one "Landenberg" in Unterwalden. Secure in their castles, they greatly oppressed the surrounding people. Landenberg caused the oxen of a peasant in Melchi (near Sarnen) to be taken from the plough by one of his men, and when the peasant's son, in self-defence, injured one of the serving-man's fingers, Landenberg, finding himself unable to catch the culprit, had the father brought to Sarnen, where his eyes were put out. In Altsellen the lord became attached to the wife of an honest man, went to the house when the husband was away, and had a bath prepared. Meanwhile, however, arrived the husband, went

E

in, and killed the bailiff in his bath with his axe. About the same time one "Staupacher" of Schwyz, who had built himself a handsome stone house, was harassed by Gesler demanding the name of the owner. His wife asked the cause of his trouble, and gave him no peace till he told her. She then urged him to go to Uri, and to join with others of like mind, reminding him specially of the families called "Fürst" and "Zur Frauen," and urging him to make enquiries in Unterwalden. Staupacher accordingly allied himself with one of the Fürsts of Uri, and with the son of the poor man of Melchi, who had fled thither. Other people joined them secretly, and they took an oath of mutual fidelity and help to defend themselves against the lords. And whenever they held their discussions, they betook themselves by night by the Mythenstein, to a place there called the Rütli. Now it happened once that Gesler came to Uri, caused a hat to be stuck upon a pole there, and bade everyone bow to the hat as though it were the lord. One of Staupacher's fellow-conspirators, and his comrade, an honest man of the name of "Tall" (or Tell), would not do this, and complaint was made of him to the lord. The lord sentenced him to shoot an apple from the head of one of his children. Tell yielded to necessity, put one arrow in his bosom, and another on his bow, asked God's help, and shot the apple off the child's head. But Gesler wanted to know why he had taken the second arrow in his bosom. Tell tried to excuse himself, and only confessed upon Gesler promising him his life, that had his first shot failed the second arrow was destined for the lord. Thereupon the latter caused Tell to be bound, in order to carry him to a place where he would see neither sun nor moon, and rowed with him and his serving-men along the lake of Uri as far as the Axen. There a terrible storm came on, and they thought they would be drowned. Gesler's men urged him to loosen Tell's bonds and make him row, for he was a strong man. This was done. Tell, however, kept his eye on his bow and arrows, which were in the stern of the boat, and when he came to Tell's rock (*Tellenplatte*) he called to the others to pull hard; if they reached that rock all danger would be over. While they obeyed his orders, he swung the little boat against the slab of rock, seized his bow and arrows, and sprang out, pushing the boat from the bank as he did so, then ran swiftly over the mountains to the "Hohle Gasse" in Küssnach, and there awaited the lord, lurking behind bushes. When the governor passed by with his train, Tell drew his bow and shot him; then, taking his way over the mountains, went home to Uri. After this, Staupacher and his fellows began to storm the castles of the lords, first in Uri, where fell Twing-Uri, then Schwanau, then on to Schwyz and Stanz. The fortress on the Rotzberg was won by a maiden. In Sarnen people came on Christmas-day to the castle, to bring presents, while the lord was at church. And when there were enough of them within the castle, they made a sign to others who had hidden themselves among the alders behind the mill, and who now came up, took the castle and destroyed it. The bailiff fled with his retainers. Thus the three states made a league together to resist the lords.

Thus far the drift of the copious work of the first chronicler; he probably drew from some older Swiss chronicle and from living tradition, but evidently did not omit to heighten the effect of his narrative with his own bright colouring till he had completed his picture. It was therefore inevitable that when this composition was used by Petermann Etterlin in his "Lucerne Chronicle" of 1507, and was reproduced in print with very little alteration, it became at once the common property of historian and people.[1]

Yet the manner in which these things were depicted in the "White Book" was not the only form in which they were imagined and related. There were essential differences in the "Traditions of Uri." According to the "Lay of Tell," of about 1470, Stauffacher is not the central figure, but Tell: his appearance and conduct forms the centre of the whole transaction, the occasion of the league, and of the revolt against the lords, and Uri is the land whence sprang the league. The

[1] Etterlin, however, always calls the bailiff Gesler "Grissler."

play of Uri of "William Tell," dating from the beginning of the sixteenth century, about 1512, which erroneously places the rising in the year 1296, went still further, and made Tell one of the three Confederates, representing him as treating with the people, inciting them to rebellion, and winning them over to the secret league. So the chronicle of Melchior Russ of Lucerne (1482), who derived his information from Uri, where he had relatives and acquaintances, and whose version, moreover, deviating from the "White Book" and being more in accordance with the actual circumstances, relates that the bailiff wanted to take Tell to Schwyz to the "castle on the lake" (*i.e.*, to Lowerz,[1] and not to Küssnach), and that Tell shot the bailiff immediately upon springing from the boat. Diebold Schilling, of Lucerne (about 1510), represents Tell as compelled by a count or lord of Seedorf to shoot the apple, and that on the 13th of the "haymonth" (July), 1334 (!). Stumpf in his Swiss chronicle (1548) also follows the Uri version by admitting Tell among the three Confederates. Instead of the fugitive from Unterwalden, he places the man of Altsellen among the three founders of the league, and shifts these events to the year 1314. Thus the traditions down to the beginning of the sixteenth century were uncertain, and to some extent contradictory.

The great chronicler Giles Tschudi of Glarus (1570) put an end to this uncertainty. Full of a lively patriotism, he desired to glorify the fame of the Confederation by a brilliant and thrilling description, and therefore treated the history of the foundation of the Swiss league with great freedom, like a romance. He set to work like a painter, who is required to paint a historical picture, but who is left perfectly free to choose his own figures and so to arrange them as to produce the desired impression.[2] He followed the description in the "White Book," but amplified and embellished it partly by verbal traditions of the country and partly by using a poet's

---

[1] The name Schwanau, which was given to a fortress near Strasburg, destroyed in 1333, has only been assigned to this castle by mistake.
[2] MEYER VON KNONAU.

licence. Then he supported the whole by a firm (but purely arbitrary) chronological framework, which even assigned exact dates to all the various incidents. Following the "White Book," which had misplaced the rising in the time after Rudolf, and a casual assertion in the "Klingenberg Chronicle" of the fifteenth century, that the league was founded in 1306, he erroneously placed the chief events in Albert's time, and even in his last years (1307 and 1308), where they seemed to him to fit in best, and from that point he divided the preceding events back to 1304, when Albert was supposed to have sent the foreign bailiffs. Albert himself (contrary to authentic history) is briefly portrayed as a tyrant of the deepest dye. Tschudi also gives the persons more exact designations than did the earlier writers. It is he who first names the man of Altsellen (probably according to popular tradition) "Conrad Baumgarten." To "Fürst," of Uri, he gives the Christian name of "Walter," to "Staupacher" that of "Werner," and to "Gessler" that of "Hermann," because he found these names in records of the time. The surnames of "Anderhalden" and "Wolfenschiess" are also first met with in his writings.

In this way Tschudi impressed upon these traditions the stamp of completeness and of absolute certainty, and obtained such credit for them as remained unshaken through many generations. His version dominated all works of history in after days, and became the common property of the civilized world through Joh. von Müller's history of Switzerland (1780) and Schiller's magnificent drama of "William Tell" (1804).

Yet criticism was soon aroused. About 1600 Franz Guillimann of Fribourg ventured to doubt the story of William Tell, on the ground of the contradictions and diversities in the accounts. In the eighteenth century it began to be noticed that in the folk-lore of Denmark and Iceland, much older traditions than those of Switzerland, there were tales of a skilful marksman (Toko, Eigil), who was forced to shoot an apple from the head of his favourite little son, and who drew out a second or third arrow in order to kill the cruel tyrant in case of failure. The first to notice this important circumstance were J. C. Iselin and Uriel Freudenberger, the latter in his pamphlet entitled *Guillaume Tell, fable danoise* (1760). Tell's advocates exerted themselves so much the more, and even resorted to forgery, in order to furnish documentary evidence for Tell's history. In the journal of Schattorf the name "*Trullo*" was altered to "*de Tello*"; in the parish register of Attinghausen "*Näll*" became "*Täll.*" A story was also invented of a decision of the *Landsgemeinde* of Uri in 1387, by which a pilgrimage to Stein was revived, and it was also ordained that in Bürglen, where stood the house of William Tell, the "first restorer of freedom," a sermon should be preached; and of testimony given by 114 persons in Uri in 1388 to the *Landsgemeinde* that they had known Tell:—as if it would have been necessary, supposing Tell to have been a historical personage, to refute doubts about him only seventy or eighty years after his existence!

Through the labours of Joseph Eutych Kopp, who from 1832 to 1835 sifted and published all the records bearing upon the origin of the Confederation, criticism gained a complete victory. It was then shown that the inhabitants of the Forest States were originally mostly serfs and dependents, and that they only obtained the freedom of the empire gradually, step by step, in the course of the thirteenth century, in close connection with the events of the history of the German empire. It became evident that the Perpetual League was concluded in 1291, and not in 1308; that it is barely conceivable that there were bailiffs in Uri appointed by the Hapsburgs after 1231, and that the Gesslers were never lords of Küssnach, &c. It is, indeed, shown that the traditions concerning the storming of the castles and the founders of the league on the Rütli[1] rest upon historical foundation, yet they can by no means lay claim to acceptance as absolutely authentic history in detail. The worth and charm of the old

[1] The Rütli may have been the historical site of the first alliance between the years 1245 and 1250. Various ruins witness to the destruction of castles, and narratives such as those of Sarnen, Lowerz and Rotzloch may rest upon a historical foundation. The characters of Stauffacher and Fürst are also historical in the main.

folk-lore, as such, was all the more recognised, at least in its earliest form, before the time of Tschudi, in the chronicle of the "White Book." In these traditions we learn to treasure the principles, ideas and customs of the primitive Swiss as the truthful and worthy product of the Swiss mind. Often have they inspired Swiss hearts to patriotic deeds, and even now no Swiss youth grows to manhood without imbibing something of the heroism and the enthusiasm for freedom ascribed to the first Confederates.

PART II.

GROWTH OF THE CONFEDERATION, EMANCIPATION FROM AUSTRIA AND FROM THE NOBILITY.

(1315-1400.)

1. COMMENCEMENT OF THE FEDERATION OF EIGHT STATES.[1]

(1315-1353.)

§ 18. **The Admission of Lucerne into the League.** Notwithstanding the violent shock which the battle of Morgarten had given to the Austrian power, the latter could not resist the temptation to form her territory into one compact principality, by striving to obtain complete possession of the Forest States. Shortly before this (1313) she had brought the Kiburgs and their landgraviate of Burgundy into subjection, and she now sought in the west to obtain forces and aid for a fresh struggle. But the Burgundian towns of Fribourg, Berne, Soleure, Morat and Bienne formed an alliance against the duke in 1318. Leopold endeavoured to reduce them by force, and in 1318 besieged Soleure; the inhabitants, however, held out bravely for ten weeks, and are said to have generously rescued their foes when the bridge over the Aar broke down beneath their weight. The plan formed against the Forest

[1] Chief sources: *Die Chronik des Johannes von Winterthur* (*Vitoduranus*), translated by Bernh. Freuler. JUSTINGER's *Berner Chronik*, edited by Studer. EBERHARD MÜLLNER's *Zürcherchronik*, edited by Ettmüller.

States was thus frustrated; and as the house of Austria was for very many years following occupied with disturbances and misfortunes elsewhere in the empire against Louis the Bavarian, the Forest States found a favourable opportunity to ally themselves with others like-minded and to enlarge their field of action. With this end in view, they entered into alliance in 1323 with the Burgundian towns, notably with Berne and Thun, to whom they were drawn by a common danger; and they then proceeded to endeavour to win to their side the very neighbour whose hostile policy had chiefly troubled them in the past, and whose friendship was now become an urgent necessity, namely, Lucerne.

As long ago as the time of the first revolt against the Hapsburgs in 1250 (*see* p. 40) Lucerne had formed an alliance with the Forest States. The frequency of intercourse by means of the lake and the requirements of trade gave rise to constant friendly relations between that town and the three Forest States. This alliance was cemented when Lucerne also rebelled against the Austrian dominion. For since this town had passed from the mild ecclesiastical rule of the monastery of Murbach to that of the Austrian house of Hapsburg (*see* p. 43), she had come under secular dominion, and into a condition of strict dependence. The perpetual demands of the inhabitants for an extension of their municipal liberties found no hearing. One party, therefore, urged an alliance with the Forest States. The breach between the town and its rulers was widened, when a few burgesses, and soon afterwards the whole community, bound themselves by a general resolution and a solemn oath to repel all encroachments in those unquiet times. The Austrian bailiff at Rotenburg, to whose jurisdiction Lucerne belonged, considered these proceedings of the burgesses dangerous to his rule, and seriously threatened the town. Thereupon the federal party took the upper hand, and on November 7th, 1332, Lucerne concluded a Perpetual League with the three Forest States. This gave rise to fierce and devastating struggles of many years' duration between Lucerne, the Forest States, and the Austrian party.

Federation of Eight States.

The bailiff of Rotenburg fell upon the men of Lucerne at Buonas, and compelled them to obedience, but it does not appear that the league with the Forest States was dissolved (June, 1336). The town was also visited by a conflagration, during which the people of Nidwalden lent their aid as faithful Confederates, notwithstanding a quarrel then existing between them and Lucerne. Meanwhile the Federal League had a severe test to undergo: on St. James's Day, 1343, the adherents of Austria formed a conspiracy against it, and raised a tumult. Their evil designs were, however, betrayed, and the conspirators were banished.[1] This league of the four Forest States formed the first introduction of towns into the confederation. Thus the latter passed beyond its mountain limits and gained a footing in the plain, the Burgundian towns having previously espoused its cause. The struggle was now resumed on all sides; in the present western Switzerland as in the east burgher and peasant alike flung down the gauntlet to their sworn enemy the noble.

§ 19. **First Victory won by Berne over the Nobility of Burgundy. Battle of Laupen.** The citizens of Berne immediately began to gain ground in the west,[2] by taking advantage of the financial and internal ruin of the nobility of Kiburg. In the dispute about the partition of the Kiburg inheritance, Hartmann von Kiburg[3] had been murdered by his younger brother Eberhard in the castle of Thun (1322). The murderer now had to fear the revenge of the Austrian government, which had been favourable to Hartmann. He therefore sought the protection of Berne, invested that town with the feudal lordship of Thun, and raised expectations with regard to Burgdorf. The Bernese enticed King Louis into the alliance against Austria, and in 1323 the Forest States also (*see* p. 56),

---

[1] This event probably gave rise to the later development of the tradition of the massacre of Lucerne.

[2] E. VON WATTENWIL-DIESBACH, *Geschichte der Stadt und Landschaft Bern*, vol. ii.

[3] For the connection between the new and the old houses of Kiburg *cf.* p. 42, note 1.

and began the struggle. In 1324 they acquired Laupen by purchase, destroyed some castles in the Jura, and joined Eberhard in attacking the counts of Neuchâtel. In 1330, however, Louis became reconciled to Austria, and Count Eberhard found his dependence upon Berne so irksome as time went on, that he finally joined the opponents of that town. The Bernese now stood almost alone, and their thirst for action was thoroughly aroused: they destroyed the castle of Gümminen, belonging to Fribourg (1332), took the field against Eberhard, attacked the lords of Weissenburg, and overthrew them completely, destroyed Strättlingen and other castles, and finally, in 1334, won the valley of Hasle from the lords of Weissenburg.

These daring enterprises on the part of Berne exasperated the entire nobility to the utmost, and the latter soon found a favourable opportunity for making their hatred felt by that town. The Emperor Louis being at this time under the papal ban, was not acknowledged by Berne, and therefore declared war against the latter. The nobles of Burgundy now readily entered into an alliance with one another and with Louis against Berne, particularly the counts of Kiburg, Nidau, Aarberg, Strassburg, Neuchâtel, Gruyère, &c., together with the dukes of Austria; the town of Fribourg also joined them, moved by jealousy against Berne. These opponents all assembled one day at Nidau, and renewed their ancient demands and claims; and upon Berne refusing to comply with all their desires, determined to destroy the town: all peaceable overtures were scornfully rejected, and when any of the nobles met a citizen of Berne they would mock him with the words: "If thou art from Berne, bow down and let us pass!"[1] In the spring of 1339 they marched upon Laupen more than 15,000 men strong: the place was bravely defended by John von Bubenberg, the younger, till the Bernese hastened to the rescue, under the skilful leadership of Rudolf von Erlach. They brought with them auxiliaries from Soleure, the Forest States, and the valleys of Hasle and Simmen,

---

[1] "*Bist von Bern, so duck' dich und lass ubergahn!*"

gathered under the banner of the White Cross—only 5000 men in all. But the enemy was forced to give way to the violent and simultaneous attacks of the Bernese and the Forest States; the infantry first yielded, and after about an hour and a half the cavalry also. This brilliant victory of Laupen, which took place on the 21st of June, 1339, the eve of the Ten Thousand Knights' Day,[1] again turned the scale completely in favour of the Bernese. They destroyed the castle of the knight, Jordan von Burgistein (who had vented his malicious joy in biting sarcasm at the distress of Berne), and richly retaliated upon the nobility for all feuds; advanced upon Fribourg, completely routed the forces of that town, and set fire to its environs. Berne was everywhere victorious; that town seemed to gain ground on all sides, and men said in amazement that God Himself had become a citizen of Berne, and was fighting for her. But both Berne and her foes soon longed for peace, which was concluded in 1340 through the intervention of Queen Agnes with Austria, and was shortly afterwards followed by a ten years' league, the Bernese engaging to furnish auxiliary troops when needed. The town also renewed her league with the Forest States, which was in no wise forbidden by the Austrian alliance; the help rendered by those states at Laupen and their common danger had linked the two parties very closely together. Berne formed as it were the western bulwark of the league of the Forest States, and the embarrassments of Austria in eastern Switzerland renewing the struggle, Berne became a permanent member of the Confederation.

§ 20. **Leagues with Zurich, Glarus, Zug and Berne.** Zurich formed the centre of operations in the east, as did Berne in the west; but, unlike Berne, Zurich first tried to gain the ascendency by a union with Austria. Ever since 1292 Austria had exerted a growing influence in eastern Switzerland, until internal affairs caused a breach between the imperial town and its rulers.

[1] *Zehntausend Rittertag.*

Here, as in other German towns, the handicraftsmen had long been endeavouring to form guilds, and to obtain equal rights with the aristocracy. The government was fiercely attacked by the citizens, and accused of divers offences. Rudolf Brun took an opportunity to possess himself of the management of the town. This clever, able and ambitious statesman in 1336 wrought a change in the constitution, which conceded certain political rights to the artisans in common with the aristocracy (for the constitution of guilds see § 23), and conferred upon himself the office of burgomaster for life. The old councillors were for the most part removed, and some of them banished. Brun now sought the support of Austria, and the latter brought about a reconciliation between the town and the exiled councillors. But these last, brooding secretly over their wrongs, obtained the assistance of Count Hans von Rapperswil, and sought the ruin of the burgomaster and his faction. Brun was on the alert, however, and sufficiently informed of their designs to take precautions. On the very night that he was to be assassinated (the night of the Zurich massacre, 23rd February, 1350), he caused the alarm-bell to be rung, and many conspirators to be massacred and put to death; a remnant only escaped. He then advanced upon Rapperswil, and administered the oath of allegiance to the inhabitants. He endeavoured to come to an understanding with Austria, and even to form an alliance with that power, but this came to nothing. A party in Zurich hostile to Brun gained the upper hand, and speedily destroyed both old and new Rapperswil (September, 1350). By this means Zurich drew upon itself the enmity of the nobility, and even of Austria its former friend, and Brun lost his essential support, and was driven to form a league with the peasants of the mountains; for Zurich, like Berne in the Laupen war, turned to the Forest States, with whom it had been occasionally connected for a century past. (See p. 40.) Brun sought to gain what advantage he might from so undesirable a connection. Thus on 1st May, 1351, the imperial free town of Zurich entered the **Perpetual League** of the Confederates, and by this means the Federation was firmly established in the plains.

It was, however, impossible that Austria should look on in silence while the Confederation increased step by step at her expense. Duke Albert, therefore, renewed the attempt (in which his brother had failed at the battle of Morgarten) to destroy the Confederation. In September, 1351, with 16,000 men, he laid siege to Zurich, which was defended by a federal garrison. The Confederates inclined to peace, but the demands of Austria were so exorbitant that negotiations were abandoned and the war was continued. In December, 1351, troops from Zurich, after devastating the baths at Baden, were surprised at Tätwil on their return journey by Austrians, and had some difficulty in making their escape. In this second struggle Zurich and the Forest States conquered Glarus. This latter territory, which belonged to Austria, having been long at variance with its rulers, and having entered into alliance with the Forest States as early as 1323, welcomed the Confederates as deliverers. The inhabitants repulsed the Austrian bailiff at Rautifeld near Näfels, and on the 4th June, 1352, joyfully entered the Perpetual League of the Confederates. Zug also, forsaken by Duke Albert, now yielded to the Confederates, and joined the league on 27th June, 1352. Upon this, Duke Albert resolved to retrieve his losses at one blow. All his adherents supplied him with troops, and Berne too was obliged to send a contingent, in accordance with the former alliance. On the 21st June, 1352, he advanced upon Zurich, as in the previous year, that being the nearest important outpost of the Confederates, but encountered such valiant resistance on the part of the men of Zurich and their allies, that in three weeks' time he raised the siege, internal dissensions arising among his own troops. But under Brun's management Zurich had assumed a sort of intermediate position between Austria and the Confederation, and felt itself rather a free imperial town than a member of the Federal League, and consequently the peace which was now concluded (Peace of Brandenburg,[1]

So called from its negotiator, the Margrave of Brandenburg.

September, 1352) was somewhat unfavourable to the Confederates. Glarus and Zug were to be once more in subjection to Austria, even Schwyz and Unterwalden were again forced to pay tribute and taxes to that power, and all the Confederates bound themselves to form no further alliances with other towns or lands belonging to the duke.

In return, the league was increased by the accession of the town of Berne. The Bernese had been obliged to furnish Austria with auxiliaries against Zurich, but they had not the slightest intention of quarrelling with the Forest States, who had befriended them at the time of the campaign of Laupen. Immediately upon the reconciliation between Austria and the Forest States by the peace of Brandenburg, Berne concluded a Perpetual League with the Confederates on 6th March, 1353; this could be done without coming into direct hostility with Austria, since the Austrian League permitted the renewal of former amities. Thus a second imperial town joined the Confederation, a town whose position and authority dominated the whole of what is now western Switzerland. Berne formed a powerful bulwark towards the south-west, as did Zurich towards the north-east. Hence the entrance of both these towns into the Federal League not only assured the continuance of the Confederation, but also secured for it a certain amount of political power in the German empire.

2. THE WAR OF LIBERATION BETWEEN AUSTRIA AND THE EIGHT ORIGINAL STATES.

(1353–1400 [1394].)

§ 21. **Conclusion of the Siege of Zurich. The Demands of Austria.** Some conditions of the peace of Brandenburg remaining unfulfilled, Duke Albert of Austria accused the Confederates of breaking the peace, carrying his complaint to the Emperor Charles IV., then at the head of the empire. The latter, after many attempts had been made to come to terms, declared war against the Confederation in the name of the empire (June, 1354). He appeared before Zurich at the head of a considerable imperial army, and was joined by Duke Albert and his adherents. Zurich now for the fourth time (since 1292) saw Austrian troops before her gates—with as little result as before, however, for the Confederates defied the enemy, though the numbers of the latter were ten times as great as their own. Owing to delay, dissensions arose in the camp of the imperial army; many of the nobility were offended by the haughty Duke of Austria; the imperial towns feared to injure their own position and to give the princes an advantage by attacking the imperial town of Zurich, and the Emperor Charles IV. was himself inclined to peace. Brun was not slow to avail himself of this disposition. He caused the imperial flag to be hoisted on the walls of Zurich, in order to call to mind the loyalty of Zurich to the empire. The feud with Zurich being thus made to appear a merely Austrian undertaking, the imperial towns withdrew their allegiance. Charles IV. therefore raised the siege, and himself offered to act as mediator; which offer Zurich, wearied by the protracted struggle with Albert, finally accepted. Terms were settled on 24th July, 1355, by the peace of Regensburg.[1] The latter was almost identical with the peace of Brandenburg; Zurich again negotiated quite as a free imperial town, and undertook to induce the Confederates to accept the peace; and the oath was taken. Brun even succeeded in persuading Zurich to enter into alliance with Austria. This equivocal demeanour on the part of Zurich only ended with the death of Brun in 1360, and the Confederates then once more advanced against Austria with one accord. Schwyz took possession of the town and territory of Zug, and Austria was forced to give her consent to this step, in 1368, by the peace of Thorberg; Zug was now once more a member of the league.

A long period of peace next followed, during which both parties recruited their strength, and even joined hands in

[1] The events of this third Austrian war have been brought to light by the researches of Prof. G. v. Wyss, and correctly described by him, contradicting hitherto existing accounts. (*Anzeiger für Schweizergeschichte Jahrgang* xii. *und* xiii.)

friendship, being unexpectedly united by the presence of a common foe. Baron Ingelram von Coucy, grandson of Leopold I. of Austria, and son-in-law of Edward III. of England, required the dukes of Austria to give up Aargau, which he claimed in his mother's right; and not obtaining it, he invaded Switzerland in 1375 with a numerous army of French and English mercenaries.[1] Terror and dismay were universal at the devastation wrought by these undisciplined troops. Wherever they went crops were destroyed, men and cattle butchered, and villages, churches and monasteries set on fire. In this emergency Austria sought reconciliation with the Confederates, and renewed the Peace of Thorberg. She also concluded an offensive and defensive alliance with the towns, from which, however, the country districts held aloof out of hatred to Austria.

The Confederates advanced immediately against the "Guglers"; in December, 1375, a few troops from Lucerne, Entlebuch and Unterwalden repulsed one division of mercenaries at Buttisholz in the district of Sursee; troops from Berne and Fribourg attacked another division at Ins (or Jens), and the Bernese alone finally gained a brilliant victory over the main army near the monastery of Fraubrunnen. The rest of the invaders, partly owing to these defeats and partly to the want of provisions and the severity of the winter, were compelled to withdraw without attaining their object. The love of war and enterprise was no little aroused in the Confederates, and notably in Berne, by these events; and the first Swiss war songs celebrated the victories of Berne over France and England. The common danger had, however, confirmed the peace with Austria.

§ 22. **The War of Kiburg, Sempach and Nafels, and its Consequences.** The second half of the fourteenth century, the period of the greatest and most rapid growth of the Confederation, was very favourable to the development of civic

---

[1] These troops received the nickname of "*Gugler*" on account of their headgear resembling a cowl (Swiss-German, "*Gugel*").

communities. In both France and Germany the towns fearlessly opposed the nobility and princes, and even seemed to aim at the government of the empire. Beyond the Rhine the town of Berne was especially disposed to wage a war of extermination against the nobility. Before this town there lay a field ripe already to harvest; for the Burgundian nobility either died out or became increasingly impoverished by the then growing want of money.[1] The counts of Kiburg, too, were much reduced, and obliged to sell or mortgage one estate after another. Count Rudolf still tried to obtain money and spoil by violent attacks upon the towns; and in 1382 he endeavoured to surprise the town of Soleure under cover of night and fog (Massacre of Soleure). But the plot was discovered, it is said by Hans Roth of Rumisberg, a peasant. Soleure and Berne called upon the Confederates for aid, and a protracted war was commenced against the house of Kiburg, which ended to the advantage of the towns, in spite of a futile siege of Burgdorf. Berne, with the help of the Confederates, destroyed the fortresses and castles of the nobility of Kiburg, and acquired the towns of Burgdorf and Thun, which were retained till 1384; and the house of Kiburg was forced to promise to commence no future war without the consent of Berne and Soleure. By this means Berne became lord of the upper and middle districts of the Aar.

But this again led to friction with Austria, since during the war with the house of Kiburg, Austria, notwithstanding promises to the contrary, had secretly supported that house, and seemed disposed to avenge its destruction. The Confederates also no longer hesitated to support the enemies of Austria. In order to be able successfully to oppose the princes and nobles of South Germany, the southern towns of Germany had formed themselves into a great alliance, and thus had come into conflict with Leopold III., Duke of Austria. In February, 1385, Zurich, Berne, Soleure, Lucerne and Zug made common cause with the allied towns in opposition to Leopold; the three Forest States held aloof, probably fearing

[1] NÜSCHELER, *Geschichte des Schweizerlandes*, ii. p. 49.

the ascendency of the towns. Leopold thought to avail himself of this division of interests among the Confederates, and endeavoured by all manner of favours to win the rural communes to his cause while venting his wrath upon the towns. Notwithstanding many urgent entreaties, he denied to Lucerne the abolition of the burdensome toll of Rothenburg. At the same time he sought to keep the peace as long as possible. The Confederates, however, who had formerly waited to be attacked, now themselves urged on the war, although the peace with Austria—renewed for eleven years in 1376—was not yet expired. War was declared by them on all sides: Zurich attacked Rapperswil; Zug the Austrian fortress of Saint-André on the lake of Zug; Lucerne on Christmas-day destroyed Rothenburg, admitted Entlebuch, then hard pressed by the lord of Thorberg, the Austrian bailiff, into a civil alliance, and finally did the same for Sempach, which was striving to free itself from the Austrian dominion (January, 1386).

After such gross violations of the treaty, Austria could hesitate no longer. The imperial towns, it is true, sought even yet to adjust matters peaceably; but these attempts at reconciliation merely caused delay, and the towns, being just then threatened by Bavaria, made terms with Austria, and forsook the Confederates. The valiant Duke Leopold now resolved to strike a decisive blow at the Confederation. The universal dislike and animosity felt by the nobility towards both townsmen and peasants favoured his desires; and a numerous body of knights joined him from the Austrian territories of Thurgau and Aargau, and from Suabia, Burgundy and Alsace. In order probably to separate the forces of the Confederates, Leopold sent a portion of his army against Zurich, while he himself, with the main body of his troops—6000 men in all—advanced, in the beginning of July, 1386, against Sempach, Rothenburg and Lucerne. The Confederates left the inhabitants of Zurich to defend their own territory, and marched against Leopold with a force of only about 1500 men.

On the 9th of July the two armies met unexpectedly at Sempach, and a battle ensued. The nobles prepared for the attack by alighting from their horses, the ground being unsuitable for the use of horses. The Austrians formed a close column, with their spears pointed against the Confederates, who were chiefly furnished with short weapons, and were drawn up in the form of a wedge. The Austrians, moreover, stood on higher ground, and hence the Confederates suffered severely at the commencement of the action, and Leopold imagined the victory secure. But then (according to later but authentic accounts) one of the Confederates, the brave Arnold Winkelried, is said to have pressed forward careless of his own life, and opened a breach in the hostile ranks. Encouraged by this heroic example, the Confederates dashed forward, their wedge shape broken, over the corpse of the slain man upon the Austrians, and dealt such blows with their halberds and clubs upon the enemy, that the latter, suffering greatly at the same time from the weight of their armour in the sultry heat of July, could not long hold out. In vain did Duke Leopold dash into the thick of the fight to arrest the flight of his men; his life was sacrificed with those of the bravest of his knights. Part of the Austrian army—mostly pages with the horses—had already taken to flight. Between 700 and 1500 Austrians had fallen, among them 600 of the highest nobility, while the Confederates lost only about 120.[1] This brilliant and encouraging victory of the Confederates made a deep and far-reaching impression. In it the fate of the Austrian power in Switzerland was determined. The Bernese, who had hitherto held aloof from the struggle because the peace of Thorberg was not yet expired, now also took up arms, and possessed themselves of the dominions of Fribourg and Austria in the Bernese Oberland (Obersimmenthal, Unterseen and Oberhofen) and in Seeland. The remainder of the Confederates joined Glarus, their ancient ally, took possession of the Austrian town of Wesen in August, 1386, and placed

[1] For the criticisms upon this question *cf.* W. OECHSLI, *Zur sempacher Schlachtfeier* (Zurich, F. Schulthess, 1886), and the works there quoted.

a garrison there. Glarus drove out the Austrian bailiffs, and in 1387 was annexed to the Confederation as an independent and free community.

Meanwhile Duke Albert, Leopold's brother, unwilling to surrender his dominions so easily, turned his force against Glarus. Wesen was first recovered by treachery and cruelty. Austrian soldiers were smuggled into the town by the help of some of the townsmen, and put the Federal garrison to death (Massacre of Wesen, 22nd February, 1388). The Austrians—6000 strong—next advanced against Glarus; and were encountered on 9th April, 1388, by 500 men of Glarus and a handful from Schwyz at Näfels. The men of Glarus posted themselves behind the "Letzi" (a rampart) which enclosed the entrance to the valley, but were forced to yield to superior numbers. While the Austrians dashed blindly up the valley in search of plunder, the men of Glarus assembled themselves at the side of the valley on a hillock on the slope of the Rautiberg. The Austrians turned hastily in that direction, but were received with a shower of stones and thrown into confusion. The men of Glarus, under Mathias Ambühl, dashed impetuously down, threw themselves upon the enemy, and drove them in a protracted struggle down the valley towards the "Letzi," and over it as far as Wesen: 1700 of the enemy are said to have perished; many were drowned in the Linth. Wesen was taken by the men of Glarus and destroyed by fire. After many castles had been destroyed, in April, 1389, the imperial towns effected a truce of seven years between Austria and the Confederates, which secured their conquests to the latter.

Austria afterwards sought to retrieve her losses by entering into alliance with the Burgomaster (Schöno) and the small council of Zurich, who were still well disposed towards Austria, as they had been in 1356. But the citizens, most of whom were loyal to the Confederation, destroyed the treaty and expelled the traitorous faction (1393). An alteration in the constitution strengthened the democratic element in Zurich, and the new union of the Confederates found worthy expression in the Convention of Sempach.[1] (*Sempacherbrief*, see § 23.) An amicable settlement was made with Austria, and on the 16th July, 1394, the seven years' peace was lengthened to twenty years. Glarus, like Zug, now formed a free member of the Confederation. The war of liberation, which had lasted almost a century, was brought to a conclusion in May, 1412, by a further extension of the peace for fifty years.

After so many struggles and hostilities the position of the Confederation was at length assured for a long time to come. Austria surrendered her claims to the dominion of Schwyz and Unterwalden, her rights over Lucerne, Zug and Glarus for as long as the peace should last. The power of the nobility in the Confederation was shattered.

3. NATURE OF THE FEDERAL LEAGUE.

§ 23. The wars of freedom of the Swiss peasants and townsfolk, which form but a link in the great chain of the struggles of those times between aristocracy and democracy, acquired a more general significance from the fact that similar democratical efforts had been suppressed in other lands. The rising of the peasants in England, and the revolt of French citizens, which took place about the same time, failed; and contemporary with the victories of Sempach and Näfels was the battle of Döffingen (1388), where the free citizens of southern Germany, when almost victorious, succumbed to the blows of their princes. Thus it was reserved to the Swiss alone to found a state of a civic and republican nature. It was to begin with greatly in their favour that the dukes of Austria were at a distance, and that their attention was claimed simultaneously on all sides. But they owed their success yet more to their warlike capacity, their readiness in battle, and their bravery. A special strength and a peculiar character were also conferred upon them by the combination between peasantry and townsfolk, a combination found nowhere else in Europe.

[1] K. HAGEN, *über die politischen Verhältnisse der Eidgenossen zur zeit der Sempacherschlacht. Archiv für Schweizergeschichte*, vol. xii.

But this very combination was the chief cause that the internal political conditions of the various members of the League differed widely, and even in some cases formed complete contrasts to one another. In the interior cantons of Uri, Schwyz, Unterwalden and Glarus, and partially also in Zug,[1] the chief power rested in the *Landsgemeinde*, which was derived from the ancient *Markgemeinde* in the thirteenth century. To this every man, from the age of sixteen, had access; it assembled every year, elected the magistrates (the Landamman, the council, the treasurer, &c.), determined taxes, and decided as to proposed laws; it also exercised judicial powers. At the same time, according to ancient German custom, there was no difference as to right of voting between the meanest peasant and the highest burgher, and the attainment of political majority was signified as among the old Germans by the bearing of weapons in the assembly.

The towns had a more aristocratic constitution. But even among them there were again great differences, especially between Zurich and Berne. In Zurich since Rudolf Brun's time the guilds (of tradesmen and artisans) had a share in the government, and much resembled the old free and knightly families or patricians, who alone had formerly been entitled to vote. The wardens, *i.e.* the masters of the thirteen guilds, with the thirteen councillors, the representatives of the "Constafel" (the society of noble citizens of ancient descent), together formed the council. By the side of this existing "small council" an enlarged "great council" (of the 200) gradually developed in course of time, privileged to represent the communes. But whereas Brun had endowed the office of a burgomaster with almost monarchical powers, divers events, especially the treachery of Schöno in 1393, led to a restriction of that office and a strengthening of the great council, as also of the college of wardens. In contrast to those of Zurich, the artisans of Berne acquired no influence whatever; the guilds could take no active part in political

[1] Zug had indeed a civic constitution of its own, but formed a *Landsgemeinde* canton collectively with Menzingen, Aegeri and Baar (the "Amt").

matters, and the government was carried on exclusively by the council, composed of members of distinguished families of the nobility. There were also great differences as to the position in the League which the various states occupied, as well as in their internal constitutional conditions.[1] The three Forest States formed a group by themselves, and became the nucleus around which the other members gathered. All the remaining states, which had concluded no special league among themselves, allied themselves to them, and they were united by the closest bond of fellowship among themselves. The provisions of the League were the same for all three. They mutually bound themselves to render constant and prompt aid to one another; none of the three might enter into foreign negotiations without the knowledge and advice of the others; the punishment of offences in matters concerning the League appertained to all in common. Being thus bound by a species of community of rights dating from the Perpetual League of 1315, they already represented a league in the modern sense of the word. The other states, on the contrary, were by no means so closely united among themselves. The Confederation was formed gradually by the accession of new members, till at last a many-sided whole was produced. The treaties of alliance were in every case regulated according to the special needs of the moment and local conditions. Thus the League of Lucerne differs essentially from others. The rendering of aid is made conditional upon the distressed state affirming itself upon oath to be in the right, and upon formal notice given. No member may interfere with the internal affairs of another, and no party to the League may conclude an alliance without the consent of all the Confederates.

The League of Zurich is the first to describe a Federal circle within which aid should be rendered—Grimsel, Aare, Rhine, Thur, Ringgenberg near Truns, Platifer near Faido, Doisel near Lax in Upper Valais—and the stipulations with regard to such

[1] S. PFAFF, *das Staatsrecht der alten Eidgenossenschaft*, Schaffhausen, 1870. *Die Bundesurkunden bei Bluntschli, Geschichte des eidgenössischen Bundesrechts*, vol. ii., and in the *Eidgenössischen Abschieden*, vol. i.

aid are fixed more definitely. Internal dissensions are to be settled by arbitration, each party to elect two judges, and they to deliberate at Einsiedeln. Should there be no majority, an arbitrator is elected, whose decision shall be final. Further, every party retains the right of forming alliances, and Zurich moreover asserts her right to demand immediate assistance of the Forest States should her guilds or her burgomaster be in danger. Finally, all ancient rights and customs are guaranteed at the outset. Every ten years both old and young shall swear to this alliance. In contrast to Zurich, Glarus is treated with scant respect in her League, and almost like a dependency, while Zug enters into the rights enjoyed by the Forest States in the Treaty of Zurich. Berne maintained a favourable position, including freedom of alliance and a guarantee for her existing territory. Thus the Confederation was by no means a political structure. It was but loosely held together; Zurich, Berne and Lucerne, for example, were not directly allied to one another at all, but only through the medium of the Forest States.

Yet, notwithstanding this slight formation, the League was durable. While the leagues of the German and Italian towns, and even of the Hans towns, fell to pieces, the Swiss Federation, after centuries of duration, is the only example of a state which had its origin in free alliances. Notwithstanding local differences, we find even in these early times essential points in common between the political aims and views of the Confederates. For instance, from the earliest times the various states would suffer no exceptional advantages to be given to the clergy, and in spite of violent protest regularly assessed the monasteries within their territory (*e.g.*, Uri laid taxes upon Wettingen, Schwyz upon Einsiedeln), and the towns likewise subjected their religious houses to the authority of the state. Twice (in 1248 and 1338) Zurich expelled the insubordinate clergy, drew taxes from their estates in spite of the prohibition of the Bishop of Constance, and kept a watchful eye upon their conduct and management. The rural communities vied with the well-to-do towns in the abolition of ground-rents and feudal rights, which they owed to divers spiritual and temporal lords, and in the course of the fourteenth century they gradually freed themselves by purchase from the greater part of these burdens, as for example Uri from Wettingen and Fraumünster, Schwyz from Einsiedeln, Kappel and Engelberg, Glarus from Seckingen. Both the towns and the rural communities were exceedingly anxious to induce the emperor to release them from their obligations to the empire and from its jurisdiction, and desired to obtain dominion and sovereign rights, such as county courts, penal judicature, and rights of coinage over their adjacent territory, and to annex the latter. The efforts of Uri, Schwyz, Lucerne, Berne and Zurich were successful, and the latter as early as the beginning of the fifteenth century had little by little acquired dominion over the greater part of the present canton, and had by strenuous efforts obtained her emancipation from imperial bailiffs, tolls and taxes.[1]

The course of events soon obliged the Confederates to establish federal principles which should be generally binding, and to enact federal laws. When Bruno Brun, Provost of the *Grossmünster* in Zurich, and his brother, Herdegen Brun, the two sons of the burgomaster, having taken part in an attack upon Peter von Gundoldingen, mayor of Lucerne, refused, as ecclesiastics, to appear before the secular court, it was ordained by the "Priests' Charter" (*Pfaffenbrief*) of 7th October, 1370, by the majority of the Confederates (six states), that ecclesiastics should be under the authority of the state, and should occupy no exceptional position; that all feuds and assaults should be forbidden, and all roads protected. On the 10th July, 1393, all the eight states united with Soleure in the formation of a common military ordinance

---

[1] The most important acquisitions of Zurich (mostly obtained by purchase) were:—1358 Zollikon, 1384 Küssnach and Goldbach, Höngg, 1385 Thalwil, 1400 Erlenbach, 1402 Greifensee, 1405 Männedorf, 1406 Maschwanden, Horgen, Rüschlikon, 1408 Grüningen, Stäfa, Hombrechtikon, Mönchaltorf, 1409 Regensberg and Bülach, 1410 Meilen, 1415 Freiamt (by conquest), 1424 Rümlang, 1424 and 1452 the county of Kiburg (Tösstal, lower Glattal, the "Wine Land"), 1484 Stein on the Rhine, 1496 Eglisau, &c., &c.

called the Convention of Sempach (*Sempacherbrief*). The voluntary enterprises of individuals, unauthorized pillage, and the ill-treatment of sacred spots and of defenceless women, were prohibited by this ordinance. This is the only example in those days of fierce and warlike passions of any statutory settlement of military discipline in the interests of order and humanity, and it testifies amply to the high purpose of the Federal League, and also to earnest endeavour towards a firmer alliance.

From all these circumstances it is evident that the Confederates had no definite preconceived idea in view, nor did they advance in full consciousness of a task to be achieved, but only sought to realise step by step whatever was attainable and possible under existing conditions. In contrast to the unbridled revolutionary attempts of the lower classes in France, England, and other parts, which occurred about this time, the Confederation, by their moderate measures, averted any strong reaction, and rendered steady progress possible.

Part III.

SWITZERLAND AT THE HEIGHT OF HER POWER.

(1400-1516.)

1. FIRST ALLIANCE WITH ADJACENT COMMUNITIES.

Had the Federal League of eight states remained unmolested after the victorious issue of the war of independence, and unnoticed by surrounding neighbours, it would hardly have expanded of itself. But it had set an example which began to kindle the surrounding countries, and aroused such desires after freedom that the Confederates could not remain inactive. Hence the League began to spread on all sides, and the Confederation soon stood, as it were, surrounded by a strong rampart of free communities, the largest and most important of which were Appenzell, Valais and the Grisons.

§ 24. **The Alliance with Appenzell and St. Gall.**[1] The right of dominion over Appenzell and over the towns of St. Gall had gradually devolved to a great extent upon the Abbot of St. Gall. But while the abbots were endeavouring to maintain, and even to extend their rights, the inhabitants of Appenzell, St. Gall, and other their dependencies were striving for greater freedom in face of the various struggles for independence going on around them. As early as 1377 Abbot George von Wildenstein was unable to hinder the people of Appenzell, Hundwil, Gais and Teufen from allying themselves with southern German towns around the lake of Constance, and from appointing a common administration freely elected by themselves. The election of this administration gradually led to the regular establishment of the so-called *Landsgemeinde*. Insubordination quickly made its appearance on all sides. The town of St. Gall, which possessed an imperial charter dating from the thirteenth century, and had for many years had its own corporation, had previously entered the League of the towns. An insurrection broke out in Wil. Abbot George's successor, however, Cuno von Stoffeln, who became abbot in 1379, seemed to have mastered the movement by skilful policy and rigid discipline. He even entered into alliance with the imperial towns, and by their help forced the inhabitants of Appenzell to do him homage, and to pay tributes, rents and tithes; double taxes were laid upon the malcontents.

This was the signal for an open and general rising. The people of Appenzell, in desperation, leagued themselves in 1401 with the town of St. Gall, and advanced upon the castle of Clanx belonging to the abbot, which was taken. By the efforts of the imperial towns, however—the abbot himself having become a burgher of Lindau—St. Gall was once more reconciled to the abbot. But the people of Appenzell persisted in their rebellion, allied themselves in 1402 with Schwyz, which sent them aid, and prepared for war, destroying many castles, and carrying their ravages almost to St. Gall

[1] ZELLWEGER, *Geschichte des appenzellischen Volkes.*

itself. Meanwhile the troops of the imperial towns, summoned by Cuno, had arrived at that town. On the 15th May, 1403, these troops, together with the abbot's retainers and the men of St. Gall—5000 men in all—advanced towards the heights of Vögelinseck on the "Letzi"[1] (near Speicher), where 200 men from Appenzell, with 300 from Schwyz and 200 from Glarus awaited them. After a brief engagement the enemy was forced to yield; 250 of them remained dead upon the field. The imperial towns then concluded a peace with the inhabitants of Appenzell, leaving the abbot to continue the struggle (1404). The latter sought help from Austria, and Duke Frederick reluctantly consented to interpose. Upon this the inhabitants of St. Gall again attached themselves to those of Appenzell, and the latter were also supported by Count Rudolf von Werdenberg, who had been (through his own fault) dispossessed of his estates by Austria.

The Austrians advanced in two divisions, one encamped before St. Gall, and the other prepared to attack Altstätten. While the former, under Duke Frederick, devastated the neighbourhood of St. Gall, the latter advanced from Altstätten towards the frontier at the Stoss.[2] The Austrians crossed the "Letzi" successfully; but the men of Appenzell and Schwyz dashed suddenly down upon them from the heights, hurling down stones and trunks of trees; the Austrians could scarcely keep their feet upon the slippery ground, and were soon put to flight, from four to five hundred being slain. The division under the duke retired from St. Gall. This was on the 17th June, 1405.

The duke, discouraged, withdrew from the war, whereupon the men of Appenzell, giving the rein to their youthful prowess, speedily achieved unexpected successes. They renewed their league with St. Gall, and in the course of their victorious march conquered the whole of the Rheintal, liberated the towns of Werdenberg, Sargans, Feldkirch and Bludenz, and concluded with them the "League above the Lake";[3] the

---

[1] A redoubt or rampart.—E. S. [2] The name of a mountain-spur.—E. S.
[3] "*Bund ob dem See.*"

province of Toggenburg also entered this alliance. This league formed as it were a second Confederation side by side with that of the Swiss, held its own diets, and acted as an independent power towards foreign countries. In the flush of victory, and in revenge for old scores, the men of Appenzell devastated the territories of neighbouring lords and hostile towns; they proclaimed liberty to the peasant everywhere, and in a brief space of time destroyed over fifty castles. Thurgau and Vorarlberg were overrun; the county of Kiburg and the whole of Suabia were thrown into alarm and excitement by the unbridled fury of the invincible mountain folk. Every effort was therefore made to oppose them. In the first instance the burgesses of Constance and the nobility of Suabia joined, fell upon the men of Appenzell suddenly in winter before Bregenz, the lake being frozen (January, 1408), and put them to flight.

In consequence of this defeat the "League above the Lake" was dissolved, and the pride of the inhabitants of Appenzell was crushed; they now desisted from further interference with neighbouring districts. But now they were again threatened on their own territory, the emperor endeavouring to force them into subjection to the abbot. The Confederates, on the other hand, supported them, and on the 24th November, 1411, they were received by the seven states (all the eight states except Berne) as a subordinate member of the League, and taken under protection by a treaty of perpetual citizenship.[1] Liberty was secured to Appenzell by its accession to the Swiss League.

In the next year the town of St. Gall followed its example, after having compelled the new abbot to acknowledge its freedom and independence. In vain did the abbots endeavour to recover their sovereign rights; they were obliged to content themselves with certain rents and taxes, which, moreover, were gradually remitted. The alliance of Appenzell and St. Gall with the Confederates was renewed after the Zurich war, in which they had served as a support against Austria, and was confirmed for all time.

[1] "*Ein ewiges Burg-und Landrecht.*"

§ 25. **Liberation of the Valais.**[1] The inhabitants of Valais, like those of Appenzell, turned to the Confederates for help in obtaining their freedom. Here, too, there had since very early times existed a tolerable number of free folk, confronted by a powerful nobility. The land was divided politically into two districts. Upper Valais, which was chiefly German, was under the Bishop of Sion; Lower Valais, with a Romance (French) population, under the Count of Savoy. The former gradually acquired a position of freedom, like the inhabitants of Appenzell under their abbot, and like so many provinces under ecclesiastical dominion; several communities called *Zehnten* acquired certain liberties which in 1354 were ratified by the Emperor Charles IV. Every *Zehnte* had its own jurisdiction, and all stood alike under one council and one governor-general.

The bishop had often formerly sought to defend himself against such efforts for freedom by a league with the counts of Savoy; the latter, however, thought to avail themselves of this alliance to extend their own rights in the Valais. With this view, Count Amadeus VII. of Savoy interfered in a dispute between the nobility and people. A devastating war broke out, in which, in 1388 (soon after the victory of the Confederates at Näfels), Amadeus and the nobility were defeated at Visp by the Valaisans. Upper Valais was by this means secured against Savoy.

But a new danger threatened from the direction of the mighty Baron von Raron. The family of Raron was at that time the most powerful in the Valais, and united the offices of a bishop and a governor-general; it was also strongly supported by Berne (in which town the family enjoyed civic rights) and by the dukes of Milan. The barons therefore expected to be easily able to subjugate the land. But in 1414, the Confederates being expelled by them in concert with Savoy from Eschental, which had been taken from Milan (*see* § 27), the Valaisans rose in revolt; the *Landsturm*[2] was

---

[1] FURRER, *Geschichte des Wallis.*
[2] A general levy of the people.—E. S.

called out, the *mazza*[1] was raised, and all flocked to their country's flag. Beauregard, the ancestral castle of the Rarons, was destroyed, and the family driven out (1415). The Raron family then seeking the help of the Duke of Savoy, the people of Upper Valais concluded a ten years' treaty of citizenship with Uri, Unterwalden and Lucerne (1416), with whom they had long been on terms of friendly alliance for purposes of trade. The Bernese, however, supported the Raron family as their fellow-citizens. War broke out afresh, and a furious struggle ensued. Now the Bernese and Witschard von Raron invaded Valais, robbing and plundering; now the men of Valais made incursions into Bernese territory. The Bernese and their allies advanced against Upper Valais in 1419 with a powerful force. Devastation followed in their train, and a fearful panic ensued. Then a gallant patriot, Thomas Riedi by name, assembled a few hundred adherents, fell upon the enemy at Ulrich, and compelled them to retreat. Valais once more was saved.

In 1420 the Confederates negotiated a peace, which, owing to the machinations of Berne and Savoy, proved unfavourable to the inhabitants of the Valais, and the latter was allotted to Berne and the Raron family as indemnification. On the other hand, the Valaisans had achieved an enduring success. The position of governor-general was thenceforth always occupied by a native of the district agreeable to the people. A new constitution gave the people a greater share in the government, such as the choice of officers, judges, sergeants, and members of council; and the bishop might not nominate his officials without the consent of the country. The Rarons left the land.

§ 26. **Alliance with the Grisons.** Hardly any other district had undergone so many territorial divisions as ancient Rhætia.[2] Upon the heights which encircle the valleys of the

[1] A club upon which was carved a human face in agony, which was carried from village to village as a symbol of revolt.—E. S.
[2] JUVALTA, *Forschungen über die Feudalzeit im curischen Rätien*, Zurich, 1871. PLANTA, *die currätischen Herrschaften*.

Rhine and its tributaries there stood numerous castles (some of which still remain as romantic ruins) in the possession of powerful nobles, as those of Razuns, Montfort, Werdenberg, Belmont, Triens, Aspermont, Montsax (Misox), Vaz, &c. The bishops of Coire owned a specially extensive territory; almost the whole land was under their rule, with the exception of the valleys of the Upper Rhine, Prätigau and Davos, and not a few noble families were their feudal vassals. But at the same time many free communes existed there, similar to the "Zehnten" in Valais; these were called Jurisdictions (*Gerichte*), and were the champions of freedom. Their gradual emancipation was favoured by the circumstance that their many lords either held one another in check or made common cause with the people, in order to restrict the power of the bishops' ecclesiastical dominion. For this reason the people of those parts mostly lived on unusually friendly terms with the nobility.

Liberty was acquired, here as elsewhere, by means of alliances, the earliest of which originated in the bishops' territory. Bishop Peter, neglecting the administration of his community, and entering the service of Austria, his subjects in 1367 concluded the "League of God's House" (*Gotteshausbund*). Later we find adherents of this League taking an active part in all important matters; they held formal diets, superintended the administration, and only tolerated the bishops at their will.

Soon after the "League of God's House," which embraced the central and southern parts (Engadine) of the present Grisons, there appeared (1395) a similar league of lords and communes in the west, in the valley of the Upper Rhine, on the territory of the monastery of Dissentis, which was afterwards designated the "Upper" or "Grey" League. This League, to which the various feuds of the lords had chiefly given rise, provided a standing court of arbitration, and was also allied to the Forest States and Glarus. In 1424 it was solemnly renewed under the maple at Trons; all participators, both high and low, enjoyed equal rights.

To these two leagues a third was afterwards added. The ten jurisdictions in the eastern part of Rhætia (Prätigau, Schanfigg and Davos), which were under the counts of Toggenburg, joined in a league in 1436, on the death of the last Toggenburg, in order to avoid dispersion. By about the middle of the century these three leagues had little by little formed themselves into one united league, which, however, left all possible liberty to the separate leagues and to the high jurisdictions. After this the united leagues held common diets, and in 1486 they jointly conquered the districts of Cleves, the Valtelline, and Worms, which afterwards became subject-lands of the three leagues in common; and Puschlav, which fell to the bishopric of Coire.

The threatening encroachments of Austria led them to form an alliance with the Confederation. Sigismund, Duke of Austria, in 1477 acquired the greater part of the Ten Jurisdictions, and Maximilian tried to obtain the whole of the Münsterthal, the jurisdiction of which he shared with the bishop, in order to enjoy safe communication with Milan. For this reason the Upper League concluded a perpetual league with the Confederates in 1497, and the League of God's House in 1498; only the Ten Jurisdictions were kept aloof by Austria. The struggle known as the Suabian War, which was thus brought about, established the alliance of the Grisons with the Confederation for all time.

§ 27. **The First Advances beyond the Alps.** The original cantons had early cultivated friendly relations with the district on the southern slope of the St. Gotthard. The traffic carried on by means of this—the latest of the great Alpine passes—brought about an ever-increasing commerce between the Forest States and Milan in Italy. Interruptions occurring in this commerce, caused Uri to turn her attention to the possession of the higher district of the Tessin, the territory of Livinen (Val Leventina). In the year 1331 it had already been found necessary to secure the Upper Tessin by a warlike campaign. Then in 1402 certain officials of the viscounts of Milan having deprived people of the Forest States of cattle, which they were taking to market at Varese (on account of their refusal to pay the appointed toll), troops from Uri and Obwalden marched over the St. Gotthard and conquered Livinen; this valley was the first possession held by the Confederates in common. After this, in 1410, some lords from Eschental, adherents of the government of Milan, having robbed some people from Faido (subjects of Uri and Obwalden) of their cattle upon one of the Alps, and let fall some mocking words against the men of Uri, all the Confederates advanced over the St. Gotthard and across the pass of Giacomo into the Eschental as far as Domo d'Ossola, and conquered the whole territory, which thus became the second common possession. Meanwhile the enemies of the Confederates in Valais, the lords of Raron and dukes of Savoy, looked on in displeasure, and in 1414 an army from Savoy, aided by the Rarons (*see* p. 78), invaded the Eschental, and drove out the Confederates. The latter, however, would not yield, and after several expeditions recovered the province in 1417. Uri and Obwalden in the following year purchased in addition the dominion of Bellinzona of the family of Sax.

Milan now exerted her powers to the utmost. The duke prepared to strike a decisive blow, and attacked Bellinzona. The Confederates immediately marched out; but at variance among themselves, and in scattered bands, they were defeated at many places in crossing the Alps. So it came to pass that the vanguard of the Confederates (from Uri, Lucerne, Zug and Unterwalden), occupying a disadvantageous position near Arbedo, above Bellinzona, was surprised by the Milanese on the 30th June, 1422, and suffered a sanguinary defeat in spite of heroic resistance (*die Koline von Zug*). The Confederates were all obliged to retire, and lost all their possessions south of the St. Gotthard. In 1425 volunteers under Peter Rissi once more ventured over the Alps, and by a bold stroke captured Domo d'Ossola, but were afterwards surrounded and hard pressed by Milanese troops. All the Confederates, even the Bernese, promptly came to their aid, but were unable to do more than rescue their distressed comrades. It was not until 1440 that Uri contrived to repossess herself of Livinen, which territory remained thenceforth a subject-land of Uri.

§ 28. **The Conquest of Aargau.** For the continuance, and the untrammelled development of the Swiss Federation, it was not sufficient merely to check the claims of Austria, for this seemed to have been already achieved by the peace of 1412. The Confederates were still surrounded on all sides and separated from one another by Austrian territory, and therefore it was soon felt to be absolutely necessary to enlarge their borders.

The first occasion of war came from without. A great Council had assembled in 1414 in the imperial town of Constance, under the auspices of King Sigismund, to discuss the subjects of schism and church reform. There were at that time three rival popes, of whom John XXIII. possessed the most rightful claims to the pontificate, but was the worst of the three as regarded character and morals. He hoped to support his position, but finding it impossible, simulated repentance, and announced his resignation. Immediately regretting this step, however, in order to embarrass the Council he formed an alliance with Frederick, Duke of Austria, a rival of Sigismund, and by his connivance, disguised as a post-boy, fled to Schaffhausen, whence he fulminated anathemas against the Council. The assembly of the church, however, took energetic measures against both pope and duke. The latter was put under the ban, and at the command of Sigismund an imperial war was forthwith commenced against Frederick in 1415. Sigismund made a special appeal to the Confederates. The latter could with difficulty bring themselves to violate the peace of 1412; and it was only after repeated and urgent warnings from Sigismund and the Council, and also after many and ample privileges and liberties had been conceded, that they silenced their conscience and undertook an expedition against Aargau. The Bernese were the first to march out, and Zofingen,

Aarburg, Aarau, Lenzburg, Brugg and Hapsburg in quick succession flocked to the imperial standard. Zurich next followed, and conquered a portion of the Free Bailiwick (the bailiwick of Knonau). Soon there was no canton which held aloof. Troops from Lucerne took Sursee, Vilmergen, Beromünster, &c., and the six cantons took Mellingen and Bremgarten. Finally, the seven cantons together with Berne took Baden by storm on the 18th May, destroying the castle by fire (the *Stein*).

All these conquests having been achieved by the Confederates as subjects of the German empire, were bestowed upon them by Sigismund as imperial estates for a money payment, and in 1418 Frederick was forced to resign all claim to them. The partition was so made that the west fell to Berne, the bailiwick of Knonau to Zurich, and the south to Lucerne; but that conquest in which all had taken part (Baden and the Free Bailiwicks) became the common property of the six, and later of the seven cantons. Thus did the Confederates acquire their first enduring "common domain." Frederick's kindred, however, refused to recognise his renunciation, and therefore saw with pleasure the dispute which soon afterwards arose about the inheritance of the last Count of Toggenburg, and did their utmost to widen the breach between the Confederates and to break up the detested League.

2. THE STRENGTHENING OF THE CONFEDERATION DURING AND AFTER THE OLD ZURICH WAR.
(1436–1468.)

§ 29. **Origin and Commencement of the Civil War.** For a long time past there had been keen antagonisms between the towns and rural districts, which had arisen out of divers causes and occurrences, and specially between Zurich and Schwyz, when the two latter states were brought into conflict with one another during their efforts at expansion, after the extinction of the line of Toggenburg.

Among all the families of the higher nobility in the territory of the Confederates, the counts of Toggenburg had not only been able to hold their own, but had even succeeded in extending their power considerably. Frederick VII. of Toggenburg (1400–1436), besides the original possessions of his house (Toggenburg, Utznach and the Upper March) and the inheritance of the Vaz family in Rhætia, which had fallen to the Toggenburgs in the fourteenth century (Prätigau, Schanfigg, Davos, Churwalden, Maienfeld and Malans), had also obtained the mortgage of the intervening lands of Sargans, Gaster, Wesen and Windegg, the Rheintal and Vorarlberg. During the strife between Austria and the Confederates, he cunningly contrived to keep in with both parties, and also succeeded in defending his own territories against the efforts after liberty of the people of Appenzell, now by menaces, now by friendship. He earnestly sought the friendship of the Confederates. At the commencement of his rule he concluded a civil alliance with Zurich for eighteen years, placing himself, his country and his people under the protection of Zurich; in 1405 he renewed this treaty for a similar period, and ten years later, in 1416, it was once more renewed, to endure till five years after the death of Frederick. In 1417 he concluded a treaty with Schwyz, but only for ten years; upon its expiration he renewed it, to endure till five years after his death.

The people of both Zurich and Schwyz exerted themselves to be of service to him, that they might by his means preserve their own lands and estates. Zurich in particular spared no trouble or sacrifice, and the count was greatly indebted to that town, Zurich endeavouring to obtain from the count in return the domains of Wesen, Windegg and Gaster. Schwyz entertained hopes of acquiring the Mark. The count being childless, and the direct line likely to die with him, the question of succession gradually became more urgent. But Frederick left his numerous kinsmen and the Confederates quite in the dark on the subject. Being repeatedly urged by Zurich to nominate a successor, he evaded the question, and when they became importunate about Wesen and Gaster, he showed more favour to Schwyz. On the 30th April, 1436, he died suddenly, leaving no will.

A vehement agitation now arose; the widowed countess claimed the inheritance, and was stoutly supported by Zurich. The count's kinsmen, however (von Mätsch, von Montfort, von Brandis, von Aarburg, von Raron, and von Razüns) maintained the will of the count to have been that the countess should have her dower and a pension, but that his lands should descend to his kinsmen. Schwyz took their part. The affairs of that state were then managed by the clever, able and sagacious Landamman Ital Reding, the elder, who was resolved not only to hinder the extension of the power of Zurich, but to gain for his own people a territory which would secure them a passage from the upper lake of Zurich to Rhætia, and to make Schwyz the dominating power in the whole of the northeast of the present Switzerland. In opposition to Reding were the ambitious, passionate and self-opinionated burgomaster Rudolph Stüssi, and the clever town clerk Michael Graf, a Suabian. Each party endeavoured to overreach the other. Wesen, Windegg and Gaster being taken back by Austria, Zurich succeeded in obtaining Utznach from the countess; Schwyz took the Mark, concluded a treaty with the inhabitants of Gaster, the little town of Sargans, Utznach and Toggenburg; Zurich was only able to effect an alliance with Wallenstadt and the province of Sargans.

After lengthy negotiations, the dispute about the inheritance was decided in 1437 in favour of the count's kinsmen, and the latter immediately hastened to form a perpetual alliance with Schwyz and Glarus, and to sell Utznach to Schwyz. In 1438 Austria also mortgaged Wesen, Windegg and Gaster to Schwyz and Glarus. Thus Schwyz saw her highest hopes fulfilled, while Zurich came off empty-handed. The latter being unable to obtain anything from the Confederates, endeavoured to coerce Schwyz by cutting them off from all means of subsistence, but without success. Schwyz proposed to Zurich to abide by the Federal decree of 1351 (*see* pp. 71, 72); but Zurich pleaded that as an imperial town it was not binding upon her, and that she could only acknowledge a decree in which the empire had taken part. Their differences were irreconcilable, and both parties became so incensed, that in May, 1439, they flew to arms. The people of Zurich were at variance among themselves, one faction adhering to the Confederates, and they were easily defeated on the Etzel. A truce gave opportunity for fresh preparations, and in the autumn of 1440 they faced one another once more on the Etzel, above Pfäffikon. Stüssi had hoped that the other Forest States and the Confederates would either decide in favour of Zurich, or else remain neutral; hence the sudden appearance of troops from Unterwalden and Uri, in aid of Schwyz and Glarus, so dismayed the men of Zurich that they left their breakfast on the tables and retreated in haste. The result of this was that the whole of the left bank of the lake, together with the bailiwick of Knonau, fell into the hands of the enemy; Zurich was moreover obliged to reopen traffic, to surrender the territory of Sargans to Schwyz and Glarus; and Pfäffikon, Wallerau, Hurden and Ufenau ("the upper farmsteads")[1] to Schwyz (1441).

This was a bitter humiliation. Thenceforth Stüssi and Graf thought of nought else but how to avenge their shame upon the Confederates, and to wrest the spoil again from Schwyz. A league with Austria seemed the most available means. Like Brun in 1356, and Schöno in 1393, so Stüssi and his faction did not scruple to depend entirely upon Austria. Under her influence (chiefly indeed through the agency of the foreign town clerk), the burgesses of Zurich, in June, 1442, concluded a formal defensive alliance with Austria (the Emperor Frederick III. and his brother Albert), in spite of the opposition of the Federal faction (led by Meiss, Trinkler and Bluntschli), and even promised to surrender to Austria the greater part of the county of Kiburg.[2] Frederick on his part undertook to secure Toggenburg and Utznach to

---

[1] *Die oberen Höfe.*
[2] The county of Kiburg had been mortgaged to Zurich by Austria in 1424. Only the New Bailiwick, the district on the left side of the Glatt, now remained to Zurich.

Zurich, and it was further intended to found a new Austrian Confederation with Zurich at its head. Frederick III. ratified the agreement by a personal visit which he paid to Zurich, which town received him joyfully with the insignia of Austria (peacocks' feathers and red crosses). The town then received Austrian governors, Thüring von Hallwil and William von Hochberg. The righteous wrath of the whole Confederation was directed against the recreant member. Zurich protested her right of free alliance, reserved to her indeed by the terms of the Zurich League of 1351, but limited by the interests of the Federal leagues: in the eyes of the Confederates it was justly regarded as an offence against the spirit of the league, against old friends and inherited principles. The conduct of Zurich gave to the hereditary enemy of the Confederates an opportunity once more to assert his authority in the midst of the Confederation. The whole German empire regarded this feud merely as an Austrian enterprise, and refused their help, in spite of all Frederick's efforts.

§ 30. **War of the Confederates against Zurich, Austria and the Armagnacs. Conclusion and Results of the War. 1443–1450.** Zurich refusing to give up the Austrian alliance, the Forest States on the 20th May, 1443, declared war against that town and Austria. The forces of Zurich, after an unfortunate engagement on the frontier near Freienbach, retreated as far as the "Letzi" on the heights of Hirzel. But here also they met with no success for want of unity among themselves, their main force being on the heights of the Albis. Thus for the second time the left bank of the lake and the Free Bailiwick fell into the hands of the Confederates.

Berne also now took part against Zurich, and all the Confederates took possession of the whole of her territory. They then withdrew to attend to their own affairs, and after a month's rest a second expedition was set on foot, intended to advance straight upon Zurich through the Free Bailiwick. The inhabitants of Zurich, contrary to the advice of their Austrian commanders, advanced across the Sihl to meet them, and on the 22nd July, 1443, they engaged in a battle near the Sihl at St. Jakob, in which, without order and without discipline, they were overcome, and soon completely routed. Stüssi himself fell while endeavouring to arrest the flight with a few faithful followers by a valiant defence of the bridge over the Sihl. The enemy was with difficulty prevented from entering the town itself. Graf, the town clerk, was stabbed by a fellow-countryman. Through the agency of the Bishop of Constance a peace was brought about, which was so little observed by either side that it obtained the name of the *böse* or "bad" peace. But in the spring of 1444, when a definite peace was about to be arranged, party strife broke out once more, and the Austrians incited their partisans in Zurich to the utmost against the leaders of the Federal party, branding them as traitors. A rising of the people ensued; Brunner, Meiss, Zörnli, Effinger, Bluntschli and other adherents of the Confederates were arrested as enemies of the "Fatherland," and several of them were executed (April).

After the expiration of the truce the Confederates took the field once more with a large force in April, 1444, and overran the territory of Zurich for the third time, devastating the whole district; they then sat down before the stronghold of Greifensee, which was bravely defended under Wildhans von Breitenlandenberg for almost four weeks. Finally, the garrison was obliged to yield, and out of sixty-two men all but ten were mercilessly beheaded at the end of May in a meadow at Nänikon. Soon afterwards, in June, Zurich itself was surrounded and besieged. The town, however, suffered little, being defended with the utmost vigilance; a party of adventurous youths of Zurich (afterwards called the *Böcke* or "Valiant") did considerable damage among the Confederates by surprises and pillage, but could not induce them to raise the siege.

In order to bring matters to some decisive issue Austria began to look for outside help, and incited Charles VII. of France to an enterprise against the Swiss. Meanwhile, and until these auxiliaries should come to their relief, the Austrians endeavoured to divert the Confederates from Zurich. In July Thomas von Falkenstein, on behalf of the Austrians, surprised the little Bernese town of Brugg, but was obliged to retire with his forces to the Farnsburg. Thereupon the Bernese, with some auxiliary troops of the Confederates, besieged that fortress.

At length, on 23rd August, the dauphin advanced upon Basle with 30,000 predatory mercenaries, called Armagnacs,[1] to the relief of the Farnsburg and Zurich, and to enable the Austrians to conquer the Confederation. A little band of about 1300 Confederates hastened to meet him from the Farnsburg and Zurich, but with injunctions not to be drawn into an engagement. After obtaining insignificant victories over the advanced guards at Pratteln and Muttenz (26th August), however, the moment they came in sight of the hostile forces on the Birs they threw themselves upon them, and, notwithstanding the prohibition of the authorities, dashed across the river with reckless confidence towards the mighty army. But, being soon hard pressed by the enemy's cavalry, they established themselves behind the garden wall of the hospital of St. Jakob an der Birs, and fought with the courage of lions. The Armagnacs flagged and desired peace. The Austrian knight, Burkhard Münch, went to the garden wall to come to terms with the Confederates; but, letting fall some scornful words, a Swiss flung a stone at him, causing a wound of which he soon afterwards died. The strife endured till the last of the Confederates had fallen. In death they were victorious, for the loss of the dauphin was so great (2000 men) that he abandoned the enterprise, made peace in October, and withdrew. The Confederates before Zurich also retired, and a desultory war was carried on until, after the lapse of two years, the Confederates having won a brilliant victory over the Austrians at Ragatz, in March, 1446, general exhaustion caused both parties to desire peace.

Zurich still obstinately continued to insist upon her rights

[1] Because one of their former leaders had been a Count of Armagnac.

as a free imperial town in regard to the Austrian League, and thus protracted the negotiations (1446-1450). At length, by the decision of Heinrich von Bubenberg, of Berne, appointed as arbitrator in the name of the imperial towns, it was finally settled that Zurich must abandon the Austrian alliance in the interests of the Confederation. Thenceforth the Swiss League was no longer to be regarded merely as a loose alliance of individual states, but as a political union, to be for ever binding upon every member. The Confederates gave back to Zurich all the lands they had conquered with the exception of the "upper farmsteads" on the lake of Zurich. In Zurich itself Federal principles once more obtained entirely; and thus it came to pass that during the celebration of Shrove Tuesday in Zurich, in 1454, Hämmerlin, the canon, was surprised by a number of Confederates, and taken a prisoner to Gottlieben, because in his writings about the nobility he had ridiculed the men of Schwyz as "effeminate cows' mouths" (*weibische Kuhmäuler*), and had represented them as a mob of detestable and depraved peasants. The spirit of the League seemed to have revived; Zurich and the Confederates held once more firmly together, and rejoiced in their newly-acquired independence of Austria. But the destructive effects and consequences of the war might long be traced in agricultural damages and a serious retrogression in the habits of the people.

§ 31. **New Leagues and Conquests.** After the old Zurich War the Federal leagues were extended. As early as 1450 Glarus had obtained a new league, placing her on an equality with the other states. In the years 1451 and 1454, Zurich, Lucerne, Schwyz and Glarus took first the abbot and then the town of St. Gall into a perpetual civil alliance. In 1452 the seven states (the eight with the exception of Berne) took Appenzell again into the League as an allied state. As soon as the Confederates were once more united among themselves they felt their strength, and let no opportunity pass of exhibiting their military prowess and extending their territory. The period now began during which they neglected the occupations of peace for the profession of arms, in which they had already so often been put to the test; the period when an overweening and almost ungovernable passion for war animated every Swiss and drew him from one war into another.[1] Young companions in arms, eager for adventure, advanced now into Hegau, now into Thurgau, to punish their neighbours for mere teasing and pestering. In this mood they were not likely to spare their old enemy, Austria. Upon the return of an expedition against Constance in 1458 (*Plappartkrieg*), forces from the Forest States offered their aid to the Federal faction in Rapperswil, where complaints were being made of the Austrian government, and conquered that town. Even earlier, in 1454, the Austrian town of Schaffhausen had also concluded a league for twenty-five years with the Confederates; Stein on the Rhine now followed suit, and in 1459 formed an alliance with the states of Zurich and Schaffhausen.

Duke Sigmund, of Austria, a son of Frederick, considered these proceedings a fresh breach of the peace, and prepared for war; a truce was, however, made. Soon afterwards the Confederates were incited against the duke by his foes, the detested Barons of Gradner, and were finally actually urged to war by Pope Pius II., who had quarrelled with the duke. In the midst of the peace youths from the Forest States, Zurich and Glarus marched into Thurgau. The main army followed, and in September, 1460, rapidly conquered the greater part of that district; Diessenhofen, too, was obliged to yield, and Winterthur only maintained a successful resistance. Appenzell simultaneously wrested from Austria the Rheintal, claimed by that power. Duke Sigmund, by a peace concluded in 1461 for fifteen years, was forced to acquiesce in the cession of all conquests to the Confederates. Austria thus lost the Rhine; a triumphant song of that time rejoices that Sigmund will now be able to throw no more bridges over the Rhine.[2]

---

[1] This fact finds special expression in the war-songs of that time; *see* GEROLD MEYER, of Knonau, *die schweizerischen historischen Volkslieder des 15 Jahrhunderts*, p. 16 *et seq.*

[2] G. MEYER, of Knonau : *die schweizerischen historischen Volkslieder*, p. 15.

Austria soon afterwards lost Mülhausen, another post on the Middle Rhine. Harassed by the nobility of Alsace, this town, in 1466, concluded a defensive alliance for twenty-five years with Berne and Soleure, and when the nobility, detesting the Swiss, inflicted all sorts of injuries on this "Swiss cowshed," the allies placed a garrison in the town. The Austrian governor thereupon wanted to take the town by force, but his attempt only resulted in all the states advancing before the town and occupying Sundgau (1468). Schaffhausen, the outpost of the Swiss towards the north, being also continually harassed by the surrounding nobles, and it being fruitless to complain to Austria, the Confederates openly declared war against Duke Sigmund, and in July, 1468, on their return from Sundgau, besieged the strong fortress of Waldshut.

The people of southern Germany were now so favourably disposed towards the Confederates, and so disaffected towards Austria and the nobility, that it seemed almost as if the whole district of the Black Forest might attach themselves to the former. But the garrison of Waldshut exhibited unexpected bravery, so that the Confederates achieved nothing, and peaceable terms were arranged. By the Peace of Waldshut, of August, 1468, Sigmund promised satisfaction to the towns of Mülhausen and Schaffhausen, and to the Confederates the sum of 10,000 florins towards the expenses of the war; Waldshut and the Black Forest were appointed pledges. Thus the struggles with the Confederates resulted in ever fresh debts and losses of territory on the part of Austria. The duke having been compelled a year previously, in 1467, to sell Winterthur to Zurich (upon the wish of the burgesses of the former), all the possessions of Austria beyond the Rhine, with the exception of Frickthal, were now alienated. Austria conceived an inveterate hatred of the Confederates, and the two parties were only to be reconciled by extraordinary events, menacing both the Confederates and Austria.

3. SWITZERLAND AS A EUROPEAN POWER.

§ 32. **The Burgundian Wars.**[1] From the time of the battle of St. Jakob an der Birs, the Confederates having measured their strength so successfully with one of the most powerful military forces of Europe, they enjoyed the respect of the Continent. The Swiss were held to be without rivals in the arts of war, and that nation was considered fortunate which could obtain their services. Experienced men and adventurous youths betook themselves in troops to foreign princes and towns and rendered their services in war. The much-harassed kingdom of France sought the friendship of the Confederates, and afterwards their arms, with the utmost eagerness. This was a great advantage to them, for whereas from the time of the battle of St. Jakob an der Birs the Confederates had had cause to fear the menacing danger of an alliance between France and Austria, they might now hope to find in France a support against Austria. They therefore (in 1452) willingly concluded a treaty of amity with Charles VII., which was renewed (in 1463) with his son Louis XI., who had made their acquaintance at St. Jakob. But Louis XI. was not the man to further the interests of the Swiss from disinterested motives; he rather desired to obtain the favour of Austria and the Confederates in order, by their help, to overthrow his mightiest vassal and mortal foe, Charles the Bold of Burgundy. The Confederates also cultivated friendly relations with Burgundy; the towns of Berne, Fribourg, Soleure and Zurich had concluded a treaty of neutrality in 1467 with Philip the Good, the father of Charles, and with the latter himself.

Matters stood thus when Austria, in 1469 (after the Peace of Waldshut had been revoked by the Emperor Frederick III.,

[1] Sources: The Chronicles of Etterlin, Schilling, Anshelm, Knebel, &c. Compilations: E. v. RODT, *die Feldzüge der Schweizer gegen Karl den Kühnen.* GINGINS, *Episodes des guerres de Bourgogne*, Lausanne, 1850. DÄNDLIKER, *Ursachen und Vorspiel der Burgunderkriege*, 1876. OCHSENBEIN, *die Kriegsgründe und Kriegsbilder des Burgunderkrieges*, 1876.

cousin of Duke Sigmund), sought in the west financial support and help in case of need in a war against the Confederates. Meeting with a refusal from Louis XI., Duke Sigmund turned to Burgundy. Charles the Bold, who thereupon began to build great hopes for an extension of his power eastwards towards Germany, seized the opportunity with avidity, entered into an alliance with Sigmund in May, 1469, paid the latter 50,000 florins, and received in exchange Alsace, Waldshut and the Black Forest. For this the Swiss received 10,000 florins indemnity. But at the same time Charles was obliged to undertake to reconcile Austria with the Confederates, and in case of hostilities on the part of the Swiss, or a war between Switzerland and Austria, to take part with and defend the latter. This completely contradicted the treaty of neutrality of 1467; Charles wantonly violated that treaty, and by that means gave great umbrage to the Confederates.

In addition to this, the new Burgundian bailiff in the mortgaged lands of Alsace, Peter von Hagenbach, offended the Confederates, provoked them by all manner of intrigues, and especially endeavoured to annul the alliance (of 1466) of the Bernese with Mühlhausen. Upon the Confederates complaining to Duke Charles, the latter gave harsh and equivocal answers, or did nothing towards their satisfaction. The intended reconciliation between the Confederates and Austria not being achieved, the breach was widened between the two parties, as also that between the Confederates and Burgundy. Berne was naturally the leading state in these matters, and watched with increasing exasperation the growing arrogance of Charles and Hagenbach. The more Burgundy repulsed the Confederates, so much more the Swiss inclined towards France and Louis XI. The lords of Diesbach earnestly advocated French interests in Berne, and in the then state of affairs they easily overcame Adrian von Bubenberg, the friend of Charles the Bold, and his faction. Louis hoped in time to induce the Swiss to enter into an offensive and defensive alliance against Burgundy, to ally Austria with Switzerland, and to take the field against Burgundy. His efforts were extraordinarily facilitated by the further course of events.

For meanwhile a breach and division had taken place between Austria and Burgundy. One day in the autumn of 1473, when Charles the Bold was awaiting at Trêves the betrothal of Max, son of the emperor, with his daughter Maria, his own elevation to the rank of king, and investment with German imperial lands, the Emperor Frederick III. suddenly left him in the lurch and withdrew, in order to rid himself of burdensome obligations. Duke Sigmund at the same time quarrelled with Charles, because the latter had not fulfilled his expectations, and was no longer willing to surrender Alsace. Sigmund and Frederick next allied themselves with Louis XI., and the latter exerted himself to the utmost to effect a permanent reconciliation between the Confederates and Austria. This was achieved by the "Perpetual Peace"[1] of March, 1474. Austria renounced everything she had lost to the Confederates, receiving in return the latter's promise of help in war and assistance in the recovery of the lands mortgaged to Burgundy. The Confederates likewise joined the "Lower Union," the alliance of the Alsatian towns.

Matters quickly came to a crisis. The people of Alsace revolted against their cruel and oppressive bailiff, and on the 9th May Hagenbach was put to death with the co-operation of the Swiss. While Charles, detained by a quarrel with Cologne and the siege of Neuss, was preparing to avenge the removal of his bailiff, Louis XI. succeeded in the autumn in forming an alliance with the Confederates for the purpose of a united struggle against Burgundy, and also summoned Frederick III., all subjects of the German empire, and more particularly the Swiss, to the war against Burgundy.

On 25th October war was declared by Berne. Barely two days afterwards the Bernese and their allies advanced from Fribourg, Soleure and Bienne into Franche Comté, and together with the rest of the Confederates (8000 in number) and the army of the Upper Rhine (18,000 men in all), besieged

[1] "*Ewige Richtung.*"

Héricourt (south-west of Belfort), and there, on the 13th November, defeated an army of 10,000 Burgundians, and took the town. Thinking they had thus fulfilled their duty to the empire, they then returned, and declined to take part in the relief of Neuss at the request of Frederick III., desiring to protect "their fatherland and the territories of Upper Germany." Louis XI. congratulated them and distributed liberal pensions; this was the first time that the Swiss reaped such alluring and dangerous fruits of their labours. In January, 1475, Savoy formed a league with Burgundy, and from thenceforth Berne and the western towns were constantly threatened from the side of the Pays de Vaud and the Jura, and in the spring there followed a succession of expeditions made by Berne and her allies into the territories of Savoy. On 2nd April, 1475, the troops of Berne, Soleure and Lucerne took Pontarlier. The Bernese already conceived the idea of the extension of the Confederation as far as the Jura, her natural boundary on the west; they conquered Grandson and Orbe, belonging to vassals of Savoy, and in the autumn of 1475, recovered one by one the places taken in the Pays de Vaud by Peter of Savoy. (*See* p. 41.) Geneva preserved herself from attack by a promise of money. A Savoyan army, which advanced as far as Sion, was repulsed by troops from Upper Valais and Berne; Lower Valais yielded to Upper Valais. The power of Savoy seemed to be suddenly banished beyond the frontier of Switzerland.

Meanwhile, however, Charles had conquered Lorraine with its capital, Nancy; and, moreover, Louis and the emperor were faithless enough to come to terms with him, and shamelessly to desert the Confederates. Charles now found himself in a position to advance in great force against the Confederates. He marched rapidly through the Vaud to Grandson, and owing to the dilatoriness of the Confederates was enabled to take the little town, and finally the castle as well. The garrison, which had been promised protection in case of surrender, was cruelly put to death. At length the Confederates and their allies, 18,000 men strong, advanced towards the army of the

H

Burgundians, at least twice as numerous as their own, and the battle of **Grandson** was fought on March 2nd, 1476. A band of men from Schwyz, Berne, Lucerne and Soleure, who had separated themselves from the main army, took up a position on the heights north-east of Grandson, among the vines, and valiantly engaged in battle, without waiting for the rest of the army. In order to entice them down into the plain and there to overwhelm them, Charles, finding the efforts of his artillery and archers unavailing, commanded a retreat from Grandson towards the plain; the rear took this for a flight, fell into confusion, and gave way. At that moment the weapons and armour of the advancing Swiss force glittered on the heights; loud blew the horns of Uri and Lucerne, spreading terror and dismay among the Burgundians. Charles tried in vain to arrest the flight of his men: attacked in the van, the rear and the flank, the Burgundians fled impetuously, and their camp, with all stores, valuables and jewels, fell into the hands of the Confederates. Charles's fine and well-disciplined army was totally defeated by the peasant folk he had so greatly despised; the confident hope of the Alsatian nobility, that the Swiss would be overthrown,[1] was dashed to the ground! This victory was one of the richest in spoil ever gained by any people.

Far from being daunted by this unprecedented defeat, Charles, with all haste, made his preparations at Lausanne for a fresh campaign, while Berne and Fribourg occupied the important outpost of Morat (*Murten*). As early as the 9th of June the duke appeared before that place. The Bernese commander, Adrian von Bubenberg, held it with only 15,000 men, but resolved to spend their last drop of blood rather than yield. By a most prudent defence, by a constant renewal of the bulwarks, by excellent discipline, and lastly by bold sallies, Bubenberg succeeded in holding the duke at bay till the forces of the Confederates—after long tarrying and many irresolute delays—advanced to the number of about 24,000 men. Charles, however, was at the head of about 35,000 men. On

---

[1] *See* KAPLAN KNEBELS' *Chronik der Burgunderkriege* (published in the *Basler Chroniken*).

the 22nd June, the Ten Thousand Knights' Day,[1] and a day after the date of the battle of Laupen, after the example of the knights, the Confederates marched from the forest of Morat to the plateau north-east of Morat (near Salvenach and Münchenwiler). There the advanced guard of the Confederates encountered that of the Burgundians, and were forced to retreat to the forest after a short resistance. The main body of the Burgundian army pursued them amid torrents of rain, and, fortified by their artillery, posted themselves behind quickset hedges. The main army of the Confederates arriving, led by Hans Waldmann, a violent struggle ensued. The Swiss van (under Hans von Hallvil) succeeded in breaking through the hedges, and the spirited and heavy advance of the Confederates compelled the Burgundians after a few hours to retire into the plain, where the terrible slaughter inflicted by the Confederates sealed their defeat. On the Burgundian side from 8000 to 10,000 men are said to have fallen, while the Swiss lost only 500! The whole of Switzerland was filled with rejoicing, and bells were rung throughout the land.

The immediate result of this victory of the Confederates was a peace concluded with them by Savoy, by which the latter surrendered to Berne and Fribourg their conquered territories of Morat, Echallens, Illens, Orbe and Grandson, released Fribourg, which had fallen to Savoy in 1452, and ceded Lower Valais to Upper Valais. No peace was as yet effected with Burgundy. Charles intended to try his fortune once more against the Confederates, but was deterred by a revolt in Lorraine. René, Duke of Lorraine, exiled by Charles, sought help from the Confederates, at whose side he had fought at Grandson; at the Diet of Lucerne he with tears implored help in holding Nancy, his capital, against Charles. No Federal aid was granted to him, but he was allowed to levy men at will; and about 8000 Swiss mercenaries, under Hans Waldmann, fought with him at Nancy, where the haughty Duke of Burgundy fell in the rout like a common soldier. This was the death-blow to the Burgundian power (January 5th, 1477).

[1] *10,000 Rittertag.*

The next question was the partition of the conquests and of the possessions of the fallen duke. The Duchy of Burgundy fell to France. The Netherlands devolved upon Maximilian of Austria, who married Maria of Burgundy, daughter of Charles the Bold. Louis XI. and Maximilian contended for Upper Burgundy or Franche Comté; and both courted the favour of the Confederates, in whose hands lay that territory. A number of the Federal States, however, and Berne in particular, were specially desirous of keeping High Burgundy for themselves, and extending the Confederation towards the west. But the states were soon divided, some, notably Zurich, considering the country too remote; and it was finally agreed to sell High Burgundy, and thus to choose France as a neighbour rather than the Austrian Hapsburgs. France obtained Franche Comté for 150,000 florins, but shortly afterwards it fell during a war to the Hapsburgs, in whose hands it remained till the seventeenth century. Meanwhile the Confederates had by this war assured their position towards the west; the barricade of Savoy was broken down by the conquest of strong places in the Vaud and in Lower Valais. Fribourg and Soleure now joined the Confederates entirely; and Neuchâtel, whose count had rendered help to the Bernese, also entered into alliance with them. Thus the western frontier of the Swiss Federation gradually approached the Jura. The Confederation had now taken its stand as a European power, and the fame of the Swiss was in every mouth as of the finest warriors in Europe.

§ 33. **The Period after the Burgundian Wars. The Covenant of Stans. Hans Waldmann.** The Burgundian wars had stirred the spirit of the people to its inmost depths, avarice and love of adventure were aroused, and the bands of discipline and order became lax. Divers causes of friction likewise arose: the states were divided as to their future political attitude, towns and rural districts filled with mutual mistrust. The towns had developed considerable power in these wars, and had assumed the position of leaders of the Confederation, and when the two towns of Fribourg and Soleure, which had fought faithfully at the side of the others during the Burgundian war, afterwards desired admission into the League, the position and influence of the towns seemed to be growing in a way that the rural states felt keenly. The latter passionately resisted this tendency, especially as the towns tried to put a stop to the liberty of foreign service, while the rural states were in favour of it. The people, too, became mistrustful of the despotic government of their lords, and in the spring of 1477 popular riots broke out in various states. In Art and Weggis particularly the malcontents assembled on Shrove Tuesday, and lamented the policy of the towns and the new rule (*Herrentum*). It was decided to fetch from Geneva the ransom money yet unpaid (*see* p. 97), and to divide it among themselves. With a wild desire for war and booty, and taking a club and a sow for the design of their banner, they formed themselves into the "Band of the Mad Life,"[1] marched through Lucerne, Berne and Fribourg, extorting entertainment wherever they went. But the diet and government of Savoy succeeded in inducing the rioters to retreat before they had attained their goal. The authorities in the rural states having favoured this undertaking, the towns in anger resolved upon the formation of a separate league (*Sonderbund*); and on 23rd May, 1477, the five towns of Zurich, Berne, Lucerne, Fribourg and Soleure united in a perpetual treaty (*Burgrecht*). They agreed to protect one another against such attacks as that of the "March of the Sow-banner," and to insist upon the admission into the League of Fribourg and Soleure. A great breach was occasioned in the Confederation; the rural states were embittered to the utmost, and tried to destroy this treaty. They specially attacked the town of Lucerne, which had no right, according to the tenor of the League, to make any alliance without the consent of the other Forest States. (*See* p. 71.) The people of Obwalden avenged themselves by inciting the subjects of Lucerne in Entlebuch to revolt. Peter Amstalden, the governor of the district, an innkeeper of Schüpfheim in Entlebuch, headed the rebels. Lucerne,

[1] *Bande vom tollen Leben.*

hearing of the affair, enticed Amstalden into the town, had him arrested and hastily executed, in November, 1478, without regular trial. Great excitement followed. The situation was so critical, that the dissolution of the Confederation was feared. Fruitless efforts were made during many diets to effect a reconciliation. At this critical moment Lucerne and the rural states turned to Nicholas von der Flüe of Einsiedeln, a man who led a godly life on the brink of a lake near Sachseln, deeply respected throughout the whole of Switzerland, and even far beyond its borders, who gave loving counsel to all, and was revered among the people as a worker of miracles. Many times were messengers sent to him to ask his advice. By the end of November, 1481, things had gone so far that a scheme was drawn up for a new League (by which, in the interest of the towns, all anarchical movements were to be suppressed), and a League was also projected with Fribourg and Soleure, in which the only restriction laid upon those two towns was that they might enter into no alliance without the consent of the eight states. These agreements needed only to be ratified by instructions from the authorities.

Assembling once more in Stans on 18th December, 1481, the old dispute was renewed with redoubled violence as to the admission of the two towns into the League, and after wrangling for three days the deputies separated on 22nd December in great irritation. In this extremity the pious pastor Heinrich Imgrund of Stans hastened to "Brother Klaus" for his advice; came back bathed in perspiration, fetched the deputies from their various inns, and in the name of the monk of Einsiedeln, prevailed upon them to assemble once more. He then brought forward the proposals of his venerable friend, and within an hour a reconciliation was effected.[1] The towns yielded and relinquished their separate league, and the rural

---

[1] The most ancient reports and a picture drawn by Schilling, an onlooker, say nothing of the personal appearance of Brother Klaus in the hall of the assembly; he acted only by the mediation of the pastor of Stans. The minutes of the diet (*Abschiede*), in accordance with the character of the diet (*see* § 36), always register the articles of debate with the formal conclusion, "Let the deputies report at home." So in this case we find, "Let every deputy report at home

states on their part consented to the admission of Fribourg and Soleure into the Perpetual League, although under the further restriction that they should be subordinate to the eight states in war. In order to avoid similar disputes in future, and to strengthen and invigorate the League, the already projected covenant of Stans was definitely accepted. What the towns had wanted to obtain by their separate league became now the concern of the whole Federal League; for every town engaged to refrain from instigating the subjects of the others to rebellion (as had been the case in the revolt of Entlebuch), and from injuring the territory of the others. Dangerous or unusual societies and assemblies, which might do harm to anyone (as, for instance, the assembly of Art, which gave rise to the "mad life"), were forbidden, and the states pledged themselves to mutual support against such attacks and insurrections. Finally, that both old and young might the more firmly bear the leagues in mind, every five years the Convention of Sempach (*see* p. 69) and this Covenant of Stans were to be renewed and confirmed by oath.

This concord formed an important advance in the life of the League, and to a certain extent strengthened its power; thereby legitimate bounds were set to all tumultuary attempts, and all arbitrary dealings, to the freebooting and licentiousness, so abundantly manifest in the Middle Ages. It is true that in later times these provisions, though directed against any actually violent breach of the peace, were abused, in that the governments, by their support, suppressed mere popular assemblies, and claimed Federal aid to repudiate the just demands of the people. This strengthening of the central power corresponded to the tendency then simultaneously manifesting itself in Spain, France, Germany and England towards the foundation of the modern state.

the faithfulness, care and labour which that godly man, Brother Klaus, has employed in these matters, and thank him sincerely for it; as every deputy can tell more fully." The feeling of the godly man of Einsiedeln himself in this matter appears from a letter he sends to Berne, in which he says, "Peace is always in God, for God is peace, and peace cannot be destroyed; but discord will be destroyed."

But the internal disquiets of the Confederation were not yet allayed by the Covenant of Stans. By the acquisition of subject lands on the part of individual states, and by the increase of the number of towns in the League, the Confederation had gradually assumed quite an altered character. There was no longer, as at the time of the battles of Morgarten and Sempach, one people of almost equal rights, but a separation was already introduced between lords and subjects. In the towns, especially in Berne and Zurich, the idea of a united executive power, exercised from one centre (as already in use in great monarchies), was gaining ground; a sense of sovereignty was beginning to make itself felt among the governments of the towns. A tendency arose to establish an absolute rule of the towns over the country. In addition to this an effort was being made within the towns themselves to strengthen the power of the burgomaster and wardens[1] among the artisan class.

This new idea was pursued in Berne by Peter Kistler. He had risen by his own efforts from the rank of a butcher to that of a standard-bearer, and in 1470 was elected mayor. Thereupon the nobler burgesses who possessed manorial estates in the country over which they exercised a despotic authority (*Twingherrschaften*), the families of Erlach, Diesbach, Bubenberg, &c., left the town in a body. Kistler endeavoured to humiliate them, to limit their jurisdiction, and to subject them to sumptuary laws. But the country folk, feeling oppressed by the town, took part with their manorial lords, and a revolution was only averted by the mediation of the Confederates. The nobles acknowledged the sovereignty of the town of Berne, but were released from the sumptuary laws (1471). The manorial lords returned amid the rejoicings of the burghers.

A similar tendency shortly afterwards found place in Zurich under Hans Waldmann. Born at Blickensdorf, in the canton of Zug, settled in Zurich, and there enfranchised, Waldmann early distinguished himself during mercenary and other military expeditions in the sixth and seventh decades of the

[1] The heads or masters of the trade guilds.—E. S.

century. He rose rapidly by his extraordinary talents, his activity and untiring energy, by his fortune and family alliances. He established his fame during the Burgundian wars, and ranked among the foremost as a leader in war and as a politician. Through the influence of the guilds he was chosen a member of council, became a landlord, chief warden, and finally burgomaster in 1483, upon the removal of the aristocratic Heinrich Göldli. Towards the aristocracy, who despised him, he bore an inveterate hatred, and he now turned old clauses of the constitution to account somewhat unfairly, in order to humble the *Constafel*[1] and to establish the supremacy of the guilds. He reduced the number of aristocrats in the council from twelve to six; he offended the Göldli family to the utmost. At the same time he kept discipline and order among the clergy, and did much towards the adornment and improvement of Zurich. In the management of the state he endeavoured to establish greater uniformity and equality in place of the glaring inequalities of mediæval times. He held the country folk in strict subordination, as had long been the custom, bound them remorselessly by statutes old and new relating to manners, clothing, agriculture, handicrafts and forestry, and thereby aroused much bitter feeling. In Federal matters he obtained for Zurich an almost absolute supremacy, endeavoured to suppress foreign service, and by so doing exasperated Lucerne and the rural states, and came into violent conflict with the leader of mercenaries, Frischhans Teiling, of Lucerne. Their antagonism dated from an expedition to Milan in 1478.

The Sforzas, who succeeded to Milan upon the extinction of the Visconti family in 1447, concluded a capitulation or treaty with the Confederates in 1467, but did not keep the promises therein made, such as the renunciation of the *Livinen* (Val Leventina), freedom from tolls, &c. Negotiations having failed of their aim, Uri prepared for war; and

[1] There were in Zurich two great electoral bodies; the first, or aristocratic class, was styled the "*Constafel*," and consisted of knights, nobles, and the more well-to-do burghers. The second class consisted of the artisans forming the thirteen guilds.—E. S.

in December, 1478, under the conduct of Hans Waldmann, 10,000 to 14,000 Confederates advanced as far as Bellinzona (*Bellenz*), and besieged it. But owing to dissensions and the cold of the winter, the Confederates were obliged to retreat, leaving only a small garrison in Giornico. Thereupon the Milanese advanced, 10,000 strong, but were opposed by the garrison (aided by 350 of the inhabitants of the Val Leventina) under the leadership of Frischhans Teiling, of Lucerne. By stopping the mountain streams, whose waters immediately froze, they had secured their position; and as the enemy advanced, they rolled down stones and rocks, fell upon their opponents, and put them to flight. It was a glorious act of heroism, and Frischhans Teiling was thenceforth honoured as a hero of war. Teiling arrogantly ridiculed the banner of Zurich as a "beggar's wallet," and the Zurich folk as "perjured wretches." Later, in 1487, when Waldmann defeated an expedition into the Eschenthal, and an attempt being nevertheless made to force a passage, 800 men were slain, he abused the burgomaster of Zurich as a "villain, a murderer and a traitor." For these things Teiling, going to mass at Zurich in the autumn of 1487, was arrested and mercilessly put to death. A cry of indignation rang through the heart of Switzerland, and the animosity against Waldmann reached its height, as an inexorable advocate of the supremacy of the towns, the chief representative of the system of pensions, and the suppressor of foreign service.

In the spring of 1489 disturbances broke out in the rural districts of Zurich, because Waldmann had been betrayed into setting proceedings on foot against the large and dangerous dogs of the peasants. The peasants held meetings on the banks of the lake of Zurich, at Meilen, Küssnach, &c., and in March advanced upon the town. Having allowed themselves to be appeased, and then finding that the town would not keep the treaty, they marched out in April for the second time. Meanwhile within the town the Göldli family and their adherents were exasperating and inciting the townsfolk against Waldmann, and the council hall was besieged by a tumultuous mob. Federal deputies hastened to intervene, but, instead of allaying the tumult, they yielded to the urgency of the people, delivered up Waldmann and his friends, and led them to the Wellenberg.[1] In a tumultuous assembly of the burgesses fresh councillors were elected, and Waldmann's opponents took the helm. General accusations against Waldmann were spread abroad, and after summary proceedings he was finally condemned to death. The hero of Morat went to his death with manly courage on 6th April, 1489.

The new council slaked its thirst for revenge by a succession of further condemnations and executions, and by its harshness and cruelty earned the name of the "Horny Council." By the intervention of Federal deputies a reconciliation was effected between the town and the rural districts. Ancient liberties and rights were confirmed to the various domains and districts by charters containing the decrees of Waldmann, by which also a number of innovations were abolished, and freedom of trade, commerce and manufacture was assured. The greatest concessions were made to the dwellers around the lake, especially the right of making their wants and wishes known to the government. Lastly, the municipal constitution was legally settled for the time to come, and, in so far as concerned the position of the aristocracy and wardens in the council, essentially in accordance with Waldmann's ideas.

The fall of Waldmann produced a general excitement throughout the Confederation, and occasioned similar agitations in several places against despotism and against the drawing of pensions. A like storm broke out against the government of Lucerne, and the council was forced to bind itself to levy no taxes, form no alliances, and commence no war without the consent of the community. In 1489 the town of St. Gall, the League of God's House, and the people of Appenzell revolted against the harsh Abbot Ulrich Rösch, reputed a friend of Waldmann, and destroyed the buildings of a new monastery commenced by the abbot at Rorschach. Burgomaster Farnbühler had already planned a great Con-

[1] The state prison of Zurich.—E. S.

federation in the east, with the addition of Thurgau, to be under the direction of the town of St. Gall. With the help of the Federal protection, however, the abbot quelled the insurrection; Farnbühler was forced to fly, and the insurgents were heavily fined (1490). Meanwhile Federal affairs were likewise in a state of fermentation. At the Diet of Lucerne a prohibition of pensions and service-money was mooted, "it being seen how much harm Waldmann had caused by pensions," and Schwyz suggested the idea of assembling the communities in all parts, even in the town cantons, in order to discuss these matters. But the towns, with Berne at their head, opposed this; and through their influence it was finally decided to abide by the Covenant of Stans, as published in 1481. The abolition of such pressing grievances as foreign service, the system of pensions and the laxity of the League was deferred.

§ 34. **The Suabian War.**[1] After Switzerland had by her own strength overthrown one of the powers of Europe in the Burgundian wars, the bonds uniting her to the German empire were gradually slackened. Hitherto no Swiss had dreamt of such a thing as separation from the empire; they all unreservedly considered themselves members of the empire, just as the Bavarians, Franks or Saxons. Their privileges were ratified by the emperor; they took part in imperial diets and imperial wars; and even in the Burgundian war they had professed to be obliged to fight, and to wish to do so, as members of the empire. But these relations had gradually become mere formalities. As a matter of fact, Switzerland had long been alienated from the empire, because she no longer needed its protection. The feeling of connection was the more readily lost that the German Empire was wanting in any firm union which could hold the different parts together.

[1] T. PROPST, *die Beziehungen der schweizerischen Eidgenossenschaft zum deutschen Reiche in den Jahren 1486-1499* (*Archiv für Schweizergeschichte*, vol. xv.). KLÜPFEL, *die Lostrennung der Schweiz von Deutschland* (in *Sybels historischer Zeitschrift*, vol. xvi.). Sources: the Chronicles of Anshelm and Schilling; WILLIBALD PIRKHEIMER's *Schweizerkrieg* (containing interesting episodes, edited by Ernest Münch, Basle, 1826).

For more than two centuries past a total dissolution had been gradually approaching. There was no generally recognised imperial authority; the princes and towns forming the individual members were almost independent. Thus the Swiss, too, were able to strike out an independent course; often enough in later times they had shirked their duties towards the empire, and gone unpunished.

Moreover, powers had gained the ascendent in Germany, which were by their very nature incompatible with Switzerland. At one time the haughty nobles of Suabia caused continual friction; the biting scorn which they poured forth upon the peasants and cowherds across the Rhine not only gave rise to reciprocal mockings, but even caused the Confederates to take to arms. Then from the year 1438 the Austrian house of Hapsburg had filled the German throne, and that house could never forget that the Confederation had become great at her expense. The long reign of Frederick III. (1440-1493) specially alienated Switzerland from the empire; for it was he who, in the first Zurich war, under pretext of imperial interests, had endeavoured to destroy the Federal League. The fresh demands made by Maximilian, Frederick's son, in the name of the empire, brought matters to a crisis. The first prince of his age to take any real interest in the affairs of the empire, he wanted to subject Switzerland, as a regular member of the empire, to the newly-established regulations for the public peace, to the Imperial Chamber and to imperial taxes (1496); and St. Gall, an allied state of the Confederates, refusing to submit to a sentence of the Imperial Chamber, was outlawed. The Confederates did not scruple to repudiate such demands. They had no need of the special precautions of Germany for the preservation of the public peace, for they were sufficiently defended by their leagues.[1] Moreover, at the new Imperial Diet the towns and burghers were but feebly represented, the peasants not at all; and Switzerland, like North America nearly 300 years later, could not recognise any obligations to

[1] C. KIND, *die Eidgenossenschaft in ihrem Verhältnis zum deutschen Reiche während des 15. Jahrhunderts* (*Deutsche Blätter*, August, 1873).

a parliamentary body from which they were, so to speak, excluded. "The way is open to find a master for you, and I will accomplish it by the pen in my hand," cried the Imperial Chancellor. But a Confederate replied: "Others formerly failed in what you now threaten, though they attempted it with halberds, which are more to be feared than goose-quills!" With yet greater indignation the Confederates rejected the suggestion that they should join the Suabian League, then under the influence of Austria and the nobility of southern Germany. The nobility now desired nothing more earnestly than the overthrow of Switzerland; north of the Rhine one vied with another in scornful ridicule and base accusations against the Swiss, and protracted, fruitless trials and processes drove them from exasperation to the thirst for war.

A trivial cause finally led to the outbreak of war. Maximilian's advisers, who were urgent for war, caused the Münsterthal (the jurisdiction of which was shared by Austria and the Bishop of Coire) to be seized in the king's absence, because the Grey League and the League of God's House had joined the Confederates in opposition to Austria (*see* p. 81); even the Suabian League was applied to for help. The Grisons sought and obtained the help of the Confederates (January, 1499), and soon the armed forces of both parties confronted one another along the banks of the Rhine from Basle to Maienfeld. The Suabian troops acquired Maienfeld by treachery and occupied Luziensteig; but on February 9th, 1499, the Confederates forded the Rhine at Triesen and repulsed the enemy. Meanwhile the Royalists had assembled at Bregenz. The Confederates attacked them at Hard or Fussach, and rushing upon the enemy, as at Grandson, with desperate courage under a heavy fire, they won a signal victory.

One month later, on 22nd March, Suabians from Sundgau and the Black Forest, attacking Soleure and retiring hastily, were totally defeated at Bruderholz, on the rising ground south of Basle. Once more the Suabian League took courage; its troops took up their position at Constance, and thence attacked

Ermatingen in Thurgau. The Suabians were, however, again surprised by the Confederates, and defeated on April 11th at Schwaderloo, south of Constance. The Swiss arms were shortly afterwards victorious in the Oberland. Austrians from the Tyrol and Wallgau assembled at Frastenz (east of Feldkirch) behind an intrenchment. The Confederates determined to make a decisive attack upon them, and on April 20th, by a skilfully planned manœuvre, executed by Heinrich Wolleb of Uri, they remained masters of the field after a hot struggle. The brave Wolleb himself was the first victim, falling when in the act of giving the signal for advance against the guns of the enemy, dealing out death and destruction. 3000 of the enemy were slain.

Meanwhile Maximilian had returned, and resolved to take the war in hand in good earnest. But there appeared small inclination for it in the empire, the war being regarded merely as an Austrian feud. Maximilian assembled his troops on the frontier between the Tyrol and the Grisons, and specially fortified the outlet of the Münsterthal into the Tyrol, in the neighbourhood of the lower Rambach. At the gorge of the latter stream (the "*Calven*") a battle took place. Only 6300 Grisons rushed upon 15,000 Imperialists, intrenched behind fortifications. Glorious deeds of heroism were done. Benedict Fontana, one of the leaders of the League of God's House, hastening at the head of his men to the attack on the intrenchment, was wounded by a bullet, but still shouted words of encouragement to his followers. The Grisons pressed forward from all sides, and the Imperialists were forced to give way (March 22nd).

While the emperor attempted another attack from Constance, Austrian troops from Sundgau advanced towards Soleure, but being surprised while feasting and bathing at Dorneck (Dornach), they were put to the rout. Both sides were now weary of the war, for in the course of eight months 20,000 soldiers had been slain, nearly 2000 places burnt, and the land devastated far and wide; and the people were terribly oppressed by want of money, scarcity and famine. All therefore longed for peace, which was concluded on September 22nd, 1499, at Basle. The emperor suspended all proceedings and decrees of the Imperial Chamber against the Swiss; he ceded to the Confederates the rural jurisdiction of Thurgau, and by that means foreign jurisdiction was entirely banished from their territory. The Ten Jurisdictions (Prätigau, Schanfigg and Davos) were obliged to do homage to the emperor as their sovereign, but remained in alliance with the Confederates, as did the other leagues of the Grisons. Nothing was indeed definitely settled as to the general position of Switzerland with regard to the German Empire; but as a matter of fact imperial regulations had no real force among the Swiss, and fresh orders being issued a hundred and fifty years later, in 1648, led to the formal separation of Switzerland from the German Empire for ever. After the Suabian War, Basle and Schaffhausen, which had been most exposed to danger during the war, joined the Perpetual League of the Confederates (on June 8th and August 10th, 1501), and so completed the Federal territory towards the north.

§ 35. **Wars of Milan.** The French kings who succeeded Louis XI. sought, as that monarch had done, to avail themselves of the warlike powers of the Swiss. In 1484 Charles VIII. renewed his father's alliance, and ten years later conquered Naples chiefly by Swiss mercenaries. His successor, Louis XII., in 1499, concluded a treaty for ten years, and thought by the help of the Confederates to conquer Milan (to which he laid just claim in right of his grandmother), and to drive out the Sforzas. (*See* p. 82.) In that same year, at the head of Swiss mercenaries, he expelled Louis Sforza, surnamed the Moor. But the latter had made an alliance with certain Federal States, and in February, 1500, succeeded in recovering Milan. Then arrived an army of 24,000 French. Louis the Moor held Novara, but suffered greatly from want. His Swiss followers shrank from fighting against their brother Confederates, and capitulated behind his back. They promised, however, to take him with them on their retreat. But by the treachery of a Swiss soldier in the French army Moro (the "Moor") was delivered up to the French, and ended his life ten years later in a French prison. In this way Milan once more became French. Louis XII. renewed the capitulation of Milan, and engaged to restore Bellinzona, which he had conquered, to the Forest States. (*See* p. 82.) But the Confederates were at length obliged to wrest it from him by a special campaign (1503).

Now, however, the powerful position which France had acquired in Italy by the possession of Milan threatened the balance of power among the nations of Europe, and offended the patriotic pride of the Italians. Hence fresh wars broke out, in which almost all the noted rulers of that time were concerned, and in which the Confederates played a specially important part. Just as in the Burgundian wars they had been led by France and the emperor to take the field against Burgundy, so in the Italian struggle they were urged by the other interested powers against France. At the same time, however, the Confederates had once more their own interests to maintain, so that they were not merely the puppets of the powers. It was to their interest to secure their possession of the territory of Ticino (Tessin), and to show France that they would not be used as a mere tool. Louis XII., following the faithless and cunning policy of Louis XI., did not keep his promises, and offended the Confederates by a haughty and despotic course of action. The alliance with France coming to an end in 1510, the Swiss thought it well to show Louis that "money is only useful to him who owns iron too," and they lent their ear to the enemies of France, and particularly to Pope Julius II., whose highest aim was the expulsion of the French from Italy.

By the order of the Pope, Matthew Schinner, Bishop of Sion, an able, intelligent and eloquent man, addressed himself to the Confederates, and induced them in 1510 to conclude a treaty with the papal throne for five years, by which they engaged to furnish troops to the papacy, to the exclusion of all others. Having further allied himself with Spain, the emperor, Venice and England (the "Holy League"), Julius opened the war against France.

Two Alpine expeditions of the Confederates failed—the campaign of Chiasso in 1510, and the "cold winter campaign" of 1511. On the 11th of April, 1512, the French defeated the army of the League at Ravenna. Julius II. now rested his hopes solely upon the Swiss, and was not disappointed. A Swiss army of 18,000 men marched across the Alps, made a successful expedition through Lombardy in concert with the Venetians, and conquered Pavia and the whole Duchy of Milan. This expedition, which took place in July, 1512, and was called the "great expedition of Pavia,"[1] met with brilliant success. For themselves the Confederates obtained Domo d'Ossola, the territory of the present canton of Ticino, Locarno, Lugano, Mendrisio and Maiental, the Grison Leagues acquiring the Valtelline, Chiavenna and Bormio. The whole range from Monte Rosa to the Wormser Joch was now brought into permanent connection with the Confederation. In Italy, however, the Confederates were greeted with rejoicings as deliverers from the yoke of France, and they were highly honoured and richly rewarded by the pope. They even decided the important question as to the possession of Milan; and Schmid, burgomaster of Zurich, delivered the key of the city to Maximilian Sforza, the son of the unfortunate Louis the Moor. They at the same time concluded a treaty with Sforza, and engaged to protect Milan. Louis XII. next attempting to recover Milan by force of arms, the Confederates were again obliged to take the field. On the 4th of June, 1513, the French bombarded Novara, which was garrisoned by Swiss troops under Sforza. The French hoped events would turn out as twelve years previously, but the garrison maintained a firm resistance until the main army of the Confederates came up. On the 6th of June a sanguinary battle took place outside the gates of the town, in which the Confederates, inspired by the heroic courage of their forefathers, defied the artillery and cavalry of the enemy, killed

[1] *Grosser Pavierzug.*

8000 Frenchmen, and put the rest to flight. This was a red-letter day for the Confederation.

The Confederates had about this time undertaken an invasion of Burgundy (known as the "Campaign of Dijon"), in concert with an imperial army, but allowed themselves to be put off with idle promises. Milan fell for the second time into the hands of the Swiss, and the French were by them a second time driven out of Italy. The Swiss, with haughty self-confidence, compared themselves already to the Romans; and one of the cleverest Italians of that day, Machiavelli the historian, prophesied that they would become the rulers of the whole of Italy. But this was not to be. Francis I., the valiant successor of Louis XII., appeared upon the scene with a fresh and powerful army, and the Swiss encountered him at Marignano. In spite of the warnings of the majority of their leaders, one division imprudently and impetuously commenced the attack on the evening of the 13th of September, 1515, and fought with lion-like courage and partial success till night put an end to the slaughter. On the following day the struggle was renewed. Once more the Confederates precipitated themselves upon an army of double their number, but they were terribly cut to pieces by the artillery and cavalry of the enemy, and were moreover menaced in the rear by a Venetian army. That they might not undergo the fate of St. Jakob, they took the wounded on their shoulders, the artillery in their midst, and withdrew towards Milan in perfect order, "bruised rather than defeated." Twelve thousand corpses—the majority of them those of Confederates—covered the field of battle.

This—the first defeat that the Confederates met with—which laid the foundations of the reputation of Francis I. and of the supremacy of France, gave a new direction to the course of Swiss affairs. Among the Confederates it began to be generally recognised that the position of power to which they had so rapidly and unexpectedly attained could not long be tenable, nor the many evils wrought by endless wars be endured; and consequently, on the 29th November, 1516, a perpetual peace was concluded between Switzerland and France, which united those two powers more closely than ever. Hostilities were to cease for ever on both sides, full freedom of trade and peaceable relations to connect the two nations, and neither party should support the enemies of the other.

Thenceforth the independent part played by Switzerland in European politics was at an end, and she maintained a neutral position in European disputes. The only lasting advantage gained was the conquest of the territories of Ticino, the Valtelline, and Cleves (*Cläven*), the possession of which was guaranteed[1] by France to the Confederates in the perpetual peace. The two last-named districts fell to the Grisons, the former became the common property of the Confederates, and from 1803 onwards formed the present canton of Ticino; and thus the Federal territory received its southern boundary.

4. INTERNAL CONDITIONS.

§ 36. **Political Development of the Confederation of Thirteen States.**[2] The fifteenth century, that time of glorious wars abroad and the dawn of intellectual progress at home, also brought important political changes; and the lax League developed gradually into a firm and well-ordered state.

In the first instance, as regarded the mutual relations of the states, the Forest States in the fourteenth century had formed as it were the only bond of union of the League. (*Cf.* p. 71.) But in the fifteenth century, states not hitherto allied concluded perpetual leagues among themselves, as for instance Berne and Lucerne in 1421, Zurich and Berne in 1423. And the five new states which joined later, Fribourg (1481), Soleure (1481), Basle (1501), Schaffhausen (1501), and Appenzell (1513), entered into agreements not only with the Forest

---

[1] Domo d'Ossola and the Eschental had to be given back.
[2] PFAFF, *das Staatsrecht der alten Eidgenossenschaft*, Schaffhausen, 1870. BLUNTSCHLI, *Geschichte des schweizerischen Bundesrechts*. SEGESSER, *Beiträge zur Geschichte des Stanzerverkommnisses*.

States, but also with all the eight. At the same time they were in many ways restricted and slighted in comparison to the older states. At the accession of Fribourg and Soleure the eight states restricted the circle of Federal aid; the two new states might enter into no foreign alliance without the consent of the rest, and were to submit themselves to the majority of the eight states in cases of peace and war. The latter stipulation was also made with Basle, Schaffhausen and Appenzell. These three states were, moreover, obliged to promise to remain neutral during any disputes among the others.

Together with these thirteen fully qualified members of the Confederation, there were also some "allied" (or "friendly") states (*Zugewandte Orte*), that is, such as were mostly only in alliance with individual members of the Confederation, and either took no part in the transactions of the Diet, or had an inferior representation (only one instead of two delegates), and moreover had their places apart. Such were the Abbot of St. Gall, who in 1451 had become allied to the four states of Zurich, Lucerne, Schwyz and Glarus; the town of St. Gall; Bienne, allied only with Berne, Soleure and Fribourg; the Grisons, Valais, the counts of Neuchâtel, allied in 1406 with the same states as Bienne; Mülhausen (1515) and Rotwil (1519), allied with all the thirteen states. All the above-named held quite different positions. All were, however, shut out from any share in the common domains.

The Confederation of the fifteenth century differs from that of the fourteenth century by the acquisition of domain lands. This also distinguished the Swiss League from other leagues in the empire which were like it in origin, and it was this which specially contributed to convert the Confederation into a compact state. At that time the liberal principle, that acquired territories should be placed on an equal footing with other states, was quite unknown; no one ever thought of such a thing. The Confederates, therefore, thought nothing of gaining as many subject lands as they could, and thus making their own position more assured. So in 1415 they had acquired the domains of Aargau, Baden and the Free Bailiwicks, in 1460

Thurgau, 1483 Sargans, 1490 Rheintal, and in 1512 the territories of Ticino, viz., Lugano, Locarno, Mendrisio and Maggiatal. All, or a large majority of the Federal states took part in the government of these territories. Every one of the participating states in turn sent a bailiff to the various subject lands to maintain the sovereign authority. The latter, however, did not extend very far; in some domains, as in Thurgau and Rheintal, the Confederates had only the execution of the higher jurisdiction (the criminal court), the control of the communal administration and commercial affairs; while the lower jurisdiction was vested in the nobility, bishops and so on; or they granted no small liberties (a council of their own election, and their own jurisdiction) to various towns, such as Baden, Bremgarten, Mellingen, Frauenfeld, Diessenhofen, Lugano, &c., to engage them in their interests. The bailiffs collected the revenue (taxes, tolls, feudal rents and fines), in time of war took the lead of the men fit for service, and executed justice in the case of crimes worthy of death, with a court of justice appointed by the Confederation. The bailiffs were obliged to give account to the Diet every year for revenue received, and any surplus over the costs of administration of the district was divided among the participating states; in doubtful cases the bailiffs were referred to the Diet.

The great development which had taken place in the political life of the Confederates, partly through their common territories, and partly by their taking part in the contests of Europe, may be seen by the increased activity and authority of the Diet. This was still, as formerly, merely a meeting of delegates or "messengers" (*Boten*) from the governments of the states, who possessed no actual power of passing legal measures. On the contrary, the delegates, convened by the capital for the time being (from the end of the 15th century Zurich was usually the capital), had to get their instructions as to their votes from their home governments. After every session the votes were given to the deputies in writing on their departure,[1]

---

[1] These writings were called "*Abschiede*," and were of the nature of reports of the proceedings of the Diet.

that they might lay them before their governments or "take them home." The decision was then made by the majority of the states, not of the delegates. In other ways, too, the assembly was not formally constituted. It was not bound to any particular time or place; an assembly was held regularly at least once a year at Baden, to which the yearly accounts of the bailiffs of common territories were brought. But besides this many extraordinary sessions were held at divers places, Zurich, Soleure, Lucerne, Schwyz, &c., and the sphere of business of the Diet gradually became almost as extensive as that of an established Federal government.

Its appointments and arrangements related in the first instance to foreign affairs; it lay in its power to send embassies and despatches to the pope and the emperor, to princes and cities, to conclude treaties, as well as to appoint frontier forces and defences in time of danger. The debates of the Diet next dealt with matters relating to trade and to public morals and public health in the widest sense; orders were issued against vagrants, beggars, thieves and tinkers; and also about the isolation of persons suffering from infectious diseases, and the stoppage of traffic during prevalent epidemics; prohibitions were issued against swearing and indecent clothing; improvements and repairs of the main roads throughout the territory of the Confederation were often ordered; and the consent of the Diet was necessary for the introduction of new tolls, or the raising of old ones. By it arrangements were frequently made as to the coinage. Even church matters were dealt with as common Federal affairs. Finally, the Diet also interposed in disputes between different states or between individuals.[1] Thus the Diet was an assembly in which prominent men from the various states gained knowledge and experience in affairs of state; and the very fact that it was incumbent upon them to care for the domains common to all exercised a beneficial influence upon many branches of the administration which might otherwise have been neglected.

---

[1] This was called Federal Intervention or Mediation.

It is true that the decisions of the Diet were often not carried out in all the states; they had mostly to be repeated again and again, being rather of the nature of suggestions or friendly advice to the various states, and were only binding upon those which agreed to them. In 1515 it was first enacted that in matters concerning the honour and well-being of the Confederation the minority should yield to the majority; but this resolution fared like many others which existed only on paper. In contrast, however, to the succeeding centuries, with all their internal dissensions and frequent friction between the towns and the rural states, the necessity of arriving at a common resolution and carrying out united measures always prevailed. The events of war naturally produced a reaction in the conditions of the Confederation both at home and abroad.

The heroic days of Grandson, Morat and Novara made the name of the Confederates famous. Their military prowess had stood the test gloriously, and was acknowledged even by their enemies. While at that time cavalry usually played the chief part in war, with the Swiss the infantry formed the main part. They drew up in closely-compact lines in perfect order, the foremost provided with long pikes—the chief weapon of the Confederates—and standing as firm as a wall. The various divisions were so arranged as not to get in one another's way during manœuvres, and that the flight of any one portion might not cause that of the rest, as had been the case at Morat on the Burgundian side. The enemy always admired in the Swiss the excellent order, in which they were themselves wanting, and the heroic courage of their men, which was never stained by cowardice. Cavalry could do nothing against the impenetrable forest of bristling pikes of their close lines; and when the van had by this means broken the enemy's order of battle, the halberds, clubs, battle-axes and heavy swords of the rear proved murderous weapons. Artillery alone could be of any use against this order; but firing was very slow work in those days, and the Confederates having escaped the effects of the first fire by stooping low, dashed immediately upon the batteries and took them from the enemy.[1] Thus, says a contemporary, they revived the fame of the bravery of foot-soldiers, and became the first warriors of the world.

This military superiority gave the Confederation great political importance abroad. Milan, Savoy, Austria, France, the popes, and even the remote Matthew Corvin of Hungary, sought their favour. The chief views of foreign powers in so doing was to obtain Swiss mercenary troops; and those who gained their help usually played a winning game in the struggle. Hence, after the middle of the fifteenth century, the fate of European wars was decided by the Swiss, and their sword often turned the scale of European policy. They themselves, indeed, had no extensive or high aim in view by these foreign connections and relations; they aimed only at easily-earned material advantages, either the drawing of annuities (pensions) for the benefit of the community in general, or advantages of trade and commerce (freedom of customs, reduction of duties, &c.); from France they desired free entry into the university of Paris, as also in their treaties with Milan and the pope.

§ 37. **Culture and Morals.** By their military and political position and their relations with the outer world, the inner life of Switzerland was benefited in many ways. We owe a large number of beautiful war-songs to the spirit of patriotism aroused to consciousness among the Swiss by their brilliant victories. Enthusiasm for the freedom and fame of the fatherland inspired many a poet among peasants and handicraftsmen, as Hans Auer, of Lucerne, about 1430, Hans Viol, and afterwards Veit Weber and Matthias Zoller, both about the time of the Burgundian wars. These had mostly earned their fame by the sword; after dangers undergone they turned homewards, and extolled the heroic days in sweet songs, which speedily went the round among the

[1] C. VON ELGGER, *Kriegswesen und Kriegskunst der schweizerischen Eidgenossen*, 1873.

people, and were sung in quiet cottages as well as on public holidays.[1] Arising entirely from the sphere of thought of the people, these poems gave a powerful popular impulse to German literature.

Side by side with the song writers we find historians, who, impelled alike by their own share in the struggles and by the triumphant fame of their nation, narrated events in a naïve and popular style. Thus Konrad Justinger in Berne (1420), Johannes Fründ in Schwyz (1450), Melchior Russ, Petermann Etterlin and Diebold Schilling in Lucerne, Diebold Schilling in Berne, before or after the wars of Burgundy, and Gerold Edlibach, the stepson of Hans Waldmann, in Zurich.

Simultaneously with this movement of the popular mind, a corresponding stir of higher scientific activity was brought about by contact with foreign parts. The enthusiasm for the study of the classics of Greece and Rome (*Humanismus*), which emanated from Italy, took firm root in France and Germany, and produced an entirely new culture, soon spread to Switzerland also. The first traces appear, though yet very imperfectly, with Felix Hemmerli, a canon of Zurich (1440), who had tasted the classics at their source in Italy, and was one of the most learned men of his time. The famous dean of the monastery of Einsiedeln, Albert von Bonstetten (*cir.* 1470), also brought the new learning into Switzerland from foreign schools. Among the Confederates it was looked upon as most important that the Swiss should study in foreign schools, and therefore in all treaties with foreign powers as to the pay of mercenaries, a stipulation was always made for the free admission of a certain number of Swiss scholars into their universities.

Basle was a great centre of learning in Switzerland, and there, by the co-operation of Pope Pius II., a university was founded, which soon gained renown in Europe. Theology,

---

[1] S. TOBLER, *über die historischen Volkslieder der Schweiz* (*Archiv des historischen Vereins des Kts. Bern*, vol. vii., part 2.), and another edition of the same in BÄCHTOLD, *Bibliothek älterer Schriftwerke der deutschen Schweiz.* G. MEYER of Knonau, *die schweizerischen historischen Volkslieder des 15 Jahrhunderts, Rathausvortrag*, 1870.

law, medicine and the "seven free arts"[1] were taught here; the most distinguished families of all the Swiss cantons sent their sons hither. The names of learned Swiss who laboured here, such as Thomas Wittenbach and Glarean (Heinrich Loriti, of Glarus), were held in repute also in other lands; and learned Germans of high fame, like Erasmus and Reuchlin, lived and laboured successfully in Basle. As early as 1460 the art of printing had established itself in Basle, its first seat in Switzerland, and this town became a chief seat of the book trade. We find it a little later in Beromünster, Burgdorf, Geneva, &c.

Both material and artistic culture flourished rapidly after the time of the wars of freedom. What had been denied to their land by the niggardly hand of Nature was supplied by the energy of its people. Foreign relations gave rise to brisk commercial intercourse, and gave an impulse to home industries. The silk industry early established itself in Zurich, and the linen industry in St. Gall; and Basle, Berne, Fribourg, Zurzach, &c., became famous for trade and industries; they had all extensive relations with the great adjacent lands on the north, west and south; as, for instance, the cloth goods of Fribourg attained great repute in Germany, France and Italy. By this means no less than by the great annuities which were received according to agreements for the pay of mercenaries, and the magnificent spoils carried off from the great wars, the wealth of the burgesses increased greatly. Hence, in Switzerland, too, both in town and country, men began to beautify existence by art. Household utensils, tables, chairs, beds, cupboards and wainscots were manufactured of beautiful wood, freely ornamented with carving; windows with beautifully painted panes, armorial bearings, stoves with allegorical and historical pictures, &c., &c.; and even the outsides of houses were often adorned with frescoes. Council and guild-houses were endowed even more richly than private dwellings with delicate carving, pictures and painted glass; and from the end of the fifteenth century onwards Switzerland produced

[1] Grammar, dialectic, rhetoric, arithmetic, geometry, astronomy and music.

much that was pleasing and really great in those arts most closely connected with actual life.

Gothic ecclesiastical architecture was yet in its second bloom: the church of St. Nicholas in Fribourg, the minster at Berne, the church of St. Oswald in Zug, the *Wasserkirche* in Zurich, &c., date from this period. But the Gothic no longer reigned alone. A preference for the beautiful forms of the Greeks and Romans gradually obtained, the so-called Renaissance style, which was for the arts what the study of the ancient classics was for learning. The new birth of art, especially as regarded painting, found an early place in Switzerland, owing to its close relations to Italy, and also owing to the skilful artists who laboured there, as Holbein in Basle, Urs Graf in Soleure, Nicholas Manuel in Berne[1] (designs for the coloured glass in the Council Hall, 1520, the Holbein frescoes on the Hertenstein's house in Lucerne, 1516).

All these circumstances also produced a reaction in social life. Foreign customs and splendid luxury were introduced, and clothing became more costly. The desire for intellectual enjoyment found vent in the introduction of the drama and the theatre, as in Lucerne in 1470; the genial sociability of the fatherland found expression in national Federal festivals, such as public shooting matches, a very large one being held in Zurich in 1504. But this desire did not degenerate into a mere pursuit of pleasure; the affairs of the fatherland were eagerly discussed, and the common people talked politics daily, even at weddings and in the parlours of inns and taverns.

Yet the splendour and the progress thus developing in every walk of life brought lamentable drawbacks in their train. Above all, the pensions paid to the Swiss by foreign powers, notably by France, had a most fatal influence on the public spirit; for besides the various states influential individuals also secretly drew such pensions for themselves, often from many princes simultaneously, as, for instance, Waldmann, who drew 400 florins from the Austrian dominions, 4000 florins from the same for distribution, and from René, of Lorraine, 100 florins.

---

[1] LÜBKE, *die deutsche Renaissance*, ii. 225 ff. For Manuel *see also* § 38.

Thus the leaders of the State were not seldom influenced in their decisions and endeavours by money.

Further, foreign influence and increased wealth fostered a laxity of morals that was most injurious. Former simplicity was despised, and men began to array themselves in silk, velvet, costly furs, silver and gold embroideries set with jewels; and Spanish and French fashions came into vogue. The mercenaries on their return home usually brought with them a habit of gossip, and much vexatious slander prevailed. The governments soon found themselves forced to issue prohibitions against unseemly and improper clothing, as also against immoderate drinking and swearing, and to punish mercenaries for insolence. Many mercenaries no longer cared to work at home, and became idlers and vagabonds, who squandered their pay, and then lived by robbery and plunder. In the year 1480 about 1500 thieves and vagabonds had to be executed in the course of a few months, most of whom were discharged mercenaries. In regard to this prevailing wantonness, and the corruption wrought by pensions and by foreign hire, a great task of reform lay before the sixteenth century.

Third Period.
INTELLECTUAL PROGRESS AND POLITICAL STAGNATION OF THE CONFEDERATION.
(1516-1798.)

PART I.
THE ERA OF THE REFORMATION.
(1516-1600.)

1. THE REFORMATION IN THE EAST OF SWITZERLAND.[1]

§ 38. **The Nature of the Reformation and its Origin.** The great changes which came about in every department of life in all the great states of Europe about the end of the fifteenth and beginning of the sixteenth centuries, soon made themselves felt in Switzerland also. The Confederates, everywhere victorious, overflowed with exuberant vitality; their national life grew more active and more varied on the stage of European politics, while private life became richer in comforts, and the arts and sciences permeated a wider circle of society. The church alone, whose guidance lay in other hands, followed the beaten track, and blemishes became apparent in social and moral life in startling contrast to the new culture and new views of life.

[1] The principal source is BULLINGER'S *Reformationsgeschichte* (published by H. H. Vögeli and Hottinger). KESSLER's *Sabbatha* (published in the *Mitteilungen des St. Galler hist. Vereins*). ANSHELM's *Berner Chronik* (newly published by the Berner hist. Verein). Newer compilations: HOTTINGER, *Fortsetzung von Müllers Schweizergeschichte* and *Ulrich Zwingli und seine Zeit.* MÖRIKOFER, *Ulrich Zwingli*, 2 vols. FINSLER, *Ulrich Zwingli*, 3 lectures. Zurich, 1873. H. ESCHER, *Die Glaubensparteien in der Eidgenossenschaft*, 1882.

The corruption of the church in Switzerland was on a par with that in Germany. In Switzerland, too, the life of the church had become torpid. Men inclined more and more to a mechanical, thoughtless following of outward ordinances, to a mere show of piety, the worship of images, credulity and superstition. The sale of indulgences, which was at that time carried on in a most shameless fashion, fostered this conception of religion as a matter of externals. The doctrine that man might be suddenly cleansed from all sin by the mere purchase of a slip of paper containing an indulgence was to many an inducement to sin. Even the clergy favoured this view, being themselves to a great extent depraved, ignorant and superstitious, particularly the monastic clergy. In 1507 the Dominicans in Berne, by means of scandalous machinations, inflicted the five stigmata of Christ upon a poor tailor named Jetzer, whom they had admitted into their order, in order to proclaim him as the living Christ, and to achieve a public success in opposition to the Franciscans, who laid claim to great miracles. Abbot Trinkler, of the monastery of Kappel, was notorious for his dissipation and immorality, as were many other principals of monasteries and convents. Even flourishing monasteries with a glorious past behind them, such as St. Gall, degenerated, and allowed the treasures of knowledge to decay. An ordinance of Bishop Hugo of Constance gives us a gloomy picture of the generally scandalous conduct of the clergy; the chief pastor complains that so many ecclesiastics and priests pay no attention to discipline and morality, sit with the laity in taverns, gamble, quarrel, get drunk, enter into unlawful contracts, &c.[1]

Many noble-minded men watched this mental and moral decay of the church and clergy with grief and indignation. As early as the time of the old Zurich War, Felix Hemmerli, the broad-minded canon of Zurich, openly blamed the negligence, frivolity and licentiousness of the clergy. In Berne the painter Nicholas Manuel scoffed at the clergy in his "Dance of Death," painted in the monastery of the Preaching

[1] MÖRIKOFER, vol. i. p. 67.

Friars, as also in his "Carnival plays" (*Fastnachtspielen*), which were performed in public; in the latter, for example, he represented Christ with the crown of thorns, followed by the poor and the sick, in contrast to the pope riding on a splendid steed, with his richly adorned retinue.

While the outward church was exhibiting so much vice and depravity, the "humanities" (*Humanismus*), reviving the spirit of antiquity, were leading men of culture to a wider conception of faith and of church teaching. Famous professors at Basle, such as Thomas Wittenbach, &c., were moved to attack existing institutions. Their untrammelled efforts rapidly kindled a spark among the youth of the schools and universities; a new generation grew up, less prejudiced and freer in thought than the former, and moreover possessing the courage to turn conviction into action. The authorities had, it is true, already set to work in Switzerland to remedy individual abuses, although, according to the teaching of the church, ecclesiastical affairs did not come under the authority of the state. The Diet, for instance, which had long since included ecclesiastical as well as political matters in the sphere of its debates, in 1479 sent a serious warning to the Abbot of Pfäffers about the ill-management of his house, and threatened to take the monastery into their own hands. In Zurich attempts had already been made under Waldmann to restrict the exorbitant claims of the clergy, and to compel them to discipline and morality by the coercion of the state. The Council of Zurich prohibited the licentiousness and idle loitering of the monks, and deprived Abbot Trinkler of his office. The government of Berne adopted a like policy.

While such ecclesiastical abuses prevailed throughout Germany, others, chiefly of a social nature, such as the oppression of the peasantry, began to make themselves felt. Switzerland was less affected in this way than the rest of Germany, but on the other hand Switzerland suffered from a peculiar political canker. From the time of the Burgundian wars she had formed the centre and aim of European policy, whence all the powers of Europe borrowed their forces for war; she was, as it were, "a great human market, where wholesale merchants sought to outbid one another."[1] Even little Glarus was traversed by envoys from the pope, the emperor, from Milan, Venice, Savoy and France. Not only did foreign service often lead the Confederates against one another in war, but it also drained the land of its best resources, introduced evil habits, and destroyed the spirit of patriotism; the Swiss became dependent upon foreign powers, and only too often their policy was determined by money.

The healthy sense of the people, it is true, early realised the uncertainty and danger of this state of things, notably at the time of Waldmann's downfall, when the selfish ends of the leaders of the mercenary bands (who were the chief gainers by the system) became apparent. In their exasperation against the dominant class which had sprung up by means of foreign pay and pensions, the people tried to obtain a prohibition of all annuities, salaries and donations; somewhat later, at the time of the battles of Novara (1513) and Marignano (1515) organized rebellions[2] took place (in Berne, Soleure and Lucerne) against the French faction. Different classes of people at various times proposed a general prohibition of pensions, but the majority was always against it. Popular risings were everywhere suppressed; the dominant class remained, and aroused dissatisfaction among the country people, whose instincts were those of freeborn Swiss. A general revolution was therefore only to be desired. A reformation which sought once more to set the truth of a Christian life in the place of its semblance could not but be welcomed with joy, and work a complete renovation of moral consciousness. But for that very reason such a reformation must necessarily meet with so much the more opposition, since not only the ecclesiastics and the ignorant ranged themselves against it, but also all the advocates of the foreign hire and pension system and of the old Federal conditions.

[1] MÖRIKOFER, *Zwingli*, vol. i. p. 18.
[2] These were styled risings against the "crown eaters" (*Kronenfresser*), *i.e.*, against those in the Council who were suspected of taking bribes in French money—crowns.

§ 39. **The Reformation of Zurich by Ulrich Zwingli. 1519-1525.** The founder of this Swiss Reformation was Ulrich Zwingli, the first among a great number of men like-minded, who dared openly and effectually to reform existing conditions. Born at Wildhaus, in Toggenburg, in 1484, son of the chief magistrate of the commune, his religious instincts were early aroused in his own home; his parents, probably through the influence of two uncles who were priests, destined him for the ecclesiastical profession. One of these uncles, Bartholomew Zwingli, dean of Wesen, a most humane and enlightened man, took charge of the talented boy, and sent him in his tenth year to a good school at Basle, and afterwards to Berne, where Zwingli enjoyed the instruction of Wölflin (Lupulus), one of the most famous humanists; and he finally attended the university of Vienna from 1500 to 1502. Animated by a keen thirst for knowledge, he became, under the teaching of Lupulus, specially enamoured of the beauties and the brilliant world of thought of the Greek and Roman classics. Classical studies took such complete possession of his mind, that we find him for a time practising as a teacher of Latin at Basle. There he found in Thomas Wittenbach a teacher in whom were united deep religious convictions with a liberal turn of mind, one who had already cast off the fetters of the scholastic methods which had hitherto prevailed and of ecclesiastical doctrine. Zwingli was strangely moved; to carry to the people such a purified creed as this would surely be for himself the noblest of tasks.

In 1506 he became a parish priest in Glarus, and besides the duties of his office he spent all his leisure time in study. He steeped himself in the philosophy of the ancients, specially that of Plato and Seneca, whose ideas he so esteemed that he says they had drunk of "the heavenly spring," even though they were not Christians. In addition, he read the New Testament in the original, and doubts arose within him as to the authenticity of the teaching of the Fathers of the Church and the papacy. He had an opportunity, moreover, of discovering political abuses as field-chaplain in the Italian

The Reformation in East Switzerland.

campaigns; he rejoiced, like a true patriot, it is true, in the great expedition to Pavia in 1512, at the prowess and bravery of his countrymen; but in the expedition of Marignano, in 1515, his inmost soul was roused to indignation by the moral corruption and profligacy of his country.

He left Glarus, where his opponents of the French faction were triumphant, and in 1516 was appointed preacher to Einsiedeln, the famous place of pilgrimage. As yet, however, he made no open attack upon the teaching of the church. It was only after Luther had ventured the first bold step in Germany, and when he himself in December, 1518, was called as a secular priest to Zurich, where a great number of the enlightened citizens already shared his views, that he resolved upon any decisive breach with established tradition. Without troubling himself about church usage, he began at once, on New Year's Day, 1519, by preaching and expounding the pure Gospel, and his hearers testified that they never heard the like. Zwingli, the humanist, had never been so much attached to the old ecclesiastical system as Luther, the monk, therefore it cost him less to tear himself from it. It was not with him, as with Luther, the anxiety of an oppressed spirit which could find no rest that led him to the Reformation, but, before all things, the reasonable love of truth which he had imbibed from the classics. Zwingli was a Republican withal, took a lively interest in political affairs, which he brought within the range of his practical efforts, and thus aimed at a reformation not in creed only, but in every department of life. Just as he attacked the immorality of the clergy, the papacy, and the indulgences, so he condemned secular abuses, the system of pensions and foreign hire, and foreign alliances; and himself now, in 1520, formally and openly resigned the pension which the pope had sent him for some years in succession as a supporter of his political interests.

He speedily met with considerable sympathy in Zurich, and in the very first year could reckon upon more than two thousand who shared his views. The Diet assembled in Zurich also denounced Bernhardin Samson, the shameless hawker of indulgences, and succeeded in keeping him out of the town. At Zwingli's instigation, and with the full consent of the *Landsgemeinden*,[1] who had to give in their votes in due form, the Council rejected the alliance with France concluded by the twelve states in May, 1521. The adherents of the old *régime*, however, now began to bestir themselves; in spite of all Zwingli's efforts, the advocates of foreign service induced Zurich to provide the pope with mercenary troops for the expedition to Piacenza in 1521. Meanwhile Zwingli's preaching began to take effect. The reformer having declared that fasting was not obligatory, certain of the inhabitants of Zurich in 1522 disregarded a mandate of the bishop enjoining a fast, for which they were punished.

Zwingli therefore wished to establish the truth of his views, and to convince everyone of the hollowness of all reasoning to the contrary, by open discussion with his opponents. Hence, on 29th January, 1523, the first disputation was held at Zurich. Faber—the episcopal vicar-general of Constance, a learned man who had formerly himself had some leanings towards the Reformation, but who had changed his attitude in order to obtain preferment—entered the lists as Zwingli's chief opponent. He was completely worsted by Zwingli's assurance and ability; the authority of councils and of popes, the authenticity of tradition, and the celibacy of the clergy, were all shown to be errors and abuses.

Henceforth began the actual Reformation. The council decided that Zwingli should continue as heretofore; and he immediately set to work to reform the monasteries, especially the Institute of Canons in the town of Zurich. For the first time an ecclesiastic, Wilhelm Röubli, of Wytikon, now ventured to be publicly married (April, 1523); soon a number of other eminent ecclesiastics followed his example: and in the following year Zwingli himself married the excellent Anna Reinhart, the widow of a nobleman of Zurich, with whom he led the happiest family life. Thenceforth marriage became the rule among the reformed clergy.

[1] *See* p. 70.

Zwingli's friends, however, being guilty of many rash proceedings and seeking to get rid of pictures and church furniture by force, violent opposition soon arose, until the second disputation at Zurich (October, 1523) established Zwingli's points more clearly, and put a stop to all violent dealings. Konrad Schmied, a friend of Zwingli's and the distinguished head of the monastery of the Order of St. John, in Küssnach,[1] urged that the weaker brethren should not be harassed, but treated with indulgence. The great council —chiefly composed of Zwingli's adherents—pursued their course of reformation with fresh courage. But just as he had established it within the city by instruction, not by violence, so in the country he secured the consent of the people. Zwingli and his friends went among the various communities, and by their influence opinions were formed which were vehemently expressed in favour of the Reformation. Consequently, almost without opposition or tumult, pictures were abolished in 1524, then the monasteries were dissolved, and in 1525 the mass was discontinued. Under Zwingli's guidance Zurich was completely reformed in a short space of time, and its political system was totally changed. The temporal possessions and rights of the canons of the *Grossmünster*, which, like a kind of small principality, had hitherto formed a state within a state, he transferred to the State. Out of the revenues he erected a school for theologians and humanists (the *Carolinum*), and invited eminent learned men as teachers (such as Pellikan, Ceporin, Myconius and Collin), who raised Zurich into a nursery of the higher culture. The religious houses, both in the city and in the country districts, were converted into hospitals, almshouses and schools, and regulations were issued for the poor and the sick, and also concerning marriage, for the whole state.

There were, however, many whom these reforms did not satisfy, specially the Anabaptists. That the latter should reject infant baptism and insist upon the baptism of adults was a deviation of little importance; but they were very zealous

[1] On the lake of Zurich.

for the strictest application of the Gospel and the conditions of primitive Christianity, and equally so against the prevailing social system, the difference between rich and poor, and against the oppressive feudal taxes (tithes and ground rents), and thus once more aroused the efforts of the oppressed peasants. To these demands, which were to some extent reasonable, they united fanatical and extravagant ideas about the coming of the kingdom of God, thought they had received revelations, imagined themselves the "chosen of the Lord," and wanted to purge the church of the "impure," or to form a church of the pure and holy. These Anabaptists appeared in Switzerland (in Zurich and St. Gall, for example) about the same time as in Germany. Their most zealous leaders were Konrad Grebel and Felix Manz, both of Zurich, learned men of spirit and understanding, but full of passionate zeal. The excesses of the Anabaptists were necessarily regarded as dangerously inimical to the Reformation. The State itself saw its very existence threatened by them, all the disputations having hitherto availed nothing for their instruction. Authoritative measures were taken against them, and severe punishments were inflicted upon them, as was the spirit of the age; some were drowned, and among them Felix Manz.

The peasants, however, next began to agitate. When in 1525 the collective peasantry of southern Germany rose in revolt, and in twelve articles demanded the abolition of tithes, of villainage, of hunting monopolies, the diminution of taxes and compulsory service, &c., these ideas spread to their neighbours of Basle, Zurich and Schaffhausen. In many places, at Eglisau, Grüningen, Rüti and Greifensee, the peasants declared that God had created water, the woods, fields, birds, wild game and fish freely for every man without distinction, and that it was but righteous and just that every man in the country districts should pursue his craft or trade as in the city, and that everyone in the country should have free access to and intercourse with the city. They complained bitterly of the oppressive innovations which had been introduced in Waldmann's time. Popular riots ensued; the monasteries of Rüti and Bubikon were attacked and plundered, and on the 5th of June a popular assembly was brought about at Töss. The authorities and Zwingli, however, allayed the storm. The gentle and conciliatory words of Rudolf Lavater, the bailiff of Kiburg in Töss, and the liberal hospitality practised by the town of Winterthur, succeeded in appeasing the vehemently excited minds of the populace. At Zwingli's instigation the Council abolished villainage, as far as lay in their power,[1] the tithes were lessened, and a prospect held out of their partial remission. The Council of Basle made similar grants, and Zurich added that from all time the city and the lake communes had been one, and that the latter should be regarded as burgesses of the town. Schaffhausen resorted to force. The unfavourable issue of the Peasants' War in Germany afterwards materially contributed to intimidate the peasants in Switzerland.

§ 40. **Spread of the Reformation, 1524-1528.** The Forest States became more and more adverse and hostile in their attitude towards the commenced work of reformation. From the outset they clung more to the glorious inheritance received from their forefathers. In their simple conditions they saw less of the depravity of the clergy, and a liberal education was unknown among them; even social abuses were not so severely felt by them as by the other states. Moreover, they saw their most important source of gain threatened by Zwingli's zeal against mercenary service and foreign alliances; and on this point the other states were at one with them, particularly Lucerne, which was strongly influenced by French money, and was striving to obtain a position of power similar to that of Zurich. Hence, when Zwingli abolished the mass and purged the churches, the Forest States prevailed upon the Diet held at Lucerne in 1524 to decide to hold fast to the old faith, and if necessary to resort to punishments. Zurich was admonished to re-establish the old religion, and as this produced no effect, the Forest States withdrew their Federal friendship;

[1] Namely, only for the bondmen who belonged to the state of Zurich, and not to outside owners.

some people even suggested publishing the Federal charters to the state so desirous of innovation.

The first conflict broke out in the common dominion of Thurgau. The Thurgau, as common subject-land, was obliged on all occasions to have recourse to Zurich as the seat of government, and through her intercourse with that town the Reformation speedily took root throughout the districts of the territory of Thurgau. But the bailiffs of the Forest towns hindered it, and availed themselves of every slightest occasion to take violent measures against the new doctrine; they specially turned their attention to Stammheim and Stein, dependencies of Zurich, which were under the high jurisdiction of the Thurgau. Both these places readily accepted the Reformation with Zurich, but when they began to abolish images, Amberg, the bailiff from Schwyz, interfered, and caused Pastor Öchslin to be imprisoned in the castle of Stein. Thereupon a popular tumult broke out, and the Carthusian monastery of Ittingen, a stronghold of the old faith, was burnt to the ground (July, 1524). The under-bailiffs, Wirth and Rüttimann, of Stammheim and Nussbaumen, were falsely accused of instigating the riot, together with the pastors there, sons of Wirth, and were thrown into prison. Zurich could effect nothing by her intercession, but was obliged to submit to the majority of the governing states; three of the innocent prisoners were condemned at Baden and mercilessly executed! Thus fell the first victims to religious hatred, and a war very nearly broke out; but the severe defeat which the Swiss mercenaries had sustained in February, 1525, with the French at Pavia at the hands of the imperialists, had damped the warlike zeal of the five states.[1]

Meanwhile, however, in spite of bitter opposition, the Reformation had already forced its way into a great part of the Confederation. As early as the second disputation delegates from Schaffhausen and St. Gall had taken its part. In Schaffhausen, where the ecclesiastical movement and a political one

[1] The five Catholic states :—Uri, Schwyz, Unterwalden, Lucerne and Zug.— E. S.

were closely connected (the victory of the guilds over the nobility), there laboured friends of Zwingli, such as Sebastian Wagner (*Hofmeister*). In St. Gall the celebrated city-physician and humanist, Joachim von Watt (Vadian), afterwards burgomaster, laboured for the Gospel, as did John Kessler, writer and saddler, who had studied with Luther and Melanchthon at Wittenberg. In Glarus the Reformation was advanced by divers liberal-minded pastors, disciples of Zwingli, notably Valentine Tschudin.

Basle soon cast off the episcopal dominion; several learned men at the university, especially Zwingli's friend, Ökolampadius ("the light of the house"), were there active on behalf of the new doctrine. Berne found a reformer in Zwingli's friend, Berthold Haller. Young priests, disciples of Zwingli, carried the new ideas even into the little state of Appenzell; the more enlightened population of the lowland portion (the present Outer Rhodes) in 1524 obtained a decision of the *Landsgemeinde* in favour of religious liberty, whereupon a number of communes accepted the Reformation. Friends of Zwingli and clergy from Zurich carried the seed of the Reformation even to the remote Grisons, where its cause was essentially advanced by an antagonism of long standing to the episcopal rule. Liberty of faith having been established at a disputation at Ilanz in 1526, the bishop and clergy were afterwards excluded from the Federal Diet, and from appointments to secular offices; by this means the Grisons also took an important step towards independence. Thus little by little the Reformation gained the ascendent in the whole of the north-east of Switzerland. In 1525 the neutral states of Basle, Schaffhausen and Appenzell separated themselves from the other Catholic states; and also Soleure, Berne and Glarus assumed either a neutral position or one favourable to the Reformation, and disapproved of the very severe decisions of the Diet against Zurich.

Meanwhile the remaining six Catholic states hoped to succeed in gaining the victory for their religion in the same way as Zwingli had in Zurich, by arranging a disputation at

Baden in May, 1526. Their plan seemed to meet with brilliant success, for Zurich held aloof, because impartial management was not to be expected, and also fears were entertained for Zwingli's life, for in 1523, at the instigation of Lucerne, a Diet had decided that he should be arrested wherever found on Federal soil. On the Catholic side there appeared Dr. Eck, the most able controversialist of Germany, and other learned men of mark, such as Faber, the vicar-general, and Murner, the Franciscan monk, who defended the ancient church with such assurance and such ability that the Catholics might well triumph in their victory. The reformers disputed the victory with their opponents, and complained of fraud in the report drawn up by the other faction.

The places which had hitherto remained neutral (with the exception of Soleure) now took up a much more decided position of hostility towards the strict Catholics, and aided Zurich. Berne in especial now took part openly with the Reformation, having quarrelled with the Forest States, who refused to publish the acts of Baden. A re-election of the Council (1527) turned completely in favour of the partisans of the Reformation, and the government arranged a disputation in January, 1528, in order to bring the wavering to a decision. On the papal side only very insignificant speakers attended; Zwingli, on the other hand, distinguished himself by his perspicuity and depth of thought. When at the close of the disputation he preached in the minster, a priest who was just preparing for the mass was so overcome by the truth of his words that he threw aside his vestments, and cried: "If it be so with the mass, then will I neither to-day nor ever henceforth hold mass!" Berne joined Zurich in carrying out the Reformation, and also concurred in insisting upon the abolition of the pension system, and such-like Federal matters. The secession of this powerful and important city with her vast territory secured the continuance of the new doctrine in the whole of Switzerland, for the step taken by Berne also led to the complete establishment of the Reformation in Basle, Schaffhausen and St. Gall. Most of the professors at Basle left the university, and the bishop removed to Porrentruy (*Pruntrut*), in the Jura.

§ 41. **The Wars of Kappel, 1528-1531.** With the increasing spread of evangelical teaching, the antagonism between the Catholic and the reformed states was heightened. The immense progress of the Reformation in the common domains, in particular, led to constant disputes. In addition to the Thurgau, evangelical doctrines had won the day in the Rheintal, belonging to the eight original states (1527), then in Sargans and Gaster, and in the common domains of Baden and the Free Bailiwicks it had likewise gained ground. Hitherto the principle had indeed been maintained that in the common dominions all things should be decided by the majority; Zurich and Berne, however, would not allow that principle to hold good in religious matters, and insisted that every commune should enjoy unconditional religious liberty. The reforming of these territories resulted in a constant decrease there of the influence of the Catholic states. Zurich meanwhile had extended her power by other measures. As early as 1527 she concluded an "Evangelical Alliance"[1] with the reformed town of Constance, thus forming a separate league; this was joined by Berne, St. Gall, Mülhausen and Bienne, after the triumph of the new doctrine in each of those states respectively. Zwingli, who by his paramount influence in Zurich held sway even in political matters, and was practically to a certain extent burgomaster, town clerk and council all in one, proceeded in consequence with even more energy. In order to make their opponents feel their supremacy, the inhabitants of Zurich punished most severely every offence against their creed, and now tried to procure the triumph of their opinions in the territory of their adversaries by force. Thus Max Wehrli, the bailiff's officer (*Landweibel*) in the Thurgau, was put to death for alleged aspersions upon Zurich, and thus a cruel revenge was taken for the sanguinary decree of Ittingen.[2]

[1] *Evangelisches Burgrecht.* [2] *See* p. 136.

Zurich specially exasperated her enemies by supporting the subjects of the Abbot of St. Gall, who were availing themselves of the Reformation to throw off the yoke of their spiritual lord, and who applied to Zurich as one of the protecting states of the abbey.[1] When the evangelicals purged the churches in Toggenburg in 1528, attacked the monastery of St. John, and drove out its abbot, Zurich encouraged the Toggenburg folk to refuse homage to the Abbot of St. Gall; a similar course was pursued in the "Old Territory," where the town of St. Gall, Rorschach and several communes abolished Catholic worship, and refused obedience to the abbot. The other states protecting the abbey, especially Schwyz, embraced contrary measures, and mutual preparations for war speedily ensued. During these disputes Murner, the Franciscan, hurled such satires, invectives and abuse at Zurich and Berne, that these states demanded satisfaction at the Diet; Lucerne, however, took Murner under her protection.

A separate league entered into by the Catholic states accelerated the rupture. In order to be able to depend upon the support of their co-religionists, these states resolved upon the fatal step taken by Zurich a hundred years earlier, namely an offensive and defensive alliance with Austria, concluded in April, 1529 ("the Christian Alliance," or the "Treaty of Ferdinand"). This union gave a greater shock to the Federal Leagues than even the union of Zurich with Constance. At this crisis the reformed pastor, Jakob Kaiser, of Schwerzenbach, being taken prisoner by the men of Schwyz and burnt to death for promulgating the new doctrine upon their territory, and Murner pouring forth fresh invectives, a civil war broke out.

Zwingli was resolved upon war; he hoped by its means to advance the cause of religion, and induced Zurich to take arms so much the more eagerly, that he believed it necessary to oppose the power of the emperor and of Ferdinand in the name of the Reformation. Zurich forestalled the enemy, speedily took possession of the Free Bailiwicks, and stationed

---

[1] The Abbey of St. Gall was under the protection of Zurich, Lucerne, Glarus and Schwyz.—E. S.

her main army at Kappel in June, 1529. The Bernese, although not so eager for war, also marched out. But the people had not lost all sense of Federal brotherhood; sentries and advanced guards encountered one another in friendly fashion; when for instance a number of boon companions from the Forest States had got possession of a large vessel full of milk, but had no bread, they placed it on the frontier, and called to the men of Zurich; the latter brought bread, and they shared milk porridge amid merry jests. Jakob Sturm, Mayor (*Stadtmeister*) of Strassburg, said of them: "You Confederates are a wonderful people; even in discord you are at one, and never forget your old friendship!" This frame of mind at that time still prevailed, and most shrank from civil war. Neither were the Catholics very eager for war, since the reformers were better armed, and had a more powerful force in the field. The Landammann Aebli of Glarus therefore succeeded in effecting a truce, and through the intervention of the neutral states, on the 25th June, 1529, the first peace of Kappel was concluded (seemingly against Zwingli's wish), which secured mutual liberty of faith; the right of decision in religious matters in the common domains was yielded to the communes on the principle of majority, and the Austrian alliance was broken off.

Still further encouraged by the concessions of their adversaries, Zwingli and his adherents endeavoured to completely subjugate the five states. Without any reference to the other protecting states (Lucerne and Schwyz), the two states of Zurich and Glarus, challenged by their opponents, declared that the Abbot of St. Gall, who had fled, had forfeited his domain, disposed absolutely of the goods of the monasteries, and gave a free constitution to the Toggenburg, the home of the Reformation. The evangelicals next concluded a league with Philip of Hesse. Zwingli, whose plan of operations extended far beyond Switzerland, had long seen with anxiety the growing power of Charles V. and his hostile intentions towards the Reformation. He wanted to effect a league to oppose him, and therefore endeavoured at the religious conference at Marburg, in October, 1529, to form an agreement and an alliance with the German Protestants. This failing, he immediately attacked his opponents in Switzerland. It was his intention to dominate the Forest States, whom he regarded as incapable, to deprive them of all right to the common domains, and to degrade them into vassals of Zurich and Berne. These two cities, which surpassed all the other states put together in extent of territory and in population, and which had formed the starting-point of the Reformation, he considered as the basis of the Confederation. It was his aim to establish a uniform Federal Government, in which the larger states should be paramount, to carry reform throughout the Confederation, and to sweep away the system of pensions and mercenary service. He once more allowed himself to be torn from these lofty aims to seek a decision at the sword's point. In the emperor and in his brother Ferdinand of Austria, with whom the five states cultivated friendly relations, he not only saw the bitterest foes of the German Reformation, but also credited them with an intention of exterminating the reformed party in Switzerland, in concert with the five states. He therefore entered into negotiations with Francis I. of France, the chief enemy of Charles V., and with Venice, and when in Germany also, to his joy, the party prepared for the struggle at Schmalcalden, he thought the moment had come for open warfare.

Various causes combined to give him his opportunity. Jacob of Medici, lord of the Castle of Musso, on the lake of Como, apparently in collusion with Austria, attacked and surprised the Valtelline, a subject-land of the Grisons. The Grisons called in the help of the Confederates, but only the Protestant states marched out (April, 1531), while the five states refused their aid. This aroused the suspicion that they were in conspiracy with the enemy, and Zurich accused them of breaking the League. Then came all manner of spiteful invectives and accusations on the part of the five states. The war with Musso now taking a favourable turn, the Confederation prepared for a second religious war. Zurich considered that peace was no longer possible, and hoped to obtain more favourable conditions by the decision of war. She was with difficulty persuaded, at the desire of the allied towns, in May, 1531, to coerce the five states by a blockade of provisions only. This measure had the opposite effect: instead of submission, the Catholics offered a most daring resistance, and on the 9th of October they declared war.

Zurich had not expected this; she had neither secured the aid of her co-religionists, nor made due preparations herself. Paralysed by dissensions within her own territories, and not less by the coolness and alienation of Berne, Zurich tardily sent 1200 men to Kappel on the 10th of October, under Captain George Göldli, who was inimical to Zwingli, with injunctions not to let himself be drawn into a battle until the main army should come up. Instead of obeying, Göldli, on October 11th, allowed himself, though occupying a most unfavourable position, to be drawn into a battle with the powerful army of the five states, numbering about 8000 men; and when about midday on the same day a reinforcement of 1500 men appeared under Rudolf Lavater, accompanied by Zwingli himself, the conflict was already almost decided. The manly courage displayed by the men of Zurich was all in vain: by a flank movement the five states rendered the position of the Zurich troops untenable.[1] Zwingli himself fell beneath a tree. Recognised by the light of the torches, the dying man received his death-blow from a captain of mercenaries from Unterwalden; but Pastor Schönbrunner, of Zug, exclaimed as he looked at the corpse: "Whatever thou hast been as to thy faith, I know thou hast been a good Confederate!" Over 500 of the men of Zurich, many of them of the foremost of the city, remained dead on the field. In vain did the Bernese and others of the reformed religion advance to the help of the Zurich troops; they were altogether wanting in unity and confidence; and the victory of the Catholics was completed by an attack made on the night of the 24th of

[1] S. E. EGLI, *die Schlacht bei Kappel.* Zurich, F. Schulthess, 1873.

October on the Gubel, near Zug, upon the men of Zurich and their allies.

The five states were at first resolved to pursue their advantage to the utmost against Zurich; but Golder, the chief magistrate of Lucerne, urged them to treat the men to Zurich as brothers and fellow Confederates, and to be lenient with them, and his advice at length prevailed. So the second Peace of Kappel (November 20th) assured the free exercise of religion to every state, and religious liberty even to the common domains; but a Protestant majority was not to be allowed to compel a Catholic minority to change their religion, and all separate leagues were abolished.

The reformed party was terribly disheartened by the result of the second war of Kappel. The adherents of the older faith became more arrogant in their bearing; not only was the scheme for the further spread of the Reformation shattered, but with it that of the political reform of the Confederation, and Zwingli's cherished hope of establishing the supremacy of Berne and Zurich was dashed to the ground. The territories of those two cities were in a state of violent fermentation, and general dissatisfaction with the arbitrary proceedings of the authorities reigned. In order to avoid an insurrection, Zurich was forced, in December, 1531, to promise by the "Charter of Kappel" to consult the rural districts on all matters of importance, and particularly to commence no war without their consent. Berne was obliged to concede the same to her country-folk, to grant free trade, and to lighten the tithes. Zwingli's place as chief pastor (*Antist*) of the church of Zurich was taken by Henry Bullinger, of Bremgarten, who, supported by Leo Jud, carried on Zwingli's ecclesiastical work with fidelity and discretion, but relinquished his political schemes and undertakings.

In consequence, however, of the pre-eminence of the five states after the battle of Kappel, a Catholic reaction rapidly ensued. In certain communes in Glarus Catholic worship was re-established, as also in Rapperswil, in the Free Bailiwicks, in Utznach, Wesen and Gaster. The Abbot of St. Gall returned to the protection of the five states, completely re-established the sway of the monastery over the "Old Territory" and Toggenburg, and partially restored Catholicism. The five states were specially successful in Soleure, where the Catholics sought to crush the Reformation completely. In October, 1532, the two factions were already in arms against one another, when Nicholas Wengi, the Catholic mayor, rushing in front of the guns of his faction, exclaimed: "If the blood of my fellow-citizens must flow, then let mine be the first!" The combatants yielded in astonishment, and civil war was averted. The reformed party, however, were so alarmed, that many left the town, and others joined the Catholics, so that the counter-reformation prevailed.

As a result of this reaction the religious conditions of Switzerland took definite shape; the five states, with Valais, the Free Bailiwicks, Rapperswil, Utznach and Gaster forming one united Catholic Federal territory, and acting as a bulwark to Fribourg and Soleure on the west, and to Inner Rhodes in Appenzell and St. Gall on the east. Separated from one another on all sides, and to a certain extent encircled by arms of the Catholic territory, or by "districts of parity"[1] (Baden, the Thurgau, Toggenburg, Rheintal and Glarus), the reformed territories of Berne, Basle, Zurich, Schaffhausen, Outer Rhodes in Appenzell, Werdenberg and the Grisons were more isolated.[2] On this account the reformed party laboured under a disadvantage, but an opportunity soon arose for a considerable extension of their power in the territories of western Switzerland.

[1] *i.e.*, recognising equality of political rights between the two confessions.—E. S.
[2] *See* map No. 10 in VÖGELIN MEYER's *historisch geographischem Atlas der Schweiz*. Zurich, F. Schulthess.

2. THE REFORMATION IN WESTERN SWITZERLAND AND ITS CONNECTION WITH EASTERN SWITZERLAND.[1]

§ 42. **The conquest of the Pays de Vaud by Berne, and commencement of the Reformation in Geneva.** Owing to the immense strides taken by the House of Savoy during the 13th century, the bond between the present western Switzerland and eastern Switzerland had grown lax (*see* p. 41), until during the Burgundian war Berne conceived the great design of restoring the old kingdom of Burgundy, and in concert with Fribourg conquered the domain of Morat, and Orbe, Grandson and Echallens in the Pays de Vaud. (*See* p. 97.) The attempts of Charles III., Duke of Savoy, to bring completely under his sway the episcopal towns of Geneva and Lausanne (then making strenuous efforts after liberty), where his house possessed certain rights of dominion conjointly with the bishops and the civic communes, next induced Lausanne (1525) and Geneva (1526) to conclude alliances with Fribourg and Berne for the protection of their liberties and rights. Since the beginning of the 16th century two opposite factions had existed in Geneva: the Savoyards (or "Mamelukes") and the "children of Geneva," the latter under the leadership of the high-minded Philibert Berthelier. Charles III. endeavoured to crush his opponents, and in 1519 caused Berthelier to be put to death. But in Bezanson Hugues the party of Berthelier found another able leader, and the civil alliance with Berne and Fribourg was the result of his initiative.

The nobles of Savoy made a fierce attack upon the town (*Löffelbund*), and Bonivard, the Genevese historian, was arrested in the Vaud, and thrown into a dungeon of the Castle of Chillon. Geneva now tried to obtain complete freedom, and in 1530 succeeded, by the help of the Confederates; the duke was forced to promise to respect the

---

[1] HIDBER, *die Waadt wird schweizerisch.* KAMPSCHULTE, *Calvin, seine Kirche und sein Staat in Genf*, 3 vols. GALIFFE, *Jean Calvin.* ROGET, *Histoire de Genève*, 7 vols. VAUCHER, *Esquisses d'histoire Suisse.*

liberties of Geneva. If the peace were not observed, the Pays de Vaud was to be surrendered (the Peace of St. Julien).

The aim of the efforts of Berne was to drive the House of Savoy completely out of the Pays de Vaud, and to annex the latter themselves, for which the Reformation afforded them a welcome expedient. Under the direction of Berne there came to the Vaud William Farel, an ardent preacher, who had been exiled from his home in the south of France. He traversed the country with unflagging zeal, preaching in Aigle (1526), Morat, Neuchâtel, Grandson and Orbe with great success. The most violent opposition did not discourage him; often surprised, beaten and imprisoned, he always returned undaunted to the struggle, and shrank from no danger. Thus in 1532 he came to Geneva, and there found a favourable soil, because the citizens were then striving to throw off all dependence upon the bishops, and had been won over to the Reformation (after the treaty of 1526) by the efforts of Berne. But while the reformed party relied upon Berne, the sympathies of their opponents were with Savoy and the bishop. Many hostile encounters took place, and victory long hung in the balance, until Berne threatened to dissolve the League and the bishop tried to take the town by surprise.

The Reformers gained the victory in a disputation; an ecclesiastical storm followed, but in 1535 the Reformation was established. Duke Charles thereupon besieging the town, the Bernese declared war upon him, advanced into the Vaud in January, 1536, with 6000 men under the conduct of Franz Nägeli, conquered the whole country almost without striking a blow, as also Gex, Genevois and Chablais, and drove out the troops of Savoy. In a second expedition they happily succeeded in releasing Bonivard from Chillon. The duke was obliged to yield the territories just named to Berne.

The town of Geneva, however, owing her deliverance to the Bernese, bound herself to enter into no alliance without the consent of Berne, so that the latter exercised a species of protective right. Thus was the foundation laid of an enduring political and intellectual alliance between those

French territories and the German Confederation. With the regulations introduced into the acquired territory by Berne, the constitution of the Vaud was gradually swept away, bailiffs were sent into the country, and the laws of Berne introduced, though with reservation of the communal liberties; the reformed teaching was disseminated throughout by force, and Catholicism interdicted. But the greatest services rendered by Berne to the Vaud were the erection of schools, the establishment of a poor fund, and the founding of the University of Lausanne, where the famous theologian, Peter Viret, of Orbe, a colleague of Farel, and Theodore Beza, a later disciple of Calvin in Geneva, taught.

§ 43. **The Appearance of Calvin in Geneva.** While the Pays de Vaud was being thus linked to Switzerland an important change was taking place in Geneva. The old order of things was indeed demolished, but everything was still in a state of ferment, and Farel, who was wanting in talent for organization, was painfully perplexed until he finally found a powerful supporter in Calvin.

John Calvin, born at Noyon, in Picardy, in 1509, and very strictly brought up, at first studied for the law, which left a lasting impression upon him in a certain austerity and consistency. The reformed doctrines reached him in the midst of his studies, and won the day after fierce inward struggles; the classics, to which he had for some time devoted himself, were soon driven out by the Bible and the early Fathers. But when he openly proclaimed his faith he found himself endangered, and was forced to fly. At Basle in 1535 he wrote his famous confession of faith,[1] in which he—a deep thinker—put aside all the imperfections and contradictions of the Lutheran teaching, and laid down a rigid system of Christian doctrine (predestination, fore-ordaining, or election). One evening he arrived, weary, at Geneva, intending to pass through it; Farel came to him and begged him to remain. Calvin refusing, Farel menaced him with the wrath of God,

[1] *Institutio Religionis Christianæ.*

until Calvin, much moved, promised to remain (1536). He was at once appointed chief preacher.

He gave great offence, however, by his violent and arbitrary proceedings, by favouring the French, and by departing too much from the doctrines and usages of German-Swiss Protestantism, which Berne had introduced into the Vaud and had joyfully extended to Geneva. When in 1538 he and Farel refused to administer the Lord's Supper to the "godless" population, they were both forced to leave the town. Farel went to Neuchâtel, Calvin to Strassburg. But after a short time Calvin's following strengthened; and the tumults increasing and the encroachments of Berne becoming dangerous, a strong, guiding hand was urgently desired, and in 1541 Calvin was recalled. Amid the violent struggles of his opponents, the "Libertines," he founded a new church.

Geneva, which ever afterwards formed a refuge for French Protestantism, assumed an entirely new character under Calvin's direction. At the head of his ecclesiastical system there stood two lay "Elders" or "Presbyters" chosen from the council, who, together with the clergy of the town, formed a moral tribunal called the "Consistorium." This exercised the strictest supervision over the conduct of the whole community, both in public and in private; every slightest offence, every careless speech, even jests, were reported and punished. Every luxury, all amusements (dancing, card-playing, singing, and the theatre), were strictly forbidden. The whole state was to be ruled by the church, as the body by the soul; anyone who did not conform, or who ventured to gainsay, might expect to be severely punished by the council, or even put to death. Between 1541 and 1546 from 800 to 900 persons were imprisoned, fifty-eight put to death, and Servet, the Spaniard, who denied the doctrine of the Trinity, was burnt. Even distinguished and eminent persons were not exempt. By such severities a system of church polity was erected which was most exemplary in externals, and which was imitated in France, Scotland, the Netherlands, and several German states (the Palatinate). Geneva, where Calvin, in

1559, founded the famous university, became the "Protestant Rome," to which numerous strangers from France found their way.

These proceedings, however, produced an estrangement between Geneva and Berne, for the latter would fain have kept Geneva in subjection. But while the political alliance between Geneva and Switzerland was being loosened a friendly union was springing up between the Calvinistic and the Zwinglian churches. In 1549 Calvin and Farel went to Zurich, and in consultation with the theologians of Zurich, notably Bullinger, drew up the "Compromise of Zurich" (*Consensus Tigurinus*)—a union of the two confessions of faith. But most of the reformed towns opposed this amalgamation of differing doctrines; and it was not till after Calvin's death (which took place in 1564) that the "Helvetic Confession," composed by Bullinger, and freer from Calvin's crudities, was accepted by the states of Zurich, Berne, Schaffhausen, St. Gall, the Grisons, Bienne, Mülhausen and Basle.[1]

3. THE GROWTH OF CIVIL AND INTELLECTUAL LIFE.[2]

§ 44. **Improvement in Morals and Increased Prosperity.** After the peace of 1516, the Confederation as such assumed the position of a neutral state; it was no longer necessary, as it had been in the fifteenth century, to take the field almost every year for the protection of their own hearths and homes, and they no longer took any direct part in the proceedings of other powers. Liberty was achieved, their territory assured and its limits defined, and the passion for war had cooled to a great extent. They therefore betook themselves rather to the occupations of peace, although indeed a portion of the population still took part in foreign wars.

This development was essentially furthered by the Reformation, which sought to permeate every department of life with

---

[1] The first Helvetic Confession was published in 1536, the second in 1566.

[2] Copious material is found in the *Gemälden der Schweiz*; also in JOH. MÜLLER's *Schweizergeschichte*, continuation by VULLIEMIN (vol. viii.), and in SCHULER's *Taten und Sitten der Eidgenossen*.

an austere moral earnestness as with leaven. Scorning all pretences, the clergy in their sermons taught the means and the way to a truly pure and honourable life; the authorities themselves from time to time published so-called "moral mandates" (*Sittenmandate*), laid severe penalties upon all excess and vice, intemperance, luxury, gambling, cursing and swearing, and kept a watchful eye upon the manners of the community. Zurich, for instance, appointed a commission for the inspection and punishment of all disorderly and extravagant households. Thus there were far fewer riotous outbreaks among the people after the Reformation than before; many hitherto customary excesses were discontinued; clothing became more decent; women and girls sought to distinguish themselves by domestic virtues. It is evident that men were thoroughly in earnest in their endeavours to improve their manner of life, for the slightest transgression was punished severely and even harshly, and the most trivial faults and offences of the clergy, censured by the synods, were visited with dismissal and heavy penalties. Many a man who had formerly led a rollicking life as a mercenary in foreign lands hung his sword on the wall and devoted himself to business—tannery, the linen industry, trade, the silk industry, &c.

The industries particularly flourished in the cantons of Zurich, St. Gall and Appenzell, where manufactures were carried on of flax, hemp and cotton. The linen trade now sprang up in Appenzell, and later manufactures of woollen and muslin fabrics. In Zurich the silk industry, which had fallen completely into decay, was revived by refugees from Locarno; the immigrant families of Muralt and Orelli were the founders of this flourishing industry. Frequent intercourse with Italy and southern Germany furnished an ample market for home manufactures, and these peaceable industries increased the general prosperity in astonishing fashion; on festive occasions almost every family, even of the middle class, could display silver vessels, embroidered cloths, gold chains, &c., &c. The outward appearance of the Swiss towns of that time bears specially certain evidence to the prevalent affluence. Montaigne, the Frenchman, considers them finer than French towns; he praises their wide streets, their squares adorned with fountains, the fronts of the houses ornamented with frescoes; the painted glass, handsome stoves, polished floors and beautiful wrought iron within the houses.[1]

A higher tone of thought and the pursuit of nobler ideals among the middle classes were also among the best fruits of the Reformation. Everywhere the sense of hospitality and benevolence was awakening. In various districts, as in Basle, Geneva and Zurich, French refugees and English Protestants found a kind asylum, and the English Protestants in particular looked back with touching gratitude upon the kindly care which they had enjoyed in Zurich. Zurich showed the same spirit towards the exiles from Locarno (*see* p. 158), whom she received and provided with all necessaries, notwithstanding a prevalent scarcity. Public spirit had now found a broader and a nobler field of action, and the money that was formerly spent upon masses, and in providing images of saints and ornaments for churches and chapels, was now bestowed upon benevolent institutions, almshouses and hospitals, &c., which were founded or enriched by legacies.

§ 45. **The Development of Swiss Science and Art.** The reorganizing and creative force, which, emanating from the Reformation, permeated the whole of political and social life, was perhaps most strongly evident in the sphere of popular education and the cultivation of the arts and sciences. The more peaceable disposition which had taken possession of the popular mind, and the increase of prosperity, must in themselves have assisted the advance of mental culture. Moreover, the Reformation fought chiefly with spiritual weapons, and therefore first awakened the desire for universal education. Hence the clergy, particularly Bullinger in Zurich, made it their duty to give instruction in reading, writing and Christian doctrine. Equal attention was paid to the training of qualified teachers and capable ministers; and this was furthered by the enthusiasm for the revival of antiquity ("Humanism"). A great impulse was consequently given to learning.

---

[1] LÜBKE, *deutsche Renaissance*, ii. 225 ff.

Formerly the youth of Switzerland had been almost always sent to the schools of other lands for every higher branch of education; there, as Thomas Platter relates of himself,[1] they were forced to gain a scanty subsistence by begging, to endure hunger and thirst, to undergo almost intolerable hardships, and often enough they fell into bad company, so that they not infrequently came very near to being miserably ruined. Now, however, schools for higher education sprang up on all sides in Switzerland itself. Zwingli took the lead in Zurich by the foundation of the "Carolinum"; and soon Schaffhausen, Berne, Basle (in addition to the university), Lausanne and Geneva erected schools for the study of the ancient classics and languages, called "gymnasiums," or "schools of the humanities." Even small towns, such as Brugg, Stein-on-the-Rhine, &c., did much in this respect. Poor and talented youths were supported by scholarships, mostly derived from former ecclesiastical institutions and donations. At the same time large libraries were established in Zurich, St. Gall and Berne.

But these efforts for universal education and the spread of learning still met with manifold hindrances; many a famous teacher of those days was forced to ply some trade in addition to his learning, as, for example, Thomas Platter, who worked as a ropemaker by day and gave lessons in the evening, and was so poorly clothed that any stranger visiting the school would certainly not have taken him for the professor. Notwithstanding such miserable conditions, the thirst and craving for knowledge were indescribably great, all difficulties and pains counted for nought in the effort to obtain the treasure of learning; even an old man of eighty learnt Hebrew with Platter. Many used all imaginable means to curtail their rest in order to satisfy their thirst for knowledge.

As regards individual studies, the Reformation in the first instance gave a special impulse to theology. In Zurich the Bible was translated into German by Leo Jud and Collin, and

[1] THOMAS PLATTER'S *Lebensbeschriebung*, published by Fechter, Basle, 1840. Boos, *Thomas und Felix Platter*, Leipzig, 1878.

a French translation appeared in Neuchâtel. Everywhere were found men ready to expound and interpret the various books of the Bible with affection, enthusiasm and thorough knowledge of the subject. The theological writings of Bullinger enjoyed the highest esteem, not only in Switzerland, but even in England and the Netherlands; the foremost men in England, Germany and France, even princes and statesmen, kept up a lively correspondence with him, and embraced his theological views. Theology in those days was not a mere matter for clergy and men of learning, but also for statesmen and even for ordinary men.

Next to the study of theology that of the Greek and Roman classics was most cultivated. These were translated and explained, and numerous copies printed in Zurich and Basle. Excellent editions of the classics were produced by Glarean, Ceporin, Vadian, Konrad Gessner, Rellikan and others. By its very novelty the resuscitation of antiquity possessed such a wonderful charm for the world of those days, and the delight in it went so far, that Latin and Greek began once more to be spoken in the classical form as the ancients spoke them; and even theatrical representations were given in the Greek or Latin tongue. For instance, at the New Year's festival of 1531, a comedy of Aristophanes, the Attic comedian, to which Collin had composed a prologue and Zwingli a musical accompaniment, was performed in the Greek language at the new school in Zurich by twelve men and youths—partly noted men of learning and professors, partly pupils.[1]

The study of antiquity also bore fruit in other branches of learning. From the ancient classics men imbibed a sense of beauty and a taste for thorough scientific research; the profound thought and observation of the old philosophers and writers aroused fresh independent thought. This was specially noticeable in historical writings. The hitherto existing chronicles were already found too inartistic and too narrow; all that distinguished the historians of antiquity was wanting

[1] A. HUG, *die Aufführung einer griechischen Komödie zu Zurich*, 1531. Zurich, Sal. Höhr, 1874.

in them—their broader manner of viewing things, their systematic arrangement of the whole, and their knowledge of manners and customs. Hence, a number of more widely comprehensive histories and descriptions of Switzerland were produced after their pattern. In 1547 Johannes Stumpf published his *Swiss Chronicle*, a history, geography and topography of Switzerland, which became a favourite book with the people, and was even circulated in other lands. With similar industry and zeal for research, Bullinger in his chronicle wrote a history of Switzerland with special reference to Zurich. His work, however, was for centuries long only circulated in manuscript; as was also the case with the Helvetic chronicle of Giles Tschudi, of Glarus, who by the help of numerous records wrote the history of Switzerland from the year 1000 to 1470, and who, full of patriotic enthusiasm, succeeded in delineating it so gracefully and so brilliantly, that when his chronicle appeared in print in 1734 it supplanted all other descriptions.

While Stumpf, Bullinger and Tschudi occupied themselves in narrating the various historical facts and notable events as they followed in course of time, Josias Simmler of Zurich, on the other hand (in his book, *Vom Regiment der löblichen Eidgenossenschaft*, 1576), endeavoured to represent the internal development of Switzerland in respect to its constitutional and political conditions; even in the sixteenth century his book was translated into many languages, and passed through quite a number of editions. This development of the art of history gives unmistakable evidence of the awakening of patriotic enthusiasm and national feeling, which also manifests itself in the fine paintings on glass, wood carvings and tiled stoves of this period, for which by preference scenes from the history of the fatherland were selected, such as the battles of Morgarten and Sempach, the story of William Tell, &c.[1]

From this time geography and the physical sciences were cultivated almost like entirely new sciences. The ancient

---

[1] LÜBKE, *Glasgemälde im Kloster Wettingen, Mitteilungen der antiquarischen Gesellschaft*, vol. xiv. p. 128.

classics had also aroused sense and interest for the contemplation and observation of Nature. Men began to scale the heights of the Lower Alps, to admire and extol their beauties, and to describe the vegetable and animal species found there (*e.g.*, Rellikan, Vadian and Konrad Gessner). Simmler devotes a separate volume to a description of Valais, while Stumpf gives the preference in his chronicle to the customs of the Alpine folk. Men saw at length the inadequateness of the methods hitherto pursued in the interpretation of Nature, according to which absolute reliance had been placed on traditional opinions, and now new paths were opened by independent research. Thus Paracelsus of Einsiedeln (about 1530) zealously opposed the prescriptions and theory of medicine handed down by tradition, and would learn only in the great school of Nature.

The greatest celebrity as a naturalist, however, was attained by Konrad Gessner, of Zurich (*ob.* 1565). In spite of poverty and ill-health, he raised himself by incredible exertions to the rank of one of the most learned men of his time. But it was after studying and comparing all earlier works on natural science that he first really noticed the great gaps in the then existing knowledge, and extended his own attainments by travel, and by getting his friends in other lands of Europe to send him pictures and descriptions of plants and animals, he was the first to try to classify them from a scientific standpoint. Famous men from every part of Europe hastened to visit him, but he remained unshaken in his modesty and simplicity.

Of the arts, special progress was made during this century (about 1570) in painting on glass, in which Swiss artists earned themselves a reputation which stretched far beyond their own borders. Their work excelled in power, lucidity and warmth of colour, in delicate and fine execution. Equally delicate and masterly are other works of Swiss artists in sculpture and wood carving, as well as the stoves of this period. And in architecture the Renaissance style now attained to brilliant development, as in the Town Hall at Lucerne, the house in Berne in the *Kirchgasse*, &c.

Great, however, as were the changes which were taking place in every sphere of life, a total transformation could not so rapidly be effected; contrasting with the light many shadows were visible, unlovely heirlooms of an earlier barbarism, forming so many obstacles to progress. Thus the Reformation could not put an end to the general and widespread superstition, or at once do away with the prevalent barbarity of the age. Even educated people believed in ghosts and all sorts of witchcraft; the authorities actually caused numberless persons in Zurich, Lucerne and Berne accused of witchcraft or of repudiating the faith of the church, to be tortured in most horrible fashion (such as having their tongues slit or being tormented with hot irons), and put to death, quartered, racked, burnt or drowned. Whippings, the rack, tortures and inhuman executions were among the customary sentences. Such barbarity and superstition hindered moral and political progress, education and humanity quite as much as the mercenary system and foreign service, which still continued in the Catholic, and even in several reformed, cantons.

4. THE COUNTER-REFORMATION AND ITS EFFECTS.

§ 46. **The Revival of Catholicism and the Borromean League.** The Catholic reaction, which in Switzerland followed the battle of Kappel, was, as it were, a prelude to the European counter-reformation which occupied the latter half of the sixteenth century. It seemed as though a new generation had arisen; the noble and conciliatory spirits of such men as Aebli, Golder, Wengi and others had vanished, and mutual intolerance increased into the utmost violence.

Berne was the first to adopt the principle—"To whom the territory belongs, let theirs be the religion" (*wessen die Gegend, dessen die Religion*)—by depriving the harmless folk of the newly-conquered valley of the Saane of their Catholic religion, and even of their pleasures and popular festivals (1555). A companion picture was formed in the same year by events in the Italian bailiwicks. The seed of the Reformation had been carried to Locarno by reformed bailiffs from Zurich and Glarus, and had there found fruitful soil; and Beccaria, a zealous preacher, soon stood at the head of a considerable congregation. The five states, however, would not suffer this, and passed a resolution at the Diet, which left no alternative to the Protestants of those parts but a return to Catholicism or banishment. The perplexed people steadfastly refused to recant, willing to sacrifice their all for their faith; and in mid-winter more than one hundred persons crossed the snow-clad Alps, and found a welcome in hospitable Zurich, and a new home there and in Basle (March, 1555). Great services were afterwards rendered by the families of Muralt and Orelli.[1]

On this occasion the Papal Legate and the Roman Inquisition were already active; thenceforth the Catholic states became more and more closely connected with the papal policy. Thus they took part in the reform of Catholicism carried out by the pope and the Jesuits at the Council of Trent (1545 to 1563), which widened the breach between Catholicism and Protestantism. Moreover, without regard to their fellow-confederates, they associated themselves with the most intolerant of the Catholic powers. In 1565 they allied themselves to Pope Pius IV. (who promised them aid in matters of faith), formed connections with Spain and Savoy, and took counsel as to ways and means of exterminating the new faith by force. The foreigners increased their zeal by secret agitation and by granting them great privileges.

Carlo Borromeo in particular, the Archbishop of Milan, who had carried on a counter-reformation in his own territory with rigour, selected Switzerland as the chief field of his activity. He introduced the counter-reformation into Misocco, tried to win over the Catholic states by his efforts for the erection of a Catholic theological seminary, and hoped in return to

[1] There is a monography on this subject by FERDINAND MEIER, *die evangelische Gemeinde in Locarno.*

introduce the Inquisition and the Jesuits into Switzerland. His restless endeavours, however, went too far even for the Catholics, and the clergy complained of the innovations and encroachments of Carlo Borromeo. The states next requested the pope to send his nuncio to set in order the affairs of the church. In 1580, therefore, Buonhomo, the first papal nuncio, appeared in Switzerland, and established himself in Lucerne. Borromeo, however, pursued his aim with untiring energy. He started upon his journey, traversed Ticino, the Val Blegno, the valley of the Upper Rhine, and the inner states; he was everywhere received by the people with enthusiasm, and everywhere encouraged them for the coming religious struggle, while everywhere vigorously combating all moral and ecclesiastical abuses. The nuncio was equally active; upon his tour he was not only attacked by the reformed states and accused of inciting others against them, but could even obtain no recognition from several of the Catholic states (Fribourg, Valais), who feared any encroachments upon their liberties; the clergy petitioned against such a foreign visitation, finding that he punished all faults and omissions with severity, so that it became necessary to recall him. Meanwhile, however, through the influence of Borromeo, and also through the leaders of the Catholic party (such as Melchior Lussi of Stans, Ludwig Pfyffer of Lucerne, &c.), formidable religious combatants were introduced into Switzerland: the Jesuits, who arrived in Lucerne in 1574 and in Fribourg in 1581, and the Capuchins, who established themselves in Altdorf (1581), Stans (1582), and Appenzell (1588). While the Jesuits were working craftily in schools and in the houses of the upper classes, the barefooted, long-bearded Capuchins, with their coarse cowls, became the darlings of the populace, and laboured in the hovels of the common people.

Thus did the breach between the two parties grow ever wider. In 1579 the Catholic states concluded a league with the Bishop of Basle, who was eagerly carrying on the counter-reformation. This annoyed the reformed party, who were just then zealously supporting the town of Geneva in a struggle against Savoy, and were assisting Henry of Navarre and the Huguenot party in France, while the Catholic states took the part of Savoy and of the French Catholics. Men's minds were still further inflamed by the dispute about the calendar, which began in 1582. A religious civil war had very nearly broken out. On the 5th October, 1586, the Catholic states of Uri, Schwyz, Unterwalden, Lucerne, Zug, Fribourg and Soleure entered into a separate offensive and defensive alliance, known as the Borromean or Golden League,[1] for the defence and maintenance of the Catholic religion. This was a skilfully laid scheme of Ludwig Pfyffer's. The states at the same time concluded an alliance with the new pope, Sixtus V., and in 1587 also with Philip II., of Spain, the great foe of heresy.

§ 47. **The Disastrous Effects of the Counter-Reformation.** Thus from the time of the Council of Trent the Catholic states had become more and more estranged from their fellow-confederates. By this means the Confederation had been split into two camps, from whom it was useless to expect any united and concerted action; on the contrary, the states constantly opposed one another, either openly or in secret. This is already evident in the period between the Council of Trent and the Borromean League; not only did the Catholic states attempt a counter-reformation in all directions, but they specially resisted the accession of new members to the League who professed the principles of the Reformation.

Supported by the Catholic states, the Bishop of Basle, who had been forced to fly to Porrentruy, endeavoured to obtain his restoration, and reintroduced Catholic worship in Laufen by force. In Valais, where as early as 1551 the reformed party had grown so strong that universal tolerance and equality of rights had been decreed, the Catholic states effected the revocation of this decision, and a partial restoration of Catholic worship; and when about the end of the century the Jesuits made their appearance here too, the Protestants were openly persecuted and driven into exile.

[1] So called in memory of Borromeo, who died in 1584, and because the initial letters of the treaty were illuminated in gold.

With the help of the Catholic states, Philibert Emmanuel, Duke of Savoy, in 1564 obtained the restitution of the districts of Chablais, Genevois and Gex (*see* p. 147), conquered by Berne in 1536, and gradually converted to the principles of the Reformation, where he caused the Catholic worship to be restored by the Jesuit Francis de Sales. Attempts were also made to alienate the Vaud from the Bernese, but the latter succeeded in retaining it; they engaged to maintain all the liberties of the Vaud, and the peace thereupon concluded was guaranteed by France (1565). In return, Charles Emmanuel of Savoy (from 1580) several times attempted to repossess himself of Geneva, and to establish the episcopal authority there, in which attempts he had the Catholic states, the pope and Spain on his side. The solicitations of Geneva to be received into the Swiss League were frustrated by the dissensions between the Federal States themselves. In 1602, after several unsuccessful attempts upon Geneva, the duke resolved to carry it by surprise, and placed an army before the town by night. A number of soldiers had already mounted the walls unnoticed by means of blackened ladders, when a shot awakened the citizens, and the Savoyards were once more repulsed. This was the so-called "Escalade" of the 21st and 22nd December. Charles Emmanuel was once more forced to acknowledge the independence of Geneva.

The efforts of the Catholics in the Grisons were equally far from attaining their object. The religious factions here also partook of a political nature, for France and Austria alternately solicited their alliance. The Austrian party (under the Plantas), which was labouring by command of the pope for the restoration of Catholicism, suffered its first defeat in 1565 at the hands of the French faction (under the Salis); from that time for centuries long the two parties opposed one another with the utmost ferocity and cruelty; whichever party was victorious would pass judgment for the banishment and persecution of its opponents. This could only occur in a country where, as in Rhætia, the jurisdiction was under the management of the communes (*Hochgerichte*). The Catholic states sympathizing with the Catholic factions, the request of the influential Protestant League of the Ten Jurisdictions,[1] in 1567, to be received into the Confederation was denied.

Strassburg was also among the places which desired to be received into the Federal League. But the Catholic members refused this, upon which the reformed states concluded a separate league with that town in 1588, after a number of young men from Zurich had given proof that Strassburg did not lie too far from the Confederation, by one day taking a boat down the Limmat, the Aar and the Rhine containing an enormous kettle full of hot lentils, which was still warm when they reached Strassburg (*Hirsbreifahrt*).

But not only were no new members received into the League on account of the breach in the Confederation, even old members were abandoned. As early as 1548 Constance was taken by storm by the Austrians in the war of Schmalcalden, and thus cut off not only from the Federal League, but even from the Reformation itself. And in 1586 the Catholic states even ejected Protestant Mülhausen from the League.

At length the secession of the canton of Appenzell followed as an evil effect of this party system. The majority in Outer Rhodes had inclined to the Reformation, while Inner Rhodes remained true to the old faith, and adhered to the seven states. On various occasions, such as the dispute about the calendar, the introduction of the Capuchins, and the conclusion of the Spanish alliance, violent conflicts arose; and in order to avoid a civil war the Diet at last found themselves forced to arrange a separation (1597). The Protestants of Inner Rhodes were driven into Outer Rhodes, and *vice versa;* and the land held in common was divided. But in Federal affairs the two halves of the canton were reckoned as having each only half a vote. In the year 1600 Inner Rhodes joined the Spanish and Borromean Leagues.

---

[1] The Grisons (or *Graubünden*) comprised three leagues, the Grey League (*Grauerbund* or *Ligue Grise*), the League of God's House (*Gotteshausbund*, *Ligue de la Maison Dieu* or *Caddea*), and the League of the Ten Jurisdictions (*Zehngerichtenbund* or *Ligue des dix Droitures*).—E. S.

Thus during the period succeeding the Council of Trent the attitude of the Confederation towards the outer world was that of a double state with conflicting halves, and moreover the Catholic states at the instigation of Lucerne and of Ludwig Pfyffer her great politician (the "Swiss King") rendered effectual aid to France in her wars against the Huguenots. Whole hosts of soldiers poured from the inner cantons into France, and helped to gain the victories of Dreux in 1562, St. Denis, Jarnac, &c.; and as the Protestants supported the Huguenots a civil war had almost ensued among the Swiss in France. The situation was only altered by the accession of Henry IV. One part of the Catholics then fought for Spain, another part inclined to Henry, who was allied to the Protestants; when in 1593 Henry formally embraced Catholicism at St. Denis he was joined by the once hostile Catholic states, and peace was for a time secured within the Confederation.

PART II.

THE ERA OF RELIGIOUS WARS AND OF THE FORMATION OF ARISTOCRATIC CONSTITUTIONS.[1]

(1600-1712.)

1. SWITZERLAND DURING THE THIRTY YEARS' WAR.

§ 48. **Condition of Affairs in general and Confusion in the Grisons.** After the division of the Confederation into two camps, and more especially after the year 1526, the periodical confirmation of the old leagues by oath—prescribed in the Federal charters—was totally neglected, and special Diets were frequently held by both Catholic and reformed states to advise upon their affairs, while general Diets became more and more rare, and lost all significance. At the same time the relations between the factions continued to be very

[1] VULLIEMIN, *Geschichte der Eidgenossenschaft während des 16 und 17. Jahrhunderts* (continuation by Joh. v. Müller). SEGESSER *Staats und Rechtsgeschichte von Luzern*, vols. ii. and iii.

strained—a condition of things which was purposely aggravated by the Jesuits, the Capuchins and the Catholic powers. Disputes were rife about the common domains and the subject-lands which belonged to both Catholic and reformed states alike, as, for instance, between Glarus and Schwyz about Utznach, Berne and Fribourg about the Vaud, Zurich and the five states about the Thurgau. Meanwhile the antagonism between France on the one hand and the Austrian Hapsburgs together with Spain on the other hand had a decisive influence upon the internal and external relations of Switzerland. In the struggle for European supremacy these powers contended with one another for the favour of Switzerland. France triumphed at first. In 1602 Henry IV. concluded an alliance with the twelve states, which was also joined by Zurich in 1614, Zwingli's principles being abandoned. The opponents of France now did their utmost. The Count of Fuentes, the Spanish governor of Milan, distributed money with a free hand, and effected a renewal of the alliance with the Catholic states (1604). At the entrance to the Valtelline he built the gigantic fortress which bore his name ("Fort Fuentes"), and endeavoured to attach the leagues of the Grisons to himself. But the Alpine passes forming a passage from Milan through the Valtelline to the Tyrol were only opened to the enemies of France by the death of Henry IV. in 1610. The Spanish and Austrian party in Rhætia, under the leadership of Rudolf Planta, triumphed over their opponents, the adherents of France and Venice. A revolt against the Plantas next broke out, headed by George Jenatsch, a minister of the reformed church, and by a decree of 1618 the Planta family and their adherents were banished to Thusis. A tumultuous reign of terror ensued, during which the Planta faction was supported by the Catholic, and their opponents by the reformed states of the Confederation.

So matters stood when the Thirty Years' War broke out in Germany. The religious schism in the empire fostered afresh the factions in Switzerland. The reformed states, it is true, notably Zurich, resolved to take no active part in the struggle, nor even to support their fellow-Protestants, in order that they might not exasperate the Catholic states, and possibly kindle a civil war, for which reason they also declined to make any league with the German Protestant Union. The Catholic states shared their desire of not meddling with that fatal war, and in order to preserve Switzerland from forming a battlefield for the combatants, merely wished to defend the frontiers. Hence the system of neutrality was for the first time adopted as a principle, though it had practically been in operation since 1516 (*see* p. 116), inasmuch as the Confederation had not since then interfered in any foreign war as an independent party. From the commencement, however, these good intentions were only half carried out; for it would frequently happen that sometimes one party, sometimes the other, would favour the powers and the troops holding their own views, especially as the central position of the Confederation made each of the belligerent powers anxious to engage its interest, and to claim the advantages of free passage and levies of mercenaries.

These circumstances so paralysed Switzerland that she was unable to fulfil her duties to her own fellow-confederates or to preserve her neutrality as was fitting. This is specially evident in the affairs of the Grisons, that state becoming in a most lamentable way the puppet of the combatants. During the passionate struggles between the two religious and political factions, after the decree of Thusis, a terrible reaction set in against the arbitrary rule of the reformers, which had its origin in the Valtelline, the subject-land of the Grisons Leagues. A relative of the Plantas, named Robustelli, who was in collusion with the Catholic powers, fell upon this valley with bands of the lowest assassins, and massacred five hundred Protestant Grisons (the massacre of the Valtelline, July, 1620). The Valtelline, Bormio and the Münsterthal were now acquired by the Spaniards and Austrians with but little trouble. In spite of the attempts of the Catholic states to block their passage, Zurich and Berne sent troops to the help of the Grisons, but they were defeated at Tirano. Mercenaries from the five states, under Beroldingen of Uri, marched to the help of their co-religionists. Now ensued the most frightful party struggle, accompanied by outbreaks of blind fury, rapine, fire and sword. Pompey Planta, the brother of Rudolf, was attacked and slain in 1621 by the Protestants in the Engadine, under the conduct of Pastor George Jenatsch. The troops of the five states and of the Spaniards were repulsed. But the very same year the tide turned: the Spaniards and Austrians made a fresh invasion; Jenatsch was obliged to fly, and now became a soldier. Once more the Austrians were driven out, and once more they returned; and in 1629, the year when the power of the emperor was at its height, an imperial army marched upon Coire (*Chur*) and conquered the leagues for the third time, while the Confederates left that land completely in the lurch.

France next endeavoured to interpose, and to undermine the Austrian power in the Grisons. By the command of Richelieu, the Duc de Rohan, the former leader of the Huguenots, appeared with an army, and in 1635, with the help of Jenatsch, who had returned and taken the command, defeated the Austrians and Spaniards.[1] But when France refused to accede to the requests of the leagues, that their subject-lands should be preserved to them unimpaired as formerly, the mood of the Grisons changed; Jenatsch deserted the French and went over to the Spanish party, raised a revolt against the French, and in 1637 drove them completely out of the country.

The strife of parties raged for some years longer. Rudolf Planta, a son of the murdered Pompey, next arrived in the land in 1639, and attacked and killed George Jenatsch at a festival, with the assistance of disguised accomplices. Tranquillity was gradually restored, and in 1639 a perpetual peace was concluded with Spain. The Valtelline was restored to the leagues, but on terms favourable to the Catholic religion;

---

[1] There is an interesting article on the events of this period in the Grisons in the *English Historical Review* for April, 1891, under the title of "Ulysses de Salis," by Signora VILLARI.

and Spain might now send bodies of troops unhindered over the passes of the Grisons. Austria, with whom peace was likewise concluded, consented to sell her rights over the Ten Jurisdictions and the Lower Engadine. It was, however, primarily due to the divisions among the Confederates that the three leagues thus became the puppets of foreign powers.

§ 49. **Events in the North of the Confederation. Peace of Westphalia.** The northern frontiers fared hardly any better as regarded protection than those of the south-east. While the five states granted frequent passage to Spanish troops, Zurich favoured those of Sweden, and this opposition often led to unpleasant collisions. On one occasion Bernese troops hastening to the relief of their fellow-confederates of Mülhausen, then hard pressed, were overtaken in the Klus, near Balsthal, by peasants of Soleure, and many of them slain (1632). A civil war was nearly breaking out in Switzerland. When in the following year the Swedish General Horn marched past Stein (Canton Zurich), and through the Thurgau to Constance, the five states took Kilian Kesselring, the Protestant governor of the Thurgau, prisoner, thinking that he had summoned the Swedes into the country, and that Zurich, of which Kesselring was a citizen, was in collusion with Horn. Kesselring was long kept a prisoner, and it was not until the Protestants threatened to prepare for war that he was released for a high ransom. The five states also renewed their league with Spain, which caused Berne and Zurich to consider the advisability of a formal alliance with Sweden, whose ruin they considered would be their own.

Basle occupied a specially difficult position, being most exposed to the enemy, and was only able to preserve her neutrality with great difficulty, since she was totally forsaken by the other states; her frontiers were violated in 1624 by Tilly's troops, and in 1636 Bernhard of Weimar crossed the territory of Basle into the Fricktal. Schaffhausen and Mülhausen were in similar situations, so that they likewise were often in great danger; and finally, in 1632, Rotwil, one of the allied states, was totally abandoned by the Protestants because it had taken part with Austria, and assisted the five states.

Thus the weakness of the Confederation became everywhere apparent, and yet this war might so well have led them to greater unity; for in moments of most serious danger (as for instance in 1636 when Basle and Soleure were threatened by Bernhard, Duke of Weimar, and in 1647 when Wrangel and Turenne approached the Swiss frontier) they recognised that unity alone could save them, and that they must for their own security make common cause to keep all foreign armies at a distance from Swiss soil. Hence in the course of the war a scheme was several times devised for a joint military system of land defence (*Defensionale*), which was at length formally drawn up in 1647. But in 1648 the much-desired peace was concluded in Münster and Osnabrück.

When the question arose as to the representation of the Confederation at Münster, and the maintenance of Swiss interests, their lack of unity seemed likely to ruin everything. Notwithstanding the Peace of Basle of 1499 (*see* p. 112), in the latter times inhabitants of Mülhausen and Basle had repeatedly been harassed and sued by the court of the Imperial Chamber; Basle therefore endeavoured to induce the rest of the states to send a joint Federal deputation to Münster, which should procure the unconditional release of all Confederate citizens from the jurisdiction of the Imperial Chamber. But the Catholic states would take no part, and it was only at the instigation of the reformed states that Rudolf Wettstein, the gallant burgomaster of Basle, conducted the negotiations at the Peace Congress. By his ability and the activity of his single-minded patriotism, and no less by the efforts of other eminent Confederates with foreign powers (Major-General Hans Ludwig von Erlach, Zwier von Evibach, Landammann of Uri, &c.), and by the co-operation of the imperial ambassador, it came to pass that in the "Peace of Westphalia" the formal declaration of the total separation of Switzerland from the German empire was published.

2. THE ARISTOCRACY AND THE PEASANTS' WAR.[1]

§ 50. **The growth of Aristocratic Governments in the towns.** In the 14th and 15th centuries, when the Confederate States were forming their leagues, the inhabitants of every town or of every state enjoyed, generally speaking, equal rights. The freedom of a city might be acquired without payment, or for a small sum, and the road to office and dignity was open to all. In the 17th century it was quite otherwise. In all parts there arose a small class within each community who gradually succeeded in obtaining exclusive possession of the rights of government, and becoming the sole bearers of political power. As early as the 16th century this phase had commenced. It had its origin in the fact that as the population increased, both in the towns and in the several villages, the original citizens and residents held more and more aloof from the mere tenants or copyholders, fixed a certain sum for the purchase of citizenship (formerly gratuitously bestowed), raised this sum increasingly, and tried in every way to hinder the admission of strangers. At the same time in many places the distribution of pensions paid to the citizens of individual states by foreign powers contributed greatly to limit the number of the "citizens," *i.e.*, of the participators. So that the influence of individual families who had attained riches and eminence by means of trade and manufactures, or by pensions and mercenary service, made itself increasingly felt, and such families by various means converted their offices into hereditary possessions, and possessed themselves exclusively of the government.

The right of the governing body to make up their number themselves served them as an effectual means to this end. Both the small and great councils in the cities had the right of completing their number themselves, or of mutually electing one another. Hence it tacitly became the rule that appointments to positions in the councils should be held for life, or

[1] The best description of the Peasants' War is that of VOCK in the *Zeitschrift Helvetia*, vols. iii. and vi. Also HEUSLER, *der Bauernkrieg von 1653 in der Landschaft Basel*.

even hereditary; in Lucerne, for instance, the son succeeded the father, and the brother the brother. But when the end could not be attained lawfully, unlawful means, such as bribery, were brought to bear. Thus the burghers separated themselves into a distinct caste, with the sole and hereditary right of governing the whole state. The road to any government appointment was totally barred to all who were not by birth freemen of the city. Members of the government took the title of "Esquire" (*Junker*), placed the attribute "*von*" before their surnames, and adopted arms and crests.

Meanwhile an important difference became evident in the various states. In the democratic cantons the *Landsgemeinden* at first formed an effectual barrier against the formation of a system of government by powerful families; they passed severe laws against the fraudulent acquisition and the inheriting of offices. Similarly in the guild cities of Zurich, Basle and Schaffhausen the guilds prevented individual families from obtaining exclusive sway, so that here the government could never be completely monopolised by a limited number who should exclude others by law. In the cities of what was formerly Burgundian Switzerland, on the other hand, where the guilds never attained any political significance, as in Berne, Fribourg and Soleure, and also in Lucerne, a purely aristocratic system was gradually formed, or as it was called (after a like system of ancient Rome) a "Patriciate." In Fribourg, for instance, it was determined in 1627 to exclude all families who were not at that time within the pale of the council from holding any public offices; a "secret chamber" of twenty-four members elected the great and small councils and all government officials, and completed itself; thus the political rights were limited to only seventy-one families.

No city, however, guarded the rights of aristocratic families more strictly than Berne, where in 1640 Frischherz, the treasurer, was executed for attacking prevalent abuses, and in 1646 Müsslin, the former bailiff, was sentenced to a heavy fine, a humble apology and banishment for making use of invectives.

The formation of these aristocracies in Switzerland was quite in keeping with the general tendency of European policy at that time, for in all parts in other countries of Europe efforts were being made to extend and strengthen the powers of government. The Reformation itself had contributed to this, for in the reformed states the power of the church had been by law transferred to the governments, while in the Catholic states the government lent her arm to the church, to defend and expand it. This union of ecclesiastical and political interests tended, both in republics and in monarchical states, to the revival of despotism, hence every Swiss state now began to look anxiously to the preservation of her sovereign rights. The chief aim of the various states was to increase their power in all directions, and to suffer no encroachments from without. They cut themselves totally adrift from one another, as from alien states.

§ 51. **The Attitude of the Authorities towards the Subject-Lands. Prognostics of the Peasants' War.** Great as were the differences between the internal conditions of the aristocracies in the towns, they all held a like position with regard to the rural population, whom they endeavoured to reduce to the condition of subjects with no voice in the government. These endeavours had become very evident by the latter half of the fifteenth century; then, however, the country folk made an energetic resistance, as in the time of Waldmann. The position of the several territories was usually settled by covenants; from the first the various districts in the common domains had enjoyed peculiar liberties, which were guaranteed to them by the Confederates when they took possession; such was also the case with the territories acquired by the various cities. If at any time these were curtailed or disregarded, the peasants would obtain from their lords fresh charters of recognition, such as the Charters of Waldmann (*Waldmannischen Spruchbriefe*) in Zurich (1489), and the "Treaties of Kappel" there (1531), and likewise in Berne by the latter treaties.

Warned by the refractoriness and vigilance of the people, the governments for a time adopted another course, and tried to establish more friendly relations with their subjects. Hence from the end of the fifteenth century it became the rule in Zurich and Berne to consult the peasantry and advise with them upon all important acts of government, such as the declaration of war, the conclusion of peace, alliances, taxes, &c. During the course of the sixteenth century, however, the idea gradually obtained that the authorities wielded the sword of protection and punishment in God's name, and that the divine law required obedience from subjects in all cases. The example of the monarchs of that time, who displayed their sovereign magnificence as "gracious lords ruling in God's stead," and who required unconditional obedience from their subjects, was imitated by the authorities in the republics. Just as the former sought to set aside the authority of parliaments and states, so the latter tried to destroy the influence of the people, more especially after an exclusive ruling faction had arisen within the cities themselves. Berne appealed to the rural district in 1589 for the last time, Zurich in 1620 and 1640; divers individuals in Zurich were of opinion that it was contrary to the liberties of the town to render any account to purchased subjects.

Every effort was made to deprive the people of the rights and liberties formerly conferred and increased, or to bury them in oblivion; thus Zurich withdrew the charters of Waldmann and of Kappel unnoticed, and Berne simply caused the charters of Kappel and the liberties of the Vaud to be effaced. The authorities next tried to abolish the many diverse customs and legal conditions, and to reduce the inhabitants of all parts of the land into a similar condition of subjection. The towns, moreover, were anxious to secure financial advantages for themselves by fresh claims and privileges. That which Waldmann had already attempted was now carried into execution; the towns appropriated numerous monopolies (such as the sale of salt and powder and the practice of industries), and restricted trade in general—the sale of cattle by a duty called *Trattengeld*,[1] the sale of wine by another called *Ungeld* or *Ohmgeld*. The taxes caused even more bitterness than these institutions. The levying of taxes from time to time had commenced indeed at the end of the fifteenth century; the subject-lands, however, were unaccustomed to it, and regarded it as an unlawful innovation.

The peasants of Switzerland prided themselves upon being, in many respects, better situated than those of other lands; after the Reformation a very small proportion of them were bondmen, the greater number being free landowners, who rejoiced in their prosperity and in the consciousness of a great past and Republican liberties. They therefore watched the temper of the authorities very carefully, and were quick to resent any encroachments upon their traditional liberties, more especially in the matter of fresh impositions. Thus in 1570 the peasantry of Lucerne marched upon the town on account of some such innovation; in 1594 Basle with difficulty succeeded in quelling an armed revolt of the peasants against the town (*Rappenkrieg*, or "War of Farthings"); in 1599 the peasantry around the lake of Zurich and in the bailiwick of Grüningen rose in revolt about a war tax. The peasants refused to admit the excuse of the towns, that the Thirty Years' War had entailed extraordinary outlay for fortifications. When in 1641 Berne levied a property tax without reference to the country district, a rising took place in the neighbourhood of Thun and in the Emmental, and a civil war must have ensued had not the reformed states interposed. Some years later Kiburg, Wädenswil and Knonau refused to pay a tax levied by Zurich, relying upon the charters of Waldmann and Kappel; they demanded greater rights and liberties equal to those of the citizens, and when these were denied they flew to arms. Zurich, however, succeeded in effecting a reconciliation with the county of Kiburg, took possession of Wädenswil in 1646 by an armed force, and represented to the inhabitants that they deserved to be cut down to a man

[1] The expression comes from *traite*; in their wrath the peasants called it scornfully *Krottengeld*.

without quarter. Four ringleaders were executed, others condemned to pay fines; the men of Wädenswil were compelled—"to the sorrow of many honourable patriots," as writes Waser, the noble burgomaster of Zurich—to implore upon their knees that their charters of liberties should be confiscated! In other bailiwicks and districts these were withdrawn by the bailiffs; but one remained, and that in Küssnach.[1]

Finding that isolated risings were easily suppressed, the peasantry took the earliest opportunity of combining for a united effort. In almost every country of Europe the lower classes were at that time in a violent ferment; efforts were being everywhere made to shake off the yoke of despotism. In England the Parliament and people were successful in their rebellion against absolute monarchy (the English revolution[2]); in France people and nobles combined against ministerial despotism (the Fronde); in Catalonia and Naples the people rose against the oppressive taxes and arbitrary rule of Spain. Might not the free peasants of Switzerland also hope for success, if they could only make common cause? An occasion offered itself immediately after the close of the Thirty Years' War.

§ 52. **The Peasants' War and their Defeat, 1653.** During the Thirty Years' War numberless fugitives established themselves in Switzerland with their fortunes, that country being but little if at all disturbed by the war, and consequently the prices of houses, land and provisions rose. The peasants of Switzerland made splendid sales, and enjoyed a period of luxury; the mercenaries, too, had ample opportunity of making money in foreign service. After the close of the war, however, the fugitives withdrew, the value and price of provisions, and consequently of land also, dropped with every year and every month, and the occasion for foreign service was also at an end. Want of money and discontent everywhere ensued.

In addition to all this peculiar innovations were now made

[1] On the lake of Zurich.   [2] Usually styled the Great Rebellion.—E. S.

in the coinage, which greatly embarrassed the peasantry. During the war, in order to raise money, the authorities had issued a base coinage. Now, in 1652, they suddenly once more debased the small coin, and even called in some. In Berne one batz[1] became worth half a batz, in Fribourg and Soleure three-quarters. This was a sensible loss to the peasants, and moreover sufficient time was not allowed them for exchange. The people of Entlebuch were the first to rise. Often enough already they had joined issue with their authorities of Lucerne, when the latter had indulged in any encroachments upon their liberties and rights. They sent delegates to the government on the 8th January, 1653, to implore help in this financial perplexity, and the abolition of the latest restrictions on trade, manufactures and commerce. They found small hearing, however; a member of the committee of the Council encountered them angrily, called them troublesome, pig-headed fellows, who must be brought to order by severity and rigour; they would never be quiet till four or five hundred French-Swiss, sword-proof and sure-footed, should be sent to bring them to reason! At a second discussion, when the people of Entlebuch further demanded the abolition of prosecutions for debt and a reduction of rents, the magistrate confronted them with the rights of the powers ordained of God. But a sturdy fellow of Entlebuch exclaimed: "Yes, yes! you are of God, if you rule righteously, but of the devil if you rule unrighteously!" Negotiations availing nothing, the men of Entlebuch proceeded to arm themselves with clubs and battle-axes. At the same time they endeavoured to form a combination and union with the other bailiwicks, and prevailed upon a large majority to join them; on 26th February, 1653, the people of ten bailiwicks assembled at a *Landsgemeinde* (*see* p. 132) at Wolhusen in Entlebuch, and solemnly pledged themselves to mutual assistance for the redress of their grievances. Certain Bernese peasants assisted at this league, and by their means the revolt spread into Bernese territory, particularly into the neighbouring Emmental, where young Nicholas Leuenberger incited the

[1] A Swiss coin=four kreutzers.—E. S.

peasants to revolt. On the 14th March peasants from Berne and Lucerne held a joint assembly at Langnau in the Emmental, declared their grievances and encouraged the Bernese Aargau to join them also, whereupon the peasants in the Aargau and in the territory of Soleure and Basle likewise rose. Then first came into use the party epithets of the "Soft ones" (*Linden*) or adherents of the government, and the "Hard ones" (*Harten*) or opponents of the government.

These early movements, however, were quickly suppressed; Lucerne, like Zurich in 1489, requested Federal mediation, and assembled troops from the territories which had remained true to her when the peasants advanced upon the town. The rebellious peasants, powerless against the fortified town, were forced to agree to a truce (18th March), declaring the League of Wolhusen null and void. In the Aargau the peasants subsided after preventing Aarau from being garrisoned by Federal troops; the governments of Basle, Berne and Soleure came to terms with the insurgents, by which certain imposts were abated.

The Diet, however, exasperated them afresh by calling their grievances "the futile excuses of bankrupts," and by resolving to lend ready aid to the authorities of every state against insurrections of the peasantry, without reference to the justice or injustice of the revolt. The lords based this decision upon the provisions of the Covenant of Stans, that the Federal states should render one another aid against rebellious subjects. This demeanour on the part of the Diet soon fanned the still glowing embers into flame. The peasants everywhere regretted that they had allowed themselves to be so easily appeased; in Entlebuch the discontent was fanned by Christian Schibi, of Escholzmatt, a hoary warrior of powerful physique; the inhabitants of the Emmental once more ranged themselves under Leuenberger, and fresh ferments arose in the territories of Soleure and Basle. In opposition to the "League of the Lords" arose the idea of a great "League of the People" (or subjects). Hence, on 23rd April, 1653, a Federal *Landsgemeinde* was assembled at Sumiswald, composed of delegates from the peasantry of Lucerne, Berne, Soleure and Basle, and made a compact, by which they engaged to defend one another with their property and their lives, to act in concert and to compel the authorities to abolish the new impositions; Nicholas Leuenberger himself was elected president, much against his will. At a fresh *Landsgemeinde* at Hutwil (30th April), attended by 5000 peasants, the people solemnly ratified this compact. The peasants vowed body and soul, life and property, for mutual defence. Conscious of a righteous cause, and full of indignation at the injustice of the new system of government, they rose above all the religious differences which had sundered the Confederation for centuries past; Catholics and Protestants realised that they were members of the same stock, one united people, as had once been the case with the Confederates at the sealing of the first leagues during the danger menaced by the Hapsburgs. The tradition of the oath on the Rütli was vividly present in their minds: three men of Entlebuch represented the "Three Tells" at an official assembly at Schüpfheim, and many a man looked back upon the "time of William Tell" as a sort of "Paradise Lost." The demands of the peasants were not exorbitant; the majority only wanted the abolition of the new imposts and restrictions, the restoration of their former better legal status, and the establishment of greater confidence between the people and their rulers. Yet even this was not to be conceded.

At the end of April and the beginning of May the Diet decreed that the rising should be suppressed by force of arms, whereupon the several states summoned their contingents. The peasants meanwhile had won the Free Bailiwicks over to their cause, and displayed the greatest activity in all directions; they assembled in crowds, and guarded all the roads and passes. Nicholas Leuenberger, their leader, at first enjoyed unqualified respect, and exercised dictatorial authority, to which a ready obedience was yielded. It was originally intended to take Berne by surprise; Leuenberger, however, confined himself to threats, and a hollow peace was concluded on the 24th May, in which Berne made many fair promises. This "Peace of

Murifeld" was broken by both parties. Leuenberger undermined his own position by this course, and had no longer sufficient authority to restrain his followers from acts of violence, and from invading the territories of Lucerne and Aargau. Berne also now broke the terms of the peace, and summoned auxiliaries from the Vaud and Fribourg. Meanwhile an army from Zurich and from the eastern states, being ignorant of the peace of Murifeld, advanced towards Mellingen, under the conduct of General Conrad Werdmüller, who had occupied Wädenswil in 1646. Thereupon the Bernese peasants combined afresh, took up arms once more under Leuenberger, and hastened to the help of the army of the rebels then in Aargau, commanded by Schibi. But Werdmüller's troops, though few in number, were better armed and better trained; they had, moreover, acquired an exact knowledge of the peasants' plan of action through a citizen of Zurich. A heated combat at Wohlenswil, on 3rd June, therefore terminated in a defeat of the peasantry. Two days later, on June 5th, General Zwier of Uri attacked the peasants of Lucerne at the bridge of Gislikon, but was forced to retreat, and on 8th June Sigmund von Erlach, the Bernese general, gained a victory at Herzogenbuchsee over the troops which Leuenberger had again assembled for the struggle. The peasants of Basle also yielded. The last act of the tragedy ended, where it began, in Entlebuch. When the government required the oath of allegiance, the "Three Tells" raised a revolt; but this ended in the death of the leaders (September, 1653).

The victorious rulers were merciless in their sentences; Leuenberger and Schibi were tortured and beheaded, and a number of prisoners were fearfully tormented, mutilated and put to death. Thus the cause of the peasants, which had made such a brilliant start, was completely shattered by dissensions, imprudence and treachery, and remained in abeyance for almost a hundred and fifty years. The struggles for liberty in Switzerland, therefore, shared the fate of those in other continental lands, all of which were obliged to succumb; and here, as in Spain and France, only afforded a fair field for despotism to strike its roots the deeper and more firmly.

The aristocratic development reached its perfection in the latter half of the century. In Berne, Soleure and Fribourg admission to the rights of citizenship was totally suspended (1680-1690), in Soleure with the express condition:—Until the number of reigning families be reduced to twenty-five! In Berne the governing families or "patricians" disputed among themselves for rank and title. Three distinct classes began to be recognised; the first and most honoured was entitled the "highly-respected nobility" (*wohledelfeste*), the second the "respected nobility" (*edelfeste*), and the third the "nobility" (*feste*) only. Violations of these formalities were considered punishable offences. The most powerful families were those of Steiger, Wattenwyl, Stürler, Graffenried, &c., by whom most of the appointments were occupied. Efforts were also made in the guild cities to establish a similar rule of powerful families, and these towns also suspended the admission of citizens. In Zurich, the most conspicuous of the guild towns, the guilds and city companies lost their original significance. The great council was no longer elected by the guilds, but only by a committee of them, who formed at the same time a portion of the council. In Schaffhausen and Basle the council, which was renewed by itself from a few families, was all powerful; at Basle, in 1666, all the more important positions in the council were in the hands of the single family of Burckhardt. Moreover, it frequently happened that individual families resorted to all sorts of intrigues and corruption in order to attain to power; and these often became so bad, that it was found necessary to introduce the ballot at elections (as in Schaffhausen in 1689, and Berne in 1710).

There was no longer any talk of communicating with the rural population about political matters; the country people were even excluded from all public appointments. All upper bailiffs and country bailiffs, officers, captains, parish clerks and ministers were citizens, and the habit of command imbued the citizens with an idea of higher rank, as though they were of better blood than the country folk, whom they had nevertheless, a hundred and fifty years earlier, declared to be equal members of the state and dear kinsmen. In the civic cantons, moreover, the whole of the public burdens pressed upon the poor country districts; the inhabitants of the towns and capitalists did not contribute a farthing; for instance, while the property of citizens might be inherited perfectly freely, legacy duty had to be paid for the very smallest inheritance in the country. The rulers, bailiffs, officials, clerks, beneficiaries and such-like grew rich upon tithes, Lenten offerings and feudal rents, but needed to pay nothing themselves. Even men holding offices and dignities ventured publicly to attack and censure this aristocratic system with its abuses, as for example Pastor (*Antistes*) Werenfels in Basle, and Pastor (*Antistes*) Breitinger in Zurich. In certain states public dissatisfaction found vent from time to time in revolutions and rebellions (as in Schaffhausen in 1688, Basle 1691 and Zurich 1713); but these efforts mostly met with small success, or were suppressed and rendered abortive.

3. PERIOD OF THE VILMERGEN WARS AND OF THE DOMINATING INFLUENCE OF LOUIS XIV.
(1656-1712.)

§ 53. **The First Vilmergen War.** The Peasants' War had called attention to many failings in the Federal laws and their administration. Remedies were devised, and in May, 1655, a proposition was made at the Diet to draw up a common uniform Federal charter. As the Confederation in the main merely represented a number of heterogeneous alliances between individual states, and therefore certain states holding unequal positions were somewhat estranged from one another, a wholesome national unity might well have been introduced had this decision been carried into execution. Waser, burgomaster of Zurich, and Colonel Sigmund von Erlach, of Berne (nephew of the major-general), drew up a *Federal Charter*, embodying the several previous alliances in one comprehensive whole. But when the time for its acceptance arrived, the older and more privileged states could not make up their minds to sacrifice their advantages in favour of a common league; moreover, men feared the supremacy of Zurich and Berne, which had once formed Zwingli's ideal, and refused to give up the separate leagues. The proposed alteration therefore fell to the ground, and as if in defiance the Catholic states renewed the Borromean League in 1655, and made a fresh alliance with France, contrary to a former prohibition of the Diet. Even the reformed states now contemplated a separate league, and entered into negotiations with Holland and England. So the two parties once more confronted one another in hostile fashion, almost as they had done just before the wars of Kappel. How differently had the despised peasants, the "heretics and rebels," stood the test, when in spite of all religious differences they had revived the Federal sense of brotherhood by a common league! The breach between the two religious camps was so great, that an event in itself insignificant led to a civil war.

Thirty-eight Protestants of Art, who had formed a secret reformed commune, and endeavoured to spread their religious tenets, fled from persecution to Zurich, and, supported by that town, demanded the restoration of their property. Schwyz, however, not only refused this, but also punished the kindred of the fugitives most cruelly and demanded the surrender of the fugitives from Zurich; presuming upon its cantonal sovereignty, it would hear nothing of Federal judicial proceedings. Finding it hopeless to attempt an amicable settlement, Zurich impetuously took the law into her own hands, and declared war on the 6th January, 1656, in the name of all the reformed states, accusing Schwyz of violating the peace of 1531. Kappel was at once garrisoned, the Aargau and Thurgau protected. General Rudolf Werdmüller (a cousin of Conrad) advanced upon Rapperswil with 10,000 men; but while he was aimlessly and hopelessly besieging that little town, he left the Bernese, who had marched slowly towards Aargau, completely exposed to the main army of the enemy. The Bernese on their part, heedless and undisciplined, next occupied Vilmergen, but were surprised and defeated on 23rd January by troops from Lucerne. Through the mediation of the neutral states and of foreign powers, a truce was effected, and by the exertions of Wettstein, burgomaster of Basle, peace was concluded at Baden on 7th March. In this peace the views of the Catholic states were adopted, as of the victorious party, and hence for centuries Federal interests were sacrificed to the separatist spirit of those states or to cantonal sovereignty. The sovereign rights of every state were to remain for ever undisputed; and above all, every state was to be at liberty to use her own discretion in matters concerning the migration of those holding different religious views. Just as in 1648 the sovereign independence of the members of the German empire had been assured, so it was now with the members of the Swiss League; with the result that the political system of Switzerland also presented a like picture of a maimed body and a powerless organism.

§ 54. **The Situation in France. The Mercenary System.** While in the internal governments of the individual states interested motives and selfishness appear as the prevalent evils of the time, an incredible inconsistency is apparent in their dealings with foreign powers, as in this respect also every state acted according to her own will and pleasure; the Swiss were never more shamelessly sold to the highest bidder than at this time. Thus France used Switzerland completely to her own advantage. The alliance of 1602 (see p. 164) expiring in 1651, the Court of Paris was anxious for its renewal. De la Barde, the envoy, by threats, promises and various artifices enlisted first the Catholic (see p. 181) and then the reformed states in his cause. Disregarding the urgent warnings of Wettstein, the patriotic burgomaster of Basle, the thirteen states renewed the old alliance with France at Soleure on 24th September, 1663. In return for certain advantages of trade and commerce, for an annuity of 3000 francs for every canton, and the pay of the troops, the Confederation engaged to allow France to levy from 6000 to 16,000 men. On the 18th November this alliance was confirmed by oath in Notre-Dame, in Paris; the Swiss, however, were grievously mortified, and Louis XIV. did not abide by the terms of the alliance. There could be no talk of the payment of arrears (30 millions), for Moulier, the crafty French ambassador, had easily succeeded in bribing the states by gifts and false promises.

For the rest, the Confederation took up a neutral position during the great wars of Louis XIV., as in the Thirty Years' War. But the task of preserving an armed neutrality was again left unfulfilled, and any uniform measures which they adopted proved but transitory.

In the first war of Louis, that in the Netherlands (1666–1668), the Confederation should have protected Franche Comté, which, according to ancient treaties, had been included in the Swiss neutrality. When, in January, 1668, it was attacked by a French army, in whose ranks were even some Swiss troops, the states actually united in a decision that the mercenaries should be withdrawn and all French levies prohibited. The reformed states at the same time revived the notion of the *Defensionale* (*see* p. 168), adopted during the Thirty Years' War; the danger brought the Catholics to their side, so that a common military system now took a definite form. A council of war, consisting of delegates from every canton or state, and a war exchequer, supplied by subsidies from the several states, were established; every state was to contribute a certain contingent of troops to the Federal army, which was affixed at 40,000 men. This course of action, if continued, might in time have proved the means of an important advance in the Federal constitution, the first step towards national unity; but France soon knew how to draw the states back to her side and to shake their good resolutions. Moulier the ambassador began by negotiating with each state separately, and the prohibition of levies immediately fell to the ground: both the Catholic and the reformed states once more sent mercenaries to Louis. By the peace of Aix-la-Chapelle the latter was obliged to restore Franche Comté.

During the second war, that against Holland (1672–1678),

Louis XIV. violated the treaties outrageously by leading Swiss mercenaries to take the field against Protestant and republican Holland. Erlach's Bernese regiment at first refused to cross the Rhine, and Captain Rahn of Zurich returned home. Louis was quietly allowed to take permanent possession of Franche Comté. The *Defensionale* was powerless to effect any practical union of the states, and remained a well-meant project. The Catholic cantons, encouraged by the pope, laboured to oppose it as a "work of heresy"; Schwyz complained that the younger states might command the older ones, and therefore withdrew from it, and was soon followed by the rest of the Catholic cantons (1676–1680).

Strassburg, the old ally of the Confederates, fell to Louis, like Franche Comté, in 1681. He even threatened the Swiss by erecting the great fortress of Hüningen opposite Basle. The Huguenots, whom he expelled in 1685, found refuge in the reformed states. Mercenaries flocked to France in crowds during the later wars of Louis. In the war in the Palatinate (1688–1697) about 35,000 fought at his side with a courage and heroism worthy of a better cause. Louis owed his brilliant victories in this war chiefly to the bravery of the Swiss mercenaries. How many of them shed their blood in the cause of the foreign despot is shown by the expressions of Stuppa, the chief mercenary leader, who, when Louvois spoke reproachfully of the amount of gold which France had bestowed upon the Swiss, saying that a military road might be paved with *thalers* from Paris to Basle, answered quickly: "That is possible; but a canal from Basle to Paris might be filled with the blood shed by the Swiss in your service!"

It was therefore vain to hope for the preservation of neutrality at home; in the moment of need unity of action was always wanting. The reformed states gradually inclined more and more to the side of the Protestant powers of the north (Holland, England and Prussia), especially in the war of the Spanish succession (1700–1713), when they combined in opposition to France. Hence they also favoured the interests of the allies with regard to the principality of

Neuchâtel. Here the reigning dynasty expired in 1707, and Louis XIV. was anxious to confer the principality upon a French prince. Neuchâtel hastily renewed her civil alliance with the Swiss towns, and favoured the hereditary claims of the Prussian king, which were likewise supported by Switzerland. On 3rd November, 1707, the estates of Neuchâtel elected King Frederick of Prussia as their prince, and this transfer of Neuchâtel to Prussia was subsequently ratified by the European Peace of Utrecht (1713). From this time forwards military service in Holland was specially popular in Switzerland; the Protestant Swiss felt themselves more akin to the Dutch in faith, in political views and in simplicity of life than to the Catholic, monarchical and aristocratic French. Meanwhile Austrian, French and English gold still exercised its force of attraction among them, and Switzerland became a recruiting ground for all nations.

§ 55. **The War of Toggenburg, or the Second War of Vilmergen.** Amid the confusion of foreign wars the states were constantly at variance among themselves about their ecclesiastical and political rights, chiefly in regard to the common domains, where their rights of dominion came into collision. Trivial occurrences often alarmed both Protestants and Catholics, so that many times civil war seemed imminent, as in 1664, when an attempt was made to interfere with Protestant worship in the neighbourhood of Wigoldingen (in the Thurgau), and in 1694, when a similar effort was made to introduce Catholic worship side by side with the Protestant at Wartau, in the Rhine valley. The Spanish war of succession accentuated religious differences, and finally troubles in the Toggenburg led to a fresh resort to arms. The religious and political liberties of this district were constantly threatened by the abbots of St. Gall and their tyrannical officials. Supported by Schwyz and Lucerne, the abbots were perpetually extending their princely power and endeavouring to secure the supremacy of the Catholic religion, to the exclusion of the influence of Zurich, which was allied to Toggenburg.

Abbot Leodegar Bürgisser now forced the inhabitants of Toggenburg, in the interests of the Catholic states, to construct a great road through the "Hummelwald," in order to facilitate communication between the five states and the territories of St. Gall, while separating Zurich, Glarus and the Grisons. Opposition arising, however, and Zurich inciting the Toggenburg folk to revolt, with his usual equivocal policy—the saying went, that he "sometimes put on Suabian breeches, sometimes Swiss"—he concluded an alliance with the emperor (1702), who had raised him to the rank of a prince of the empire. By this he made enemies of the states of Schwyz and Glarus, and so defeated his own ends. Nothing daunted, however, he ingratiated himself with Zurich and Berne as easily as with the emperor, alarmed the Catholic states by this alliance, and forced them to conform to his will. Schwyz engaged to render help to the abbot, and required Toggenburg to separate from Zurich and Berne, to whom she had applied in the cause of religious liberty. But the Toggenburg folk considered their liberty in danger, took up arms and called Zurich and Berne to their aid. The latter immediately took up their cause. Troops from Zurich occupied the old district of St. Gall, took Wil (22nd May), the monastery of St. Gall and the Rheintal. The Bernese occupied the Free Bailiwicks, took Mellingen, Bremgarten, and also Baden, where they demolished the fortress. The Catholic states were divided, and when some suggested a peace, the exasperated Catholic populace arose, and 4000 armed men precipitated themselves upon the Free Bailiwicks. Once again, as in 1656, a battle was fought at Vilmergen, but this time the Protestants were victorious (25th July, 1712). The Catholics, however, were only induced to yield by the advance of the Zurich troops upon Rapperswil, Schwyz and Zug, and by fresh expeditions on the part of the Bernese. By the Peace of Aarau, on 11th August, the five states were excluded from any share in the government of the county of Baden and the lower part of the Free Bailiwicks, while Berne was admitted to the share in the government of the Thurgau, the Rheintal, and the upper and lower Free Bailiwicks. Zurich, with Berne and Glarus, took Rapperswil and Hurden under her protection, and thus obtained a strong point of support against Catholic Schwyz. Peace was not effected between Toggenburg and the abbot till 1718; the political and religious liberties of the district were secured, and in return it submitted to the abbot.

This event destroyed the supremacy of the Catholic states established by the first war of Vilmergen. Henceforward success and power lay on the side of the reformed party, and Zwingli's plan of making Zurich and Berne sovereign states seemed about to be realised. But the Catholic states felt the sting deeply, and therefore mutual aversion afterwards grew into an actual division and breach, so that thenceforth there were literally two Confederations in existence side by side.

§ 56. Culture and Customs of the Seventeenth Century. Outwardly considered, the aristocracy developed a certain splendour and opulence, and presented an appearance of no inconsiderable prosperity, especially in the administration. The general conditions and necessities of the time led to many useful institutions. France, in particular, under Richelieu and Louis XIV., presented an example of an ostentatious political administration, which was eagerly imitated both by princes and by Republican governments. In Berne, Zurich, Zug, Basle, and even in Soleure, Lucerne, Stans, &c., public almshouses, hospitals, orphan asylums, improved houses of correction, prisons, &c., were established. The governments of Zurich, Berne, Basle and Zug made more extensive provision than formerly for scholastic institutions, scientific collections and libraries, for commerce and industry. In Berne and Zurich the government bought up large stores of fruit to aid the country districts in times of need and scarcity; about the middle of the century a postal system, imitating that of other lands, was adopted in those states; and in 1690 Berne also introduced manufactures at the expense of the state. A number of splendid public buildings of that period (in the late Renaissance style) yet adorn the principal towns of Switzerland, as for example the *Rathaüser* in Zurich and Lucerne. Berne drained the Kander, raised Morges into a place of considerable trade, and endeavoured to connect the lakes of Neuchâtel and Geneva.[1]

Soleure, the seat of the French ambassadors, and Berne, the haughty patrician city, attained the greatest magnificence. The former state amassed considerable treasure, so that it was able to lend vast sums to the French government, and to erect many handsome buildings, such as the arsenal, the embassy, the town-hall, water supply (*Brunnenleitung*), and the bridge of Olten; while Berne made all the arrangements of a great state. The government managed the several branches of the administration by means of separate chambers—the chambers of war, of salt, of corn, of trade and of appeal; Berne was also able to lend to all the banks of Europe, and her public treasure excited the envy and covetousness of other nations.

The authorities of the various states vied with one another in their efforts to further the material welfare of their subjects in "fatherly" fashion, to support them in times of misfortune, of bad harvests, of famine, &c., and to check beggary, pauperism and such-like by numerous mandates. Viewed externally, many parts of Switzerland presented a more cheering appearance than the numerous provinces of other lands, mostly depopulated and devastated by war.

Together with the administration, the aristocracy paid special attention to science and art. Beautiful private houses, some of them absolute palaces, arose, as in Berne, Frauenfeld and Schaffhausen, and the Freuler palace in Näfels. The apartments of wealthy burghers and of officials and all public buildings were beautifully decorated and furnished. Paintings on glass and artistic stoves formed the chief decoration, representing historical scenes, studies from nature and from daily life with wonderful delicacy and refinement, and bearing witty verses and merry proverbs.[2]

---

[1] Much matter concerning these things is found in SCHULER'S *Thaten und Sitten der Eidgenossen*, vol. ii.

[2] LÜBKE, *über alte Öfen in der Schweiz*.

Manifold progress was made in the higher studies. A society in Zurich established in 1630 the public library for citizens (the town library at the *Wasserkirche*), which about thirty years later already numbered 6000 volumes; in 1636 the town library of Schaffhausen was founded, while the libraries of Berne and Basle were considerably increased and extended. From the ranks of the aristocracy, especially in Zurich, arose notable men of learning, who cultivated theology, and in close connection with that the study of languages and history. Johann Heinrich Hottinger, of Zurich (1620–1667), was one of the most celebrated masters of oriental languages, and wrote a copious universal church history; his son, Johann Jakob, wrote a history of the church in Switzerland. Johann Heinrich Heidegger acquired European fame by his theological writings, as did Kaspar Schweizer by his knowledge of Greek. A like celebrity was attained by professors of languages and theology in western Switzerland, such as Turretin, Tonchin, &c. In natural sciences, J. J. Scheuchzer, of Zurich (*see* p. 193), and the Bernoullis in Basle specially distinguished themselves; as chroniclers, J. H. Rahn of Zurich and Michael Stettler of Berne; as topographer, Mathias Merian of Basle, &c.

Once more for every ray of light there was also a shadow; narrow-mindedness and bigotry reigned supreme, in a way which it is now hardly possible to conceive. As regarded intellectual life, much was written by learned men, almost without exception members of the aristocracy, of the dominating families, mostly in Latin, and therefore intended only for their peers and not for the people. The subjects of their writings were likewise suited almost entirely to learned men and their colleagues; the sciences were confined to the study and the lecture hall, and did not come in contact with life. Higher schools were, indeed, provided, but on the other hand hardly anything was done towards educating the people. The teachers in the popular schools were ignorant artisans, discharged soldiers or uneducated youths; the education consisted merely in learning mechanically by rote and without understanding religious matter out of the catechism and various devotional books.

By this means ignorance was systematically cultivated, and the mind of the people was stifled rather than awakened. Intellectual life was entirely under the control of the authorities, secular and religious; it was feared that a liberal education might open the eyes of the people. Writings which displeased the authorities, even innocent poems and popular songs, were unhesitatingly suppressed; everything had to undergo the censorship of severe masters. The teaching of Copernicus, the tenets of the new philosophers, Spinoza, Descartes, &c., were prohibited under pain of the most severe punishments. Rahn of Zurich was not allowed to print a large Federal history, because it contained much that was offensive to the authorities; political history was in itself considered so dangerous, that it was in many states not admitted among the professorships.

Theology presented still greater difficulties, for the clergy wielded the sword of the executioner as well as the government. It was not enough to declare the very letter of the Bible and of the church prayers holy and infallible, everything was condemned which did not absolutely agree with those letters. (Consensus formula of 1675.) Scheuchzer and Bernoulli suffered many attacks on this account on the part of the clergy; even the expression of Scheuchzer: "God is everywhere present!" was reckoned as heresy, because the words of the Lord's Prayer say "in heaven." Thus a religious coercion was practised which almost equalled the Inquisition: a Jew was put to death for saying that Christ was the son of a Jew; General Rudolf Werdmüller, a remarkable man, one who rose far above the superstitions of the age and indulged in rough jests about the church and the clergy, suspected of heresy, of witchcraft and of forming a league with the devil, was condemned, after a trial of six years' duration, and forced to quit his country. Michael Zingg, a kindly minister, and professor of mathematics in Zurich, was called to account in 1661 for rejecting the decisions of the synod of Dortrecht (1618), which sanctioned strictly Calvinistic views; they threatened to behead him, and even to immure him; he was compelled to fly, and to gain a scanty subsistence as an exile.

All other symptoms of life among the people were as carefully watched as their opinions and confessions of faith. The restraints which had been put upon industrial activity were even increased; foreign imports were prohibited, as also free competition. Raw material might not be procured from without, but must be bought in the town; and the peasant was not allowed to sell his agricultural produce where he would, but had to take it to the market in the town. In the municipal cantons trade and manufactures might only be carried on at all in the towns; if anyone wished to transact business elsewhere, he was obliged to get permission from the guild concerned, and any opposition was severely punished.

No less heavy were the fetters which lay upon social and civic life. The authorities forbade showy and fashionable dress; they prescribed the exact form and colour of garments; dancing, card-playing, skittles, &c., were punished by fines and imprisonment, smoking and snuff were forbidden. The evil moral consequences of misgovernment were not wanting. Johann Kaspar Escher, the philanthropic bailiff of Kiburg, about 1720, lays great stress upon this in his account of the time of his administration. Such prohibitions, he says, gave rise to secret revels; the younger generation lost all heart and love for and all delight in their fatherland, thinking that in other lands there was more liberty; and even the country folk were embittered by the townsmen being in all things preferred before them, which was most unjust, and by the rich being free to indulge in such pleasures openly on payment of money. But the voice of Escher died away, like that of many a nobler-minded man, and no attempt was made to check the source of these abuses.

PART III.

PRESAGES OF MODERN TIMES.
(1712-1798.)

1. INTELLECTUAL REGENERATION.[1]

§ 57. **Ideas of Reform and the Helvetic Society.** The political conditions of the Confederation in the eighteenth century were somewhat miserable. After the Toggenburg war, the one constant thought and aim of the Catholic states was to recover what they had lost in that war (see p. 187). They pursued their efforts for this restitution for about eighty years without intermission. In 1715 they concluded the *Trückli-bund*[2] with France, in order by the help of that power to coerce Zurich and Berne. But also on the part of the Protestants, who indulged in a malicious triumph after the war of Toggenburg, there reigned only hatred against all holding other views than their own. Both sides regarded their fellow-confederates of the other faith not as brothers in league, but as heretics and heathen, from whom they must keep as far aloof as possible. The antagonism rose to such a height, that in Zurich and Berne the most severe punishments were laid upon marriages with Catholics by order of the state.

In consequence of this want of unity, the neutrality of Switzerland could with difficulty be preserved during the foreign wars which affected her in any way, such as the Polish and Austrian war of succession, and the Seven Years' War. Only once during this century was any united action taken towards a foreign land, and that was in August, 1777, when the French alliance of 1663 was renewed by all the thirteen cantons at Soleure. But this was only a patched-up agreement due to foreign influence, for the French had resorted to every

---

[1] C. MORELL, *Karl von Bonstetten; Ein schweizerisches Zeit-und Lebensbild; Die helvetische Gesellschaft.* MÖRIKOFER, *die schweizerische Literatur des 18 Jahrhunderts.* J. J. MÜLLER, *der Geist der Ahnen oder die Einheitsbestrebungen in der Schweiz vor der helvetischen Revolution,* Zurich, 1874.

[2] So called because the document was preserved in a closed box.

possible art of bribery and corruption in order to reconcile all the states of that league; the Confederates had not united of themselves, and a hopeless want of union prevailed after as before. "Every man for himself!" was their motto, according to a contemporary. Individuals only felt themselves to be citizens of their state or adherents of the Catholic or Protestant party, but never Swiss. Every state had its own coinage, its own law; if a Swiss wanted to settle in another canton, he was there accounted almost as a foreigner. The *Defensionale* (*see* p. 168) remained forgotten, the Diet was a ponderous machine; the execution of any uniform arrangements (in coinage, the police, military and legal systems) was always frustrated by the want of unity and selfishness of the states. The most important affairs were thus protracted for years and years, either not settled at all, or only after many years; and in the common domains the most urgent reforms were neglected.

Thus in the eighteenth century the Confederation resembled a weather-beaten ruin, ready to fall. But just as "out of ruins there springs forth a new young world of fresh verdure," so even in this apparently hopeless period "bright visions began to appear, prophetically foretelling the new and regenerate Switzerland of the nineteenth century."[1]

Although in political matters dissensions prevailed, yet in intellectual and scientific life a sense of the unity of the fatherland was beginning to arise, notably in the reformed towns, where intellectual life had made great strides since the success of the war of Toggenburg. Men began to study their own position, learnt to know the individuality of Switzerland, and drew thence the hope of a brighter future. The pioneers of the movement were Scheuchzer of Zurich, and Haller of Berne. J. J. Scheuchzer (1672–1733), physician and naturalist, made himself famous by various journeys into the Swiss Alps, wrote the first natural history of Switzerland, and also completed a large map of Switzerland, by which labours he put new life into patriotism. Albrecht von Haller (*ob.* 1777), the

[1] MORELL, *Karl von Bonstetten*, pp. 4, 5.

great poet and naturalist, by unrivalled industry acquired an extensive and learned education; he also possessed a strong poetic vein, and a warm and patriotic heart. Among his poems which appeared in 1732, *die Alpen* ("The Alps") made a great impression by its poetic depth and the novelty of its ideas. Full of indignation at the depravity of the time, and yearning for natural and unspoiled conditions, he there depicts with vigorous touches the life of nature and of men in the Alps, the simple beautiful customs of the Alpine folk, with a patriotic warmth and enthusiasm before unknown. In another poem, *der Mann der Welt* ("The Man of the World"), he laments the degeneration of his fatherland; in a third, *die verdorbenen Sitten* ("Demoralization"), in contradistinction to the good old times, he apostrophises the decay of his own day, exclaiming—" O, Helvetia! once the land of heroes, how is it possible that the men whom we now behold could have descended from thy former inhabitants?"[1] By his poems and his researches in natural science Haller became so famous in other lands, that he received a number of honourable calls, yet he declined them all; he wanted to devote his powers to his beloved country, and from 1753 until his end he served her as a government official with affectionate devotion and self-sacrifice.

In addition to these motions on the part of the Swiss themselves we find the influence of other lands, England, France and Germany, in whose newly-awakened intellectual life the learned men of Switzerland took a lively interest. The writings of Montesquieu and Rousseau, and of all those men, burning with love of liberty and of their fellow-men, who in England and France were fighting against the intellectual bondage and political oppression under which the people lay, were eagerly read; Rousseau himself, a chief supporter of the new political and social ideas as to the welfare of the people and popular government, was a citizen of Geneva, hence his writings made

---

[1] *Sag an, Helvetien, du Heldenvaterland,
Wie ist dein altes Volk dem jetzigen verwandt!*
(Translation by Mrs. Howorth, 1794.)

a great sensation in western Switzerland. On the lovely shores of the lake of Geneva eminent writers from both France and England spent much time together (as Voltaire at Lausanne and Ferney, and Gibbon, the historian of the Roman empire, at Lausanne), and disseminated their views; and intellectual societies, such as were in vogue in France, here also invited both natives and foreigners to enjoyments of a high order.

Switzerland took no less interest in the development of German literature. Just at that time a close connection was formed between German and Swiss literature, inasmuch as J. J. Bodmer and J. J. Breitinger, both of Zurich, incited by English authors, opened a contest with Gottsched and his school, in 1740, in order to establish the principles of the art of genuine, true and pure poetry, and thus prepared the way for the great classical poets of Germany—Klopstock, Herder and Goethe. Following the example of England and Germany, Bodmer also brought about the formation of learned societies, which facilitated a more lively exchange of thought among Swiss men of letters. Thus Zurich became the centre of an active and eminently productive intellectual life, and here, too, German writers, such as Klopstock, Wieland, Kleist, Goethe, Fichte, &c., loved to sojourn.

All these stirring influences gradually led to the intellectual regeneration of the whole Swiss people. Day began to dawn on all sides. Existing conditions were measured by the requirements of the new ideas, actual facts aroused numerous complaints, and from theories men proceeded to practical suggestions for the improvement of matters in the state, the church, and in social and intellectual life.

Bodmer was already working zealously in this direction, and gave a great impulse to all efforts aiming at the public good and the improvement of the conditions of the people. In Basle Isaak Iselin, the philanthropist, laboured, both by his words and writings, for the improvement of social conditions. Then, in 1758, Franz Urs Balthasar of Lucerne published his work: *Patriotische Träume eines Eidgenossen von einem Mittel, die veraltete Eidgenossenschaft wieder zu verjüngen*,[1] in which

[1] "The patriotic dreams of a Confederate of a way to rejuvenate the ancient Confederation."

he recommends the erection of a national Swiss institute of education, where youthful aristocrats should be trained to become useful citizens and politicians, and should be taught the history and politics of Switzerland and military science. Only by such means could love and unity, long torpid, be re-awakened, and Switzerland preserved from threatened ruin. Salomon Gessner, poet of Zurich, wrote at this same time his widely-read "Idylls," in which he extolled the simple, contented rural and shepherd life as compared with the pleasure-seeking, luxurious life of the rich and great. A definite example in illustration of this was given by his friend, Dr. Hans Kaspar Hirzel, the famous physician of Zurich, a noble and genial philanthropist, in his story of the so-called Farmer Kleinjogg. Kleinjogg, really Jacob Gujer, was a farmer at Wermatsweil (in the commune of Uster), distinguished by his penetration, his wit, and also by his diligence, who by his thrift and his admirably sensible agricultural management converted the worst farm of the neighbourhood into a flourishing model farm. "He made use of every blade of straw, every twig of pine-wood, every moment." By his representation and description of the activity of this remarkable peasant Hirzel sought to influence a wider circle, and to put before "the selfish, idle aristocracy a faithful picture of Swiss manhood and ability, such as was still to be found among the people." Such words and hints quickly kindled all noble spirits, and soon the scattered voices of the friends of reform were joined in one chorus "to make hearts tremble with the thunder of patriotic enthusiasm."

In the year 1762 a circle of zealous patriots, incited by Balthasar's work, was formed at Schinznach, called the "Helvetic Society," and including Gessner, Hirzel and Iselin. As time went on this society united all the most famous men both of French and German Switzerland in annual meetings, whose aim was the enthusiastic awakening of the consciousness of Swiss interdependence. While, broadly speaking, religious differences still divided the Confederation into two hostile camps, in this society reformed and Catholic Swiss lived together on terms of cordiality; in familiar intercourse they learnt mutual respect, and in pure love of their country they felt themselves at one. Hence after their gatherings they always returned home encouraged, and disseminated their public spirit throughout the states, and the scattered seed slowly sprang up. Under the auspices of the society the young J. C. Lavater, of Zurich, composed the popular *Schweizerlieder*, condemning dissensions, and extolling unity as the chief source of national prosperity.

> "What is it alone can save us
> When all power and wealth do fail?
> Union only, brothers, union!
> Pray for this, and thus prevail!
> Steadfast in the midst of danger,
> Conquering ever in the fight,
> Never missed the Swiss their purpose
> By the force of union's might." [1]

These songs became "Songs of the People" in a very real sense, and were sung almost throughout Switzerland by men and women, old and young. The Helvetic Society, however, went still further, and sometimes included within the sphere of its labours criticisms upon the degradation in public matters, the improvement of morals, and the removal of prejudices; within it were focussed all efforts at reform in the domains of intellect and of public utility, partly because it prompted such efforts itself, and partly because it was joined by most of the advocates of reform.

Iselin of Basle, one of the founders of the society, who had imbibed enlightened principles from French authors, ventured early, though indeed diffidently, to attack the privileges of the governing class and the inequalities of rank. The energetic

[1] "*Wer ist's, der uns schützt und rettet,
Wenn es Macht und Gold nicht kann?
Eintracht! Eintracht! Brüder betet,
Fleht Gott nur um Eintracht an.
Unbeweglich in Gefahren,
Unbesiegbar in dem Streit,
Alles, was sie wollten, waren
Schweizer stets durch Einigkeit.*"

younger generation, however, threw itself cheerfully and
unhesitatingly into the new movement, and adopted his views
in thorough earnest. Some young men of Zurich (Lavater,
Schinz, Füssli, Escher and Pestalozzi) formed a league, in
order to initiate immediate reforms in the territory of Zurich;
they prosecuted all instances of oppression and injustice on
the part of bailiffs and municipal officers, and attacked worthless ministers, while seeking to support the poor and lowly
in their demands to extend the rights of the people, &c.[1]
When Grebel, the aristocratic bailiff in Grüningen, like some
of his colleagues, practised extortion and corruption, and the
complainants could get no redress, Lavater, then a youth of
one-and-twenty, burning with a noble indignation, wrote his
work, *der ungerechte Landvogt, oder Klagen eines Patrioten*,[2] and
would not rest till Grebel was put upon his trial. This bold
course of action created a great sensation throughout Switzerland. Individual leaders of the Helvetic Society went still
further in their demands. Canon Gugger of Soleure (1773), as
president of the society, vigorously opposed place-hunting and
office-seeking, and also all ideas of subjection, and maintained
Rousseau's principle—that the highest authority lies with the
people. Stockar of Schaffhausen lamented bitterly (1777)
that the noble ideal of a common fatherland was as yet
unrealised, and desired national representation; he expressed
the daring wish that had as yet escaped the lips of no man,
that the divers free states of Switzerland might be merged
in one single state, whose burghers should all have equal
rights, and be under equal obligations. Others denounced
foreign military service, and were eager for an increase of the
Swiss military force and a uniform military system. Such
manifestations seemed dangerous to the alarmed authorities,
who trembled for their privileges; Berne, Soleure and Fribourg therefore issued formal prohibitions against the society.
The latter, however, defied all persecution, and remained the
steadfast refuge of all efforts of high purpose. Besides the

---

[1] *See* Morf's *Biography of Pestalozzi*, ii. p. 17.
[2] "The Unjust Bailiff, or the Complaint of a Patriot."

improvement of public conditions, its chief aim was the advancement of education and the system of schools; the ideas of Bodmer and Balthasar were discussed, and Iselin, in particular, was urgent for an improvement in education. The society encouraged various practical attempts at a new method of education and instruction (*see* p. 202), and within its ranks the notion of a common Federal university, and of the introduction of better popular schools, found many adherents and supporters.

§ 58. **The First Practical Results of Enlightenment.** The chief effect on private life of this tendency towards a general reorganization was an increase of industrial activity. In Zurich, in addition to the silk industry, a remarkable impulse was given to cotton and woollen manufactures, in Basle to the weaving of silk ribbons; while St. Gall became one of the most flourishing towns through its linen trade, cotton manufactures and embroidery. Muslin embroidery was brought to great perfection in Appenzell, Outer Rhodes. The industrial spirit even spread to the mountainous districts of Switzerland, hitherto quite shut off. In the high-lying district of La Chaux de Fonds manufactures of watches and jewellery were commenced, as also in Geneva; in Glarus cotton-spinning formed the most considerable branch of industry; in the canton of Berne the fabrication of velvets, silks and cloths was commenced; even in the remote valleys of Emmen and Engelberg weaving and spinning were established, and about the middle of the century Schwyz and Gersau also applied themselves to these industries. Switzerland adopted the use of machinery at an early period. This peaceable industrial activity soon led to the decline of mercenary service; the French cabinet expressed its regret that the inhabitants of the Swiss cantons had become merchants rather than soldiers, and that the Swiss were retiring more and more from military service, and working peacefully in factories.

The advancement of industry was followed by that of agriculture. The agricultural societies (in Berne, Zurich and

Basle) laboured specially to this end; through their exertions the cultivation of new products, such as clover, lucerne, esparcet and potatoes was introduced, in addition to the artificial irrigation of meadows, stall-feeding, the breaking up of fallow ground and other innovations, now long since become general. The authorities and societies further laboured zealously to facilitate traffic by improving the roads. Good roads were become so much the more necessary since in other lands men were beginning to appreciate the beauties of the Swiss Alps and glaciers, and to travel frequently in Switzerland. There were certainly great difficulties to be overcome—chasms must be filled in, rocks and boulders blasted, and costly bridges built; but skill and perseverance overcame them. The states of Berne, Zurich, the Grisons, Basle and Glarus distinguished themselves by their good roads; over the Passwang, the Gemmi, the Hauenstein, &c., highways were constructed. The brothers Grubenmann, of Appenzell, were among the most accomplished builders of bridges of that day: the bridge over the Rhine at Schaffhausen, that over the Limmat at Wettingen, and many of the bridges in Glarus are their work (about 1750-60). In the course of the eighteenth century, moreover, and especially in the latter half, numerous benevolent institutions and public buildings were erected, such as orphanages, infirmaries, magazines, loan offices and savings banks.

Hand in hand with such material progress we find an improvement in social life. In individual cantons smaller societies were labouring, like the Helvetic Society throughout Switzerland, towards intellectual and economical progress, and were inculcating a love for the arts and sciences, enlightenment and public utility. In 1779, at the instigation of the Helvetic Society, a Swiss military association was started, aiming at a fundamental improvement of the Swiss military system with a view to greater uniformity. In Zurich, Basle, Berne, Geneva and Lausanne reading clubs were formed, and societies of all kinds—naturalist, agricultural, beneficent, musical, &c., and in Zurich a society of artists; while even smaller places, such as Rolle and Yverdon in the Vaud, and Wädenswil, Stäfa, Winterthur, &c., in the canton of Zurich, had their reading and musical societies, and realised the necessity of intellectual education. Printing offices increased in number, and were kept fully occupied in satisfying this intellectual craving. Thus an exceedingly abundant and enlightened literature was produced, which permeated all classes, and produced an essential alteration in the views of that time. The different societies themselves started periodicals (*Museen, Bibliotheken*) for the instruction of the people by means of reliable treatises on historical, philosophical and public subjects. Fäsi and Füssli produced excellent Swiss political and physical geographies; Saussure, the great naturalist of Geneva, graphic descriptions of travels; Ebel, a German, wrote the first Swiss guide book; the æsthetic Sulzer, of Winterthur, propagated new ideas on art, J. C. Lavater on religion, philosophy and physiognomy; but the greatest notoriety was attained by the Swiss history of Johann von Müller of Schaffhausen (1780). This was the first attempt at a popular history that could be enjoyed by all classes. Müller embraced the history of the Confederation as a great whole, and wrote it in the lofty, fine and thrilling style of the ancient classics, for the invigorating and strengthening of patriotic feeling. His contemporaries felt its elevating influence, and "once more believed in their fatherland."[1]

A splendid impulse was given to art as well as to literature. A number of very remarkable churches in the baroque and old-fashioned[2] or antique style date from that period in Schwyz, St. Gall, Berne, Soleure, &c. There are also handsome secular buildings in the antique style which are even yet worthy of note, such as the houses in Zurich *zur Krone* and *zur Meise*,[3] the white and blue house in Basle, and houses in Soleure, Frauenfeld, &c. Landscape and portrait painting were greatly developed, as also the art of copper-

---

[1] An expression used by Mülinen, then studying in foreign lands. *See Illustrirte Schweiz*, 1874, No. 2, p. 97.
[2] Somewhat similar to the contemporaneous Georgian style in England.—E. S.
[3] The "Crown" and the "Titmouse."

plate engraving. Men talked and wrote about art and the history of art. Churches and schools, too, were fain to fall in with the new modes of thought. A more liberal spirit sprang up in them, and orthodoxy was confronted by rationalism. Little by little men threw off the restraints of church and creed, little by little modern tolerance forced its way. In the Catholic church a storm broke out against the Jesuits, which led to the suppression of the order in 1773. The improvement of the scholastic and educational system was zealously pursued. A brilliant commencement was made by Dr. Planta, a Grison, who founded an educational institution at Haldenstein in 1761, in which the way was paved for instruction by object-lessons according to the principles of philanthropists, and special preference was given to the sciences most useful in daily life; while at the same time the sense of a common humanity, patriotic virtues and religious toleration were strengthened and nourished. The Helvetic Society encouraged this establishment, which seemed to realise Balthasar's dream, and a number of distinguished men, who laboured in succession for the reformation of their country, were trained at this fine institution. Other institutions beside Haldenstein soon sprang into existence, and the various states, such as Zurich and Berne, also improved their schools, both the higher town schools and the lower rural schools (1770–1780), special attention being paid to the education and development of girls.

For the better advancement of their plans and ideas, the Helvetic Society offered prizes for the best suggestions for the improvement of the educational system. This had a specially stirring influence upon the man who (more than any other) devoted his whole life to the task of educating the people, viz., Johann Heinrich Pestalozzi of Zurich. The ignorance of the school-teachers, the unkind treatment of the children, and the stultifying, arbitrary methods of instruction filled him with disgust; the hitherto existing institutions for popular education seemed to him to be merely "artful machines for suffocation." He was thus moved to put his own hand to the work; he resolved to begin where the need was greatest—with the lowest and most abandoned classes of the population. He therefore began in 1776 to gather poor children around him on his country estate of "Neuhof" near Habsburg in the Aargau, and endeavoured to arouse and develope their physical, mental and moral powers by manual labour, mental and verbal exercises, mental arithmetic, reading and writing. But not being sufficiently supported by the authorities, this fine undertaking fell through in 1780 for want of means for its maintenance. He now tried to spread his views by his words and writings, and amongst other things wrote his famous and popular book *Lienhard and Gertrud* (1781), in which he draws, in the portrait of Hummel the bailiff, a thrilling picture of the degeneracy of the governmental system, while on the other hand in Gertrud and her household he represents the beneficial effects of a loving and religious moral training.

But in spite of all efforts Pestalozzi was unable to achieve any new practical results, and was still forced to build all his hopes of support upon the future. It was useless to think of any Federal measures being taken so long as the old and rotten political fabric existed. And this remained absolutely untouched, in spite of the urgent wishes and entreaties which were from time to time expressed in the Helvetic Society. No attempt was ventured to strengthen the central authority, and to give the people a share in the government. It is true that in 1778 certain patricians of Berne made the suggestion that the subject-lands should at least be put upon an equal footing with the allied states, but the matter ended in good intentions. Men preached to deaf ears; the majority of the governing body were unwilling to deprive themselves of their privileges, and did their utmost towards the preservation of existing conditions. Thus there remained to the oppressed no means but those of violence of acquiring their rights.

2. POLITICAL FERMENTS AND REVOLTS.

§ 59. In the course of the eighteenth century the aristocracy became only more bigoted, wilfully closing its eyes to the evil results of the system of government. In Berne the circle of families entitled to a share in the government became ever narrower; in 1776 there were only eighteen families represented in the Council of the Two Hundred, among whom were six of the family of Erlach, eight of Diesbach, eleven of Tscharner, twelve of Stürler, thirteen of Wattenwyl, of Graffenried, &c. Under pain of imprisonment artisans and other persons were forbidden to carry any wares under the arcades (arbours or walks), that the patricians and their wives might be able to walk in comfort; and they always first of all chose the finest and best at the daily vegetable market, while other citizens were not admitted until eleven o'clock, and were obliged to content themselves with what was left. Hunting was permitted to patricians only, they alone might give balls as often as they pleased; exception after exception was made in their favour in the sumptuary laws, and if a patrician offended against the laws of the state, he was treated far more leniently than other people; in severe cases at the utmost he was banished to his country estate, or secretly ordered to absent himself from his home. In Lucerne, too, the patricians mutually winked at one another's offences and defalcations. The arrogant bearing of the citizens of Zurich towards the country folk likewise increased, and they even grudged to the town of Winterthur the development of her industry, and prevented the introduction of silk manufactures there; the citizens of Zurich claimed a monopoly of the latter, and whoever infringed their privilege was severely punished.

During the course of the eighteenth century a spirit of opposition was aroused against such narrow-mindedness, which became more and more pronounced. The sense of injustice, the ever-increasing enlightenment, the new views concerning the welfare and sovereign rights of the people which had found their way from England and France by means of numerous pamphlets, and were eagerly welcomed—all combined to arouse the bitterest hatred among the people, and to drive them at length to action.

The first impulse to violent revolt against the aristocracy was given by Geneva, which state was, in fact, only connected with the Confederation at all through Zurich and Berne, and had hitherto had little influence upon the course of Federal affairs. The power of the Genevese aristocracy was vested in the smaller council, which filled any vacancies in the great council and almost all other offices, while the *conseil général* itself (or the *Bürgergemeinde*)[1] had lost the right of legislation. The small council consisted of twenty-five members, who were appointed from the few governing families. Meanwhile a democratic and antagonistic element had sprung up gradually among the many French settlers who had found a new home in Geneva. Quite at the beginning of the century (1707) a committee of the council, at whose head was Pierre Fatio the lawyer, under pressure from the people, required the abolition of the one-sided system of government by families, the regular assembling of the *conseil général*, and free initiative. The movement, however, was suppressed by military interference, imprisonment and executions, Fatio himself being thrown into prison. Afterwards, when the government caused costly fortifications to be erected in a despotical manner, the democratic party arose, and in 1737 were victorious in the struggle, and extorted a recognition of the principle that the highest authority, the choice of officers, the right of making war and peace, and the right of legislation and taxation should rest with the burghers (*Bürgergemeinde*).

This victory of the popular faction in Geneva soon had its effect upon Berne. From the year 1710 attack after attack, lampoon after lampoon, had followed one another in quick succession, directed against the aristocracy; special exception was taken to the claim made by the patricians of the sole right over official appointments. The patricians mockingly

[1] The community of the burghers.

observed that the citizens must be stripped of their feathers, that they might not want to fly. New petitions were, however, presented, and in 1744 a proclamation was issued, calling upon the burghers to help themselves as the Genevese had done. Those concerned were punished by banishment, among them Samuel Henzi, a cultivated and enlightened citizen, famous as a clever French poet and author. The latter being pardoned before the expiration of his term, thought of entering the Modenese service as a means of earning a livelihood, but being prevented, and so remaining in Berne, was entangled in fresh political agitations in 1749. He showed some disposition to take part in fresh efforts at petitions; but the leaders, Wernier and Fueter, spoke of a conspiracy, the overthrow of the government, burning of the town, &c. Everything was betrayed, and the name of Samuel Henzi was specially coupled with those of Wernier and Fueter as one of the chief ringleaders. The government, filled with terror and dismay, took stringent measures, and all those already named paid the penalty with their lives upon the scaffold.[1] But such severity did not avail to restore respect for the patricians, and thenceforward the government was never safe from conspiracies.

Violent storms shook the patriciate of Lucerne. The citizens there had long complained that the authorities purchased domains, concluded alliances, appropriated French annuities, &c., without consulting them. An ecclesiastical dispute added fuel to the fire of dissension. A patrician of Lucerne had in 1768 published a work on the rights of the state as opposed to those of the church, and showed how the Swiss should guard against the encroachments of Rome; another work demanded the abolition of the religious orders and restrictions upon monasteries. A family quarrel was added to these agitations, for at the head of the patricians at that time stood the family of Meyer, which was attacked with great violence by the family of Schuhmacher. Placidus Schuhmacher, whose father had been ruined by one of the

[1] BÄBLER, *Samuel Henzi, ein Lebensbild.*

Meyers, sought help from the burgesses during the despotism of Valentine Meyer by adopting their cause and seeking to defend their rights; he was, however, executed in 1764 on the plea of his having concocted a secret plot. The Schuhmacher family next tried to get at their mortal enemies from another point. Valentine Meyer being held to be the author of the work against the monasteries, they availed themselves of the agitation stirred up by the clergy for the overthrow of their foes. There was nothing to be gained for the popular rights from these disputes; these were forgotten: it was even forbidden to talk over the sentences and mandates of the authorities.

The government of Soleure pursued a similar course, upon some citizens censuring prevalent abuses; and Zurich too was not behind the rest in severity. When in 1777 the authorities violated the right of the community legally established in 1713 of being consulted in alliances, by concluding the French alliance, disturbances arose among the citizens, in which the old Pastor Waser played a leading part. The latter had been previously unjustly deprived of his office, and threw himself with zeal and success into all researches in natural history, history, agriculture and statistics. In revenge he wrote articles in the journal of statistics of Professor Schlözer in Göttingen, touching upon divers abuses in the political system of Zurich,[1] and revealing political conditions hitherto kept secret. For this he was brought to trial, found guilty of high treason, and condemned to death in 1780.

Opposition against the aristocracy and the governing class was about this time aroused among the burghers of Fribourg, and once more broke out in Geneva. In the year 1762 the government of Geneva caused Rousseau's *Contrat Social* setting forth the democratic principles of liberty and equality as the right of all men, to be burnt. The popular faction thereupon rose, and in 1768 forced the government to restore to the *conseil général* the right of electing councillors. But this provision was made only with respect to the citizens of long stand-

[1] C. K. MÜLLER, *Joh Heinrich Waser.*

ing, and the new citizens (or "natives"),[1] hitherto slighted in every way, now rose and demanded at least a share in these rights, while Voltaire from his seat in Ferney added fuel to the flame. A rebellion broke out; the government summoned troops from Berne, Savoy and France for its suppression. These struggles in the little republic formed as it were a prelude to the great French Revolution, and all the rest of Switzerland took great interest in them. The people considered the cause of the opposition their own; for instance, while the population of Zurich had willingly marched out in the Peasants' War for the suppression of the populace in other cantons, they refused to do so when summoned against Geneva, and Berne had reason to fear that the disaffection would spread to the Vaud.

In the rural cantons, too, struggles were rife like those of the town cantons, in which the adherents of the oligarchical government styled themselves the *Linden* and their opponents the *Harten* as in the time of the Peasants' War.[2] In Outer Rhodes of Appenzell and in Zug a dispute about various portions of land was interwoven with this party strife. In the first-named little canton the *Harten* accused the government of neglecting to consult their *Landsgemeinde* at the peace of Toggenburg, and they gained a victory in 1732. They had taken up their position by preference in the portion west of the Sitter, the *Linden* in that east of the Sitter. For some time the defeated faction adhered to their separate government under violent persecution from the *Harten*, till both parties were exhausted.

In Zug the *Harten* (who found their chief support in the bailiwicks in opposition to the town) overthrew the family of Zurlauben, who were in receipt of French pensions; but they having introduced a "reign of terror" under Joseph Anton Schuhmacher, the *Linden* once more gained the upper hand, and in 1735 Schuhmacher was sent to the galleys. Owing to the changed conditions of French service, the *Harten*

---

[1] *Natifs* or *habitans*, old inhabitants of Geneva, excluded by birth from taking part in public affairs.—LARDNER.
[2] *See* p. 176.

were victorious in 1764 in a tumultuous popular assembly; the *Landgemeinden* of Zug demanded an equal division of pensions among the people, and established an extraordinary tribunal which settled matters peaceably. Meanwhile in Schwyz, too, the battle raged between *Linden* and *Harten*, the latter being victorious, and the dominion of the Reding family was for a time severely shaken. In Inner Rhodes of Appenzell the popular party gained the upper hand under Anton Joseph Suter, who became bailiff of the Rheintal, and in 1762 Landammann in opposition to a candidate of the aristocratic faction. But Suter incurring blame for certain blunders, the *Linden* stirred up an agitation against him and effected his overthrow. Suter was forced to leave the country, but was afterwards treacherously captured by his foes, brought to trial, and executed in 1784.

Not only were the aristocrats attacked by their slighted fellow-citizens, but for a long time past those from whom they had most to fear had been clamouring at the doors, viz., the oppressed subjects. These also endeavoured to secure and extend their rights by revolts and demonstrations, and did not scruple to proceed to extremities. For instance, the community of Wilchingen in Schaffhausen (1717-1729), the towns of Winterthur and Stein on the Rhine (1783), (the two latter being subjects of Zurich), in conflict with their rulers even turned to the emperor for help. The risings, however, were mostly put down by force of arms.

The inhabitants of Werdenberg complained that they were deprived by Glarus of their charter of liberties, but they found no hearing, and Glarus discovering a plot in 1721, caused the whole district to be occupied by the military and the conspirators to be severely punished. Major Daniel Abraham Davel, of the Pays de Vaud, an enthusiastic but good-natured and harmless advocate of liberty, availed himself of the opportunity of a muster to call upon his countrymen to emancipate themselves, and endeavoured to raise the Vaud into an independent canton, but was taken prisoner by subtlety and beheaded (1723). The inhabitants of Livinen had in 1713 extorted certain liberties,

P

and in 1755, deeming these infringed by Uri, they rose in resolute resistance. The government of Uri, however, sent an armed force, and disarmed the men of Livinen; the latter were forced once more to render homage on their knees, and to watch the execution of their leaders, and the district was deprived of all its liberties.

Although, however, the people had not obtained their rights, they were at least aroused; they learnt that the proceedings of their lords and rulers were no longer to be deemed infallible; while the latter had in many parts sown the seeds of hatred and bitterness. In the Vaud especially the fuel of discontent was heaped high; in the Italian bailiwicks, well-nigh devastated by the negligence of the Diet and the harshness of the bailiffs,[1] it was only with the deepest resentment that the population bore the yoke of the Federal bailiffs, against whom elsewhere also many a man chafed in secret. Only the kindling spark was wanting to set the whole political fabric in flames.

[1] For a description of the condition of the Italian bailiwicks *see* MORELL *Karl von Bonstetten*, chapter vi. STRICKLER, ii. (1st edition, p. 283 *et seq.*).

Fourth Period.
PHASES OF THE NEW DEVELOPMENT.
(1798–1874.)

Part I.
THE REVOLUTION, AND ATTEMPTED REORGANIZATION UNDER FOREIGN INFLUENCE.
(1798–1830.)

1. THE INVASION OF THE FRENCH, AND THE "HELVETIC REPUBLIC ONE AND INDIVISIBLE."[1]
(1798–1800.)

§ 60. **The First Agitations.** The rosy dawn of a new era rose over mankind as the French Revolution sounded the call to liberty and equality, to the shaking off of every tyranny and the destruction of feudal rights. The reforming efforts of enlightened men had prepared the soil in Switzerland, too, so that from the beginning the Revolution found warm sympathy among many cultured men of high position in Switzerland. Meyer von Schauensee, an aristocrat of Lucerne, pointed out in a thrilling speech before the Helvetic Society the wholesome effects of that society upon the civic and political equality of all classes. Revolutionary ideas were specially warmly welcomed and upheld by three advocates, bound by the closest

---

[1] HOTTINGER, *Vorlesungen über den Untergang der alten Eidgenossenschaft*, 1844. MORELL, *Karl von Bonstetten.* HENNE-AMRHYN, *Schweizergeschichte*, vol. iii. TILLIER, *Geschichte der helvetischen Republik*, 3 vols., 1843. HODLER, *Geschichte des Schweizervolkes, neuere Zeit*, vol. i., 1865. HILTY, *Vorlesungen über die Helvetik*, Berne, 1878. DR. STRICKLER, *Aktensammlung der helvetischen Republik*.

ties of fellowship: Dr. Albrecht Rengger of Brugg, Konrad Escher ("von der Linth") and Paul Usteri of Zurich. These not only gave energetic and enthusiastic expression in the Helvetic Society to their conviction of the wholesomeness of the aim of the Revolution, but also sought by their writings to overthrow existing prejudices. Escher expressed his desire that Switzerland might enjoy more than the mere shade of the French tree of liberty! Revolutionary notions were disseminated among the people, particularly in 1791 and 1792, during the occupation of the frontier in the time of the war of the coalition. For here, in the immediate vicinity of the great events, the Swiss soldiers, too, were seized by the fiery zeal of the neighbouring people; the cry of victory: "Liberté, egalité," the trees of liberty, the language of democratic clubs, kindled the warmest emotions in every liberal-minded Swiss. There was soon no Swiss town where there might not be found some who had a fellow-feeling for the French, and soon the watchwords "liberty and equality" were in the mouth of almost every Swiss. On the other hand the new ideas gave a great shock to the governing class, and many of them not only feared the overthrow of existing conditions, but apprehended danger from the west to the freedom of their country.

The first attempt towards the realisation of these ideas in Switzerland originated in the Swiss Club at Paris. This was a society chiefly composed of men from the Pays de Vaud and Fribourg, who, long dissatisfied with things at home and specially with their subject condition, wanted to extend the revolution to their native land. For this purpose they entered into correspondence with those like-minded at home, as also with the leading statesmen of France, and sent French speeches to Switzerland, which awakened lively sympathy, particularly in the western and Romance districts. The earliest results were seen in the French Lower Valais. This district ever since the Burgundian wars had been under the rule of German Upper Valais, and was harassed and fleeced by harsh bailiffs. Hence it needed only the slightest encouragement from Paris to cause the population of Monthey and St. Maurice to revolt (September, 1790), to plant trees of liberty, and to drive out the bailiffs. Soon afterwards, under similar instigation, the people of Porrentruy rebelled against their harsh ruler, the Bishop of Basle. The revolt of the Valais folk was, however, suppressed with the help of Berne; Porrentruy indeed proclaimed itself free under the title of the "Rauracian Republic," but in order to avoid total anarchy, was obliged to annex itself to France in 1793 as the department Mont Terrible. Revolutionary movements sprang up simultaneously in Geneva and in the Pays de Vaud. In Geneva the "natives" once more revolted (see p. 208); the example of France was here faithfully imitated both for good and evil, and among the perilous waves of party strife many endeavoured to form connections with France.

The determining influence chiefly at work in the Vaud was that of Frederick Cæsar Laharpe of Rolle.[1] Filled even as a boy with burning indignation against all injustice, at the seminary at Haldenstein (see p. 202) Laharpe imbibed enthusiasm for a united Helvetic Republic through the influence of historical studies and liberal-minded teachers. As a lawyer in Berne he gained a fuller knowledge of the narrow-minded and selfish aristocratic government, and he himself relates the deep impression made upon him by the harsh reply he received from one of the noblest patricians in speaking of the spirit of innovation: "Remember that you are our subjects!" Deeply affronted, he left his home, and through the recommendation of an acquaintance was received at the Russian court, where the Empress Catherine appointed him tutor to her grandsons. But like a stout republican, he did not renounce his liberty even at the foot of the throne, and laboured unceasingly by his writings for the good of his countrymen, who first declared their sympathy with the events in France by banquets. He at length returned in 1796, poor and without means of subsistence, to liberate his ardently loved country by the power of his words and of his arm. But the watchful policy of

[1] Cf. *Mémoires de Frédéric Cæsar Laharpe*. (Swiss historical studies by J. VOGEL, Berne, 1864).

Berne was before him, and refused him entrance to his fatherland as a rebel. Often he would sit and rest upon a boundary-stone on the Swiss frontier, and cast longing glances over into the Vaud; he heard how his friends and relatives were condemned and banished; finally he felt no longer safe on the frontier, and fled to Paris, where, having resolved upon a life and death struggle with Berne and the aristocracy, he laboured indefatigably for the emancipation of the Vaud.

The movements which took place in the territory of Zurich were far more serious and proved more enduring than all those of western Switzerland. On their return from the occupation of the frontiers (*see* p. 212) many of the men of Zurich were filled with enthusiasm for the French, notably those dwelling around the lake, who, as formerly in the days of Waldmann, of the wars of Kappel, and of the Thirty Years' War, were once more the most zealous for the liberty of their country. They took an intense interest in the proceedings in France, and frequently assembled to talk over political affairs. The more zealous among them founded a reading society at Stäfa, where they discussed historical and political subjects, and read the pamphlets and speeches of the leaders of the French Revolution. In 1794 they presented a memorial to the government setting forth their chief grievances, insisting that the town and the rural district should be placed upon an equality in one common constitution, and demanding freedom of trade, liberty to study, relief from feudal burdens, and the admission of country people into the body of officials. They called attention to their ancient charters of liberty of 1489 and 1531, of which they had been deprived by the government. The government, however, thought it necessary to encounter the rapidly-spreading spirit of revolution with severity, and caused those chiefly implicated—Pfenninger of Stäfa, Stapfer of Horgen, and Neeracher a potter of Stäfa, the author of the memorial—to be arrested, fined and banished. But these methods of intimidation had quite a contrary effect to what was intended; a yet more eager search was made for the ancient charters, and these being actually found among the archives at Küssnach,[1] were rapidly disseminated by means of copies, and once more the government was required to abide by these charters (1795). By way of reply, preparations were made to suppress the new "rebellion" by force of arms, whereupon the community of Stäfa resolved to stand by one another "all for each, and each for all." The government, fearing the consequences of this demeanour, immediately despatched a body of troops 1700 strong; the community of Stäfa was disarmed, a sword was brandished over the head of Bodmer, the treasurer, as one of the chief leaders; he was condemned to imprisonment for life, and about 250 citizens in all were punished. "Rulers must command, people obey without question," proclaimed the unyielding authorities.

The country folk of St. Gall found more indulgence from their lord, the princely Abbot Beda of St Gall. Provoked by the useless extravagance of the latter, and incited by John Künzle, a letter-carrier, an enlightened and eloquent man, they revolted against their superior lord. Beda was good-natured and patriotic enough to yield, but in so doing neglected to consult the chapter, or assembly of monks of the monastery, who were hostile to him (1795). They therefore protested against his action, and Pancraz Forster, the new abbot who soon succeeded, one of Beda's chief opponents, would not hold to the terms made by Beda with the people. The states protecting the monastery, however, seeking to mediate, finally ranged themselves on the side of the people, the latter giving vent to their excitement in menaces and imprecations. The people obtained the right of electing a rural council, of which Künzle himself became president in 1797, and peace was restored. This might well have formed an example for other governments, showing how they might come to an understanding with the people in peaceable fashion, and make their rule more popular. But the latter remained inexorable. They did not even seem to notice the dangers threatening from without; mistrust and dissension reigned everywhere. So much the easier was it for the French to spread their net further and further over

[1] On the lake of Zurich.

Switzerland. Just as they had before taken rebellious Porrentruy, so now in the Italian wars of 1797, under their general Napoleon Bonaparte, they liberated the lands subject to the Grisons, the Valtelline, Bormio and Chiavenna, which had revolted against their harsh rulers, and annexed them to the kindred states of the Cisalpine Republic. In the same way in April, 1798, Geneva became the prey of the French. The latter very nearly took possession of the Vaud; but the governments had no suspicion of this, and lulled themselves in comfortable security till the thunder of French cannon in Switzerland roused them roughly enough from their slumber.

§ 61. **The Downfall of the Old Confederation.** (*a*) **Designs of the French and the "Patriots." Perplexity and Infatuation of the Governments.** The fugitive democrats of the Pays de Vaud, notably Laharpe, continually laboured while in France to influence public opinion in the "home-land." Laharpe published a treatise on the situation of the Pays de Vaud, and demanded its restoration from Berne. His hopes and those of his colleagues, of obtaining their liberty by the help of France, were much raised when, by the *coup d'état* of 18 Fructidor (5th September), 1797, the war party took the helm in France. Reubel, an Alsatian, and a member of the Directory, who as a barrister had once lost a suit in the courts of Berne, and therefore cordially hated the Bernese, specially urged a war against Switzerland, and the Directory soon issued menacing notes to the Confederation concerning favours alleged to have been shown to the Allies and emigrants. The exiles from the Vaud encouraged this action, and desired not only an intervention in their favour, but also violent interference on the part of the French in Swiss affairs. In their name Laharpe requested the Directory to intervene, with a not very apt allusion to the treaty of 1564 (*see* p. 161). It was undoubtedly Laharpe's honest conviction that France would aid the people in gaining liberty, not in order to abuse it, but simply for their benefit. The Directory, however, was induced to invade Switzerland by no such ideal and unselfish motives, but by certain private, and mostly selfish interests. For it was above all things important to the warlike operations of France to be able to hold Switzerland in a state of dependence, and at her disposal; and the Directory, in need of money, specially coveted the rich treasure of Berne, the value of which was greatly exaggerated by common report. It actually consisted of about seven millions in money and twelve millions in bonds.

The designs and aims of France took more definite form, and became more evident, after the Congress of Rastadt, where the affairs of Europe were to be arranged after the splendid conquests of Bonaparte in Italy. The Confederation desired from the Congress a guarantee of their territorial position and of their constitution. They were not, however, permitted to send a representative; on the contrary, their fate was arbitrarily settled in Paris, and that chiefly by the influence of Napoleon Bonaparte and Peter Ochs of Basle, who drew up their plans during the Congress. Bonaparte being privy to the designs of the Directory, purposely took his journey to Rastadt by way of Switzerland (November, 1797), in order to discover the disposition of the people and to make a preliminary survey of the land. He was everywhere received with enthusiasm as an honoured hero; in the Vaud, in Liestal and Basle he was openly welcomed as their "Deliverer," or "Liberator," which seemed to him to promise a favourable issue for the French. He had also confidential interviews with eminent malcontents, particularly with Peter Ochs, the chief guild-master of Basle, who, like Laharpe and many other Swiss, had become convinced that the difference between citizens and subjects must be abolished at all costs, even though it were by the help of foreigners. Ochs soon afterwards went to Paris as envoy from Basle on secret affairs (about the surrender of Fricktal to Basle); there he was also drawn into the interests of the Directory, and became thenceforth a devoted servant of France. Hence, directly after the return of Bonaparte the schemes against Switzerland were finally settled. Ochs, as leader of the "Patriots," discussed the reorganization of Switzerland with Napoleon and the Director Reubel. The Directory had been hitherto undecided whether to make of Switzerland one united state, or to divide it. The "Patriots" now urged their project of a united state, the threads of which might be easily kept in hand by France, and which would make Switzerland a strong bulwark of France. Finally, on 28th December, 1797, the Directory issued a notice to Switzerland concerning the Vaud, and resolved upon the complete annexation of the Val de Moutier, which was immediately put under military occupation. By this means Swiss neutrality was violated, and practically war was declared against the Confederation.

Nothwithstanding these menacing dangers, Switzerland remained incomprehensibly quiet and inactive, totally crippled by the old want of unity. Warnings and admonitions were certainly not wanting. Johann von Müller, the historian, in eloquent words exhorted them to a unity which should ignore all boundaries between cantons, all walls between towns and rural districts. Doctor Ebel, too, the author of the first Swiss guide-book (*see* p. 201), who, though a German by birth, entertained a warm feeling for Switzerland, exhorted men to come forward to support the ancient Confederation in the face of the growing danger, and to give up the old system of government of their own accord—but all in vain! The nearer the danger came, the greater was the blindness, the more helpless the attitude. In alarm, an assurance was given to France that her wishes should be followed; at length, on 27th December, a general Diet was assembled at Aarau. This, however, instead of negotiating, instead of generously striving after a free constitution, and throwing aside all mutual mistrust and all exaggerated fears, determined upon a renewal of the ancient Federal charters, which had not been confirmed since 1526. The Federal oath was taken with great solemnity on January 25th. The Diet hoped thus "to show the foreigner how united and happy Switzerland was under her existing constitution." But what availed a renewal of the letter of the old leagues, when Federal feeling and spirit were long since dead? As an actual fact the boasted unity seemed very doubtful; among the democracies there prevailed a deep mistrust of the policy of the aristocracies; Appenzell, Glarus and other democratic states opposed the renewal of the Federal oath, Basle formally abstained from taking part in it; and while the lords of the Diet were drinking toasts to the existing constitution at the taking of the oath, the friends of Ochs in Basle were drinking to the democratic reorganization of Switzerland. Moreover, the governments of the various states were no less divided, the adherents of the old and the new standing in sharp opposition to one another. The people, too, remained quite unconcerned by the act of the Diet, since their wishes were not regarded; in the Federal oath they only saw the union of lords against subjects, for indeed the League had long since ceased to be a really popular league.

(b) **The Revolution and the Victorious Advance of the French.** Therefore, since nothing was achieved by peaceful methods, a violent revolution became necessary. In January and February, 1798, the subjects rose on all sides, encouraged by the conduct of France; while Mengaud, the crafty French ambassador, openly fanned the flame and laboured for the revolution. Basle was the first place to come to terms with its subjects, by proclaiming equality of rights on January 20th. Once more disturbances broke out along the lake of Zurich, and the government was forced to release the prisoners arrested in 1795; the people of Schaffhausen next rebelled, and compelled their government to resign; while the ancient territory of St. Gall and Toggenburg emancipated itself, besides Thurgau, Rheintal, Sargans and the bailiwicks of Ticino, and constituted themselves independent communities. Glarus was obliged for herself to give up Werdenberg, and in concert with Schwyz to surrender Gaster and Utznach. The patrician government of Lucerne, terrified by a movement which was spreading like wild-fire, resigned to make room for one more modern and more liberal-minded.

Thus the whole fabric was suddenly on fire, the flames raging most wildly in the Vaud. Here committees were formed in every town to circulate and obtain signatures to petitions requiring the restoration of ancient rights; and when Berne hesitated and assembled troops, the populace arose in many parts to carry the revolution by force. On 25th January the arms and portraits of the governing families were demolished in almost every place, trees of liberty planted, and the green colours of the Vaud hoisted in the place of the colours of Berne; the Vaud was now to form a separate state, independent of Berne, under the title of the " République du Léman." The committees entered into correspondence with the French troops then in the Pays de Gex under the command of Menard, and on the 28th January Menard entered the Vaud with 15,000 men, Berne being unable to take any effectual step to oppose him, all appeals for help to her fellow-Confederates having remained unanswered. It now became impossible to continue the Diet; revolutions breaking out on all sides, and the French, whom no one ventured to oppose, commencing hostilities, the ground gave way beneath its feet, so that on the last day of January, 1798, it was dissolved. Hardly had the Federal delegates departed when Aarau, at the instigation of Mengaud, planted the tree of liberty, which had already been held in readiness for some days. The last hour of the Confederation was drawing near!

Berne—thrown upon her own resources by the Diet—stood almost alone against the foe, and the eyes of the adherents of the old *régime* were now fixed upon that state as upon the stronghold of Switzerland. Meanwhile, Berne herself was undecided how to meet the French; the latter, however, desired not peace, but war, and prepared for an overwhelming assault. In February Menard was replaced in the Vaud by Brune, under whom was General Schauenburg, who advanced with a division of troops from the Jura. Both together were to coerce by force of arms those governments which would not voluntarily accept democracy, and to convert the whole of Switzerland into a united republic. By craft and duplicity

Brune maintained a truce with Berne, and issued an ultimatum containing specific demands; then, when the latter were only partially fulfilled, he broke the truce and set his troops in motion.

Soleure and Fribourg capitulated at once in the beginning of March; but Berne, where there were two opposing parties in the councils (the peace party under von Frisching the treasurer, and the war party under von Steiger the mayor), hesitated whether to make a vigorous resistance, or to adopt a shameful policy of *laissez-faire;* and it was only the brave conduct of General K. L. von Erlach which succeeded in bringing his native town to the honourable decision to take up arms for their liberties. Of the other states, Zurich, Uri, Schwyz, Glarus, Appenzell and the town of St. Gall alone sent any auxiliary troops; the rest had no desire to protect the aristocracy of Berne. But Berne could not even rely upon her own troops, for these were not only very few in number and widely scattered, but were also torn by dissensions and ready to mutiny: many of the soldiers would not obey their leaders, and fostered mistrust of them and of the government; even the life of Erlach himself was threatened! The issue, therefore, could not be doubtful. Notwithstanding their weakness and paucity, the Bernese troops yet bore themselves bravely in the battle itself: at Neueneck, south-west of Berne, to which a division of Brune's army had advanced, they gave battle under Johannes Weber, adjutant-general of Colonel von Graffenried, with truly heroic courage, and put the enemy to flight (5th March). On the north side of the town, however, against which Schauenburg's troops had advanced, all was lost: Erlach's outposts yielded at Fraubrunnen; in the little wood of Grauholz, two hours' march from Berne, Erlach, after a brief but valiant resistance, was obliged to retire before a flank movement of the French, who were four times as strong as himself. At Breitfeld he assembled his men once more; but in the town all resistance had already been abandoned, and on the 5th March a capitulation ensued. Unfortunate as was the end of the struggle, the Bernese did at least save the honour of ancient Switzerland; but in their fall the Bernese aristocracy carried with them the whole of the Switzerland of old days. The other states immediately gave up all opposition.

§ 62. **The Period of the First United Helvetic Constitution, 1798-1800.** (*a*) **Introduction of the Helvetic Constitution.** While Brune and Schauenburg were occupying Switzerland, zealous attempts were being made in Paris to settle the details of the new order of things in Swiss affairs. From the pen of Ochs, the cultured and clever politician, came a scheme of a united Helvetic Constitution, abolishing cantonal differences and establishing a uniform government. The Directory and Bonaparte assented to the scheme with very slight alterations. It was drawn up after the pattern of the constitution of the French Directory. Switzerland was to form a state "one and indivisible," with a central government. All citizens of the former states or cantons were to be Swiss citizens without distinction or difference. All conditions of dependence were abolished; subjects and allied states received equal rights with the hitherto governing states, and the political power or sovereignty was vested in the hands of all the citizens. As in France, the form of government was a representative democracy with two chambers. The legislative power was to be exercised by a Senate and a greater council, the executive by a Directory of five members, assisted by four ministers; while the judicial power was vested in a high court of justice. Lucerne was made the capital.

For purposes of administration, jurisdiction and election the whole of Switzerland was divided into twenty-two cantons or jurisdictions defined by geographical boundaries; to the thirteen states were added Leman (Vaud), Aargau, Thurgau, Bellinzona, Lugano, Sargans with Rheintal, St. Gall, Valais and Rhætia. The cantons were further divided into districts. At the head of every canton there was a governor appointed by the Directory, and an administrative chamber. The constitution was submitted to the general vote of the citizens; universal suffrage was established for the election of district and communal officials: in the communes there were primary assemblies, in the jurisdictions electoral assemblies of delegates elected by the people. The personal rights of the citizens were exactly like those in France. Privileges, prerogatives of the nobility, titles and such-like were abolished. Anyone might be admitted to office; restrictions were taken off trade and manufactures, and feudal burdens were swept away. To every citizen were guaranteed liberty of conscience and of religion, freedom of the press and the right of petition as inalienable rights.

The lofty aim of the whole constitution was to further the welfare, the ennobling and the enlightenment of the people, and to induce every individual without distinction to take an active part in political life. But the French themselves discredited their work and procured enemies to the constitution by at once treating Switzerland as conquered territory, seizing the hoarded treasures, levying contributions and harassing the population. From the cantons of Berne, Fribourg, Soleure, Lucerne and Zurich alone they extorted a war tax of fifteen millions; the public chests and arsenals were robbed right and left; in Berne (according to a computation of 1815) in all over seventeen million francs were stolen. Laharpe himself was appalled at the faithless and shameful course of action adopted by the deliverers of his country.

This circumstance more than anything else strengthened the opposition already existing in Switzerland against the united constitution; the "deliverance" seemed more like subjugation. When therefore the French commissary invited all the cantons to send their delegates to Aarau on 12th April to accept the constitution, only the ten cantons of Zurich, Berne, Lucerne, Soleure, Fribourg, Basle, Schaffhausen, Aargau, Oberland and the Vaud complied, the interior and eastern cantons holding aloof. This assembly in Aarau elected the new officials, the Directory, and the ministers. Admonished by the Directory, the states of eastern Switzerland next embraced the constitution; only the original cantons,[1] where the sense of independence had for centuries been strong,

[1] Uri, Schwyz, Unterwalden.—E. S.

resisted with an obstinacy born of an affronted sense of honour and liberty; but they lost the historical and lawful precedence which they had maintained for centuries! In these cantons, too, the priests had great influence, and certain of the Catholic church took advantage of unfavourable clauses of the constitution (such as the confiscation of the monastic treasures and the licensing of mixed marriages) to arouse fanaticism among the people. A separate Diet at Schwyz protested against the Helvetic Constitution; and Schauenburg adopting violent measures, Schwyz actually fixed upon the bold plan of restoring the old Confederation and making head against the victorious nation. A violent patriotic and religious enthusiasm took possession of all classes; young and old, women and children took up arms, and ecclesiastics, like Marianus Herzog of Einsiedeln and the Capuchin Paul Styger, placed themselves at their head. A commencement was made by invading the neighbouring territories of Zug, Rapperswil and Lucerne, in order to wrench the country piece by piece from the Helvetic Republic. Schauenburg on the other hand now conceived the plan of an attack to be made on all sides, and the men of Schwyz were forced to give way. Part of the French troops advanced from Zurich along the lake, took Wollerau and Pfäffikon by storm (30th April, 1798), and marched against the Etzel and the Schindellegi. Pastor Marianus Herzog was the first to treacherously desert his post, and thus to open the way to Einsiedeln to the enemy; hence the remaining forces of Schwyz, under Alois Reding, after defending themselves most valiantly and successfully, to avoid being surrounded were forced to retire upon Rothenthurm and Morgarten, where meanwhile another division of the French had been successfully encountered; and, almost frantic with enthusiasm, on May 2nd they again defeated the united hosts of the enemy. The French forces, however, far outnumbered those of Schwyz, and the latter were moreover cut off from their fellows. When, therefore, after a truce, it became necessary for the *Landsgemeinde* of Schwyz to come to a decision, they arranged an honourable peace (4th May).

The time soon came when the whole of Switzerland was required to swear to the Helvetic Constitution, and then the resentment broke out afresh in Schwyz, and also in Nidwalden. The latter, incited by the clergy, flew to arms; Schauenburg, however, invaded the little territory with from 9000 to 10,000 men, and conquered it in a short time (9th September), though it is true with much difficulty; for, mindful of the deeds of their ancestors, the descendants of the heroes of Morgarten, Sempach and Murten did not yield till they could carry the fame of incomparable bravery with them to the grave. Terrible indeed was the fate of the country: wherever the French bayonets appeared, the ground was dyed with streams of blood; dwellings were burnt down, and misery knew no bounds ("the days of terror of Nidwalden"). Thus was the Helvetic Constitution only imposed upon them by force.

(b) **Internal Arrangements.** Meanwhile the Directory and its ministers applied themselves vigorously to the performance of their task. Specially serviceable were the efforts of the two ministers, Dr. Albrecht Rengger and Albrecht Stapfer, both natives of the little (formerly Bernese) town of Brugg. While Rengger, as minister of the interior, busied himself with the introduction of new regulations in the communes, Stapfer, minister of the arts and sciences, was untiring in his endeavours to improve the educational system. A clause of the Helvetic Constitution defines enlightenment as the chief foundation of public welfare, speaking of it as preferable to all outward prosperity. It was in this spirit that Stapfer embarked upon his task, and the intense activity which was now displayed in the sphere of education is one of the finest points of the Helvetic system; the ideas which then sprang into existence were as the first tokens of the spring of modern times, and have to some extent been only quite lately carried into execution. Stapfer caused all the cantons to send him reports of the condition of their system of schools and education, together with ideas and suggestions for their improvement. Federal regulations for schools were drawn up, which embraced all scientific and pedagogic institutions, and produced a very great advance as compared with conditions existing prior to 1798. In the chief town of every canton a council of education was established consisting of seven members; a commissioner or inspector of public instruction chosen by the council of education watched over every district, to see that the communal schools were provided with capable teachers; and in every canton a seminary was to be erected for the training of good teachers. Pestalozzi now gained his opportunity of labouring effectually for the renovation of the method of teaching by publishing a popular paper at the request of Stapfer. Stapfer specially directed his efforts towards curing the evils wrought by the war; with this aim he erected a house of education at Stans for poor orphan children, which was entrusted to the direction of Pestalozzi; here the latter laboured night and day, full of love and devotion for the little ones. Stapfer was also anxious to effectually promote higher education, the arts and sciences. He provided for the erection of "gymnasiums,"[1] and even suggested the establishment of a Swiss university or academy; he endeavoured also to establish in all parts literary societies for the promotion of public spirit, enlightenment and culture. Besides all this, he made arrangements for the foundation of a Swiss society of arts, and directed his energy towards preserving and throwing open the monastic libraries and collections (National Museum). The number of daily papers increased, and Federal newspapers sprang into existence, such as the *Schweizerischer Republikaner*,[2] of Escher and Usteri, and the *Journal von und für Helvetien*.[3]

These praiseworthy efforts, however, did not always meet with a favourable reception. The means were not adequate to the plans; the finances of the central government were altogether insufficient for the carrying out of the proposed institutions, and moreover much prejudice against all innovations still prevailed among the people; even Pestalozzi, not-

---

[1] Or grammar-schools.—E. S.   [2] The "Swiss Republican."
[3] The "Helvetic Journal."

withstanding his self-sacrificing activity, was so combated and hampered in the original cantons,[1] that he was almost in despair. But the new seed suffered most from the boundless misery left everywhere by the French invasion. Many districts were deprived of all means of subsistence; gardens and fields were laid waste, and disease and famine followed like dismal spectres in the wake of the French armies. The efforts of the Directory to help by contributions of produce and money were as a drop in the ocean; the contributions required by the French for transport, provisions and fortifications swallowed up all, and increased from day to day. For Switzerland having in August, 1798, abandoned her neutrality and concluded an alliance with France, had become the battlefield of the second European war of coalition, which harassed the land terribly, and which, although in the main quite foreign to the particular interests of Switzerland, yet had a distinct effect upon the course of political events there.

At the commencement of the war of 1799 the Austrians were at first victorious; the Archduke Charles crossed the Rhine and forced his way through the territories of Schaffhausen, Thurgau and Zurich, driving the French before him; while from the Grisons in the south-east a division advanced under Hotze (a native of Richterswil) and drove back the enemy from the districts of the interior. After a fierce encounter near Zurich on 4th June, 1799, Massena was obliged to retire before Charles and Hotze behind the Limmat. A reaction ensued in the east of Switzerland; the opponents of the Helvetic Constitution and of the French received the Austrians with rejoicings and bore themselves triumphantly; Abbot Pancras Forster revoked his former concessions to the people and once more established his dominion; in Thurgau, the numerous lords of manors and squires again possessed themselves of their privileges; the canton or district of St. Gall was abolished, and the constitution of Appenzell restored by the help of the Austrians, while the trees of liberty were destroyed.

[1] Uri, Schwyz, Unterwalden.—E. S.

But the joy of the reactionary party was not of long duration. For scarcely had the Archduke Charles been recalled from Switzerland, and marched away along the Rhine to Germany, when Massena successfully assumed the offensive, and defeated the Russians under Korsakow on 26th September, in the second battle near Zurich, whereupon Zurich and the whole of the north-east of Switzerland fell into his hands. Suworow, the Russian general, endeavouring to lead his own troops and the Austrian auxiliaries from Italy over the St. Gotthard, found his way blocked at the Lake of the Four Cantons, and it was only after indescribable difficulties and by a desperate march across the Alps (over the Kinzigkulm, Pragel, and the pass of Panix) that he succeeded in striking out a circuitous route towards the east. By this means Switzerland once more falling completely into the hands of the French, the Helvetic Republic was again established in its entirety. But the unhappy land had yet to suffer grievously for having become the battlefield of foreign armies. Great excesses were committed by the soldiers of both sides, and the demands for the maintenance of the army became more and more oppressive. In the short time from September to December Thurgau alone was forced to disburse almost a million and a half of florins for the French army; while the town of Arbon had to pay 75,000 francs, and Zurich and Basle as much as 800,000 francs! All this was not calculated to reconcile the people to the new order of things; every evil was ascribed chiefly to the new constitution. Hence, after the close of the war of the coalition there arose a conflict between the factions in Switzerland itself, which at length brought about the downfall of the Helvetic Constitution.

2. THE END OF THE HELVETIC CONSTITUTION, AND PEACEABLE DEVELOPMENT UNDER THE CONSTITUTION OF MEDIATION.
(1800-1813.)

§ 63. **Struggles between the Federalists and Centralists; Transition to the Government of Mediation, 1800-1802.** After the introduction of the united Helvetic Constitution two parties bitterly opposed one another throughout the whole of Switzerland: the Unionists or Centralists, adherents of the uniform system, and the Federalists, or adherents of the old Federal Constitution and of the Confederation. This schism was specially troublesome in the councils and in the government; while at the same time the friends of the new order of things were split up into various smaller divisions, perpetually at strife amongst themselves, and alternately seeking to obtain a leading influence in the government, and to alter the constitution to suit their own views. Four *coups d'état* succeeded one another in five years, and four changes of the constitution.

At first the government was entirely central, but after changing several of the persons composing it, the leading members themselves—Ochs and Laharpe—were expelled; the Directory then dissolved, and in its stead, on the 8th January, 1800, an executive committee of seven members (mostly "Moderates") was established by the legislative councils. This came about by the help of Napoleon Bonaparte, who had likewise abolished the Directory in France, and had raised himself to the position of First Consul. But the Centralists in the legislative councils becoming once more active, the Moderate party went further, and by the help of French troops compassed the dissolution of the councils, whereupon, on the 7th August, 1800, a council of legislation of fifty members was set up. With the attempt to establish a new constitution, however, the bitterest party strife broke out, and the influence of France became very active. The First Consul was gradually adopting the views of the Federalists, and at length, by a new constitution of the 29th May, 1801 (styled the "Scheme of Malmaison"),[1] he almost entirely restored the sovereignty of the cantons and the Diet. This constitution, however, did not last; the Centralists, under Usteri, succeeded at the Diet called together to receive the constitution in re-modelling it according to their own ideas. A counter-stroke on the part of the Federalists (Reding, Reinhard, &c.) quickly followed; they drove out the Helvetic officials, established a senate of their own party, and drew up a constitution, which was really still more Federal than the scheme of Napoleon (November, 1801, to February, 1802). But in the spring of 1802 the Centralists again rallied, and once more obtained a united constitution.

This exasperated the Federalists, and they braced themselves for a desperate struggle. The withdrawal of the French troops, which took place in consequence of the Peace of Amiens, in the summer of 1802, gave the signal for the outbreak. Under the name of a "Swiss Brotherhood" a conspiracy was formed against the Centralists and the Helvetic Government, the two states of Berne and Zurich supporting the democratic cantons. Twelve cantons assembled at a Diet at Schwyz, Zurich, as the capital, taking the lead. The Helvetic Government found itself confronted by an open revolt, which it endeavoured to quell by force of arms; but the troops were defeated by those of Unterwalden at the Rengg (27th-28th August), upon which it called upon the French to intervene.

It was in vain that Zurich was besieged in September, 1802, by the Helvetic general Andermatt. No longer safe even in Berne, the Government was forced to fly to the Vaud, where, however, the troops under General Bachmann were likewise defeated at Morat and Avenches by the troops of the "Swiss Brotherhood" under Rudolf von Erlach.[2] The Centralists now began to give way, and the Helvetic Government, no

---

[1] A country seat of Napoleon's in the vicinity of Paris.
[2] This war is commonly called the "Stecklikrieg," or "Guerre aux Batons," from the insurgents having armed themselves with sticks (*stöcke*) and clubs.

longer safe in Lausanne, was about to take refuge in Savoy, when General Rapp, Napoleon's plenipotentiary, suddenly arrived, and in the name of the First Consul, who offered himself as a mediator between the parties, commanded a halt. The revolted districts were occupied by a French army, the leaders of the revolt beheaded, and the Helvetic Government re-entered Berne in October, 1802, under the protection of French troops.

The French Consul had now got the exhausted Switzerland completely into his power. With a view to the reorganization of Swiss affairs he summoned delegates of both parties to a consultation at Paris to advise with him as to guiding principles, which might, if possible, satisfy both Federalists and Centralists. The late struggles had convinced him that the united Helvetic Constitution could not be maintained, since it endeavoured too rapidly to efface with one stroke all the conditions which had become historical, and offended too many interests and views; he was even of opinion that the very diversity of nature in Switzerland was opposed to a uniform system. Above all, he considered the constitution of the democratic *Landsgemeinde* a fine and historically noteworthy peculiarity, of which Switzerland ought not to be deprived. But just as little did he desire the mere restoration of the old order of things; the fundamental idea of the French Revolution was the benefit of humanity, and the promotion of liberty, equality and the welfare of the people; and he could not suffer a system to be adopted in Switzerland which was favoured by Austria and in direct opposition to France, or in which adherents of the enemies of France took the lead. He therefore adopted a middle course, in which proceeding he was constantly encouraged by his conferences and discussions with the members of the "Consulta." He paid no heed to any opposition, and with rare sagacity succeeded in silencing or overawing his opponents. After mature consideration, on 19th February, 1803, he submitted to the committee of consultation an Act of Mediation compiled by himself, which he desired should be deemed unalterable without any enquiry into the will of the nation itself. At the same time he did not fail to remind the delegates that only in this way could Switzerland be saved from shipwreck, and find in him a happy refuge.[1] In the constitution itself everything tended inevitably to make Switzerland dependent upon France.

As regarded the settlement of details, six new cantons were added to the thirteen old ones, formed out of former common domains, subject-lands or allied states, namely, St. Gall, Thurgau, the Grisons, Ticino, the Vaud and Aargau (to which was added the Fricktal, the last Austrian possession in Switzerland). Then the Diet was re-established, in which the people as such was not represented at all, the delegates being bound by the instructions of the governments of the cantons. Yet the Federal power was strengthened by penalties laid upon all rebellion against the decisions of the Diet, and unity found expression in the person of a "Landammann." There were to be six seats of government,[2] each for one year —Fribourg, Berne, Soleure, Basle, Zurich and Lucerne. The burgomaster, or mayor of the capital, was the Landammann for the time being. The subject-lands and all privileges of nobility, birth or family were swept away. On the other hand, very few popular rights were preserved: there was no mention of the right of petition or of liberty of the press, nor even of the sovereignty of the people. The constitutions of the cantons reverted to old historical conditions (*Landsgemeinde*, the guilds and patricians), while the constitutions of the new cantons were more liberal, the purchase of tithes and ground-rent was rendered difficult, and the suffrage was confined to those paying a certain amount of taxes.

In consequence of its combination and fusion of the old with the new, the "Mediation" was a characterless middle course, and, as was inevitable, many traces of former conditions

---

[1] *Cf.* TILLIER, *Geschichte der Eidgenossenchaft während der Herrschaft der Vermittlungsakte*, 2 vols. HODLER, *Geschichte des Schweizervolkes, neuere Zeit*, vol. i. 1865. MURALT, *Hans von Reinhard*. HILTY, *Polit. Jahrbuch der Eidgenossenchaft*, I. F. v. WYSS, *Leben der beiden Bürgermeister David v. Wyss, Vater und Sohn*.

[2] *Cantons directeurs* or capitals.

soon came once more to the fore, such as titles, torture, the obligation imposed upon artisans to join a guild, the public censorship, &c. Violent irritation was also aroused by the curtailing of popular privileges with regard to tithes and suffrage. In the canton of Zurich the population along the left bank of the lake showed signs of insubordination, especially those of Horgen under one Willi, a shoemaker. The military advanced against them, and took possession of Horgen, but were obliged to retire before Willi and his troops to the heights of Bocken (April, 1804). The country folk now became alarmed; Willi could get no reinforcements, and the troops succeeded on their second march in completely disarming the insurgents. The leaders were taken, brought before an extraordinary court-martial, and put to death without mercy. The spirit of 1795 seemed about to return. With the exception of this rising, Switzerland, after the reception of the constitution, enjoyed eleven years of peace and of salutary development, and was happily enabled to recover gradually from the wounds inflicted upon her.

§ 64. **Intellectual and Material Revival.** Under the protection of the peace, an increased intellectual advancement became evident in every respect during the time of the "Mediation." The new ideas propagated by the patriots of the eighteenth century silently permeated life, and gradually transformed the old historical conditions. Now again, as in the eighteenth century, progress was chiefly brought about by individual societies. The Helvetic Society, their jubilant songs and merry clinking of glasses drowned in the thunder of the cannon of Neueneck and Grauholz, had had no time to assemble during the party strife of the Helvetic Constitution, but they now met once more, and endeavoured to effect a reconciliation of all parties upon a national basis. For the improvement of regulations concerning the relief of the poor, education and industrial life the Swiss Society for Public Benefit sprang into existence; the Swiss society of artists, founded by Martin Usteri, aimed at giving a national direction to Swiss art; a society for historical research, and a society of Swiss teachers were also started. As a distraction from the dreary political outlook, men immersed themselves in the life of the people, the natural beauties of their land and its glorious past, and a patriotic public spirit dominated the arts and sciences. The lofty peaks of the Alps were scaled, measured and described. General Pfyffer and Müller, an engineer of Engelberg, completed high-relief maps of the greater part of Switzerland; Swiss atlases appeared (such as that of Rudolf Meier), Swiss maps (of Heinrich Keller), descriptions of Swiss plants (of Hegetschweiler), and delicate, finely engraved pictures of Swiss towns, Swiss costumes and popular festivals (*Alpenrosen, helvetischer Almanach*). As a historian, Johann von Müller led the van; full of an intense love of his country, he laboured at this time upon the flourishing period of the fourteenth and fifteenth centuries, as if to lay a wreath upon the tomb of the old Confederation. This period is characterised by the special attention paid to Swiss history; popular histories of Switzerland and histories for the young (of Zschokke, Schuler, &c.,) were written and eagerly read. Pastor Stalder of Escholzmatt laid the foundation of a Swiss *Idiotikon* (dictionary of dialects); a separate Swiss poetry sprang into existence in the popular dialect, specially through the amiable poet and artist Martin Usteri of Zurich ("*de Herr Heiri*," "*de Vikari*"). With the popular poetry there arose also a nobler order of popular songs, of which the composer, Hs. Georg Nägeli of Wetzikon (canton Zurich), is still honoured as the founder. "His melodies ring out in merry companies, at excursions on our lakes, from boys in the streets, and the low and worthless songs which had formerly been sung could never have been extirpated by any prohibition as they were by the 'Nägeli-Lieder' (songs of Nägeli).[1] His melodies were even appreciated in other lands; in Switzerland itself Nägeli became the founder of choral societies, and a great favourite with the people, who called him "Father Nägeli."

[1] G. MEYER VON KNONAU, *der Kanton Zurich*, ii. 76.

The beneficent and educational efforts of this period proved a lasting blessing to the whole life of the people. In 1810 the Swiss Society for Public Benefit was founded; it numbered members from every canton, who now pledged themselves to labour, each in his own sphere, for the relief of the poor, the starving and the wretched, and to promote the establishment of almshouses, orphanages, poor-funds, storehouses, &c. Savings banks came into existence (the first at Zurich in 1805), insurance offices, &c. Moreover, in the domain of material culture progress was made in various ways common to the period; forestry and agriculture underwent a rational improvement, the latter particularly through the exertions of the Bernese Emanuel von Fellenberg, who erected an agricultural school and model-institute with all the best agricultural appliances, on his estate of Hofwil; the monasteries of Kreuzlingen in the Thurgau and Altenryf in Fribourg followed his example. Machines were introduced for cotton manufactures in Zurich and St. Gall. But the greatest undertaking of this time was the Linth canal, which was achieved (1804-1822) through the untiring and philanthropic exertions of the self-sacrificing Hs. Konrad Escher of Zurich (hence styled "von der Linth"), and which for ever rescued the population of that district from the depths of misery.[1]

In educational and scholastic matters the activity of Pestalozzi, first in Burgdorf, and afterwards in Yverdon, attracted more and more attention; with him laboured also his pupils Fellenberg and Wehrli. His method of object-teaching, training the mind to think and find out for itself, was recognised as the best by the greatest thinkers and schoolmen of the day, and soon called forth imitation, both in Switzerland and other lands. But he was himself wanting in the necessary practical ability for the management of an educational institute for the poor. In this his friend Emanuel von Fellenberg succeeded better, who during his agricultural exertions had noted with the deepest pain the impoverishment

[1] This canal connects the lake of Zurich with the lake of Wallenstadt.—E. S.

and neglect of the lower classes, and founded a charitable institution upon his already-mentioned estate. From 1810 he entrusted the management of the latter to the able and gifted friend of the poor, J. J. Wehrli, of whom Pestalozzi joyfully asserted that he had realised his idea of a school for the poor.[1] In addition to this, Fellenberg also founded an institute for boys of the upper classes, which was greatly sought after, and held courses of instruction for training teachers for popular schools. It was reserved to the canton of Aargau to erect, in 1810, the first training college for teachers in Switzerland. Noteworthy improvements were also effected in the system of higher instruction. Cantonal schools arose in Coire and Aarau, grammar-schools (*Gymnasien*) in the Vaud and other parts, an institute for higher education in St. Gall, a political institute in Zurich for lawyers and statesmen; Berne also introduced new and excellent regulations for schools.[2]

While as regarded internal matters Switzerland managed her own affairs, towards the outer world she took up rather the position of a province of France, to which country she was bound by a defensive alliance and a military capitulation. She had come under the yoke of her powerful mediator, Napoleon (who had risen to the rank of emperor in 1804), and shared the fortunes of the Napoleonic Empire. Swiss trade suffered severely under the continental blockade: Napoleon suddenly and most despotically placed a military occupation in Ticino, under pretence of hindering English contraband trade. Swiss territory seemed to exist only to serve the interests of France: Neuchâtel became a subject principality of France, and in 1810 the great emperor arbitrarily annexed Valais to his empire as the "Département du Simplon," in order to hold unconditional sway over the road which he had constructed across the Simplon. Switzerland was also the market where the French found

---

[1] PUPIKOFER, *Leben und Wirken des Joh. Jak. Wehrli.*
[2] J. J. HOTTINGER, *das Wiedererwachen der wissenschaftlichen Bestrebungen in der Schweiz während der Mediations und Restaurationsepoche.*

their soldiers. Federal troops, always from 12,000 to 16,000 in number, were forced to fight for the glory and aggrandizement of France in Spain, Austria, and lastly in Russia, where they displayed heroic courage and unrivalled valour in 1812, but finally shared the miserable fate of the great army, out of 12,000 only 2200 remaining! Any powerful or independent action on the part of Switzerland was impossible; "neutrality" was to Napoleon a "word without meaning"; Switzerland must be guided by France alone. The emperor, therefore, purposely hindered the formation of a strong Federal military force. His agents maintained a strict supervision over the Swiss press and all freedom of speech, and the policy of Swiss statesmen was determined by his will.

3. THE PERIOD OF RESTORATION.[1]
(1813-1830.)

§ 65. **The Downfall of the "Mediation."** From the time of the overthrow of the "great army" upon the snowfields of Russia, the power of the "Emperor of the Universe" was on the wane. Prussia, Austria and England rose to assist Russia, and after the "Battle of the Nations" at Leipzig (16th-18th October, 1813), the allies advanced towards the Rhine in order to penetrate into France. Napoleon's plans were thus frustrated, and the question was raised in Switzerland, too, whether the constitution imposed by Napoleon should or should not be any longer preserved. An inclination in its favour, however, prevailed; it had procured peace to the country, preserved certain liberal principles, and given life and existence to six new cantons. Fresh storms and troubles were feared. The Diet, therefore, declined to join the allies, and decided to observe their neutrality and to raise an army.

But the adherents of the old conditions, previous to 1798, in Zurich, Berne, &c., desired an invasion on the part of the allies, by whose help they hoped to gain their end. They

[1] TILLIER, *Geschichte der Eidgenossenschaft während der sogenannten Restaurationsepoche.* HILTY, *Polit. Jahrbuch*, vol. iii.

formed the "Society of Restoration," a secret committee of which negotiated with the allies at Waldshut. The Swiss army was destined to guard the Rhine frontier from Basle to Schaffhausen and the Grisons. But the military force of Switzerland had been crippled by Napoleon, and from motives of economy Landammann Reinhard put insufficient troops in the field. Swiss statesmen, too, allowed themselves to be deceived by the allies into thinking that there was no question of any invasion of Switzerland. Hence they were lamentably taken by surprise and overcome.

When the allies announced their intention of invading the country, General von Wattenwil, who, considering the disproportionate inequality of his forces (12,500 against 160,000 men), deemed any resistance not only futile, but dangerous, ordered a retreat from the frontier on December 20th, when not a shot had been fired for the preservation of neutrality. The allies passed quietly along the Rhine from Basle to Schaffhausen, and poured into Swiss territory without finding any opposition! The immediate result of this was the downfall of the constitution of "Mediation." Metternich, the Austrian minister, was specially active towards its abolition, in spite of promises made to Switzerland that her internal concerns should not be interfered with. Under repeated pressure from the Austrian ambassador and from an insolent emissary of Metternich, the Count of Senft-Pilsach, the "Mediation" government in Berne resigned on December 23rd, and its downfall was followed by that of the governments of Soleure, Fribourg, Lucerne, &c. At the end of December an extraordinary Diet assembled in Zurich, and formally declared the Constitution of Mediation extinct.

But when it came to the establishment of a new order of things, opinions were widely divided. Berne wanted totally to ignore all that had passed since the Revolution, desired to get back her former subject-lands of the Vaud and Aargau, and demanded the restoration of the old Confederation of Thirteen Cantons, in which she was supported by the patrician states and the formerly privileged democratic cantons. The liberal towns on the other hand adopted a middle course, while the new cantons wished if possible to maintain existing conditions. In opposition to the liberal Diet in Zurich a reactionary one was soon assembled in Lucerne (20th March), and only the menaces of the powers, declaring themselves in favour of a Confederation of nineteen cantons, succeeded in effecting an outward reconciliation of the two Diets, in the beginning of April, 1814. Internal dissensions, however, continued, Berne and the cantons of similar opinions persisting in their claims upon the subject-lands. The cantons of Aargau and Vaud, finding their very existence thus threatened, prepared for an armed resistance. The claims of Schwyz and Glarus gave rise to tumults in Utznach and Sargans, parts of the new canton of St. Gall; as did those of Uri in Livinen (*Val Leventina*), belonging to the canton of Ticino. The canton of Ticino threatened to separate itself; the Grisons sought to repossess themselves of their former domains in the Valtelline, Cleves and Worms; Bienne and the former bishopric of Basle endeavoured to obtain a union with Switzerland, as did Neuchâtel, Valais and Geneva.

The Diet earnestly endeavouring to quell the disturbances, was for a long time prevented from completing the scheme of the new constitution, and the representatives of Prussia, Austria and Russia were forced repeatedly to urge dispatch. It seemed impossible in Switzerland to settle conflicting claims, and to agree upon territorial changes. At length the Congress of Vienna, which had been sitting since the autumn of 1814, interposed, in order to remove the chief causes of dispute. Switzerland had sent delegates to Vienna, but even they could not agree among themselves, and actually opposed one another's measures, which caused great delay in Swiss affairs.

Meanwhile Napoleon had been deposed and banished to Elba. Suddenly, however, he returned, and in March, 1815, attempted to reinstate his empire. The powers quickly combined: and Switzerland, too, occupied her western frontier, under General Bachmann. On 20th March, 1815, Swiss matters were adjusted by the Congress. The powers started from the assumption that Switzerland needed strengthening that she might act as a buffer against France. Valais, Neuchâtel and Geneva were, therefore, added as new cantons to the nineteen already existing, and thus the foundation was laid once for all of the Confederation of twenty-two states. On the other hand, the Valtelline, Chiavenna and Worms had to be surrendered to Austria, and the Grisons were forced to content themselves with the hitherto Austrian domain of Räzüns. In regard to internal affairs, all claims upon the formerly subject lands were declared null and void. Berne was indemnified for the loss of hers by receiving the greater part of the bishopric of Basle, together with Bienne; the remainder of the bishopric fell to Basle. The indemnities of the remaining cantons were discharged in money.

Under foreign pressure, Switzerland in the summer of 1815 forsook her policy of neutrality, and took part in the struggle against Napoleon by invading Upper Burgundy, and also by her co-operation in besieging and taking Hüningen.[1] Thus fully satisfied, the powers appointed fixed limits to the territory of Geneva, and forced France to pay an indemnity for her depredations in 1798; moreover they, on 20th November, 1815, took the territorial position of Switzerland under their protection, and acknowledged her perpetual neutrality, in which the two provinces of Savoy, Faucigny and Chablais (*see* pp. 147, 161), conquered by Berne in the sixteenth century, were included.

§ 66. **The Federal Pact of 1815, and the New Constitutions of the Cantons. Reaction and Liberalism till 1830.** During these events the "Long Diet" at Zurich was evolving a new Federal constitution, the so-called "Federal Pact," which, approved by the Congress of Vienna, was signed and accepted in August, 1815. During the deliberations, many voices had been raised in favour of maintaining a strong Federal authority, but the majority of the members of the Diet were enthusiastically attached to the system of petty states which had prevailed before 1798; the cantons hankered

---

[1] This fortress, erected by Louis XIV. (1679-1681), had always been a thorn in the side to the Swiss. (*See* p. 184.)—E. S.

after their old sovereign rights, and the aristocracy after their privileges. Thus the broad basis of the Federal State was totally abandoned, and Switzerland was transformed into a loose Confederation, in which all the twenty-two cantons enjoyed the full right of self-government, and only acted in concert in matters of foreign policy, and for the maintenance of peace and order in the interior. The system of rendering assistance and levying troops was much the same as in the time of the old Confederation, before 1798, as was also the mode of settling internal disputes. There was no distinct and unmistakable prohibition of the privileges of certain states and of birth, no mention of the people being at liberty to choose their place of residence, or of free trade, nor were the rights of Swiss citizenship established. It is true that the holding of lands in subjection was forbidden, but in the enjoyment of political privileges exclusiveness alone was prohibited.

The Diet returned to the old and cumbersome system of "Instructions," and the interchange of commerce between certain leading states. Zurich, Berne and Lucerne were to become capitals in rotation, changing every two years. The continuance of the religious houses was guaranteed, so far as depended upon the cantonal governments; but a very wide latitude was given to mercenary service, by the fact that the settlement of military capitulations was left to the option of the states. The constitution of the cantons was left to the discretion of the various states themselves, and in them very few concessions were made to the less privileged classes. Four cantons almost entirely restored the old patrician constitution (Berne, Fribourg, Soleure and Lucerne), and the new cantons also approached more nearly to the aristocratic system than during the period of the "Mediation." Among the civic cantons the chief cities once more obtained the ascendency. In Soleure the town had sixty-eight representatives, the rural district only thirty-three; in Zurich the city had one hundred and thirty representatives, the country eighty-two; in Fribourg the town had one hundred and eight, the country only thirty-six; in Berne the city two hundred, the country only ninety-nine! The franchise, as also the right to be elected, was still more restricted, according to the amount of property (*Census*), and thus the dominion of the higher classes and of the rich was once more established, though slightly enfeebled.

There was no more talk of popular liberties. The elections were excessively indirect, and the freedom of the communes was almost extinct. The obligation of belonging to a guild was once more enforced, and torture also reappeared.

This reaction corresponded to the alarm at all radical innovations, and the universal lassitude and stagnation which prevailed everywhere after the great revolution. At this time the Bernese Professor K. L. v. Haller successfully advocated opposition to all liberal institutions, and the "Restoration of the Middle Ages." Liberal teachers were persecuted. Professor Troxler, of Lucerne, who in his book "*Fürst und Volk*"[1] propagated democratic opinions, was, in 1821, deprived of his appointment. This reaction was chiefly owing to the influence of the "Holy Alliance," which Switzerland had joined in 1817. Liberal agitations becoming rife in the surrounding countries, the governments interposed with persecutions, and numberless fugitives gathered in Switzerland. Liberal pamphlets indulged freely in criticism of the "Restoration" policy of other lands, and the fugitives also, safe on Swiss soil, incited to rebellion against their home governments; till at last Switzerland, long threatened by the powers, by a decision of the Diet (*Konklusum*), in 1823, published strict regulations for the press, and laid restrictions upon the liberty of harbouring refugees. Switzerland lay for years under the ban of the surrounding countries.

The church, too, helped the reaction. In 1818 the Jesuits established themselves in Fribourg, as they had formerly done in Valais, and commenced their intrigues. Father Girard, a noble Franciscan, and a friend of Pestalozzi, who had improved and renovated the instruction in the schools of Fribourg, was by them persecuted, and finally in 1823 ruthlessly expelled.

[1] "Prince and People."

Similar attacks were made, chiefly at the instigation of the papal nuncio in Lucerne, upon the philanthropical Baron von Wessenberg, vicar-general of the Bishop of Constance, who was labouring to further the culture and enlightenment of the clergy, and to establish a more popular form of divine service, having the sermon and the mass in the mother-tongue, hymns, and exposition of the gospels. In order to withdraw his influence from Switzerland, he was removed from the bishopric of Constance in 1815 by a papal decree, and placed under an apostolical vicar, Göldlin, provost of Beromünster. After the death of Göldlin, in 1819, the Catholics of the east of Switzerland came under the direction of the Bishop of Coire; in 1828, however, a number of cantons (Berne, Soleure, Lucerne, Zug, Aargau, Thurgau and Basle) revived the bishopric of Basle, and placed its seat in Soleure. From this time the papal system struck its roots deeper and deeper in Catholic Switzerland, and "Ultramontanism"[1] prevailed, while the relations between Catholics and Protestants were almost as strained as in the seventeenth century.

Thus beneath the weight of the policy of restoration it seemed as though all free development must be stifled:—yet the spirit of the people could not remain for ever fettered, and even during the time of oppression it was gathering strength in order the sooner to gain a free field. Patriotic enthusiasm, which had shown itself in many ways during the time of the "Mediation," was still at work; for instance, creative art still gave the preference to patriotic subjects— witness the painters Vogel in Zurich, and Disteli in Olten. The poets, too, chose subjects which kindled the people: Abraham Emanuel Fröhlich, of Aargau, in his fables lashed the abuses of the time, and the Bernese J. Rudolf Wyss the younger gave Switzerland her thrilling national anthem in the song "*Rufst du mein Vaterland.*"[2] Men turned once more to seek their country, and finding its very conception lost to all

[1] From *ultra montes*, "beyond the mountains," meaning the papal seat south of the Alps.
[2] "Callest thou, O my fatherland."

appearance, they lived upon the memory of their splendid past, erecting monuments to patriotic heroes, such as the obelisk at Morat, the Wengistein, the monument at St. Jakob an der Birs, &c. The younger generation was imbued with a spirit of exertion and creation, "free progress" was written on their banners, and a number of newly-founded societies grew into workshops where the times were remodelled. From 1815 the Society for Natural Research had united the learned forces of Switzerland; the Association of Zofingen, founded in 1819, united all the students of Switzerland upon the basis of scientific effort and patriotic enthusiasm. Patriotic feeling was strengthened by the Society of Sempach, and by the shooting matches which were held regularly after 1824, when the first gathering of the Rifle Association took place in Aarau. A similar effect was everywhere produced by gymnastic and choral societies.

None of these societies, however, took up so determined and aggressive an attitude as did the Helvetic Society. Since its reassembling at Schinznach in 1819, when the noise of war had ceased, the policy of a merely hesitating and cautious opposition against existing conditions was abandoned, all aristocratic tendencies were shaken off, and it was formally converted into a political association, its chief aim being to combat the abuses of the "Restoration." Thaddäus Müller, a minister of the town of Lucerne, as president of the society, in 1821 attacked the intrigues of the hierarchy, while Troxler combated the condition of intellectual tutelage: Joh. Kasp. Orelli, the philologist of Zurich, drew a lively picture before a large assembly of friends of the disgraceful policy of "Restoration" as a whole, its intellectual darkness, the censure of the press, mercenary service, the spirit of persecution, &c., urging his hearers to exert themselves for the revival of mental culture, and comforting the more enlightened with the assurance that truth had always proved victorious in spite of scorn and opposition.

The Federal Pact of 1815 became in 1829 the subject of a cutting criticism by Zschokke, who lauded national unity, which he considered better expressed in the Act of Mediation than in the Pact, and placed before the society the noble aim of labouring for such national unity. In May, 1830, Dr. Schinz, the chief justice of Zurich, proclaimed the absolute necessity of a general alteration, and would have all governments recognise that they "exist only from the people, by the people, and for the people." Thus was expressed the principle of the new revolution, the establishment of a representative democracy.

The press chiefly contributed to this revolution, having acquired considerable influence over public life since the French Revolution. Liberal movements found advocates in the *Neue Zürche Zeitung* of Paul Usteri, in Zschokke's *Schweizerbote*, and in the *Appenzelle Zeitung*, established in Trogen in 1828.[1] The latter became the organ of all the Swiss radicals; they criticised mercilessly the abuses which were coming to light on all sides, and that in no measured terms.

But before the reform was introduced into Federal territory, several states had attempted to remodel the cantons; these were specially Lucerne, Appenzell, the Vaud and Ticino. The new aristocracy in Lucerne was overthrown in 1829 by the efforts of the brothers Pfyffer (Kasimir and Eduard), and a division of power was undertaken; the small council lost the right of recruiting itself, and the title of "Town and Republic" was abolished. In Inner Rhodes of Appenzell a revision was pushed through in 1829, extending the rights of the *Landsgemeinde*. Through the influence of the dauntless Paul Usteri the censure was abolished in Zurich, upon which, in 1829, the Diet also abandoned the *Konklusum* (*see* p. 242), while the authority of the great council was strengthened. In the Vaud the demand for reform became more and more urgent, especially after it had been proposed by Laharpe in May, 1829. But in Ticino the most fundamental alterations were necessary, for here the old abuses which had existed

[1] The "New Zurich Gazette," the "Swiss Messenger," and the "Appenzell Gazette."

before 1798, such as corruption, waste and nepotism, had been brought back. Under the direction of the teacher and editor Franscini a total revision in a democratic spirit was drawn up, which in June, 1830, was accepted by the people.

PART II.

INTERNAL REORGANIZATION OR REGENERATION OF THE CANTONS AND OF THE LEAGUE.[1]

(1830-1848.)

1. THE REMODELLING OF THE CANTONS.

§ 67. **Effects of the Revolution of July, and the Great Days of the People in 1830.** In Switzerland as elsewhere the "Revolution of July" in France gave a great impulse to the movements which were already in agitation, and lent them great force. They were welcomed with joy by the reform party, and the current soon spread through every rank of society. Demands for revision increased daily; the press revived with redoubled vigour: the sovereignty of the people, equality of rights, separation of the powers, publicity of discussion and the freedom of the press became watchwords. Tumultuous movements now followed one another in quick succession in the hitherto quiet cantons. In Aargau an assembly of Liberals at Lenzburg directed a petition to the government on 12th September, 1830, desiring that a revision might be taken in hand; and the government receiving it coldly and with hesitation, a popular assembly at Wohlenswil on 7th November emphatically demanded a thorough change

[1] MÜLLER-FRIEDBERG, *Schweiz. Annalen* (6 vols.). BAUMGARTNER, *die Schweiz in ihren Kämpfen und Umgestaltungen*, 1830-1850. L. MEYER VON KNONAU, *Lebenserinnerungen*. TILLIER, *Geschichte der Eidgenossenschaft während der Zeit des sogeheissenen Fortschritts*. FEDDERSEN, *Geschichte der schweiz. Regeneration*. BLUNTSCHLI, *Geschichte des schweiz. Bundesrechts*. BLUMER, *Handbuch des schweiz. Bundesstaatsrechts*. J. MEYER, *Geschichte des schweiz. Bundesrechtes* (2 vols).

of constitution. In Thurgau Pastor Bornhauser, of Matzingen, proclaimed the rosy dawn of a new day with enthusiasm, and appealed to his hearers to better the constitution. The first popular assembly in Weinfelden (22nd October) voted for a total revision, and a second at the same place, on November 18th, required direct popular elections of new officials and publicity of discussions. The council of Burgdorf, headed by the brothers Ludwig Schnell, town clerk, and Karl Schnell, barrister, demanded of the Bernese government a reform of the constitution (October); and in Porrentruy violent tumults took place, purporting to effect their separation from Berne. In Basle, too, the country district, led by Liestal, demanded full equality of rights with the town, and an assembly of delegates from the communes in Bubendorfer-Bade, on 18th November, required a revision of the constitution. A similar demand was made by an assembly at Olten, in Soleure. In Lucerne the exiled Professor Troxler fanned the flame by spreading broadcast through the land a pamphlet requiring full restoration of popular rights. A popular assembly at Sursee on 21st November espoused the same cause with one consent.

These efforts, however, did not mostly reach the goal at once; the aristocracies clung fast to existing conditions. The governments of Lucerne and Thurgau hesitated, the councils of Soleure and Basle resisted, and Berne actually made preparations to suppress all by the help of the military; and being the seat of government, even exhorted the members of the Federation by a public appeal to take measures against the movement. In this danger Zurich placed herself at the head of Swiss liberalism, rejected the suggestions of Berne, and aided the victory of freedom. Not altogether in vain had such men as Paul Usteri, Escher von der Linth, Hirzel the magistrate, J. J. Hottinger and Prof. J. C. Orelli been labouring for Liberal reform ever since about 1820. Even had the attempt been vain to improve the common system of schools, they had at least succeeded in abolishing the censure and arousing political thought.

There was still great uncertainty as to how to adjust the relative positions of the towns and the country districts; an assembly of councillors from the rural district held at Uster in October formulated very moderate demands as to the revision of constitution required by them, and still yielded precedence to the town in the matter of representation. It was reserved to a fugitive stranger from Nassau, Dr. Ludwig Snell,[1] to give the movement a wider aim. As a German professor he had taken part in the patriotic struggles for liberty of the years 1817–1820; but when these were frustrated he was driven out by the prevailing spirit of persecution, and finally banished to Switzerland, where he allied himself to the zealous partisans of reform, fought for the liberty of the press, and endeavoured specially to influence Zurich, which he looked upon as the intellectual head of the Confederation. At the time of the revolution in Paris he met with some of the most influential citizens of Zurich upon the Rigi; their narrow-minded views of the reforms to be undertaken induced him to try to convert Zurich to the principles of equality of rights for the citizens of every canton, the sovereignty of the people, and popular education. He wanted to establish "Constitutional Councils" (*Verfassungsräte*), and was the first to use this expression. Enlightened as to the general condition of things in the canton of Zurich by his interview with some of her citizens, he was made more intimately acquainted with the discontent and desires of the population around the lake of Zurich by his friend Dr. Streuli in Küssnach, and when pressed by Dr. Streuli to formulate their wishes publicly in a definite form, he drew up the "Memorial of Küssnach" in concert with the communal association of Küssnach, setting forth the programme of reform, which produced a great effect. According to this memorial, the country district was to elect by universal suffrage two-thirds of the 212 representatives in the great council, who should thus form the representatives of the sovereign people; the division of powers, publicity of administration, the abolition of the "Census,"[2] the

---

[1] *Dr. Ludwig Snell's Leben und Wirken*, Zurich, Meyer u. Zeller, 1858.
[2] Or limited suffrage. (*See* p. 242.)

right of petition and liberty of the press were further required. In order to work upon the Government by a popular public demonstration, an assembly in Stäfa summoned a popular assembly. At the latter, which took place on 22nd November, 1830, at Uster, 12,000 burghers were present. Jakob Gujer, of Bauma, opened the assembly, asserting its purpose to be to remodel the hitherto imperfect and insufficient constitution according to the needs of the people and the spirit of the time. Hegetschweiler, of Stäfa, recalled the words of Schiller:—

"Ye may dread the slave when his fetters break,
But in face of the Freeman never shake!"[1]

Steffan von Wädenswil spoke in favour of material alleviations and educational reforms. The assembly bore itself with gravity and dignity, and unanimously declared itself in favour of the wishes expressed, which were subsequently embodied in a new form as the "Memorial of Uster," and laid before the great council. This "Day of Uster" made a decisive impression; the government did not dare to defy the power of public opinion, and therefore, to meet the requirements of the assembly of Uster, ordered the immediate election of a new great council. Snell's scheme was taken as the basis of the deliberations upon the new constitution, and with this regeneration or transformation of public conditions a new era in the history of Zurich was introduced.

These events in Zurich made a powerful impression upon the rest of Switzerland, and turned the scale in favour of the Liberal cause. Fresh agitations immediately commenced in the other cantons. Morat, the active and Protestant German town in the canton of Fribourg, was the first to raise its voice against the existing constitution (25th November), and the great council hesitating, the exasperated populace rushed in arms upon the capital and extorted a revision, while the "*Landsturm*"[2] of the cantons of Aargau and Vaud forced the towns

[1] "*Vor dem Sklaven, welcher die Kette bricht,
Vor dem freien Manne erzittere nicht!*"
("Die Worte des Glaubens." Transl. by J. H. MERIVALE.)
[2] Local militia.

to yield (December). The excitement of the factions so wrought upon the governments of St. Gall and Lucerne that they could no longer remain passive. In St. Gall the revision was mooted by Jakob Baumgartner, the chancellor (*Staatsschreiber*), and the government hesitating (especially the Landammann Müller-Friedberg), various popular assemblies in Wattwil, Altstätten (5th December), and St. Gallenkappel,. demanded radical reforms, and the government yielded. The government of Lucerne, too, after fresh menaces, complied with the demands of the people by summoning a constitutional council (10th December). On 22nd December a popular assembly at Balsthal, in Soleure, where Joseph Munzinger proclaimed the sovereignty of the people in impassioned words, declared itself in favour of revision, and the *Landsturm* also bringing its threats to bear, the great council ceded the request.

§ 68. **Counter-attempts, and Cantonal Disturbances in Basle and Schwyz.** The greatest opposition to all Liberal efforts still continued at Berne, which was prepared to suppress the movement, and continued to encourage the other cantons to withstand the revision. The Bernese government had recourse to an extraordinary Diet, which assembled on the 23rd of December, in order to consult upon the military measures to be taken on account of the menacing danger of a war in France and Germany; and the government endeavoured to further the cause of reaction by requiring the Diet to interpose in favour of former conditions. Zurich, however, the head of Liberalism, entered an energetic protest against the placing of any hindrance in the way of the efforts of the cantons for the improvement of their constitutions, alleging that only the speedy and unhindered completion of the work could secure peace at home, and that combined warlike measures were out of place except in the case of attacks from without. This view was upheld by those cantons where the revolution was either completed or already in train; and hence, to the great dissatisfaction of the foreign powers, the Diet decided to preserve unanimously with life and property a strict neutrality towards the storm and strife of other lands, but not to interfere in any way with the constitutional reforms of the cantons. This served as a distinct warning for Berne, and while the revolutionary movement was encouraged, the Bernese government realised that its power was shattered. A popular assembly conducted by the brothers Schnell at Münsingen (10th January, 1831), threatened violent action if a constitutional council were not summoned and the sovereignty of the people acknowledged, upon which the great council yielded.

Thus hopes were everywhere aroused that the reform might be peaceably accomplished; but in Basle it was less successful. Here the great council obstinately maintained the precedence of the town; the country-folk, however, adhered with equal firmness to their radical demands. On 4th January, 1831, a popular assembly at Liestal protested, and determined to establish a separate government, which actually came to pass. The town, exasperated, made military preparations, and a battle ensued. The townspeople got the start of the country-folk, and gained the victory; the insurgents were dispersed, Liestal received a military occupation, and the rural district was completely subjugated (13th-15th January, 1831). A Federal deputation established a hollow peace in the town's favour, making the representation of the latter almost equal to that of the rural district (the country seventy-nine, the town seventy-five). This defeat of the country-folk of Basle, however, appealed to all the Liberals of Switzerland to throw themselves into the struggle, and a plan was formed for a great popular expedition of riflemen against Basle; but this, happily, was not carried into execution.

In the course of the year 1831 constitutional councils met almost everywhere, and in the first half of the year the constitutions of Soleure, Aargau, Zurich, St. Gall, Thurgau, the Vaud, Schaffhausen and Berne (partially) were successively accepted by a splendid majority of the people. So much the less could the country people in the canton of Basle now be pacified.

The town refused to grant an unconditional amnesty; the civil war broke out afresh, and the two districts actually confronted one another as two states with separate governments. The town of Basle, however, refusing all concessions, the calm was but temporary. After repeated excesses had been committed by the country-folk in August, 1831, the town undertook a second expedition, which, however, failed, and led to a complete separation (February, 1832). Only after a third encounter, which took place at Gelterkinden on 6th and 7th April, and again proved disastrous for the town, and after the failure of repeated efforts at mediation, did the Diet at length resolve, on 14th September, 1832, upon a division of the canton into two parts—the town with the twenty-one communes which still adhered to it, and the rural district with forty-six communes,[1] while in twelve other communes the separation had still to be put to the vote. Similar disturbances agitated the canton of Schwyz. Here also a separation took place, but it proved only temporary. In April, 1832, the "outer districts," that is to say, the purchased or conquered portions, which were in many ways at a disadvantage compared to the old original communes of Schwyz, and enjoyed fewer privileges, separated themselves, and became the "outer country," consisting of the districts of March, Einsiedeln, Pfäffikon and (later) Küssnach, under the direction of Lachen, and received the assent of the Diet.

As in the case of the town and rural districts of Basle, and the inner and outer lands of Schwyz, so Upper and Lower Valais threatened to separate, the former still refusing to abandon all supremacy over the latter. But the attempt at separation made by the Lower Valais was frustrated by Federal troops.

A violent conflict took place in monarchical Neuchâtel. A republican faction there desired to be separated from Prussia, and in September, 1831, endeavoured to accomplish their end by force, but without success. A second outbreak in December

[1] These two halves, forming one canton, are known as Baselstadt (the town of Basle), and Baselland (the rural district of Basle).—E. S.

resulted in the defeat of the Republicans; the Prussian faction gained the upper hand, and in 1832 urged a separation from Switzerland.

During these disturbances in Basle, Schwyz and Neuchâtel the revision of the cantonal constitutions was brought to a conclusion. The cantons of Geneva, the Grisons, Unterwalden, Uri and Zug remained comparatively undisturbed, and made no changes in their constitutions; some, like Geneva and the Grisons, because no pressing grievances presented themselves; others, because a powerful and predominant faction, chiefly clerical, nipped every innovation in the bud. But wherever new constitutions were introduced, the sovereignty of the people and equality of rights were accepted as first principles.

In all parts great stress was now laid upon the political representation of the people, which was no longer regulated by the government, but on the contrary exercised a species of control over that body. Baselland and St. Gall even introduced the veto. All the constitutions alike established publicity of administration, the publication of the debates of the great council and of judicial affairs, and a proportionate division of the public burdens, and endeavoured to institute more liberal communal regulations. Liberty of the press and of assembly, the right of petition, liberty of trade, and free choice of residence were guaranteed. Finally, a fundamental improvement of the educational system was projected.

But the constitutions of all the different cantons did not carry these principles into execution with equal thoroughness. Many towns, such as Lucerne, Zurich, Schaffhausen, Soleure and St. Gall still possessed certain privileges in the way of representation, and in most cantons the system of direct election was not immediately introduced, but a mixed system, and in Fribourg and Berne the elections were indirect only. In like manner the three powers were not at first equally sharply defined in all the cantons, nor religious liberty fully established; for instance, in Lucerne the franchise was only extended to Catholics, and in Fribourg the suffrage was withdrawn from those undergoing ecclesiastical penance. Thus in most of the cantons only a stage of transition had been reached, in which preparations could be made for the gradual expansion of the constitution with progressive experience, for all the constitutions provided for a future revision, and that at no very distant date in many cases.

§ 69. **The Question of Federal Revision, the League of the Seven Cantons** (*Siebner-Konkordat*), **and the League of Sarnen.** From the very beginning of these cantonal reforms efforts had been made to carry reform into the sphere of the Federal constitution. All noble spirits were once more inspired by the beautiful dream of those Swiss patriots of the middle of the previous century. (*See* p. 198.) That which had been exaggerated by the Helvetic Constitution and lightly discarded by the Restoration, seemed now capable of realisation: national unity, the creation of a united and strong political system in Switzerland. Under the Restoration, Zschokke had specially urged the necessity of strengthening the Federal authority, which was also advocated by Paul Usteri in Zurich during the tumults of 1830. Then, in January, 1831, when the Diet removed to Lucerne, Dr. Kasimir Pfyffer in eloquent words encouraged his native town to move the revision of the Confederation, complained that the people were not represented in the Confederation, and required that the lax political league should be converted into a firm Federal state with national institutions. The idea was eagerly discussed first of all in the Helvetic Society, of which Pfyffer was president; Dr. Ludwig Keller in Zurich, Landammann Sidler in Zug, and Joseph Munzinger in Soleure allied themselves with Pfyffer for the purpose of preparing the soil for a revision of the Confederation.

On 25th May, 1831, the government of Thurgau gave official expression to this demand by moving a revision of the Federal Pact of 1815 in an address to the capital. The Diet, indeed, received the suggestion coldly, but it was loudly echoed by public opinion. In September, 1831, a Swiss Rifle Association was started throughout the country with a view to paving the way for Federal revision. Almost immediately afterwards, on 17th March, 1832, the seven Liberal cantons of Lucerne, Zurich, Berne, Soleure, St. Gall, Aargau and Thurgau formed an alliance for the mutual security of their new constitutions, and for the carrying out of Federal reform (*Siebnerkonkordat*). This was done in self-defence, but it had very bad results. An address in favour of revision, with almost 10,000 votes attached, was forwarded to the Diet. The latter finally yielded by passing a resolution in favour of revision on 17th July, 1832, and appointing a commission to draw up a scheme. After wearisome discussions, the commission acquitted itself of its task by the following December. Its work was essentially the product of the predominating faction in the commission, the so-called *juste-milieu* party, the advocates of a middle course, who only desired a partial improvement of existing conditions; hence it was but a patchwork of half-measures, which satisfied no one.

Many among the Liberals were against the scheme, because it did not go far enough (especially in the matter of popular representation); the more so as the propositions of the commission were afterwards still further curtailed at the conference of the Diet. Among the adherents of the old *régime*, on the other hand, the efforts of centralization aroused the alarm of their old bugbear, the united Helvetic State, and at last most of the cantons absolutely declined to cede in the interests of the whole community any of the rights and privileges which they had hitherto enjoyed.

Unfortunately, too, foreign influence was brought to bear upon the matter. After the leading powers, Prussia and Austria, had introduced the most complete reaction into Germany, and suppressed the revolutionary movements, they turned their attention to the efforts for reform which were being made in Switzerland, and used all their influence in favour of the maintenance of the Federal Pact of 1815. Thus encouraged, the delegates of the six states of Basle, Uri, Schwyz, Unterwalden, Valais and Neuchâtel assembled at Sarnen on 14th November, and at once announced their opposition to the division of Basle, and to the admission to the Diet of delegates from the rural district of Basle and from Outer Schwyz, such divisions being a breach of the League. They hoped thus to bring the whole matter of Federal revision to the ground at once; then, relying upon foreign powers, they sedulously opposed the scheme at the Federal Diet, and poured their scorn upon the *Ochsenbüchlein*, or "Little Book of Ochs," and upon the *Kasimirfütterung*,[1] or "cashmere lining" of the Federal shepherd's shirt.

Finally, they assembled a special Diet at Schwyz, and there formed a formal *Sonderbund*, or separate League. The Diet of Zurich held its ground, and in April decreed also the division of Schwyz. But in July, 1833, there being no enthusiasm in any party in favour of the Federal constitution, it was rejected by popular vote. This gave the signal for a fresh reaction. Disregarding the decision of the Diet concerning the separation of Schwyz, Colonel Abyberg, one of the chief leaders of the leaguers of Sarnen, summoned by the distressed Conservatives, advanced with troops from Schwyz upon Küssnach, and occupied it (31st July, 1833). This open defiance of the Federal authority aroused an immense sensation, and had the effect of an evil example upon the already strained relations between the half-cantons of Basle. Under pressure from the Conservatives, Colonel Vischer advanced upon Liestal with troops and artillery, in order to protect the adherents of the town in the country, but was repulsed on 3rd August in a sanguinary battle on the heights of Pratteln. The Diet thereupon declared both proceedings to be a breach of the Federal League, and sent military forces and commissioners into both cantons: the members of the League of Sarnen evacuated Schwyz, and the Diet, maintaining its position with energy, decreed the dissolution of the League of Sarnen; whereupon most of the emissaries forming the conference of Sarnen resumed their places in the Diet.

The disturbances in Basle and Schwyz, and also in Neuchâtel,

[1] The first an allusion to the Helvetic Constitution drawn up by Ochs in 1798, the second to the appeal of Dr. Kasimir Pfyffer.

were happily settled for the moment. In Schwyz a reunion of the two parts was effected; in Basle a fresh partition was made, by which Baselstadt kept only the three communes of Riehen, Bettingen and Klein-Hüningen. Federal revision, however, was frustrated for a long time to come. Zurich made one more effort in its favour, and urged the establishment of a Swiss constitutional council; the Swiss National Society was also formed from within the circle of the already-existing Rifle Association, for the purpose of founding a united national state; the whole was, however, frustrated by the obstinate resistance of the inner cantons, the absolutely antagonistic views of the others, and above all by the serious conflicts and complications with other countries concerning the matter of fugitives such as Mazzini, Snell, Conseil and Louis Napoleon, 1834–1838.

§ 70. **The Fruits of Regeneration.** Meanwhile some compensation was afforded for the frustration of the Federal revision by the manifold reorganization in the internal conditions of individual cantons—the best preparation for the future progress of the whole. In 1834 Outer Rhodes of Appenzell accepted the very constitutional revision which had been rejected a year previously; Schaffhausen extended the franchise in the country district; subsequently in 1837 and 1838 Zurich swept away the last barrier between town and country, and established absolutely equal popular representation; in 1836 the principle of perfect equality of rights and the separation of powers was realised by the revision of Glarus, where the educational system was improved in most exemplary fashion. Thurgau abolished the institution of a separate ecclesiastical jurisdiction. Encouraging reforms also met with success in other spheres, specially in the educational system, in which the time had come for a fundamental and universal reorganization. All ranks were affected by it, from the highest to the lowest, and in many states the authorities, people and professors alike were seized with a veritable enthusiasm for the improvement of the methods of instruction.

S

A beginning was made by the foundation of seminaries for teachers that should train a body of efficient teachers, as in Zurich (at Küssnach in 1832, under the direction of Dr. Thomas Scherr), in Thurgau (at Kreuzlingen in 1833, under Wehrli), in Berne (at Münchenbuchsee in 1833), in Soleure, the Vaud, &c. The inspection of schools was made obligatory, scholastic institutions were carefully classified and comprised in one organic whole; while new subjects were taken up (especially the exact and historical sciences), new methods of teaching were invented, and the modern principles of education of Pestalozzi, Fellenberg, &c., were introduced. In Zurich the Director of the Seminary, Dr. Thomas Scherr (chosen for this high office by the Liberal leaders, Melchior Hirzel the burgomaster, Dr. Keller, &c.), was the soul of every effort connected with popular education; he also organized a system of popular schools, which became the model for other cantons, and likewise introduced the modern appliances for teaching in popular schools. On the other hand the noble-spirited Professor von Orelli devoted all his powers to the erection of the cantonal school and the formation of a university in 1832. This example was followed by Berne, where a cantonal school and a university were established in 1833.

In ecclesiastical matters the Liberal tendency was specially evinced in the Catholic cantons. Thus in Rapperswil two liberal-minded ecclesiastics, Alois Fuchs and Christopher Fuchs, laboured to emancipate the church from the Roman yoke; and through the exertions of the Pfyffer family Lucerne became the starting-point of a Liberal-Catholic propaganda. A conference held in 1834 at Baden of delegates from Lucerne, Berne, Soleure, Baselland, St. Gall, Aargau and Thurgau, emphatically declared itself against the pretensions of the papal court, and in favour of the erection of a Swiss archbishopric, and passed a resolution to resist the interference of the nuncio within the episcopal jurisdiction, to exercise political control over all ecclesiastical arrangements, and in general to place restrictions upon the spiritual jurisdiction.

It was next desired to deprive the religious houses of the right of self-government, to place them under episcopal jurisdiction, and compel them to pay taxes. A diminution in the number of *fête* days was likewise decided upon, and a desire expressed for the abolition of the nunciature. The papal court strained every nerve to withstand these radical proceedings; in the Bernese Jura a tumult was raised by the Ultramontanists or advocates of the papal rights, and the foreign powers also interposed in favour of the hierarchy, so that the resolutions could not be carried into effect. Nevertheless they bore some fruit, for thenceforward several governments adopted a more energetic attitude towards the pretensions of Rome, and afforded more powerful support to the principle of toleration. The first result was that the religious houses of Aargau were placed under state supervision; St. Gall proceeded to abolish the monastery of Pfäffers; Berne, however, only succeeded in quelling the tumults in the Jura by force.

Traffic was also included in the universal reform, a fine network of roads being constructed; the commercial system was improved, and the whole range of intellectual and material culture entered upon a stage of brilliant development.

2. THE STRUGGLES BETWEEN RADICALS AND CONSERVATIVES. ESTABLISHMENT OF THE MODERN FEDERAL STATE.

(1839–1848.)

§ 71. **The First Storms of Reaction, notably in Zurich and Lucerne.** United as the Liberal party had been in 1829 and 1830 in favour of progress, in the course of events the Radical branch broke loose from them, desiring to carry innovations much further. In opposition to both stood the Conservative or reactionary party, which, though defeated, was by no means annihilated; on the contrary, the more eagerly the Radicals advanced, the more impetuous, reckless, and violent their proceedings, the more they rode rough-shod over the will of the people, so much the more ground did the Conservatives gain in public opinion. By these proceedings of the extreme factions the tension was brought to a crisis, while at the same time questions of an ecclesiastical nature came to the fore and inflamed men's minds.

The Conservatives regained their ascendency first in Schwyz. In 1834 their leader and chief, Abyberg, became Landammann, and in 1836 the Jesuits were summoned to Schwyz by his direction. The Liberal party under old Landammann Reding opposed this proceeding; a dispute about the partition and appropriations of the estates of the "Allmend"[1] still further embittered both parties (the "Klauenmänner" and "Hornmänner"),[2] and at the *Landsgemeinde* at Rothenthurm in 1838 a riot took place, in consequence of which the country district was disarmed by order of Lucerne, the capital. But the matter being left in suspense, the predominant "Horn" party gained the day, and Abyberg remained Landammann.

Far more attention was aroused by the victory of reaction in Zurich. Here Liberalism seemed to have taken deeper root than anywhere else; yet it exhibited distinctly Radical tendencies, and filled not only the adherents of the old *régime*, but even the moderate party, with fears which were only too well grounded. In a very short space of time an entirely new and exemplary system of education had been brought into being; the criminal jurisdiction, military system, and divers other branches of the adminstration completely reorganized.[3] But these reforms being often harshly and inconsiderately carried out, a silent discontent began gradually to prevail on all sides. The older generation followed the rapid advance of the younger most unwillingly, while many interests were injured and many wishes left unfulfilled. As early as 1832 a reaction was threatened, and the anniversary of the "Day of Uster" was disturbed by exasperated artisans setting fire to a large factory

---

[1] *See* p. 34.

[2] The party of the "Horn-men," so called because they drove horned cattle to pasture, consisted of the rich aristocracy; while the "Claw-men," who could only drive small cattle, such as sheep and goats, to graze on the "Allmend," consisted of poor country-folk.

[3] WEISS, *Ein Beitrag zur Geschichte des 6 September*, 1839.

(*Usterbrand*). The greatest offence was given by the open endeavours of leading statesmen to emancipate the schools from the tutelage of the church and to annihilate orthodoxy. Actual insurrections took place when the "*Lehrmeister*" (a religious educational work), the catechism and the testament were abolished from the day schools and the educational appliances prepared by Scherr in accordance with modern Liberal ideas were introduced. Many considered the old faith of the church to be thereby seriously threatened, and the discontent was fanned by both laity and clergy belonging to the aristocratic families in Zurich, who hoped thus to bring the Radical government to the ground.

The government, however, and the Board of Education in particular, consisting of intellectually gifted advocates of progress, such as Melchior Hirzel, Ludwig Keller, Professor v. Orelli, Scherr, the director of the seminary, &c., rather carelessly neglected this opposition; and the chair of theology at the university becoming vacant, they hastily seized the opportunity to introduce the most extreme Liberal tendencies in theology into the highest institution in the state. They therefore summoned Dr. David Strauss, who in his "*Leben Jesu*" had applied the sharp knife of criticism to the narratives of the New Testament, had called many of them legends, and endeavoured to divest the person of Christ of its supernatural character. This abrupt act was naturally deemed a fresh outrage upon the church and Christianity; there was a simultaneous outcry throughout the land, and the majority of the clergy urged resistance. Addresses and petitions poured in against Strauss, against the Board of Education, the free-thinking seminary, and against the government; "Committees of Faith" were formed under the direction of Hürlimann-Landis, a manufacturer of Richterswil, who was on friendly terms with the aristocracy of the town, and open rebellion already threatened. The government next sought to allay the storm by pensioning off Strauss before he had so much as seen Zurich.

It soon became evident, however, that in many circles there

were other motives in close connection with the movement against Strauss, and what was really aimed at was the overthrow of the one-sided Radical system. Hürlimann-Landis, Dr. Rahn-Escher, and Spöndli the advocate, the leaders of the "Central Committee," had pressed their demands still further touching religious instruction, the seminary and the university, and their desires having been only partially satisfied by the government, a popular agitation was set in motion on 2nd September at the popular assembly at Kloten. The government still failing to comply, resistance was openly urged. The idle rumour, probably wilfully spread, that the government had summoned foreign troops, was all that was wanting to heighten the excitement to the utmost. In the night of 5th to 6th September Pastor Bernhard Hirzel, a learned but somewhat impulsive and ambitious man, had the alarm bell rung at Pfäffikon; the neighbouring communes immediately followed suit, and before dawn from the whole *Oberland* numberless armed hosts poured upon the town, while at the same time the storm broke out in other parts of the canton. This blow proved decisive; a small skirmish which took place on the cathedral square between the *Landsturm* and the troops of the government ended, indeed, in favour of the latter, but the government, timid and divided, resigned, and made room for a new Conservative party, formed of youthful members of the aristocracy, with Dr. Bluntschli at their head; a new, and, as it was popularly styled, "faithful" Board of Education was appointed, Scherr was forced to leave the seminary, and the Liberals had to bear the consequences of their indiscreet and premature proceedings for many a year. Zurich withdrew from the League of the Seven Cantons (*Siebnerkonkordat*).

These proceedings on the part of Zurich, the place which had hitherto led the van in the Liberal movement, gave rise to a succession of tumults, particularly as Zurich was at that time the capital. The first symptoms appeared in Valais. The Diet had previously expressly established the unity of this canton under a Liberal constitution: Upper Valais, however, offered resistance, and accomplished a fresh separation. The Diet remaining inactive, war broke out. In March, 1840, the troops of Lower Valais subdued Upper Valais, dispersed the old government, and forced the state to acknowledge the Liberal constitution. Struggles in Ticino and Soleure led to similar victories on the side of the Liberals. In May, 1839, the Conservatives in Ticino regained the upper hand, and drove out the Radicals. The latter (Franscini, Luvini), strong in numbers in Lugano and Mendrisio, the southern portions of the canton, made their preparations, and the government showing unfair partiality, they marched with an armed force upon Bellinzona and Locarno, on 6th December, and set up a distinctly Liberal government. In Soleure, as in Zurich, the Conservatives formed committees on the occasion of the revision, arranged popular assemblies in 1840 in Mümliswil and Mariastein, and endeavoured to overturn the government. The latter, however, took most energetic steps, frustrated a rising, and enforced a Liberal constitution.

So much the greater, therefore, was the triumph of the victorious reaction in Lucerne. Two men here took the lead as champions of the Ultramontanists: Joseph Leu of Ebersol, a councillor, a well-to-do farmer, but illiterate and a strong partisan of the church, and Konstantin Siegwart-Müller, the chancellor (*Staatsschreiber*), who had formerly been a most zealous Radical in his political and religious views, but having taken fright at the triumph of the "faithful" in Zurich, changed his colours: with them was associated Bernhard Meyer, the *Staatsschreiber*. They conceived the prevailing system to be one which would undermine the Catholic faith, and demanded the repeal of the resolutions of Baden, the recall of the Jesuits, and a new democratic constitution. Rejected at first (November, 1839), the Conservatives here, too, formed a committee (the Committee of Russwil), and when, in January, 1841, votes were taken upon constitutional revision they were to a large extent successful; a new constitution favourable to the clergy was accepted, by which means Lucerne cut itself adrift both from Baden and from the League of the Seven Cantons, in order to subjugate itself to the dominion of a strictly ecclesiastical spirit.

§ 72. **The Questions of the Religious Houses, the Jesuits, and the Separate League** (*Sonderbund*). After the riots in Zurich ("*Züriputsch*") the reactionary party in Aargau began to bestir itself. The revision of the constitution coming under discussion, the Conservatives established the Committee of Buntzen, and in the popular assemblies of 1840 all sorts of ecclesiastical and democratic wishes were brought forward. The government party, however, succeeded in effecting the adoption of a Liberal constitution on 5th January, 1841. The Committee of Buntzen protested, whereupon the government proceeded to arrest some of them. This aroused an uproar in the Free Bailiwick; at the instigation of the monasteries, notably Muri, the *Landsturm* broke out, but was defeated on 11th January by the troops of the government. The Free Bailiwick was occupied. The energetic government then took a step which must have been regarded as a throwing down of the gauntlet to all Swiss Conservatives, for, at the suggestion of the passionately excited director of the seminary, Augustin Keller, the fatal resolution was adopted of the dissolution of the religious houses. A cry of indignation at this act of violence rang through the ranks of the Conservatives in Switzerland. The advocates of the monastic system protested, and appealed to the article concerning religious houses in the Federal Pact. (*See* p. 240.) The Diet, too, in April and July, denounced the decision of the government of Aargau as incompatible with the Federal constitution. Thus Aargau was forced to partially yield, and to re-establish some of the religious houses.

In the meantime a strong agitation was spreading throughout Switzerland. Demonstrations in favour of the government of Aargau were organized in all parts by the Radicals. In Zurich the situation was peculiarly altered. The Radical leaders and newspapers and the Liberal professors opposed the reaction with all their might, and succeeded in re-awakening the memory of the great day of Uster. In contrast to the "September government," a popular assembly at Schwamendingen, at which 20,000 men took part, voted for the hearty support of the government of Aargau (August, 1841); other cantons also followed suit, and the canton of Aargau having reinstated part of the religious houses, the majority of the states in August, 1843, declared themselves satisfied. But the cantons of Lucerne, Uri, Schwyz, Unterwalden, Zug, Fribourg and Valais, which were greatly under the influence of the clergy, entered a protest, held a special conference in 1843, and "for the defence of the outraged rights of Catholic Switzerland" concluded a *Sonderbund*, or Separate League, the second since 1832: it was almost entirely composed of the very same states which had concluded the Borromean League of former days. The remaining cantons made an attempt at intimidation by threatening a formal separation. Men's minds were not as yet, however, so far inflamed as not to shrink mutually from civil war, had not a second urgent matter been added to the monastic question, which drove the factions to war—this was the question of the Jesuits.

The Jesuits everywhere strenuously opposed the Liberal policy, and it was to their influence that the Liberals ascribed the fact that in one canton, viz., Valais, which had at first held a little aloof, a sanguinary strife afterwards ensued, and finally it definitely joined the *Sonderbund*. The inhabitants of Upper Valais yearned for satisfaction for the blow dealt them in 1840. Two associations confronted one another, the so-called "Young Switzerland" or Liberals, and "Old Switzerland" or Conservatives, and did their utmost to exasperate one another. Finally in May, 1844, through the fault of Lucerne, the capital, and its representative, Bernhard Meyer, who favoured the cause of Upper Valais, a pitched battle ensued at Trientbach, in which the Liberals were defeated with much slaughter, and a military occupation was established in Lower Valais.

Soon afterwards the prolonged efforts of Leu's party to obtain the recall of the Jesuits were at last successful. The

Liberals who endeavoured to avert this step were suppressed. The tide having now turned so completely in favour of Ultramontanism and reaction, the Swiss Liberal party rose to the occasion with energy. Fellenberg demanded that measures should be taken to emancipate Valais from the Jesuits, and Augustin Keller at the Diet painted in glowing colours the dangerous nature of that order, whose detestable principles and dependency upon Rome threatened to stifle all free republican feeling.

The Diet, however, would venture no step at this juncture, and on 24th October, 1844, the Jesuits were summoned to undertake the management of higher education in Zurich. Exasperated beyond endurance, the Liberals of Lucerne conceived the unfortunate idea of pushing their cause by force of arms, in conjunction with those of like views in the neighbouring cantons. A first attempt made on the 8th December, 1844, by insurrectionary troops from Aargau and Lucerne, to take the city by surprise and drive out the Jesuits, failed. Numerous popular assemblies, specially those of the cantons of Berne and Zurich, next proffered a unanimous request to the Diet that the Jesuits might be expelled and Federal revision once more taken in hand. A profound impression was made by a proclamation issued 26th January, 1845, by an assembly of 20,000 men at Unterstrass, near Zurich. The existing government in the Vaud was overturned by the *Landsturm*, and its place taken by Radicals. Thereupon Berne, Zurich, the Vaud and Aargau unanimously voted for the expulsion of the Jesuits, but it was still opposed by the majority of the states.

In Lucerne, however, the victorious Ultramontanists exercised an absolute reign of terror. Many of their opponents were forced to fly for refuge to the surrounding cantons. Every injunction of the Diet recommending moderation proving futile, revolutionary troops once more assembled, particularly from the cantons of Aargau, Baselland, Soleure and Berne, under the conduct of Colonels Ochsenbein of Nidau and Rothpletz of Aarau, in order to take possession of the town by the help of the fugitives from Lucerne; unity and discipline were, however, wanting, and time was wasted, so that the second insurrectionary expedition failed like the first (31st March, 1845). Lucerne, on the other hand, took the opportunity to proceed to still greater extremities. Dr. Steiger, the chief of the Liberals, was condemned to death, but succeeded in escaping to Zurich, and a considerable number were forced to undergo penal servitude. Subsequently, on 20th July, 1845, Joseph Leu was treacherously shot by a depraved wretch, who imagined himself to be thus rendering a service to the Liberals; this was the occasion of fresh executions, and hundreds of persons were imprisoned, among them Dr. Kasimir Pfyffer. In consequence of the victory over the insurrectionary troops, the other cantons which were in alliance with Lucerne were also much emboldened. In the summer of 1845 the *Sonderbund* having assumed a more definite form, the allies resolved to take unanimous measures against all attacks upon their sovereign and territorial rights, and established a council of war. This step was brought about by Siegwart-Müller, and was unquestionably a gross violation of the Confederation.

§ 73. **The War of the Sonderbund.**[1] During the triumph of reaction, the strength of the Liberal cause was silently increasing. The Liberal party in Zurich had completely regained their ascendency, the leaders of the "September system" (notably Bluntschli) had been forced to resign, and Dr. Furrer, a strong advocate of reform, was now at the head of the state. In Berne, where many Radicals had been elected in the great council, the government could no longer resist the demands of the people for the extension of the franchise and increase of their rights, and in July, 1846, a new Constitution was granted. At the head of the Liberal government, side by side with Ochsenbein, the insurrectionary leader, stood Niggeler and Stämpfli. Berne and Zurich were now become the mainstay of the Liberals in Switzerland.

[1] RUDOLF, *Geschichte der Ereignisse in der Schweiz seit 1841.* BURKLI, A., *Oberst Ed. Ziegler.* General G. H. DUFOUR, *der Sonderbundskrieg.* OCHSENBEIN, *General G. H. Dufour.* DR. KERN, *Souvenirs politiques.*

In the summer of 1846, however, when the attitude of the *Sonderbund* was discussed at the Diet, the votes of two states were wanting to procure a majority against that League and against the Jesuits, and it was not until the Radical party had prevailed in Geneva through the efforts of James Fazy, and until Baumgartner (who since 1839 had attached himself to the Conservatives) had been removed from St. Gall and a Liberal majority formed in that government, and thus those two states won over to the progressive party, that the latter lawfully obtained the ascendency.

At the Diet held at Berne on 5th July, 1847, President Ochsenbein, the leader of the insurrectionary troops, once again spoke with great eloquence upon the question of progress *versus* stability, whereupon the Diet decreed the dissolution of the *Sonderbund*. This decision was received with great rejoicing by the crowds surrounding the building where the Diet was assembled, and also by all the Liberals throughout Switzerland. National life had gained a great accession of strength even in the Diet, which next summoned up courage to issue a decree against the Jesuits, and appointed a commission to draw up a scheme of Federal revision based upon the former decree of July, 1832 (*see* p. 255).

The *Sonderbund*, however, still remained defiant, and, relying upon the sympathy of foreign powers, with whom it had entered into negotiations, prepared for war. After futile attempts at a peaceable accommodation, the Diet decided to put their decree into execution by force of arms, and after adjourning for some time in order to complete their instructions, they assembled for a final general session on 18th October amid the clash of arms. Even yet the delegates of the *Sonderbund* stubbornly persisted in their demands for the repeal of the decrees already issued, and the re-establishment of the religious houses, laying great stress upon what they considered their lawful rights and their just cause, and finally on October 29th they left the hall in violent excitement, led by Bernhard Meyer. The Diet completed the preparations already commenced, and chose Heinrich Dufour of Geneva for their general. They urged upon the Confederation the necessity of unity in the struggle against that faction which "had already in 1813 opened the doors to foreign armies, had refused to guarantee the Liberal constitutions of 1831, had been indefatigable in their machinations in the cause of reaction, stirred up revolts in the Jura and other parts of Switzerland, raised an Ultramontane sedition in Aargau, and recalled the Jesuits to Valais, Fribourg, Schwyz and Lucerne; and by whose triumph the country would gradually lose all those institutions upon which depended its true freedom, its intellectual development, its power and its honour."

The adherents of the *Sonderbund* placed their forces under the command of a Grison, General von Salis-Soglio, a man whose gifts were far inferior to those of General Dufour, a soldier trained in the school of the first Napoleon. The Liberals were also stronger in numbers than the Leaguers,[1] and the latter were at variance among themselves. Dufour, with admirable speed and discretion, immediately reduced Fribourg by a double attack, and on 14th November that state announced its secession from the separate League. He next ordered an attack upon Lucerne. The Leaguers had already achieved some small successes in Ticino and the Free Bailiwick. Dufour advanced swiftly upon Aargau, in order to give battle to the main army of the *Sonderbund*, then stationed near Gislikon and the Rooter Berg. Zug, being now completely surrounded, capitulated on 21st November. On the 23rd the main attack took place. The Leaguers had an excellent and almost impregnable position. Honau was taken after a violent struggle. At Gislikon the first attack proved unsuccessful; certain battalions were forced to give way, and it was only by the courageous personal interposition and advance of Colonels Egloff and Ziegler that the enemy was repulsed from the western side of the Rooter Berg. The Leaguers were simultaneously driven back from the eastern

---

[1] Dufour's army numbered (without the *Landsturm*) about 98,000 men, that of the leaguers 37,000, but the latter were joined by the *Landsturm* to the number of 47,000 men.

side at Meyerskappel after a short struggle, the issue of which was at first doubtful. Lucerne was besieged on all sides. The leaders of the *Sonderbund* fled, the town capitulated, and on 24th November the main body of the Federal army entered. The remaining cantons yielded and complied with the demands of the victors, Valais being the last to do so. The Jesuits were expelled, Liberal governments established, and the constitutions of the various cantons altered accordingly. Thus that for which men had been striving in the cantons ever since 1830 was now first fully attained.

§ 74. **The Modern Federal Constitution.** After the defeat of the *Sonderbund* and the revolution in the inner cantons, the one hindrance in the way of the long-desired Federal revision lay in the unfavourable disposition of the majority of the foreign powers, without whose consent the Federal Pact of 1815 could hardly be altered. Austria and France had already attempted to interpose in favour of the Leaguers during the war of the *Sonderbund*, and on the part of England alone had any support been bestowed upon the Liberals; a menacing note received from the powers was delayed by England (Palmerston) until the issue had been decided against the *Sonderbund*. Even after the close of the war, in January, 1848, France, Prussia and Austria interposed as advocates of the cantonal sovereignty in favour of the defeated states.

Now, however, it was not only too late, but also the needful vigour was wanting to give force to their advocacy, for in the course of the very next month of February the revolution ensued in Paris, which spread like wild-fire to the surrounding countries, overturned existing governments, and laid the foundations of modern political conditions. While this movement frustrated the intervention of the foreigner, it essentially assisted the already-commenced work of the reformation of the Swiss Federation, and gave a powerful impulse to the Liberal cause, particularly in Neuchâtel, where the Republicans, encouraged by the events in Paris, possessed themselves on March 1st of the capital and the castle, and introduced a new and Republican constitution; all of which Prussia was powerless to prevent.

The commission appointed for Federal revision now laboured zealously at the scheme. No one any longer doubted that the Swiss people, as such, must be duly represented in the Confederation, as had for years past been required and been manifestly needful. But opinions were divided as to the desirability of uniform national representation, and as to how far centralization should be put in practice. Finally a compromise was agreed upon midway between the national and cantonal principles, or between the two systems of unity and federation, such as had already been expressed in the constitution of "Mediation"; and for this purpose the constitution of the United States of America, with its system of two chambers, was taken as a model, as had already been recommended by Dr. Troxler and others between 1830 and 1840, and was now advocated by James Fazy and Munzinger of Soleure.

The work of the commission was brought to a close in April in accordance with these leading points of view. The following were the chief stipulations. Cantonal sovereignty was guaranteed, but restricted by a strong Federal authority. The Federation no longer merely aimed at maintaining the independence of their country towards the outer world, and preserving peace and order in the interior, but also endeavoured to support the liberties and rights of the Confederates, and to further their common welfare. Accordingly, the Federation alone has the right to declare war and make peace, to conclude alliances and political treaties, especially those relating to customs and commerce, with other countries. Particular alliances and treaties of a political nature between the several cantons are prohibited; official intercourse between the cantons and foreign countries is also placed under the supervision of the Federation, and in the case of violent disturbances in the cantons the Federation exercises the right of intervention. The following are guaranteed as inalienable rights of the

Swiss people: the equality of all men in the eye of the law, freedom of domicile, liberty of the press, religious liberty, and the rights of association and of petition. Federal affairs further include the customs, coinage and postal system, the settlement of weights and measures, and the disposal of the Federal army, formed out of contingents from the cantons. Finally, the Federation also received the right of erecting a university and a polytechnic, and in general to establish or cause to be established any public works in the interest of the Confederation, or of the greater part of it. Thus a formidable barrier was set up against all efforts at separation and individualism, and the foundation laid of a necessary unification of the powers.

The executive of the Federal authority was so organized that the legislative power was placed in the hands of two councils: the National Council (*Nationalrat*) as representing the Swiss people, and the Council of the States (*Ständerat*) as representing the cantons. In the former each representative is chosen by 20,000 Swiss citizens, in the latter every canton elects two representatives (every half-canton electing one). The decisions of both councils are determined by the majority of votes, but the agreement of the two councils is requisite to render their decisions valid. The highest executive and directing authority is that of the Federal Council, consisting of seven members elected by the Federal Assembly,[1] presided over by the President of the Confederation. For the administration of the law, so far as it falls within the province of the Confederation, a Federal tribunal was established. Thus the people was now represented in the Confederation, and had at the same time acquired its essential rights, assured by the Federation: the foundation was laid of a universal Swiss citizenship, though still hampered by many limitations. The guarantee of free movement in the interior was of the greatest importance for the advancement of industry and manufactures, giving facilities for settlement, greater freedom of buying and selling, the abolition of inland customs, and

[1] The National Council and the Council of the States combined.—E. S.

free entry, exit, and transit from one canton to another, though still encumbered by slight restrictions.

It is true that when the time came for this Federal constitution to be accepted, many were dissatisfied with what had been attained. While the inner cantons still cherished the idea of the old Confederation, the Radicals wanted absolutely uniform national representation, and a greater advance in the direction of centralization. They were of opinion that the Helvetic united government, universally detested as it had been under the circumstances then prevailing, had yet projected and initiated much that was good, and that in order to inculcate true Federal principles, not only must the restrictions yet remaining upon free intercourse and popular rights be removed, but also such matters as the educational, legal and military systems must be completely in the hands of the Federation. In general, however, the idea prevailed that it was better not to go too far, lest through any rashness everything should once more be called in question. Even the advocates of uniformity consoled themselves by the consideration of what had been already attained, which they regarded as a transition stage leading to further progress.

Therefore, on the 12th September, 1848, the constitution was accepted by the majority of the cantons and of the voters from among the people.[1] The firing of cannon proclaimed the splendid result, and beacon fires blazed upon the mountains. The Swiss people entered upon an entirely new epoch, the most important since the founding of the Confederation. The League, formerly so lax, instituted in times of danger for purposes of defence, and chiefly useful in time of war, had for ever given place to a permanent political system organized upon modern principles, having for its aim the advance of civilization in every respect, its strength and value depending solely upon the education and capacity for work of its people and upon the cultivation of humanity.

[1] 15½ cantons accepted, 6½ rejected it (including those of the Sonderbund, with the exception of Fribourg.) The people took a very feeble part in the voting, almost half absenting themselves. The result was 169,743 ayes to 71,899 noes.

PART III.

THE CONSOLIDATION OF THE FEDERAL STATE AND PROGRESS OF MODERN TIMES.
(1848-1874.)

§ 75. **Introduction of the Federal Constitution.**[1] Europe looked on in wonderment at this transformation. Switzerland had remained exempt from the cruel agitations and terrible convulsions of other states, and, thanks to Dufour's judicious conduct in the war and the dissolution of the *Sonderbund*, had passed the crisis speedily and safely, and without (or rather notwithstanding) foreign interference had procured for herself a popular constitution. Equally speedily and safely there now followed the introduction of the new constitution. On 22nd September, 1848, the Diet finally resigned, giving place to the new Federal Assembly. The latter then nominated Berne, the mediator between French and German Switzerland, to be the permanent Federal capital. The highest Federal offices were filled entirely by men who had rendered good service in the dissolution of the *Sonderbund* and the establishment of the constitution; Jonas Furrer of Winterthur was elected President of the Confederation, whose portrait even yet preserves in many a home the memory of the joyful transformation of the fatherland; while the Federal councillors were Druey of the Vaud, Munzinger of Soleure, Franscini of Ticino, Ochsenbein of Berne, Frei-Herosé of Aargau and Näff of St. Gall.

The next question was to find a suitable form by which to enforce the details of the Federal constitution, and specially those branches of the administration which had come into the hands of the Confederation. The establishment of a uniform postal system was a very simple matter; Switzerland was divided into postal districts, and taxes and tariffs were fixed in due proportion. "Brightly coloured

[1] Dr. P. C. v. PLANTA, *Die Schweiz in ihrer Entwicklung zum Einheitsstaate.*

stamps began to adorn the letters, while along all the high roads and over the cold heights of the Alpine passes rolled the large and roomy postal vans of the Confederation."[1] The newly-established telegraph system was next transferred to the Confederation in 1851, and electric wires passed from Berne throughout the whole of Switzerland.

Some disputes with regard to the railway system were terminated in 1852 by a decision in favour of leaving the construction of railways in private hands, and it was not until 1873 that the Confederation assumed the licensing and control of the railways.

The abolition of all restrictions upon commerce in the interior proceeded with some rapidity, and in some cantons there only remained the so-called *Ohmgelder*, duties paid upon the importation of wine, brandy, &c.

The establishment of a uniform system of coinage presented greater difficulties. All the various sorts of Swiss money, the *Doublon*, the *Bock*, the *Batz*, the *Schilling*, the *Angster*, &c., had to be called in and carefully exchanged; and after long discussion it was decided that the new Swiss coinage should follow the French decimal system, which predominated in the commercial world; and thenceforth all Swiss money, copper, nickel and silver, bore the Swiss arms with a wreath of oak leaves, or Helvetia enthroned, pointing to the mountains: gold coinage there was none, it being only introduced into Switzerland quite lately.

With the framing of the article about the rights of domicile it became necessary to establish some legal protection for mixed marriages, hitherto interdicted. It was now seen to be a violent infringement of the liberty of mankind that religious creed should remain any hindrance to marriage. A Radical party therefore arose among the Federal authorities, which insisted upon the abolition of this restriction, and passing beyond the letter of the Federal constitution, obtained in 1850 a Federal law for the protection of mixed marriages.

The article as to a Federal educational institution was at

[1] Henne-Amrhyn III. 503.

length carried into at least partial execution. It is true that the project of a Federal university was rejected by the Council of States, but on the other hand the proposition of a Federal polytechnic was accepted by the majority. Zurich was fixed upon as its seat, for this city not having been made the seat of the Federal government, it was thought to make amends by giving it the Federal academy. The institution was opened in 1855, and in 1864 took possession of the spacious edifice built by Zurich in the style of the Acropolis.

Such satisfactory developments gained more and more friends to the new order of things; the evil consequences predicted by the opposition party did not ensue, and many opponents were themselves forced to acknowledge the advantages of greater unity and freer motion. No sort of attempt was made to return to the old standpoint previous to 1848; on the contrary, the former opponents of Federal reform, as "Conservatives" or "Moderates," clung with all their might to the new constitution for protection against further innovations. The Radicals, on the other hand, to whom the new Confederation actually owed its existence, soon made a further forward movement, partly in order to obtain demands which had been put forward earlier but suppressed, and partly to open the way for further progress.

§ 76. **The Confederation tested by the Outer World. The Affair of Neuchâtel.**[1] The Conservative governments of other countries resented the rapid and fundamental changes in Switzerland; and when, during the revolutionary storms in the neighbouring countries in 1848 and 1849, fugitives once more involved Switzerland in difficulties, they made their irritation distinctly felt. Switzerland, however, preserved her neutrality as far as possible, and about 1855 it seemed as though the storm-clouds had quite passed away, when suddenly a formidable embarrassment was presented by the affair of Neuchâtel, such as had not been experienced since

[1] Dr. A. HIRZEL, *Die Schweiz seit 1848 in ihrer Stellung zum Auslande* (R. WEBER's *Helvetia Jahrang*, 5 and 6).

the wars of liberty and the invasion of the French. This territory, which had formerly (from 1406) been an allied state, had fallen to Prussia by inheritance in 1707, and in 1815 became a canton of Switzerland, with sovereign rights reserved to Prussia. Between 1830 and 1840 a republican party came to the fore, and the principality was convulsed by numerous revolutionary attempts. (*See* p. 252.) Shortly after the outbreak of the February revolution in Paris, however, by a revolution of the 1st March the Republicans declared the rights of Prussia extinct. When, therefore, the Confederation was reorganized, Neuchâtel was inserted among the states of the modern Confederation, without any formal reservation of the rights of Prussia.

For a long time the king of Prussia was hindered from paying any attention to Neuchâtel by the revolutions in his own country and the constitutional struggles in Germany; but afterwards, having in 1852 induced the powers to guarantee his rights in Neuchâtel, he encouraged the royalist party, which was in the minority, to resistance, and on 3rd September, 1856, the Royalists took possession of the castle, just as the Republicans had done in 1848. The Republicans of the mountain district immediately broke out, besieged the castle and took it. Most of the royalist leaders were taken prisoners.

Judicial proceedings were at once instituted by the Confederation against the instigators of the rebellion, and the canton was occupied by Federal troops. Prussia protested, and was supported by the great powers. The French Emperor Napoleon III. endeavoured to induce Switzerland to liberate the prisoners, and to give up all judicial proceedings, promising in return to prevail upon Prussia to abandon Neuchâtel. Switzerland, however, was anxious before all things to save her honour, and required first the renunciation of the Prussian king. To this Napoleon would not agree, and Prussia prepared for war, appointing the 2nd of January as the final date when the negotiations should terminate; should Switzerland by that time not have yielded, war would ensue. In Switzerland itself the entire population with unanimous enthusiasm proclaimed itself in favour of the Republicans of Neuchâtel, and awaited the war with heroic composure and an almost religious calm. All the cantons prepared without hesitation to assist the one in need, as though the cause had been their own. In December the Federal assembly ordered military preparations, and in a short time the whole of Switzerland was one great camp. Old and young hastened to the standards; members of the Polytechnic, students and gymnasts, practised drilling daily at the barracks; high and low vied with one another in willing self-surrender to their country; even the school-children, with touching enthusiasm, brought money, clothing and linen. By the beginning of January 30,000 men were already stationed on the northern frontier; the whole army under the command of Dufour numbered over 100,000 men. Meanwhile Prussia had been forced to defer putting her threats into execution; the states of southern Germany had, it is true, consented to give passage to the troops, but Austria kept Prussia at bay, and threw all sorts of obstacles in the way. Then on 8th January, 1857, at a conference held between the Swiss envoys (Barmann and Dr. Kern) and Napoleon III., a treaty was effected, by which Switzerland engaged to liberate the prisoners, but the latter were to remain in exile until the affair of Neuchâtel should be settled. The authorities accepted these proposals; this acceptance gave great umbrage to many of the people, but it was the only right thing to do. At a conference held in Paris, which lasted till the 20th April, the powers succeeded in inducing Prussia to renounce all rights of sovereignty in Neuchâtel in return for certain small concessions. Under the old Confederation such vigorous action would never have been possible, and thus the new Confederation stood its first test successfully.

It was again put to the proof, and came out no less brilliantly, throughout the course of the foreign relations during the ten years next ensuing. Switzerland now enjoyed a happy period of peace, which was particularly favourable to internal development. Whereas formerly, as a Confederation of states, she had completely followed in the wake of foreign powers, she now began with energy to evolve an independent national policy, and all parties united in maintaining Swiss independence.

Foreign military service was next abolished as unworthy of a free republican state. The Federal Constitution of 1848 had only prohibited the conclusion of any fresh engagements; in 1849, however, Naples having levied Swiss troops for the suppression of revolts in Lower Italy, the Radical party extorted a prohibition of levies; and in 1859, on the occasion of the Italian War, a formal prohibition was issued against the enlisting of Swiss soldiers in foreign mercenary armies, and thus the "traffic in Swiss blood," pursued for four centuries, was legally abolished.

Switzerland next found herself involved in troublesome disputes with France, but, thanks to the moderate and energetic attitude of the Federal Council, these were peaceably adjusted. These disputes arose as follows. Soon after the settlement of the question of Neuchâtel Napoleon III. engaged in some vexatious intrigues against Switzerland, because the latter, in consequence of the right of asylum conceded, had become a rallying-point for French refugees; he accused Switzerland of encouraging these disturbers of the peace, and punished her by restricting the freedom of traffic on the frontier (1858). Against this, however, the Federal Council warmly protested, and even succeeded in effecting a partial modification of the passport regulations. But in 1859 war broke out between Italy and Austria concerning Lombardy, and Napoleon engaged to help King Victor Emmanuel, receiving in return a promise of the surrender of Savoy. Switzerland was in the highest degree interested in this transaction, for by the Congress of Vienna the two provinces of northern Savoy, Faucigny and Chablais (which had been conquered by Berne in 1536, but had afterwards to be given back) were included in the Swiss neutrality, and to Switzerland had been granted the right of placing a military occupation in these territories in case of war. The Federal authorities therefore immediately instituted military measures for the protection of the southern frontier of the Confederation, and once more appointed Dufour as general; their precautions in favour of northern Savoy were to all appearances favourably received by Napoleon, but were practically quite disregarded. This gave rise to great indignation in Switzerland; various widely-spread societies, such as the "Helvetia" and "Grütli" societies, and numerous popular assemblies, openly advocated armed interference, and that with a view to the conquest of North Savoy. In the Federal council Dr. Stämpfli also advocated war. But in the Federal assembly the opinion prevailed that Switzerland had no right to the occupation of North Savoy, and that it would be sheer foolhardiness to provoke a war on that account. Napoleon caused the matter to be put to the vote in Savoy, and brought the influence of French agents to bear, and in June, 1860, he took possession of Savoy. The rest of the powers not daring to take any action against France, the situation remained unchanged, France undertaking to come to terms with Switzerland.

A simultaneous dispute with France about the Dappental terminated more successfully for Switzerland. This territory had been annexed by France during the time of the "Mediation," but restored to Switzerland by the Congress of Vienna. France, however, had never vacated it, but still kept a military occupation there, and otherwise infringed the territorial rights of the Swiss. Switzerland therefore demanded definite satisfaction, and finally in 1862 effected a peaceable division of the territory, France being at the same time forced to promise to erect no fortress there and levy no customs.

Switzerland remained thenceforth unmolested, and when danger threatened was able to set it aside by a determined and forcible attitude, and to make her position honoured and respected by the outer world. In earlier times, since the Reformation, neutrality had been a necessity on account of internal dissensions and instability; now, however, it was consciously embraced as the noblest attitude, and the one most worthy of a popular Republic: and whereas it had been formerly either carelessly preserved or not maintained at all, now all parties united to defend it, and Switzerland moreover possessed an efficient military force for the purpose. This was shown during the wars between Prussia and Austria in 1866, and between Germany and France in 1870–1871. During the former their chief concern was to cover the south-east frontier; the Münstertal in the Grisons was occupied by Federal troops, and preparations were made for a levy of the whole Federal army; but the speedy termination put to the war by Prussia made further proceedings unnecessary. During the Franco-German war Switzerland was still more exposed, for it was easily possible for either of the two powers to use her as a bridge, and she had reason to fear a fate similar to that of the coalition period.

The whole of Switzerland, therefore, as well as the foreign powers, heard with rejoicing the proclamation of the Federal Council that an armed neutrality would be strictly preserved under all circumstances. Colonel Herzog of Aargau was appointed general by the Federal Assembly, and with the greatest rapidity a body of about 50,000 men was placed on the western and northern frontiers, to repel any attack which might be made upon Switzerland. Only the fugitive army of Bourbaki, of 80,000 men, passed the frontier, and was disarmed (February, 1871), that it might be sheltered in the country; Switzerland exercised her right of hospitality in friendly fashion, and was indefatigable in rendering aid and nursing the wounded. The storm which shook the neighbouring lands to their foundations was once more happily averted by Switzerland. Meanwhile, in both these perils of war of 1866 and 1870–1871, Switzerland recognised the serious defects of her somewhat neglected military system, and saw that it was only by keeping pace with foreign powers in the improvement of arms and tactics, and only by the possession of an army which should be as far as possible uniform in discipline, that she could feel secure against all attempts from without.

No party any longer maintained that Switzerland should play an independent part in foreign wars, as she had done in the fifteenth century. Rather is it characteristic that all should have united in recognising that the one and only task for Switzerland should be to secure the blessings of peace to herself, and to labour also in the cause of peace for other lands.

A succession of treaties and transactions between Switzerland and other countries from 1860 to 1880 testify to the carrying out of this idea. Thus in 1864 the "Convention of Geneva" was called into existence by Switzerland, by which the powers bound themselves to improve the condition of the soldiers wounded in war (the "Red Cross League"). In 1865 Switzerland formed the centre of a European telegraph treaty, later (in 1874 and 1878) of the postal system (International Postal Union).

In 1872 she came once more to the fore, in order to settle by arbitration a dispute which had arisen between England and North America about the steam vessel *Alabama*, constructed in England for the Southern States, which did great damage to the United States during the civil war (*Alabama* arbitration tribunal in Geneva, where Dr. Stämpfli represented Switzerland).

This attitude of Switzerland, this her task of becoming the promoter and the centre of the interests of international civilization, finds its noblest and most distinct expression in the undertaking of the St. Gotthard railway, which, initiated by Switzerland, was rendered possible by the assistance of Italy and Germany (1869 and 1871), the direction of the work being entrusted to Switzerland. The Federal Council took up a position far above all cantonal interests, which were in favour of other lines, and decreed for this highly important international work, in subsidies, the sum of twenty million francs.

1848-1874] *Establishment of the Federal State.* 283

§ 77. **Cantonal Reforms and the Federal Revision of 1874.**[1] After the introduction of the new Federation it became specially necessary for the several cantons to guard their Liberal institutions, since Switzerland also suffered from the influence of the general European reaction which set in after 1848, and threatened manifold injury to the fine achievements of the past. In Berne the Radical government, with Stämpfli at its head, was forced to make room for the Conservatives in 1850; the latter attacked the training school for teachers in Münchenbuchsee, which was managed on principles too liberal for the people, and expelled its director, Grunholzer of Zurich, thus imitating the proceedings of the September government in Zurich. In St. Gall the Ultramontanists violently opposed every constitutional revision, and specially directed their attacks against the cantonal school founded in 1856. The Liberal government of Fribourg, which had been appointed by the Federation in 1847, could find no firm footing. During the years 1848 to 1853 no fewer than four Ultramontane riots ("*Putsche*") followed one another in quick succession, under Carrard, Wuilleret and Perrier, which finally, in 1857, led to the victory of reaction; in consequence of which the religious houses and the educational system favourable to the Jesuits were again restored, and more privileges were bestowed upon the bishops and clergy.

In the face of these events the Liberals of Switzerland roused themselves to make a desperate effort; the need of closer union began to be realised, and hence in October, 1858, the men's society, called "Helvetia," was formed in Langenthal, which took for its object a war of progress against Ultramontanism and reaction, for the elevation of Swiss intellectual and social life, and which for a time exhibited great activity. Meanwhile the general tendency of the public mind was moving forwards, and by about 1860 much progress had already been

---

[1] CURTI, *Geschichte der schweizerischen Volksgesetzgebung.* BLUMER, *Handbuch der Geschichte des schweizerischen Bundesstaatsrechts.* DUBS, *Das öffentliche Recht der Eidgenossenschaft.* A. V. ORELLI, *Das Staatsrecht der schweizerischen Eidgenossenschaft.*

made in cantonal affairs. Thus fundamental changes, both internal and external, were brought about in Geneva by the great popular leader James Fazy. In Soleure the popular party under Landammann Wilhelm Vigier extended the rights of the people and promoted education and culture. Almost all the cantons revised their constitutions with a view to the increase and improvement of popular rights. In St. Gall, too, the Liberals now prevailed, and in 1861 inserted in their constitution the election of the great council according to political instead of communal divisions, the direction of the educational system by the state, mutual independence of the creeds in ecclesiastical affairs, an improved veto and the like. In 1863 the numerous Jews in Aargau received the rights of citizens.

The years 1860–1880 brought fundamental changes in political life. The Liberal governments, which had given a violent impetus to trade and industry, seemed to concern themselves rather with the interests of the higher classes, and to trouble themselves less about the wishes and interests of the people. Moreover, they consistently held fast to the principles of representative constitutions, and opposed all demands for an extension of the part taken by the people in legislation in the form of the Veto, the Referendum, and the Initiative.

Moreover fresh needs began to arise, both agricultural and social. The peasantry and artisan class being seen to be starving and in want, improvements in the material conditions of the people were demanded, such as the alleviation of military duty, the abolition of school fees, the reduction of the price of salt, equal division of taxes, the establishment of cantonal banks, the enlargement of the popular schools, the erection of technical and secondary schools, &c.

A Democratic party was thus formed almost everywhere, which endeavoured to thrust aside the representative system, and to comply with these popular requirements. A succession of great constitutional changes ensued. Baselland took the lead in 1863; here the Democratic party gained the day, under

Christoph Rolle, and carried the compulsory Referendum, the Initiative, the election of the government by the people, &c. Zurich next followed. After making many futile attacks upon the so-called "system" then existing under the auspices of Alfred Escher, the people was at length aroused in 1867. The leaders (Bleuler, Zangger, &c.) determined to organize four great *Landsgemeinden* in Zurich, Uster, Winterthur and Bülach on 15th December. Between 26,000 and 27,000 signatures were given in favour of revision. The people accepted it by 50,000 votes against 7,300, and in 1869 a Constitutional Council drew up a new constitution, with the Referendum, Initiative, free education, a cantonal bank, free military outfits, abolition of the holding of offices for life, &c.

In the same year revisions were adopted in the cantons of Thurgau (where the influence of Fürsprech Häberlin was undermined, and a popular union under the direction of Sulzberger, Deucher, Anderwert and others, set the revision in motion), Berne, Soleure and Lucerne, and in 1870 in Canton Aargau.

After the Federal revision of 1874 a number of cantons, being forced to alter their constitutions, proceeded to introduce the Initiative or Referendum, or both together—Baselstadt in 1875, Schaffhausen in 1876, Geneva in 1881, Neuchâtel in 1882, and Ticino in 1883. Counting the *Landsgemeinde* cantons,[1] there are in all twenty-four cantons which allow the people a share in the legislation in one form or another; one canton only—that of Fribourg—still adheres to the representative system. This introduction of the popular state and popular government forms a distinctive feature of the home policy of this country.

As had been the case between 1830 and 1840, so again now progress in the cantons was followed by further efforts for Federal reorganization. It was not only required that the Federation should be made more uniform, and greater centralization effected in those departments where experience

[1] Uri, Unterwalden (Obwalden and Nidwalden), Appenzell (Innerrhoden and Ausserrhoden) and Glarus.—E. S.

had proved it to be necessary, but a desire was also expressed that the democratic principles already established in several cantons (the Veto, Referendum and Initiative) should be adopted by the Federation. A first and partial attempt was made in 1866, when, on the occasion of a commercial treaty with France, it was desired to expand the articles on the subjects of domicile and trade. But at the voting all the proposals contained in nine articles were rejected, with the exception of one which concerned the commercial treaty, namely, the one guaranteeing to the Jews rights of domicile equal to those of Christians.

Soon, however, further needs made themselves felt, notably at the time of the Franco-German war, when the modern German empire came into existence, and the absolute necessity of a uniform organization in the army and in the legal system became evident. From the year 1869 onwards various circumstances had conspired to smooth the way for a fundamental reformation, and hence in 1872 a total revision was effected. The deliberations of the Federal authorities resulted in the drawing up of an entirely new Federal Constitution, which in every way fulfilled the wishes of the Progressive, Centralist, and Democratic party: there was to be but *one* army and *one* law, and the Referendum and Initiative in the Federation itself were to be guaranteed to the people. But just on account of its extreme tendency the scheme met with violent opposition, and was rejected when put to the vote.

This, however, by no means brought matters to a standstill. On the contrary, almost half the voters (about 250,000) having agreed to this new scheme, men took courage, and redoubled their exertions. Societies uniting the Swiss of all parts had already often carried the day in progressive questions; similar methods were now once more adopted, and at a popular assembly held at Soleure on 15th June, 1873, at which Augustin Keller spoke, a *Volksverein* (Popular Association) was founded, which, being taken up with enthusiasm, united the Swiss of all parties and of every tongue under the banner of revision, and cleared the way boldly in all directions.

The struggle against the ascendency of the church in the state (the so-called *Kulturkampf*), which exerted no small influence upon the cause of revision, broke out simultaneously in Germany and in Switzerland. The Catholic Church was making violent efforts to reassert her power. By the publication of the papal "Syllabus" (the condemnation of all modern institutions), and of the dogma of the infallibility of the Pope (1870), the Ultramontane party exasperated the Liberals throughout the country. The governments hastily resolved not to acknowledge the new doctrine, involving as it did a certain amount of danger to the state; and even among the Catholics themselves it met with some opposition: communities were formed of "Old Catholics," who adhered to the old position, before the publication of the papal infallibility, and these were protected by the state (communities of Christian Catholics, under Bishop Herzog).

This question was taken up with special earnestness by the Catholics of Switzerland. With great rigour, here and there even with harshness, the authorities defended their rights against all intended encroachments. Mermillod, a priest, venturing to style himself "Bishop of Geneva" (although the bishopric of Geneva had been previously abolished by the Pope "for ever"), was banished from the country by the Federation; the states belonging to the bishopric of Basle deposed Bishop Lachat in Soleure, because he had deprived certain ecclesiastics who refused to acknowledge the doctrine of infallibility: Berne, which carried on the struggle between church and state with much excitement and great vehemence, deprived more than sixty clergy in the district of the Jura for protesting against the authority of the state; and in 1873 the Federal authorities went so far as to expel the papal nuncio from Switzerland, because the Pope condemned these proceedings in strong terms.

All these events led men to hold more firmly together, and to recognise the necessity for closer union; and the more the Catholic clergy declaimed against the government, so much the more did the *Volksverein* and revision gain ground. In the struggle against the common foe, the progressive parties, Liberals and Radicals, Federalists and Centralists, French and German Swiss, stretched out a helping hand to one another, and in a new scheme for the Federal Constitution, drawn up in 1873, a work of reconciliation was effected, combining definite progress with discreet moderation. On Sunday, 19th April, 1874, this constitution was accepted by an overwhelming majority of the Swiss people (about 340,000 votes against 198,000), and of the cantons (fourteen and a half against seven and a half); and the joyful event was celebrated on the first lovely day of spring, 20th April, by the thunder of cannon, beacon fires, and patriotic songs which resounded from mountain to mountain and from valley to valley.

The principles contained in the newly-accepted constitution established before all things greater centralization in the legal and military systems. Laws relating to bonds, commerce and exchange were taken over by the Federal Government, as also the entire military system, including the training, equipment and legislation of the whole army. The Confederation received more authority in ecclesiastical matters: liberty of faith and of conscience was more warmly embraced, and sacred and secular affairs were more sharply defined, especially by the establishment of the "civil estate" (*Civilstand*). The prohibition of the Jesuits was emphasised, the establishment of new religious houses was forbidden, and the erection of fresh bishoprics was made to depend upon the consent of the Federal Council.

More extensive powers were also conferred upon the Federal Government in matters of political economy, relating to railways, the system of banknotes, water-works and forest regulations in the Alps, hunting and fishing, the factory system and the condition of artisans, &c. The jurisdiction of the Federation was extended in regard to intellectual culture, including the supervision of the system of primary schools, and the right of founding a Federal university and other institutions for higher education, or of supporting those already existing.

The rights of the people were also extended, as, for example, those of settlement and liberty of marriage, and the optional Referendum was introduced by the stipulation that Federal laws must be submitted to the popular vote, if required by 30,000 Swiss citizens entitled to vote, or by eight cantons. Finally, the Federal tribunal, with powers materially augmented, was made into a permanent court of justice, holding its sessions in Lausanne.

§ 78. **The Development of National Life.** The great political changes in the cantons, and still more the remodelling of the Confederation, were the results of a great advance in public spirit. The struggles after 1840, the great Federal reforms after 1850, the effects, so inspiriting to patriotism, of the so-called "Prussian war," and the agitation for Federal reform from 1869-1874, taught the people to interest themselves in national questions, and to think and feel like Confederates in a manner hitherto almost unknown. A lively interest in politics began to show itself in all parts among the great mass of the people, and everywhere men began eagerly to concern themselves about the weal and woe of the whole community. The press did its utmost to keep alive and to increase this interest; and also the many political clubs and great national associations for singing, shooting and gymnastics, with their regularly recurring national festivals, formed a no less important political school for the people.

From time to time, after some violent party strife, a closer union, and a reconciled co-operation for the solving of the problems of national civilization, would be observable. Was the country at any time attacked or injured, was it a question of making some sacrifice for a patriotic purpose (such as the purchase of the Rütli in 1861, the erection of the Winkelried monument at Stans, the collection for the Winkelried fund), were oppressed fellow-Confederates in need of help and support (as after the conflagration in Glarus in 1861, the landslip of Elm in 1881, the destruction of the quay in Zug in 1887, &c.), ever in such cases a devoted and self-sacrificing sympathy has been shown by all sections of the population.

The Swiss will inevitably feel, ever more and more deeply, the truth of those great and beautiful words:—

> "*An's Vaterland, an's teure, schliess dich an;
> Dort sind die Wurzeln deiner kraft!*"[1]

Thus are gradually vanishing those antagonisms of the cantons, of creeds and of party opinion which have in the past wrought such havoc among the Swiss people.

From time to time, too, a warm interest was manifested in educational questions. Mindful of the truth of Zschokke's expression: "*Volksbildung ist Volksbefreiung*,"[2] the statesmen of 1830-40 caused the requirements of the schools to be laid before them *en masse*, which might well serve as an example for all future time. Since then also, frequently between 1850 and 1870, various cantons made great efforts and many sacrifices for the improvement of the education of children, the enlargement of the popular schools, and the promoting of scientific and artistic culture. Great scientific establishments and institutes arose: the cantonal universities and academies, the Federal polytechnic, the cantonal and Federal collections of every kind, of natural science, archæology, and the history of art. From various centres of intellectual life brilliant results were produced. Though, indeed, there still remains much for which to wish and to strive, though there are yet considerable gaps to be filled and failings to be mended, though great progress is often checked by the indolence of individual cantons, or the flagging of the spirit of the age, yet the educational system of Switzerland has often met with due recognition.

[1] "*Die angebornen Bande knüpfe fest,
Ans Vaterland, ans theure, schliess' dich an,
Das halte fest mit deinem ganzen Herzen,
Hier sind die starken Wurzeln deiner kraft.*"

"Knit fast the ties which form your heritage,
And cleave to your beloved fatherland;
Hold to it firm with all your heart and soul;
Here are the hardy roots of all your power."

(*William Tell.* Translated by Major-General Patrick Maxwell.)

[2] "Popular education is popular emancipation."

In certain sciences and branches of literature excellent results have been achieved. Since the year 1830 Switzerland has produced a succession of learned men and poets whose fame has spread far beyond the borders of their own land, such as the theologians Alexander Schweizer, J. C. Biedermann and K. Hagenbach; the learned chaplain P. Gall Morell; the natural historians Merian, Studer, Escher, Desor and Oswald Heer; the philologist Orelli; the professor of constitutional law J. C. Bluntschli; the antiquarian Ferd. Keller; the poets Jeremiah Gotthelf, Konrad Ferd. Meyer, Gottfried Keller, &c. For the cultivation and extension of learning numerous clubs, reading societies, scientific, popular and juvenile libraries were active: in 1868 the number of public libraries rose to nearly 3000.

This intellectual transformation called into existence a corresponding improvement in externals and in material culture. The towns underwent a change in accordance with modern tastes and the necessities of life. From about the year 1830 the fortifications, mediæval walls, towers and gates were gradually abolished, old quarters pulled down and newly built. There arose everywhere fine broad streets, bordered by tasteful buildings; handsome school-houses, churches, town-halls and museums were erected; magnificent hotels, fitted with every comfort, fine promenades and quays, monuments and statues became the ornaments of modern towns. He who had only seen our towns and villages before 1830 would hardly be able to recognise them to-day.

Since 1840 great zeal has been exhibited in the construction of carriage roads and highroads, and of good passes over the Alps. The fame which Berne and the Grisons had enjoyed in this respect during the eighteenth century has been gradually extended to a great number of the cantons, and the Federation has expended great sums upon the making of mountain roads. Artistic bridges of stone and iron of wonderful construction have replaced the old wooden bridges and foot-bridges.

Since 1830, too, traffic has been facilitated by the use of steam.

The appearance of the lakes has been enlivened by steamers (of which there are now over a hundred in all[1]), and the land has been intersected by numberless railroads. The first independent national railway of Switzerland was the line between Zurich and Baden, opened in 1847. Unfortunately the railway dispute between 1850 and 1870 did not end in the railways being taken over by the Federal Government, but they were left under private management. Joint-stock companies were formed in all parts, and between 1854 and 1859 the main lines of the great network of Swiss railways came into existence, the Central and North-Eastern, the United Swiss lines, the Western lines, &c. By-and-by a veritable "railway fever" raged; the network of railways was carried to a length of nearly 3000 km.;[2] obstacles and difficulties, however, were not wanting.

The mountain railways of Switzerland are very remarkable, and a world-wide reputation attaches to the international railroad through the St. Gotthard. The plans for this undertaking having been matured, chiefly through the efforts of Dr. Alfred Escher, and their execution having been rendered possible by the treaty of Italy and Germany with Switzerland (*see* p. 282), the Gotthard Company was formed, and issued stock and bonds. In the summer of 1872 the first works were commenced on the St. Gotthard tunnel, the construction of which had been undertaken by the engineer Favre of Geneva. But many a difficulty had yet to be overcome; the work of excavation was much harder, and the cost of the whole amounted to much more, than had been expected. In 1878 and 1879 supplementary contributions had to be supplied, eight millions by Switzerland, ten millions by Germany and Italy. The "Gotthard crisis" was successfully passed through the patriotism of the Swiss people, and on 29th February, 1880, the piercing of the St. Gotthard tunnel was achieved. Favre, however, did not live to see it, having died of heart disease a short time previously in the tunnel itself. The inauguration of the main section followed in 1880, and the

[1] 1889.   [2] 1875 English miles.

opening in 1882. The marvellous structure of this Alpine railway, its windings above and beneath the earth, its imposing bridges, its tunnels, of which about fifty smaller ones may be counted—and no less its significance for the traffic of the whole world—all combine to elevate this into one of the most magnificent undertakings of modern times, and Switzerland enjoys the honour of having done the greater part of the work of its construction.

The acceleration of traffic had a beneficial effect upon trade and manufactures. The tranquillity which Switzerland had enjoyed since 1848, the free institutions in the interior, the diligence and enterprise of the people, acted as powerful levers upon industrial life. Certain branches of industry, such as the cotton and silk industry, the art of watchmaking, the making of machinery, straw-plaiting and wood-carving, attained international importance, and grew to be chief sources of the national wealth. Industry increased and spread even into the mountainous regions as far as the highest villages in the Alps, where often in the heart of the mountains one may catch sight of a factory worked by water-power, or see looms in motion. The Swiss people no longer consists merely of shepherds, peasants, and a very small number of tradespeople, but is becoming more and more an industrial people, willing to enter into competition with other lands. At exhibitions (in London, Paris, &c.) Switzerland has obtained recognition. The Swiss have sought and found purchasers for the products of their industry in all lands, even in the most remote parts beyond the seas. Commercial treaties have been concluded with all important civilized states, not only of Europe, but also of other continents, America, Australia, the East Indies, and even with China and Japan (1868).

If a distinct falling off is observable in certain spheres of industry, it may serve to remind us with what difficulties this country has to contend in competition with her powerful neighbours, and to incite us to redoubled zeal. Our forefathers were forced to pass through severe struggles in order to win for us the priceless blessings of liberty and independence, and for this they made great sacrifices and shed much blood. We, too, have a like struggle to carry on, but now a peaceful one—the contest of the nations on the field of labour, both intellectual and material.

Switzerland, small and by nature sparingly endowed, surrounded by large and wealthy states by which she is almost stifled, can only keep that which she has already acquired, and only attain to that which remains to be achieved in her institutions, her culture, and her military system, by all her members and all her citizens being equally imbued with a sense of the high and holy responsibilities laid upon them by their fatherland and its history.

SYNOPTICAL TABLE OF THE HISTORY OF FEDERAL AFFAIRS.

A. FEDERAL SYSTEM OF THE OLD CONFEDERATION
(DOWN TO 1798).

1. **The Governing States :—**

(a) The eight old states:—
Three Forest states . 1 Aug., 1291, and 9 Dec., 1315.
Lucerne . . 7 Nov., 1332.
Zurich . . 1 May, 1351.
Glarus . . 4 June, 1352.
Zug . . . 27 June, 1352.
Berne . . . 6 March, 1353.

(b) The five new states :—
Fribourg }
Soleure } . . 22 Dec., 1481.
Basle . . . 9 June, 1501, taking rank before Fribourg and Soleure.
Schaffhausen . . 10 Aug., 1501.
Appenzell . . 17 Dec., 1513.

(c) Common leagues and covenants :—
The Monks' (or Priests')
Charter . . 7 Oct., 1370 (six states ; eight with the exception of Berne and Glarus).
The Convention of
Sempach . . 10 July, 1393 (eight states besides Soleure).
The Covenant of Stans 22 Dec., 1481 (eight states).
Pensionenbrief . 1502.
The First Peace (of
Kappel) . . 26 June, 1529.
The Second Peace (of
Kappel) . . 20 Nov., 1531.
Defensionale . . March, 1668.
The Third Peace (of
Aarau) . . 11 Aug., 1712.

2. The Allied States:—

Bienne	(14th century).
Neuchâtel	1406.
Valais	1416.
The abbey of St. Gall	1451.
The town of St. Gall	1454.
Mülhausen	1466 and 1515.
The Leagues in Rhætia	1497 and 1498.
Rotwil	1519.

3. The Common Domains:—

(a) Those subject to a number of states :—

The Free Bailiwicks and Baden, 1415. The former under six and seven states at first; divided 1712; the lower ones (Vilmergen, Wohlen, Mellingen and Bremgarten) remaining only under the reformed states Zurich, Berne and Glarus; the upper ones (Hitzkirch, Muri and Merischwand) under the eight states. Baden at first under the seven, then eight, states; after 1712 belonging only to Zurich, Berne and Glarus.

Thurgau	1460 (seven, later (1712) eight, states).
Sargans	1483 (seven, later (1712) eight, states).
Rheintal	1490 (seven, later (1712) eight, states besides Appenzell).
The Bailiwicks of Ticino (Lugano, Locarno, Mendrisio, and Maggiatal)	1512 (twelve states).

(b) Those subject to two or three states :—

Utznach and Gaster	1438 (under Schwyz and Glarus).
Morat (Murten), Orbe, Grandson, Eschallens, and Illens	1476 (under Berne and Fribourg).
Bellinzona (Bellenz)	1503 (under Uri, Schwyz and Nidwalden).

B. ALLIANCES AND CONSTITUTIONS OF MODERN TIMES.

1. 1798, April 12. First United Helvetic Constitution.

1801, May 29	"Scheme of Malmaison" (a compromise between federalism and centralization).
1801, Oct. 24	New scheme of the Helvetic Diet (with a view to a united state).
1802, Feb. 27	The (federalistic) scheme of Reding
1802, May 20	Second Helvetic Constitution.

Synoptical Table. 297

2. 1803, Feb. 19. **Napoleon's "Act of Mediation"** (or "Compromise") and the *Consulta*. Constitutions of the Federation and of the nineteen Cantons.

3. 1815, Aug. 7. **Federal Pact of the Twenty-two Cantons.**[*]

    1832, 1833 . . Unsuccessful revision of the Federal Pact.

4. 1848, Sept. 12. **New Federal Constitution.**

    The Federal State:—

    1866, Jan. . . The first revision (to a great extent unsuccessful).

    1872, March 5 . . Scheme for a new Federal Constitution (rejected).

5. 1874, May 29. **Latest Federal Constitution** (revision of that of 1848).

---

[*] The order in which the cantons have usually been reckoned since 1815 follows to some extent a decision of 1803, which is determined partly according to former rank, partly according to historical sequence. The thirteen states were first reckoned, the three old chief states being placed first (the oldest at the head): Zurich, Berne and Lucerne. Then follow the others in the order of their joining the Confederation, except that Basle (as had been before determined in 1501) is placed before Fribourg and Soleure. Next come the six new cantons of the Mediation in historical succession according to their connection with the Confederates, but so that the "Allied States" come before the former "Subject Lands": St. Gall, the Grisons, Aargau, Thurgau, Ticino and the Vaud. At the end come the three cantons added in 1815, those of the oldest historical relations taking precedence: Valais, Neuchâtel and Geneva.

CHRONOLOGICAL TABLE.

1. Celtic and Roman Period, B.C. 107–A.D. 400.

B.C. 107	Defeat of the Helvetians by the Romans in Southern Gaul (Agen on the Garonne).
B.C. 58	Subjection of the Helvetians by Cæsar. **Roman Dominion**; military organization; fortresses and castles on the Rhine.
A.D. 100–250	Period of peace; progress of civilization. Western Switzerland becomes Roman.
A.D. 300–400	Introduction of **Christianity**.

2. Settlement of the Teutonic Tribes, 400–700.

A.D. 406	Invasion of the **Alamanni**; their permanent establishment in the country.
A.D. 443	Settlement of the **Burgundians** in the south-west of Switzerland.
A.D. 600–650	The Alamanni converted to Christianity; Columban and Gallus; Christian legislation.

3. The Supremacy of the Carlovingians, the German Emperors, and the Zäringens, 700–1200.

[Introduction of the feudal system. Progress of the arts and sciences in the monasteries of St. Gall, Reichenau, Rheinau and Pfäffers.]

A.D. 800	The influence of Charles the Great.
A.D. 843	The partition of Verdun. Western Switzerland falls to Lothaire, later to France; Eastern Switzerland with Rhætia falls to Germany.
A.D. 853	Foundation of the Fraumünster in Zurich. [gundy.
A.D. 888	Foundation of the kingdom of Bur-
A.D. 917	Alamanni an independent Duchy.
A.D. 1038	Burgundy, Alamannia, and Rhætia fall to Henry III.
A.D. 1097	Peace; Zurich falls to the Zäringens.
A.D. 1127	The rectorate of the Zäringens in
A.D. 1177	Foundation of Fribourg. [Burgundy.
A.D. 1191	Foundation of Berne.

4. Rise of the Confederation, 1200-1400.

[Growth of chivalrous poetry; troubadours; collection of songs of Manegg.]

A.D. 1218 . . The line of Zäringen becomes extinct. Zurich and Berne obtain imperial freedom.

A.D. 1245-1250 . War between the papal and imperial factions. Alliances of the towns; first League of the three Forest states. Struggles with the imperial bailiffs.

A.D. 1256-1273 Interregnum; club law; encroachments of Savoy in Western Switzerland; opposition of Zurich to the barons of Regensberg.

[Progress of municipal freedom.]

A.D. 1264 . Foundation of the power of Hapsburg through the inheritance of Kiburg.

A.D. 1291 . Death of Rudolf of Hapsburg. First **Perpetual League of the three Forest States** (Uri, Schwyz, Unterwalden), 1 Aug. Alliance with Zurich; war with Austria.

A.D. 1315, 15 Nov. . Victory of the Forest states at **Morgarten.** Renewal of the League of 1291.

A.D. 1332 . **Perpetual League of the Forest States with Lucerne.**

A.D. 1351, 1 May **Perpetual League of the Forest States with Zurich.**

A.D. 1352 . Alliance of **Glarus** and **Zug** with the Confederates.

A.D. 1353 . **Perpetual League of the Forest States with Berne.**

A.D. 1370 . The Monks' Charter; abolition of ecclesiastical privileges.

A.D. 1386, 9 July . Battle of **Sempach.**

A.D. 1388 . . Battle of **Näfels**; liberation of Glarus.

A.D. 1393 . . **Covenant of Sempach**; common Federal charters of the eight original states; military regulations.

A.D. 1394 . . Twenty years' peace with Austria.

5. The Confederation at the Height of its Power, 1400-1516.

A.D. 1415 . . The Confederates conquer the Austrian Aargau. First common domain.

A.D. 1436–1450   Civil war between Zurich and Schwyz.

[Development of Swiss literature, warlike songs and chronicles.]

A.D. 1460 . . The Confederates conquer the Austrian Thurgau. Second common domain. The university of Basle; spread of the "humanities."

[Development of Swiss art and industry; carving, painting, stoves; silk and linen manufactures.]

A.D. 1474–1477 . **Wars with Charles the Bold of Burgundy.**

A.D. 1481 . **Perpetual League with Fribourg and Soleure. Covenant of Stans;** strengthening of political power; mutual assistance against insurrection and dangerous assemblies, Federal oath.

A.D. 1489   Rebellion under Waldmann. The Confederates favour the demands of the rural district of Zurich for greater liberties, as opposed to Waldmann's efforts at concentration. Exasperation against the Covenant of Stans and pensions.

A.D. 1499 . Suabian War. Peace of Basle. Emancipation from German imperial regulations; the Confederates establish their rights in the Thurgau.

A.D. 1500 . The Swiss assist Louis XII. in the conquest of Milan.

A.D. 1501 . **Perpetual League with Basle and Schaffhausen.**

A.D. 1512 . . Conquest of Milan; Ticino falls to the Confederates, the Valtelline, Cleves and Bormio to the Grison Leagues.

A.D. 1513 . . **Appenzell admitted to the League; the Confederation of Thirteen States.** Victory of the Confederates at Novara.

A.D. 1515 . Defeat of the Swiss at Marignano. Perpetual peace with France; commencement of the policy of neutrality.

Chronological Table. 301

6. The Time of the Reformation, 1516–1600.

A.D. 1519	The appearance of Zwingli in Zurich.
A.D. 1523	Two "disputations" at Zurich.
A.D. 1525	Peasant agitations.
A.D. 1527	Evangelical alliance.
A.D. 1528	Berne converted to the principles of the Reformation.
A.D. 1529	Conference of Marburg. First War of Kappel. Separate League of the five states with Austria.
A.D. 1531	Second War of Kappel. A reaction sets in.
A.D. 1536	Conquest and reform of the Vaud by Berne. Calvin; first Helvetic Confession.
A.D. 1555	Protestant exiles from Locarno take refuge in Zurich.
A.D. 1566	Second Helvetic Confession.
A.D. 1586	Borromean League.
A.D. 1597	Appenzell divided into Outer Rhodes and Inner Rhodes.

7. The Period of Aristocracy, 1600–1798.

[Patriciates in Berne, Fribourg, Soleure and Lucerne. Civic aristocracies in Basle, Zurich and Schaffhausen. Oppression of the peasantry.]

A.D. 1618–1639	Confusion in the Grisons. Neutrality of Switzerland during the Thirty Years' War.
A.D. 1648	**Switzerland formally separated from Germany.**
A.D. 1653	**The Peasants' War.** League of the peasants at Summiswald; defeat at Wohlenswil.
A.D. 1656	First War of Vilmergen. Victory of the Catholic states.
A.D. 1663	League with France.
A.D. 1668–1680	The *Defensionale* put into execution.
A.D. 1712	The second War of Vilmergen, or the War of Toggenburg.
A.D. 1723	Davel's conspiracy in the Vaud against Berne.
A.D. 1749	Henzi's conspiracy in Berne.

[The commencement of public-spirited efforts. Switzerland influenced by the enlightenment of France and Germany.]

A.D. 1762	The foundation of the Helvetic **Society**.
A.D. 1777	**Alliance of the Thirteen States with France.**

[Opposition against privilege. Spread of the principles of the French Revolution.]

A.D. 1794, 1795	Troubles in Stäfa.
A.D. 1798	**The Revolution.** Invasion of the French. The fall of Berne. Introduction of the **Helvetic Constitution.**
A.D. 1799	The wars of the coalition in Switzerland.
A.D. 1802	Party strife between Centralists and Federalists. The downfall of the Helvetic Constitution.
A.D. 1803–1815	The Constitution of "**Mediation**" by Napoleon.
A.D. 1814	Invasion of Switzerland by the Allies; the downfall of the "Mediation."
A.D. 1815	The **Federal Pact**; political league of twenty-two cantons.
A.D. 1815–1830	The policy of "Restoration." New aristocracies. Decay of the Confederation. Intellectual reaction.
A.D. 1829	Commencement of constitutional revision.
A.D. 1830, Nov. 22	Assembly of Uster.
A.D. 1830–1848	Regeneration; fundamental reorganization of the educational system.
A.D. 1832	Division of Basle. League of the seven reformed cantons (*Siebener-Concordat*).
A.D. 1833	League of Sarnen. Opposition against Federal revision.
A.D. 1843	Separate league against the suppression of religious houses and Federal revision (*Sonderbund*).
A.D. 1847	**War of the Sonderbund.** First Swiss railway (Zurich to Baden).
A.D. 1848	New Federal Constitution. **Switzerland becomes a Federal State.**
A.D. 1855	Opening of the Federal Polytechnic in Zurich.

Appendix. 303

[Rapid and unparalleled development of industries. Improvement in the educational system.]

A.D. 1856, 1857	. Settlement of the dispute about Neuchâtel.
A.D. 1862	. . The Dappenthal divided between Switzerland and France.
A.D. 1866	. . Attempted Federal revision.
A.D. 1870, 1871	. Preservation of neutrality during the Franco - Prussian War. Struggle against Ultramontanism in regard to papal infallibility.
A.D. 1872	. . Alabama Arbitration Commission in Geneva.
A.D. 1874, April 1	. Brilliant victory of **Federal revision**.

APPENDIX.

A.D. 1874–1876. Legislation concerning civil marriages and divorce.

A.D. 1878. Death of James Fazy (statesman.)

A.D. 1881. Legislation concerning bank-notes.

A.D. 1882. Opening of the **St. Gotthard railway**.

A.D. 1883. National Exhibition at Zurich.

A.D. 1884. International conference held at Berne for the protection of copyright.

A.D. 1886. The Federal Government assumes the monopoly of alcohol.

A.D. 1888. Law passed for protection of patents.

A.D. 1889–1891. International Catholic university established in Fribourg.

A.D. 1890. Invalid and accident Insurance undertaken by the Federal Government.

A.D. 1891. The Federal Government assumes the monopoly of bank-notes. Six hundredth anniversary of the foundation of the Confederation celebrated in Schwyz. **Popular initiative** introduced into the Constitution.

A.D. 1893. Killing of animals in Jewish fashion prohibited.

INDEX.

Aar, The, 27, 28, 43, 55, 65, 71, 162.
Aarau, 84, 176, 186, 218, 220, 223(2), 236, 244, 266.
— Diet at, 218.
Aarberg, Count of, 58.
Aarburg, 84.
— von, 86.
Aargau, the, xi, 17, 22, 32, 38(2), 39, 42, 64, 66, 117, 176(3), 178(2), 181(2), 203, 222, 223, 232, 236, 238, 239, 243(2), 246, 249, 251, 255, 258, 259, 264(2), 265, 266(3), 269(2), 274, 281, 284, 285.
— conquest of, 83, 84.
— government of, 264(2), 265.
Abyberg, Colonel, 256, 260(2).
Ad fines. See Pfin.
Aebli, Landammann of Glarus, 141, 157.
Ætius the Roman, 12.
Agen, 4.
Aginnum. See Agen.
Agnes, Queen, 59.
Aigle, 147.
Aix la Chapelle, Peace of, 183.
Alabama dispute, the, 282.
Alamanni, the, 9(2), 11-16, 32.
Alamannia, 15, 16, 17, 19(3), 21(4), 22(3), 23(2), 24, 25, 26(3).
— Duchess of: Hedwig, 24.
— Dukes of:
    Burkhard I., 19, 22(4).
    — II., 22.
    Liudolf, 22(2).
Albis, the, 5, 88.
Alienus Cäcina, 6.
Allerheiligen (Schaffhausen), monastery of, 26.
Allobroges, the, 3, 4, 5, 6(2), 8.
Almend, the, 13, 32, 34, 260(2).
Alps, the, xi, xiv(2), 4, 8, 11, 19, 43, 81, 82(3), 114, 156, 158, 193, 194, 200, 228, 234, 243, 288, 291, 293.
Alsace (Elsass), 9, 11, 32, 39, 42, 66, 93, 95(2), 96.
Altdorf, 159.

Altenryf (in Fribourg), monastery of, 235.
Altsellen, 49, 52, 53.
Altstätten, 76(2), 250.
Ambühl, Mathias, 68.
America, 109, 282, 293.
Amiens, Peace of, 230.
Amstalden, Peter, 101, 102.
Anabaptists, the, 133, 134.
Anderhalden, ——, 53.
Andermatt, General, 230.
Anderwert, 285.
Appenzell, 12, 74, 78(2), 85, 92, 107, 117, 137(2), 151(2), 159, 162, 200, 219, 221, 227, 245, 285.
— enters the League, 75-77, 91, 116.
— Inner Rhodes, 145, 162(2), 209, 245, 285.
— Outer Rhodes, 137, 145, 162(3), 199, 208, 257, 285.
Aquæ. See Baden.
Arbedo, 82.
Arbon, 7(2), 9, 16, 228.
Architecture, Baroque, 201.
— Gothic, 36, 124.
— Renaissance, 124, 156, 187.
— Romanesque, 36.
Arianism, 14.
Aristophanes, 154.
Armagnacs, the, 88-91.
Art, 46, 101, 103, 181.
Aspermont, 80.
Attinghausen (Canton Uri), 54.
— Werner von, 45.
Auer, Hans, 121.
Augstgau, the, 17.
Augusta Rauricorum. See Basel-Augst.
Australia, 293.
Austria, 43, 45-47, 57-64, 76, 77, 80, 81, 83, 85-94, 96, 110(4), 121, 140, 142, 161, 167, 168, 231, 237(2), 239, 240, 255, 270(2), 278, 279, 281.
— Dukes and Archdukes of, 46, 58, 61, 64:
    Albert II., 61-63, 68, 87.
    Charles, 227, 228.

Austria—*cont.*:
— Dukes and Archdukes of—*cont.*:
Ferdinand I., 140, 142.
Frederick I., 46(2).
— II., 76(3), 83, 84.
— III., 87, 88, 92.
Leopold I., 46, 47, 55, 64.
— III., 65-67.
Maximilian I., 81, 100(2).
Sigismund (Sigmund), 81, 83.
— emancipation of Switzerland from, 55-74.
— first war with, 44-47.
— house of, 45, 56.
— insignia of, 88.
— John of, 45.
— loses possessions in Switzerland, 93.
— wars with Confederation of eight States, 62-69.
Autun, 5, 14.
Avenches (*Aventicum*), 5, 6, 7, 8(3), 9, 10, 15(2), 27, 230.
Aventicum. *See* Avenches.
Axen, the, 50.

Baar, 70.
Bachmann, General, 230, 239.
Baden (Canton Aargau), 6, 7, 38, 61, 84(2), 117-119, 136, 138(2), 139, 145, 182, 186(2), 263(2), 292.
Balm, Rudolf von, 45.
Balsthal, 167, 250.
Balthasar, Franz Urs, 195, 196, 199, 202.
"Band of the Mad Life," the, 101, 103.
Barde, De la, 182.
Bärentswil, 12.
Barmann, the envoy, 278.
Basel-Augst (*Augusta Rauricorum*), 6, 7(3), 8-10.
Baselland, 252, 253, 258, 266, 284.
Baselstadt, 252, 257, 285.
Basle (Bâle, Basel), 3, 5, 9, 19, 24, 33, 41, 42, 90, 110(2), 112(2), 117, 122, 123(3), 124, 130(2), 134, 137(2), 138(2), 145, 148, 150, 152, 154, 158, 167, 168(3), 170, 173, 176(3), 177, 178, 179(2), 180(2), 184(3), 187(2), 189(3), 195, 197, 200(3), 201, 217(4), 219(3), 223, 228, 232, 238(2), 240, 243, 255, 256.
— bishopric of, 239, 240, 243, 287.
— bishops of, 18(2), 26, 31, 42, 159, 160, 213.
— burgomaster of, 168, 182(2).
— cathedral of, 22.
— council of, 135, 247.
— disturbances in, 250-254, 256.
— division of the Canton, 252, 256, 257.

Basle, enters the League, 112, 116.
— industries in, 199.
— Peace of, 168.
— university of, 122, 128, 137-139, 153.
Bauma, 249.
Baumgarten, Conrad, 53.
Baumgartner, Jakob, 250, 263.
Bavaria, 6, 66.
— Duke of, 26.
Beauregard, castle of, 79.
Beccaria, 158.
Beda, Abbot of St. Gall, 215(4).
Belfort, 97.
Belgium, 1.
Bellelay, monastery of, 35.
Bellinzona (Bellenz), 82(3), 106, 113, 222, 263.
Belmont, 80.
Benedictines, the, 16, 35.
Berchtold (of Thurgau), 19.
Berne, xv, 28, 33, 36, 37, 40, 41, 45, 55-59, 61, 64, 65, 70(2), 72, 73, 77, 78, 84(2), 91(2), 93-101, 103, 104, 108, 116, 117, 122-124, 127, 129, 130, 137-140, 142-150, 153(2), 157(2), 161, 164, 165, 170-173, 175-181, 186-189, 192, 193, 198-203, 205, 206, 208(2), 213, 214, 216, 217, 220, 221, 223(3), 230-232, 236-241, 243, 247(3), 250, 251, 253, 255, 258, 259, 266, 267, 274, 275, 279, 285, 287, 291.
— conquers the Vaud, 146-148.
— council of, 129, 138, 204, 267.
— — hall of, 124.
— Diets held at, 250, 268.
— Dominicans in, 127.
— enters the League, 59-62.
— government of, 128, 204, 206, 250, 283.
— industries of, 199.
— the *Kirchgasse*, 156.
— mayor of, 221.
— minster at, 124.
— name of (derivation), 28.
— Preaching Friars in, 128.
— Reformation in, 138.
— sieges of, 43, 221.
— university of, 258.
Bernouilli, 189, 190.
Beroldingen of Uri, 166.
Beromünster, 84, 123.
— Provost of, 143.
Bertha, Queen of Burgundy, 22(2), 23(4).
Berthelier, Philibert, 146(3).
Besançon, 12.

Bettingen, 257.
Beuvrais, Mount, 5.
Beza, Theodore, 148.
Bibracte. *See* Beuvrais, Mount.
Biedermann, J. C., 291.
Bienne (Biel), 55, 96, 117(2), 139, 150, 239, 240.
— Lake of, 3(2).
Birs, the, 90(2).
Black Forest, the, 93, 95, 110.
Bleuler, 285.
Blickensdorf, 104.
Bludenz, 76.
Bluntschli, ——, 87, 89.
— Dr., 262, 267.
— J. C., 291.
Bocken, 233.
Bodmer, J. J., 195(3), 199, 215.
Bohemia, 45.
Bondmen, 13, 30, 31(2), 34, 135.
Bonivard, the Genevese historian, 146, 147.
Bonstetten, Albert von, 122.
Bormio, 114, 165, 216.
Bornhauser, Pastor, 247.
Borromean (or Golden) League, the, 157-160, 162, 181, 265.
Borromeo, Carlo, 158, 159(3), 160.
Bourbaki, army of, 281.
Bözberg, the, 6.
Brandenburg, Margrave of, 61.
— Peace of, 61, 62(2), 63.
Braudis, von, 86.
Bregenz, 7(2), 16, 77, 110.
Breitenlandenberg, Wildhans von, 89.
Breitfeld, 221.
Breitinger, J. J., 195.
— Pastor, 180.
Bremgarten, 84, 118, 144, 186.
Bruderholz, 110.
Brugg. 45, 84, 90, 153, 212, 225.
Brun, Bruno, 73.
— Herdegen, 73.
— Rudolf, 60(6), 61, 63(3), 70(2), 87.
Brune, the French general, 220, 221(2), 222.
Brunig Pass, the, 46, 47.
Brunnen, 47.
Brunner, ——, 89.
Bubenberg, Adrian von, 95, 98(2).
— family of, 104.
— Hein. von, 91.
— Joh. von, 58.
Bubendorfer-Bade, 247.
Bubikon, monastery of, 134.
Buchegg, counts of, 37.
Bülach, 73, 285.

Bullinger, Henry, 144, 150(2), 152, 154, 155(2).
Buntzen, committee of, 264(2).
Buonas, 57.
Buonhomo, papal nuncio, 159(2).
Burckhardt, family of, 179.
Burgdorf, 27, 37, 57, 65(2), 123, 235.
— council of, 247.
Bürgisser, Leodegar, Abbot of St. Gall, 186.
Burgistein, Jordan von, 59.
Bürglen, 54.
Burgundy, 17, 19, 21(2), 22-25, 27, 37, 43, 55, 58, 66, 94, 100, 115, 145.
— Berchtold IV. of, 27.
— — V. of, 27(3), 28, 37.
— Charles the Bold of, 94-100.
— — — Maria, daughter of, 96, 100.
— Conrad of, 22(2).
— dukes of, 27.
— Gundobad, King of, 12, 14(3).
— Philip the Good of, 94.
— Rudolph I., King of, 19.
— — II., King of, 22(3).
— — III., King of, 23(2).
— Sigismund, King of, 14, 15.
— Upper (or High), 100(3), 240.
— — — counts of, 27.
— — — William IV., count of, 27.
— Wars of, xii, 94-100, 113, 122, 128.
Buttisholz, 64.

Cæsar, 4, 5(2), 6.
Calvin, John, 148-150.
Capuchins, the, 159(2), 162, 164, 224.
Carlovingian dynasty, 19.
— — period, 1.
— — rule in Switzerland, 17, 18.
Carrard, 283.
Carthusian order, the, 35, 136.
Catalonia, 174.
Cave dwellers, 2.
Celtic population, the, 1.
— ruins, 3.
— tongue, 11.
— tribes, 3-5.
— worship, 8.
Celts, the, 3(2), 4, 5(2), 8, 15.
Centralists (or Unionists), 229-233, 286, 288.
Ceporin, 133, 154.
Chablais, 147, 161, 240, 279.
Charles the Great (Charlemagne), 17, 18, 20.
Chaux de fonds, la, 199.
Chiasso, 114.
Chiavenna, 114, 216, 240.
Chillon, castle of, 146, 147.

China, 293.
"Christian Alliance," the (1529), 140.
Christianity, introduction of, 9-11.
Churwalden, 85.
Cimbri, the, 4(3).
Cisalpine Republic, the, 216.
Cistercian order, the, 35.
Claux, castle of, 75.
Cleves (Cläven), 81, 116, 239.
Clotaire IV., King of the Franks, 14.
Clovis, King of the Franks, 14(4).
Cluny, 26.
— the monks of, 26, 35.
Coalition, wars of the, 212, 227, 228.
Coire (Chur), 5, 7, 10, 17, 19, 33, 36, 166, 236.
— Bishop Peter of, 80.
— bishopric of, 14, 81.
— bishops of, 18, 31, 80, 110, 243.
Coire-Rhætia, 14(3), 17, 19, 21.
— counts of, 22(2).
Collin, 133, 153, 154.
Cologne, 96.
Columban, 16(3).
Communes, 32, 34, 38, 40, 43, 135, 161, 223, 225, 242, 247, 252, 257, 262.
— formation of, 32, 39.
Como, lake of, 142.
Condat, monastery of (St. Claude), 15(2).
Confederation (or Federation), the Swiss, xv(2), 40, 44, 59, 66, 71, 97, 187, 193.
— of eight States, 52-62, 74.
— — — war of, with Austria, 62-69.
— of thirteen States, 116-121, 238.
— of nineteen Cantons, 239.
— of twenty-two Cantons, 222, 240, 241.
— constitution of, 17-25, 222-225, 240, 241, 270-276, 279, 288.
— downfall of, 216-219.
— growth of, 55-74.
— origin of, xi, 37-55.
— President of, 274.
— reformation of, 270.
— rise and development of, 37-126.
— strengthening of, 84-93.
Conseil, 257.
Constance, 10, 16, 18, 24, 26, 77, 92, 110, 111, 139, 140, 162, 167.
— bishops of, 18-20, 31, 43, 72, 89, 243.
— bishopric of, 243.
— council of, 83(4).
— Hugo, bishop of, 127.
— lake of, 4, 5, 7-9, 16, 75.
— Solomon III., bishop of, 19.
— vicar-general of, 132, 138.

Constitutional Councils, 248, 250, 251, 257, 285.
Copernicus, 190.
Corvin, Matthew, 121.
Cossus, the Helvetic envoy, 7.
Coucy, Baron Ingelram von, 64.
Council, the Federal, 272, 279(2), 280-282, 288.
— the National, 272(2).
— of the States, the, 272(2), 276.
Counter-Reformation, the, 157-163.

Dänikon, 13.
Danube, the, 7, 9.
Dappental, 280.
Davel, Daniel Abraham, 209.
Davos, 80, 81, 85, 112.
Defensionale, the, 168, 183, 184, 193.
Denmark, 53.
Descartes, 190.
Desor, the naturalist, 291.
Deucher, 285.
Diesbach, 95.
— family of, 104.
Diessenhofen, 33, 92, 118.
Diet, the, 117, 128, 137, 163, 176, 193, 218, 220, 230, 232, 237, 252, 256, 274.
— proceedings of, 102, 118, 119.
— the Long, 240.
Dijon, campaign of, 115.
Dissentis, 36.
— monastery of, 16, 35, 80.
Disteli, the artist, 243.
Divico, 4(2).
Döffingen, 69.
Doisel, 71.
Dominicans, the, 35, 40, 127.
Domo d'Ossola, 82(2), 114, 116.
Dornbühl, battle of, 45.
Dorneck (Dornach), 111.
Dortrecht, 190.
Doubs, the, 16.
Dresbach, family of, 204.
Dreux, 163.
Druey, of the Vaud, 274.
Drusus, 5.
Dufour, Heinrich, general, 263, 269(3), 274, 278, 280.

Ebel, Dr., 201, 218.
Ebersol, 263.
Echallens, 99, 146.
Eck, Dr., 138.
Edlibach, Gerold, 122.
Effinger, ——, 89.
Egeri (Aegeri), 70.
— lake of, 46.
Eglisau, 73, 134.

Index. 309

Egloff, Colonel, 269.
Eigil, 53.
Einsiedeln, 43, 72, 73, 102(2), 103, 131, 156, 224, 252.
— abbot of, 31.
— monastery of, 25, 26, 34(2), 35, 46, 72, 122.
Ekkehard I. (of St. Gall), 24.
— II. (of St. Gall), 24.
— IV. (of St. Gall), 24.
Elba, 239.
Elm, 289.
Emmental, the, 173, 175, 176(2), 199.
Engadine, the, 80, 166.
— — Lower, 167.
Engelberg, 25, 73, 199, 234.
— abbot of, 31.
— monastery of, 35.
England, 64, 69, 74, 103, 114, 154(2), 174, 181, 184, 194(2), 195(2), 205, 270(2), 282(2).
— King of: Edward III., 64.
Entlebuch, 64, 66, 101(2), 103, 175(5), 176, 177, 178.
Erasmus, 123.
Erchanger (of Thurgau), 19.
Erlach, family of, 104, 204.
— General K. L. von, 221(4).
— Hans Ludwig von, 168.
— Rudolf von, 58, 230.
— Sigmund von, 178.
— — — the younger, 180, 184.
Erlenbach, 73.
Ermatingen, 111.
Eschenbach, Walter von, 45.
Eschental, 78, 82(3), 116.
Escher, Alfred, 285, 292.
— Johann Kaspar, 191(2), 198.
— Konrad ("von der Linth"), 212(2), 226, 235, 247.
— the naturalist, 291.
Escholzmatt, 176, 234.
Etruscans, the, 3.
Etterlin, Petermann, 51(2), 122.
Etzel, the, 87(2), 224.
Europe, xv, 1, 3, 69, 94, 100, 108, 113, 118, 122, 126, 128, 156(2), 171, 174, 188, 217, 274, 293.
Evibach, Zwier von, 168.

Faber, vicar-general of Constance, 132.
Faenza, 39.   [138.
Faido, 71, 82.
Falkenstein, Thomas von, 90.
Farel, William, 147, 148(3), 149(2), 150.
Farnbühler, burgomaster of St. Gall, 107, 108.

Farnsburg, the, 90(3).
Fäsi, 201.
Fatio, Pierre, 205(2).
Faucigny, 240, 279.
Favre, the engineer, 292(2).
Fazy, James, 268, 271, 284.
Federal Assembly, the, 272, 274, 277, 280, 281.
— Pact, the, 240-245, 254, 255, 264, 270.
Federalists, 229-233, 288.
Feldkirch, 76, 111.
Felix, the Martyr, 10.
Fellenberg, Emanuel von, 235(3), 236, 258, 266.
Ferdinand, Treaty of. See Christian Alliance.
Ferney, 195, 208.
Feudal System, the, 17, 29, 34.
Fichte, 195.
Flüe, Nicholas von der, 102(3), 103(2).
Fontana, Benedict, 111.
Forest States, the, 32, 38, 39, 40(2), 42, 44, 45(4), 46(5), 47-54, 55, 56(6), 57(3), 58, 59(3), 60, 61(2), 62(2), 65, 71, 72(3), 80, 81, 82, 87, 88, 92(2), 101, 113, 116(2), 135(3), 138, 141, 142.
— — Perpetual League of, 42-44, 54, 71.
Forster, Pancraz, 215, 227.
Four Cantons, lake of the (Vierwaldstättersee), 40, 228.
France, 1, 8, 19, 64, 65, 74, 94(3), 95, 100(3), 103, 113(6), 114(2), 115, 116(2), 121(2), 122, 123, 124, 129, 132, 147, 149, 150, 154, 160, 161(2), 163(3), 164(5), 166(2), 178, 181, 182-185, 187, 192, 194(2), 195(2), 205, 208, 212, 213(4), 214, 216-225, 227, 229(2), 231(2), 232, 236(3), 237(3), 240(2), 246, 250, 270(2), 279, 280(6), 286.
— the Fronde, 174.
— Kings of:
   Charles VII., 89, 94.
   — VIII., 112.
   Francis I., 115(2), 142.
   Henry IV., 163(3), 164(2).
   Louis XI., 94(2), 95(3), 96(2), 97(2), 100, 112, 113.
   — XII., 112, 113(2), 114, 115.
   — XIV., 183(4), 184(5), 185, 187.
Fribourg (Freiburg), 27, 28, 33, 35, 37, 40(2), 43, 53, 55, 58(2), 59, 64, 67, 94, 96, 98, 99(2), 100(2), 101(3),

Fribourg (Freiburg)—*cont.:*
  102, 117(2), 123(2), 145, 146(3), 159(2), 160, 164, 170(2), 175, 178, 179, 198, 207, 212, 221, 223(2), 232, 235, 238, 241(2), 242(2), 249, 253(2), 265, 269(2), 273.
— council of, 249.
— enters the League, 103, 116.
— government of, 283, 285.
— St. Nicholas' in, 124.
Franche-Comté, 96, 100(2), 183(2), 184(2).
Franciscans, the, 36, 127, 242.
Franco-Carlovingian empire, 17-21.
— German War, 281, 286.
Franks, the, 13-16, 29, 108.
— — East, 19.
— — West, 19.
Franscini, 246, 263, 274.
Frastenz, 111.
Fraubrunnen, 221.
— monastery of, 64.
Frauenfeld, 33, 118, 188, 201.
Free Bailiwick (*Freiamt*), canton Zurich, 73, 84, 88(2), 264(2), 269.
Free Bailiwicks, the, 84, 117, 139, 140, 144, 145, 177, 186(3), 187.
Freedmen, 13, 31(2), 33, 34.
Freedom of the Empire (*Reichsfreiheit*), 31, 33, 37, 39, 41, 43, 45, 46, 48.
— Wars of, 1, 44-55, 123.
Freemen, 13(3), 18, 20, 29, 31, 33, 34, 39.
"Freiamt." *See* Free Bailiwick.
Freienbach, 88.
Frei-Herosé, of Aargau, 274.
Freudenberger, Uriel, 54.
Freya, the goddess, 23.
Frickthal, the, 93, 167, 217, 232.
Frischherz (of Berne), 170.
Frisching, von, of Berne, 221.
Fröhlich, Abraham Emanuel, 243.
Fründ, Joh., 122.
Fuchs, Alois, 258.
— Christopher, 258.
Fuentes, Count of, 164.
— Fort, 164.
Fueter, 206(2).
Furrer, Dr., 267.
— Jonas, 274.
Fürst, family of, 50(2).
— Walter, 53, 54.
Fussach, 110.
Füssli, 198, 201.

Gais, 75.
Galba, 6(2).
Gallicnus, 9.

Gallus, 16.
Garonne, the, 4.
Gaster, 85(3), 86(3), 139, 144, 145, 219.
Gaul, 4-6, 8, 10, 15, 16.
— Belgian, 6.
Gauls, the, 4.
Gelterkinden, 252.
Gemmi, the, 200.
Geneva, 3-5, 10(2), 17, 25, 27, 33, 36, 38, 97, 101, 123, 146(5), 152, 153, 159, 161(3), 188, 194, 200, 201, 205(2), 207, 208, 213, 216, 239, 240(2), 253(2), 268, 284, 285, 292.
— arbitration tribunal in, 282.
— bishop of, 287.
— bishopric of, 287.
— cathedral, 23.
— "Consistorium," 149.
— Convention of, 282.
— counts, 32.
— "Escalade," 161.
— government of, 205, 207.
— industries of, 199.
— lake of, 4, 8, 12, 19, 188, 195.
— "Natives" of, 208, 213.
— Reformation in, 146-150.
— refugees in, 205.
Genevois, 147, 161.
German migration, the, 4.
— writers, 195.
Germany, 4, 8, 11, 21, 22, 25, 28, 44, 65(3), 94, 95, 97, 103, 109(2), 110, 122, 123, 127, 128(2), 131, 134(2), 138, 142, 154, 164, 194, 195, 228, 250, 255, 277, 278, 281, 282, 287, 292(2).
— Agnes, Empress of, 25.
— Kings and Emperors of, 21-25 :
  Adolf of Nassau, 45(3).
  Charles IV., 62, 63(2), 78.
  — V., 141, 142.
  Conrad I., 20.
  — II., 23.
  — III., 34.
  Frederick II., 38, 39(3), 40(2), 43, 44.
  — — Henry, son of, 39.
  — III., 94, 96, 97, 109(2). *And see* Austria.
  — — Maximilian, son of, 96, 109-111.
  Henry I., 21, 22(2).
  — II., 22(2), 23(2).
  — — Kunigunde, wife of, 22.
  — III., 23-25, 27.
  — IV., 26(2), 39.
  — V., 34.
  — VII., 45, 46(2).

Index. 311

Germany—*cont.*:
— Kings and Emperors of—*cont.*:
Lothaire, 19, 27.
Louis II., the German, 18, 19.
— IV., the Bavarian, 46, 47, 56-58.
Otto I., 22(4), 24(2), 28.
Sigismund, 83, 84.
— literature of, 195.
— Peasants' War in, 135.
Grisons, the (Graubünden), xiv, 7, 11, 16, 74, 110, 111(3), 112, 114, 116, 117, 137(2), 142, 145, 150, 161, 163-167, 186, 200, 216, 227, 232, 238, 240, 253(2), 291.
— admission to the League, 79-81.
— Leagues of, 164:
    Grey or Upper League, 80, 81, 110, 162.
    League of God's House, 80(2), 81, 107, 110, 111, 162.
    League of the Ten Jurisdictions, 81(2), 112, 162(2), 167.
Gersau, 199.
Gesler (Gessler), family of, 54.
— Hermann, 49, 50(5), 51, 53.
Gessner, Konrad, 154, 156(2).
— Salomon, 196.
Gex, 147, 161, 220.
Ghibellines, the, 40.
Giacomo, the pass of, 82.
Gibbon, the historian, 195.
Giornico, 106.
Girard, Father, 242.
Gislikon, 178, 269(2).
Glarean. *See* Loriti.
Glarus, 34, 43, 52, 61, 62, 67, 68(8), 69(2), 70, 73, 76, 80, 86(2), 87(2), 91(2), 92, 117, 123, 128, 130, 131, 137(2), 140, 141(2), 144, 145, 155, 158, 164, 186(2), 187, 200(2), 209(2), 219(2), 221, 239, 257, 285.
— conflagration in, 289.
— enters the League, 59-62.
— the League, 72.
— industries of, 199.
Glatt, the, 87.
Glatthal, the, 73.
Goethe, 195(2).
Goldbach, 73.
Golder, 157.
Göldli, Capt. Geo., 143(2).
— family of, 105, 106.
— Heinrich, 105.
Göldlin, provost of Beromünster, 143(2).
Gotteshausleute, 34.
Gotthelf, Jeremiah, 291.
Göttingen, 207.

Gottlieben, 91.
Gottsched, 195.
Gradner, Barons of, 92.
Graf, Michael, 86, 87, 89.
— Urs, 124.
Graffenried, Colonel von, 221.
— family of, 179, 204.
Grandson, 27, 97, 99(2), 146, 147.
— battle of, 97, 98, 110, 120.
Granval, monastery of, 16.
Grauholz, 221.
Grebel, bailiff in Grüningen, 198(2).
— Konrad, 134.
Greece, 122.
Greeks, the, 3, 124.
Greifensee, 73, 89, 134.
Grimsel, 71.
Grindelwald, 27.
Grubenmann, 200.
Grunholzer of Zurich, 283.
Grüningen, 73, 134, 173, 198.
Grütli Society, the, 280.
Gruyères (Greyerz), 27.
— Counts of, 32, 58.
Gubel, the (near Zug), 144.
Guelfs, the, 19, 26, 38, 40.
"Guerre aux Batons." *See* "Stecklikrieg."
Gugger, Canon, 198.
"Guglers," the, 64.
Guilds, the, 60, 70, 72, 104, 105, 137, 170, 179, 191, 232, 233, 242.
Guillimann, Franz, 53.
Gujer, Jacob, 197, 249.
Gümminen, 27, 37, 58.
Gundoldingen, Peter von, 73.
Gütikhausen, 13.

Häberlin, Fürsprech, 285.
Hadlaub, John, 42.
Hagenbach, K., 291.
— Peter von, 95(2), 96.
Haldenstein, 202(2), 213.
Haller, Albrecht von, 193(2), 194.
— Berthold, 137.
— K. L. von, 242.
Hallwil, Hans von, 99.
— Thuring von, 88.
Hämmerlin (Hemmerli), Felix, canon of Zurich, 49, 91, 122, 127.
Hans towns, the, 72.
Hapsburg, 84, 203.
— Albert of, 45(4), 53(3).
— counts of, 32, 40(2), 49.
— house of, 38, 39(5), 41, 42-46, 48, 49(6), 54, 56, 100(2), 109, 164, 177.
— — genealogical table of, 38.
— — revolts against, 48, 56.

Hapsburg, New, castle of, 40.
— Rudolf the old of, 38.
— — II. of, 40.
— — III. of, 41(2), 42-44, 45(3), 49, 53.
Hard, 110.
Hasle, valley of, 34, 58(2).
Hatto, Bishop of Basle, 18.
Hauenstein, the, 200.
Hauterêt (Canton Vaud), monastery of, 35.
Hauterive, monastery of, 35.
Heer, Oswald, 291.
Hegau, 92.
Hegetschweiler, the botanist, 234, 249.
Heidegger, Johann Heinrich, 189.
Helvetia, 194, 275, 280, 283.
Helvetians, the, 3-5, 6(4), 7, 11.
Helvetic Confession, the, 150(2).
— Constitution, the, 222-225, 227, 228, 229-237, 254, 273.
— Republic, the, 211, 213, 228.
— Society, the, 192-199, 211, 212, 233, 244, 254.
— State, the, 255.
Henzi, Samuel, 206(2).
Herder, 195.
Héricourt, 97.
Herzog, Bishop, 287.
— Colonel, 281.
— Marianus, 224.
Herzogenbuchsee, 37, 178.
Hesse, Philip of, 141.
Hirzel, ——, 88.
— Bernhard, pastor, 262.
— Dr. Hans Kaspar, 196(3), 247.
— Melchior, 258, 261.
Hochberg, William von, 88.
Hofwil, 235.
Hohentwiel, 24.
Holbein, 124(2).
Holland, 181, 183, 184(2), 185.
Holy Alliance, the, 242.
— League, the, 114(2).
Homberg, Werner von, 46.
Hombrechtikon, 73.
Honau, 269.
Höngg, 73.
Horgen, 73, 214, 233(2).
Horn, General, 167(2).
Hottinger, Johann Heinrich, 189.
— — Jakob, 189, 247.
Hotze, General, 227(2).
Huguenots, the, 160, 163(2), 166, 184.
Hummelwald, the, 186.
Hundwil, 75.
Hungarians, the, 19.
Hungary, 121.

Hüningen, fortress of, 184, 240.
Huns, the, 11.
Hurden, 87, 187.
Hürlimann-Landis, 261, 262.
Hutwil, 177.

Iceland, 53.
Ilanz, 137.
Illens, 99.
Imgrund, Heinrich, 102.
"Immunity," 19, 29, 31(2), 33, 39.
Indies, East, 293.
Indo-European race, the, 3.
Initiative, the, 205, 284, 285(3), 286(2).
Inquisition, the, 158, 159, 190.
Ins (Jens), 64.
Irgenhusen, 13.
Irish monks, 16.
Iselin, Isaak, 195, 196, 197, 199.
— J. C., 54.
Italian Art, 9.
Italy, 7, 8, 10(2), 11, 16, 39, 44, 81, 113(2), 114, 115(2), 122(2), 123, 124, 151, 228, 279(2), 282, 292(2).
— Adelaide, Queen of, 23(2).
Ittingen, 139.
— monastery of, 35, 136.

Japan, 293.
Jarnac, 163.
Jenatsch, Geo., 164, 166(5).
Jens. *See* Ins.
Jesuits, the, 158, 159(3), 160, 161, 164, 202, 242, 260, 263, 264-267, 268(2), 269, 283.
— expulsion of, 270, 288.
Jetzer, ——, a tailor, 127.
Jews, the, 190, 284, 286.
Jud, Leo, 144, 153.
Julia, Alpinula, 6.
Julier, the, 8.
Julius Alpinus, 6.
Jura, the, xiv, 3, 5, 15, 16, 19, 25, 43, 58, 97(2), 100, 139, 220, 259(2), 269, 287.
Justinger, Conrad, 48, 122.

Kaiser, Jakob, 140.
Kamor, 5.
Kander, the, 188.
Kappel, 36, 73, 157, 171, 181.
— charters of, 144, 172(2), 173.
— First Peace of, 141.
— monastery of, 35, 127.
— Second Peace of, 144.
— Wars of, 139-145, 181, 214.
Katzis, 36.

Index. 313

Keller, Augustin, 264, 266, 286.
— Ferdinand, 291.
— Gottfried, 291.
— Heinrich, 234.
— Dr. Ludwig, 254, 258, 261.
Kern, Dr., 278.
Kesselring, Kilian, 167(3).
Kessler, John, 137.
Kiburg, 135, 191.
— counts of, 32, 41, 58, 65.
— county of, 41, 73, 77, 87(2), 173(2).
— Eberhard von, 57, 58(3).
— Hartmann von, 41, 42, 57(2).
— house of, 32, 33, 37, 38(3), 40-42, 55, 57(3), 65(5).
— Rudolf von, 65.
— war of, 64-69.
Kinzigkulm, the, 228.
Kistler, Peter, 104(2).
Kleinjogg, Farmer, 196(2).
Klein-Hüningen, 257.
Kleist, 195.
Klingenberg, 42.
— Chronicle, 53.
Klopstock, 195(2).
Kloten, 262.
Klus, the, 167.
Knonau, xiii, 84(2), 87, 173.
Kopp, Joseph Eutych, 54.
Korsakow, the Russian general, 228.
Kreuzlingen (in the Thurgau), 258.
— monastery of, 235.
Künzle, John, 215(2).
Küssnach (canton Schwyz), 52, 252, 256.
— "Hohle Gasse" in, 51, 54.
Küssnach (canton Zürich), 73, 106, 174, 215, 248(2), 258.
— — — Memorial of, 248.
— — — monastery of, 133.

Lachat, Bishop, 287.
Lachen, 252.
Laharpe, Frederick Cæsar, 213(2), 216(4), 217, 223, 229, 245.
Lake (or Pile) Dwellings, 1-3.
La Lance, monastery of, 35.
Landenberg, 49(4).
Landsgemeinden, 54(2), 70(2), 75, 132, 137, 170, 175, 176, 177, 224, 231, 232, 245, 260, 285(2).
Langenthal, 283.
Langnau, 176.
Langres, 12.
Laufen, 160.
Laufenburg, house of, 39, 42(2).
Laupen, 27, 37, 58, 60, 62.
— battle of, 57-59, 99.

Lausanne, 5, 15(2), 33, 36, 98, 146(2), 153, 195(2), 200, 231, 289.
— bishop of, 26, 31.
— university of, 148.
Lavater, J. C., 197, 198(2), 201.
— Rudolf, 134, 143.
Lax, 71.
"League above the Lake," the, 76, 77.
Leipzig, battle of, 237.
Léman, 222.
— République du, 220.
Lenzburg, 43, 84, 246.
— counts of, 32.
Leu, Joseph, 263, 265, 267.
Leuenberger, Nicholas, 175, 176, 177 (3), 178(4).
"Libertines," the, 149.
Liestal, 217, 247, 251(2), 256.
Limmat, the, 162, 200, 227.
Lindau, 75.
Lindenhof (Zurich), 41.
Linth, the, 68, 235.
— Escher von der, 212(2), 235, 247.
Livinen. *See* Val Leventina.
Locarno, 114, 118, 151, 152, 158, 263.
Lombardy, 4, 114, 279.
London, 293.
Loriti, Heinrich (Glarean), 123, 154.
Lorraine, 97, 99.
— René, Duke of, 99, 124.
Louvois, 184.
Lowerz, 52.
— castle of, 49, 54.
Lucerne, 33, 38, 40, 41, 43, 45, 46, 52, 64-66(3), 69, 72, 73, 79, 82, 84(2), 91, 97, 98(2), 101, 102, 105, 106, 110(2), 116, 117, 119, 121, 124, 129, 135, 136, 138, 140, 141, 157, 159, 160, 163, 170(2), 173, 175-178, 182, 185, 187, 195, 204, 206, 211, 222-224, 232, 241-245, 247, 253(2), 255, 258(2), 259-267, 269, 270, 285.
— council of, 107, 175, 245.
— Diets held at, 99, 108, 135, 239, 254.
— enters the League, 55-57.
— government of, 206, 219, 247, 250(2).
— *Hertenstein* house in, 124.
— League of, 71.
— massacre of, 57.
— mayor of, 73.
— *Rathaus* in, 188.
— Town Hall of, 156.
Lugano, 114, 118(2), 222, 263.
Lupicinus, 15.
Lupulus. *See* Wölflin.
Lussi, Melchior, 159.
Luther, Martin, 131(3), 137.

x 2

Lützel, monastery of, 35.
Luvini, 263.
Luziensteig, 110.
Lyons, council of, 39.

Machiavelli, 115.
Maggiatal, 118.
Maienfeld, 85, 110(2).
Maiental, 114.
Main, the, 4, 11.
Malans, 85.
Malmaison, Scheme of, 230.
"Mamelukes," the, 146.
Männedorf, 73.
Manuel, Nicholas, 124, 127.
Manz, Felix, 134(2).
Marburg, 142.
March, 86, 252.
Mariastein, 263.
Marignano, 115, 129, 131.
Marius, Bishop, 15.
— the Roman general, 4.
Mark, the, 13, 32(2), 85.
Markgenossenschaft, the, 13, 32.
Martigny (*Octodurum*), 6, 10, 15(2).
Martyrs, Christian, 10, 25.
Maschwanden, 73.
Massena, 227, 228.
Mätsch, von, 86.
Matzingen, 247.
Mayence, 24.
Mazzini, 257.
"Mediation," Act of, 231, 245.
— Constitution of, 229-240, 241, 243, 271, 280.
Medici, Jacob of, 142.
Meier, Rudolf, 234.
Meilen, 73, 106.
Meiss, ——, 87, 89.
Melanchthon, Philip, 137.
Melchi, 49, 50.
Mellingen, 84, 118, 178, 186.
Menard, the French general, 220(3).
Mendrisio, 114, 118, 263.
Mengaud, the French ambassador, 219, 220.
Menzingen, 70.
Meracher, of Stäfa, 214.
Mercenaries, 64, 99, 112, 121, 122, 123, 125, 129, 132, 136, 143, 151, 165, 166, 174, 182-185, 241, 279.
Merian, Mathias, 189.
— the naturalist, 291.
Mermillod, a priest, 287.
Merovingians, the, 14, 17(2).
Metternich, the Austrian minister, 238(2).
Meyer, Bernhard, 263, 265, 268.

Meyer, family of, 206, 207.
— Prof. Dr. Gerold, of Knonau, xiii.
— Konrad Ferd., 291,
— Valentine, 207(2).
Meyerskappel, 270.
Milan, xii, 78, 81(2), 82(3), 105, 121(2), 129, 164.
— archbishops of, 158.
— dukes of, 178.
— expeditions to, xi, 105.
— Spanish governor of, 164.
— wars of, 112-116.
Misocco, 158.
Mönchaltorf, 73.
Montaigne, 151, 152.
Monte Rosa, 114.
Montesquieu, 194.
Montfort, 42, 80.
— von, 86.
Monthey, 212.
Montsax (Misox), 80.
Mont Terrible (Department), 213.
Morat (Murten), 23, 37, 40, 41, 55, 98, 99(3), 107, 120(2), 146, 147, 225, 230, 244, 249.
— Peace of, 42.
Morell, P. Gall, 291.
Morgarten, 224.
— battle of, 44-47, 55, 61, 104, 155, 225.
Morges, 188.
Moudon, 27.
Moulier, French ambassador, 183(2).
Mülhausen, 93(2), 95, 117, 139, 150, 162, 167(2), 168.
Müller, Johann von, 53, 201(2), 213, 234.
— Thaddäus, 244.
— the engineer, 234.
Müller-Friedberg, Landammann, 250.
Mümliswil, 263.
Münch, Burkhard, 90.
Münchenbuchsee, 258, 283.
Münchenwiler, 99.
Münsingen, 251.
Münster, 168(3).
Münsterthal, the (Grisons), 81, 110, 111, 165.
Munzinger, Joseph, 250, 254, 271, 274.
Muralt, family of, 151, 158.
Murbach, abbey of, 43, 56.
— abbot of, 40, 41.
Mure, Conrad von, 42.
Muri, abbot of, 31.
— monastery of, 26, 35, 264.
Murifeld, Peace of, 177, 178.
Murner, a Franciscan monk, 138, 140(3).

Index. 315

Musslin (of Berne), 170.
Musso, 142.
— castle of, 142.
Muttenz, 90.
Myconius, 133.
Mythenstein, the, 50.

Näfels, 61, 6.
— battle of, 68, 69, 78.
— Freuler palace in, 188.
— war of, 64-69.
Naff, of St. Gall, 274.
Nägeli, Franz, 147.
— Hans Georg, 234(3).
Nancy, 97, 99(2).
Nänikon, 89.
Naples, 174, 279.
Napoleon Bonaparte, 216-218, 222, 229-231, 236-240, 269.
— Louis, 257.
— III., 277(2), 278, 279, 280(2).
Narbonne (Provence), 6.
Nassau, 248.
Navarre, Henry of, 160. *And see* France.
Netherlands, the, 100, 149, 154, 183.
Neuchâtel (Neuenburg), 23, 36, 37, 43, 100, 149, 154, 185(4). 236, 239, 252, 253, 255, 256, 270, 276-282, 285.
— counts of, 32, 58(2), 100, 117, 147.
— lake of, 3(2), 188.
Neueneck, 221.
Neuhof, 203.
Neuss, siege of, 96, 97.
New Bailiwick, the, 87.
Nidau, 58, 266.
— counts of, 58.
Nidegg (Berne), 41.
Nidwalden. *See* Unterwalden.
Niggeler, 267.
Notker, the "Stammerer" or the "Saint," 20.
— III., the "Thick-lipped," 24.
Novara, 112, 114, 120, 129.
Noviodunum. *See* Nyon.
Noyon, 148.
Nussbaumen, 136.
Nyon, 6.

Oberland, the Bernese, 25(2), 67, 111, 223.
Oberhofen, 67.
Obersimmenthal, 67.
Oberwinterthur, 9.
Obwalden. *See* Unterwalden.
Ochs, Peter, 217, 218, 222, 229, 256.
Ochsenbein, Colonel, 266-268, 274.
Octodurum. *See* Martigny.

Ohmgeld or Ungeld, 173.
Ökolampadius, 137.
Olten (Soleure), 243, 247.
— bridge of, 188.
Orbe, 97, 146-148.
Orelli, family of, 151, 158.
— Joh. Kasp., 244, 247, 258, 261, 291.
Orgetorix, 4.
Osnabrück, 168.
Ostrogoths, the, 14.
Oswalden, 101.
Othmar, 16.
Ottingen, 27.
Overmeilen (canton Zurich), 2.

Palatinate, the, 149, 184.
Palmerston, Lord, 270.
Panix, pass of, 228.
Paracelsus, 156.
Paris, 182, 184(2), 212, 214, 217(2), 222, 230, 231, 248, 270(2), 277, 278, 293.
— Notre Dame, 183.
— Swiss club at, 212.
— university of, 121.
Parity, districts of, 145.
Passwang, the, 200.
"Patriciates," 170, 206.
Pavia, 114(2), 131, 136,
Payerne, 15, 23(2), 26, 36.
Peasants' War, the, 169-180, 208(2).
Pellikan, 133.
Perpetual Peace, the, 96.
Perrier, 283.
Pestalozzi, Johann Heinrich, 198, 202, 203, 226(3), 235, 236, 242, 258.
Pfäffers, 43.
— abbot of, 128.
— monastery of, 16, 19, 21, 35, 259.
Pfäffikon (canton Schwyz), 87(2), 224, 252.
Pfäffikon (canton Zurich), 262.
Pfenninger of Stäfa, 214.
Pfin (*Ad Fines*), 7.
Pfyffer, Edward, 245.
— family of, 258.
— General, 234.
— Kasimir, 245, 254(3), 256, 267.
— Ludwig, 159, 160, 163.
Piacenza, 132.
Picardy, 148.
Pile-dwellings. *See* Lake-dwellings.
Pirminius, 16.
Planta, Dr., 202.
— family of 161, 164, 165.
— Pompey, 166(2).
— Rudolf, 164, 166.
— — the Younger, 166.

Platifer, 71.
Plato, 130.
Platter, Thomas, 153(3).
Po, the, 5.
Pontarlier, 97.
Pope Innocent IV., 39, 40.
— John XXIII., 83.
— Julius II., 113, 114(2).
— Pius II., 92, 122.
— — IV., 158.
— Sixtus V., 160.
Porrentruy (Pruntrut), 139, 160, 213(2), 216, 247.
Pragel, 228.
Prätigau, 80, 81, 85, 112.
Pratteln, 90, 256.
Premonstratensian order, the, 35.
Priests' Charter, the, 73.
Printing, introduction of, 123.
Provence, 6, 12.
Prussia, 184, 185, 239, 252, 255, 270, 271, 277, 278, 281(2).
— King Frederick of, 185.
Puschlav, 81.

Ragatz, 90.
Rahn, Capt., 184.
— J. H., 189, 190.
Rahn-Escher, Dr., 262.
Rambach, the, 111.
Rapp, General, 231.
Rapperswil, 60(2), 66, 92, 144, 145, 181, 186, 187, 224, 258.
— counts of, 32, 60.
— family of, 32.
Raron, barons of, 78, 82.
— family of, 78, 79(5), 86.
— Witschard von, 79.
Rastadt, 217.
— Congress of, 217(3).
Ratbert of Zurich, 20.
Rauracian Republic, the, 213.
Raurici, the, 3, 6.
Rautiberg, the, 68.
Rautifeld, 61.
Ravenna, 114.
Razüns, 80, 240.
— von, 86.
Red Cross League, the, 282.
Reding, Alois, 224, 230, 260.
— family of, 209.
— Ital, 86(2).
Referendum, the, 284, 285(3), 286(2), 289.
Reformation, the, 126-162, 280.
— in Berne, 138.
— in Zurich, 130-135.
Reformation in Geneva, 146-150.

Refugees in Switzerland, 152, 242, 257, 276, 279.
Regensberg, 42, 73.
— barons of, 32, 41(2).
Regensburg, Peace of, 63.
Regula, the martyr, 10.
Reichenau, monastery of, 16, 18, 20, 21, 24.
Reinhard (federalist), 230.
— Landammann, 238.
Reinhart, Anna, 132.
Rellikan, 154, 156.
Rengg, 230.
Reugger, Dr. Albrecht, 212, 225(2).
"Restoration," the, 237-246, 254.
Reubel, an Alsatian, 216, 218.
Reuchlin, 123.
Reuss, the, 5, 27, 38.
Revision, Constitutional, 246-257, 264, 266, 268, 270, 271, 283-289.
Revolution, the French, 208, 211, 212(2), 214, 216-225, 231, 242, 245.
— — of July, 246-250.
Rhætia, xv, 6(2), 10(2), 11(2), 16, 17, 19, 22, 23, 79, 81, 85, 86, 161, 164, 222.
Rhætians, the, 3, 5(2), 8.
Rhæo-Romans, the, 11-16.
Rhæto-Romance race, xiv.
Rheinau, monastery of, 20, 21, 26, 35.
Rheinfeld, Rudolf of, 25-28.
— house of, 26, 27, 32.
Rheintal, the, 7, 8, 76, 85, 92, 118(2), 139, 145, 186(2), 219, 222.
Rhine, the, xiv, 5(2), 7(4), 9(3), 11(4), 14, 15, 25, 42, 43(2), 65, 71, 73, 80, 92(3), 93, 109, 110(3), 162, 184, 185, 200, 209, 227, 228, 237, 238.
— frontier, 5, 11, 238.
— Middle, 93.
— Upper, 80(2), 96, 159.
Rhone, the, 3, 5.
Richelieu, Cardinal, 166, 187.
Richterswil, 227, 261.
Riedi, Thomas, 79.
Richen, 257.
Rigi, the, 248.
Ringgenberg, 71.
Rissi, Peter, 82.
Rohan, Duc de, 166.
Rolle (canton Vaud), 200, 213.
Rolle, Christoph, 285.
Romainmotier (canton Vaud), monastery of, 15(2), 26.
Roman civilization, 5-11.
— — effaced, 12.
— Empire, 7.

Index. 317

Roman power, fall of the, 9–11.
— roads, 7, 9.
Romance districts, xiv, 25, 41, 212.
— people, xiv, xv, 78.
Romans, the, 3(3), 4(3), 5–13, 15, 115, 124.
Romanus, 15(3).
Rome, 8(2), 9, 122, 206, 259, 266.
— Emperors of:
    Augustus, 5.
    Constantine Chlorus, 9.
    Diocletian, 9, 10.
    Domitian, 7.
    Gratian, 9.
    Julian, 9.
    Maximian, 9.
    Nero, 6.
    Valentinian I., 9.
Rooter Berg, The, 269(2).
Rorschach, 107, 140.
Rösch, Abbot Ulrich, 107.
Rotenburg (Rothenburg), 56, 57, 66(3).
Roth, Hans, 65.
Rothenthurm, 224, 260.
Rothpletz, Colonel, 266.
Rotwil 117, 167.
Rotzberg, the, 51.
Rotzloch, 54.
Röubli, Wilhelm, 132.
Rougemont, monastery of, 26.
Rousseau, 194(2), 198, 207.
Rüeggisberg, monastery of, 26.
Rumisberg, 65.
Rümlang, 73.
Rüschlikon, 73.
Rüttimann, under-bailiff of Nussbaumen, 136.
Russ, Melchior, 52, 122.
Russia, 237(3), 239.
— Catherine, empress of, 213.
Russwil, committee of, 263.
Rüti, 134.
— monastery of, 35, 134.
Rütli, the, 44, 50, 54(2), 177, 289.

Saane, the, 12, 25(2).
— valley of, 157.
Sabaudia. See Savoy.
Sachseln, 102.
Säckingen, 15(2), 43, 73.
St. Bernard, 8.
— the great, 7, 25.
St. Denis, 163(2).
St. Fridolin, 15.
St. Gall, 26, 33, 91, 107–109, 123, 134, 136–139, 145, 150, 151, 153, 186(2), 201, 215, 219, 222, 227, 232, 239, 250, 251, 253, 255, 258, 259, 268, 274, 283.

St. Gall, abbey of, 16, 18(2), 19, 20(2), 21(4), 24, 25, 35, 43, 127, 140, 186.
— abbots of, 19, 31, 75, 91, 117, 140(3), 141, 144, 185, 186, 215(5).
— burgomaster of, 137.
— council of, 284.
— enters the League, 75–77.
— government of, 250.
— industries of, 199, 235.
— town of, 117, 140, 221, 236, 253.
Savoy, 12, 43, 78(2), 79, 82, 97(4), 99(2), 100, 121, 129, 146, 147(2), 158, 160(2), 208, 231, 240, 279(2), 280(5).
— counts of, 32, 78:
    Amadeus VII., 78(2).
    Peter II., 41, 42, 97.
— dukes of, 79, 82:
    Charles III., 146(3), 147.
    Charles Emmanuel, 161.
    Philibert Emmanuel, 161.
— house of, 28, 38, 41, 42, 43, 146, 147.
— Margaret of, 42.
St. Gallenkappel, 250.
— Gotthard, 81, 82(3), 228.
— — railway, 282, 292, 293.
— Jakob an der Birs, 90, 94(3), 115, 244.
— — (on the Sihl), 89.
— John, order of, 133, 140.
— Julien, Peace of, 147.
— Martin, 15.
— Maurice (the saint), 10.
— Maurice (Valais), 6, 10, 19, 212.
— — monastery of, 15.
— Meinrad, 25.
— Urban, monastery of, 35.
— Ursanne, monastery of, 16.
Sales, Francis de, 161.
Salis, family of, 161.
— Ulysses de, 166.
Salis-Soglio, General von, 269.
Salvenach, 99.
Samson, Bernhardin, 131.
Saracens, the, 19.
Sargans, 76, 85, 86(2), 87, 118, 139, 219, 222, 239.
Sarnen, 34, 40, 49(4), 51, 54.
— League of, 254–257.
Saussure, the naturalist, 201.
Sax, 42.
— family of, 82.
Saxons, the, 108.
Schaffhausen, 26, 83, 92, 93(2), 117, 134–136, 137, 138, 145, 150, 153, 167, 170, 179(2), 180, 188, 189, 198, 200, 209, 219, 223, 227, 238(2), 251, 253, 257, 285.

Schaffhausen enters the League, 112, 116.
Schanfigg, 81, 85, 112.
Schattorf, 54.
Schauenburg, General, 220-222, 224(2), 225.
Schauensee, Meyer von, 211.
Scherr, Dr. Thomas, 258(2), 261(2), 262.
Scheuchzer, J. J., 189, 190(2), 193(2).
Schibi, Christian, 176, 178(2).
Schiller, 44, 53, 249.
Schilling, ——, 102.
— Diebold, 52, 122.
Schindellegi, the, 224.
Schinner, Matthew, bishop of Sion, 113.
Schinz, 198.
— Dr., 245.
Schinznach, 196, 244.
Schlözer, Professor, 207.
Schmalcalden, 142, 162.
Schmid, ——, burgomaster of Zurich, 114.
Schmied, Konrad, 133.
Schnell, Karl, 247, 251.
— Ludwig, 247, 251.
Schönbrunner, Pastor, 143.
Schöno, burgomaster of Zurich, 68, 70, 87.
Schoosshalde, 43.
Schuhmacher, family of, 206, 207.
— Joseph Anton, 208(2).
— Placidus, 206.
Schuler, the historian, 234.
Schüpfheim, 101, 177.
Schwaderloo, 111.
Schwanau, 51, 52.
Schweizer, Alexander, 291.
— Kaspar, 189.
Schwerzenbach, 140.
Schwyz, 34(4), 38, 39(3), 40(2), 41, 43, 44(2), 45(2), 46(5), 47-49(6), 50-52, 62, 63, 68-70, 72, 73(2), 75, 76, 84, 85(3), 86(10), 87(4), 91(2), 98, 108, 117, 119, 122, 136, 140(3), 141, 160, 164, 181(2), 184-186, 187, 201, 209, 219, 221, 223, 224(3), 225, 227, 239, 255, 256, 260(2), 265, 269.
— Diets at, 224, 230, 256.
— disturbances in, 250-254, 256.
— division of, 252, 256.
— industries of, 199.
— *Landsgemeinde of*, 224.
— Outer, 252, 256.
— reunion of, 257.
Soleure (Solothurn), 5, 7, 10, 23, 33, 35, 37, 55, 58, 65(4), 73, 93, 94, 96, 97, 98, 100(2), 101(2), 102, 110, 111, 117(2), 119, 124, 129, 137, 138, 145(2), 160, 167, 168, 170, 175, 176(3), 177, 179(2), 182, 187, 188, 192, 198(2), 201(2), 221, 223(2), 232, 238, 241(2), 243(2), 247, 250, 251, 253, 254, 255, 258(2), 263(2), 266, 274, 285, 286, 287.
Soleure, council of, 247, 250.
— Diets held at, 24.
— enters the League, 103, 116.
— government of, 207.
— massacre of, 65.
— mayor of, 145, 157.
— siege of, 55.
Scotland, 149.
Seduin, the, 4.
Seedorf, Count of, 52.
Seeland, 67.
Sempach, 66, 244.
— battle of, 67, 69, 104, 155, 225.
— Convention of, 69, 74, 103.
— war of, 64-69.
Seneca, 130.
Senft-Pilsach, Count of, 238.
Sentis, 5.
Septimer, the, 8.
Sequani, the, 3, 6.
Serfs, 13(2).
Servet, 149.
Seven Cantons, League of the, 254-257, 262, 264.
Seven Years' War, the, 192.
Sforza, family of, 105, 112.
— Louis (the Moor), 112(2), 113, 114.
— Maximilian, 114(3).
Sidler, Landammann in Zug, 254.
Siegwart-Müller, Konstantin, 263, 267.
Sihl, the, 88, 89(2).
Simmental, the, 58.
Simmler, Josias, 155, 156.
Simplon, the, 236.
— Département du, 236.
Sion (Sitten), 15, 31, 33, 36, 97.
— bishops of, 78, 113.
Sitter, the, 208(2).
Snell, Dr. Ludwig, 248, 249, 257.
Sonderbund, the, 256, 264-267, 273, 274(2).
— War of the, 267-270.
Spain, 103, 113, 158, 161, 163, 164, 166, 167(2), 174, 178, 237.
— Philip II., King of, 160.
Speicher, 76.
Spinoza, 190.
Splügen, the, 8.
Spöndli, the advocate, 262.
Stäfa, 73, 200, 214(3), 215(2), 249(2).

Stalder, Pastor, 234.
Stammheim, 136(2).
Stämpfli, 267, 280, 282, 283.
Stans, 34, 51, 102(3), 159(2), 187.
— Covenant of, xii, 100-108, 176.
Stapfer, Albrecht, 225(4), 226(3).
— of Horgen, 214.
Staufen, Frederick of, 26(2).
— Faction, the, 26.
Stauffach, family of, 45.
Stauffacher ("Staupacher"), Werner, 50(3), 51(2), 53, 54.
"Staupacher." *See* Stauffacher.
"Stecklikreig," 230.
Steiger, Dr., 267.
— family of, 179.
— von, Mayor of Berne, 221.
Stein, 7, 9, 54, 73, 92, 136.
— (canton Zurich), 167.
— castle of, 136.
Stein on the Rhine, 153, 209.
Steinach, 16.
Stettler, Michael, 189.
Stockar, 198.
Stoffeln, Cuno von, abbot of St. Gall, 75, 76.
Stoss, the, 76.
Strasburg, 52, 149, 162(3), 184.
— count of, 58.
— mayor of, 141.
Strättlingen, castle of, 58.
Strauss, Dr. David, 261(3), 262.
Streuli, Dr., 248(2).
Studer, the naturalist, 291.
Stumpf, Johannes, a chronicler, 52, 155, 156.
Stuppa, 184.
Stürler, family of, 179, 204.
Sturm, Jakob, mayor of Strassburg, 141.
Stüssi, Rudolf, 86, 87(3), 89.
Styger, Paul, 224.
Suabia, 19, 22, 27, 66, 77(2), 109.
— duke of, 26.
Suabian League, the, 110.
— War, the, 81, 108-112.
Sulzberger, 285.
Sulzer, 201.
Sumiswald, 176.
Sundgau, 93(2), 110, 111.
Sursee, 64, 84.
Suter, Anton Joseph, 209(3).
Suworow, the Russian general, 223.
Sweden, 167(2).
Swiss People, Manual of the History of, by Dr. Karl Dändliker, xi.
Switzerland, Burgundian, 19, 170.
— Early history of, 1-37.

Switzerland, a European power, 94-116.
— French, 196, 274.
— German, 19, 22, 25. 196, 274.
— incorporation into the German Empire, 21.
— invasions of, 211-228, 238, 276.
— neutrality of, 116, 165, 183, 192, 218, 227, 237, 238, 240, 276, 279, 280.
— separation from the German Empire, 112, 168.

Tal Glarus, 15.
Tanninghofen, 13.
Tätwil, 61.
Tegerfeld, Conrad von, 45.
Teiling, Frischhans, 105, 106(4).
Tell, William, 44, 50(7), 51(3), 52(6), 53(2), 54(6), 155, 177.
Tessin, the, 81.
— — Upper, 81.
Teufen, 42, 75.
Teutonic tribes, 3, 4, 9, 11-13.
Thalwil, 73.
Thäyngen (canton Schaffhausen), 1.
"Thebans," the, 10, 15.
Thirty Years' War, the, 163-168, 174(2), 183(2), 214.
Thorberg, 66.
— Peace of, 63, 64, 67.
Thun, 27, 37, 56, 57, 65, 173.
Thur, the, 5, 71.
Thurgau, the, 17, 19, 27, 38, 42, 66, 77, 92(2), 108, 111, 112, 118(2), 136(4), 139(2), 145, 164, 167(2), 181, 185, 186, 219, 222, 227(2), 228, 232, 235, 243, 247, 251, 254, 255, 257, 258(2), 285.
Thusis, 164, 165.
Tiberius, 5.
Ticino (Tessin), xv, 113, 114, 116(2), 118, 159, 219, 232, 236, 245(2), 263(2), 269, 274, 285.
Tigorini, the, 4.
Tilly, General, 167.
Tirano, 165.
Toggenburg, 12, 24, 42, 77, 85-87, 140(2), 141, 145(2), 208, 219.
— counts of, 32, 81(2), 84(2), 85(2), 86.
— Frederick VII. of, 85(3).
— War of, 185-187, 192(2), 193.
Toko, 5.
Tonchin, 189.
Töss, 134.
— bailiff of, 135.
— the, 5.
Tösstal, the, 73.

Trajan, the Emperor, 7.
Trattengeld, 173.
Trent, Council of, 158, 160(2), 163.
Trèves (Trier), 96.
Triens, 80.
Trientbach, 265.
Triesen, 110.
Trinkler, abbot of Kappel, 127, 128.
— of Zurich, 87.
Trogen, 245.
Troglodytes. *See* Cave-dwellers.
Trons, 80.
Troxler, Prof., 242, 244, 271.
Trücklibund, the, 192.
Truns, 71.
Tscharner, family of, 204.
Tschudi, Giles, 52, 53(2), 55, 155(2).
Tschudin, Valentine, 137.
Tuggen, 16.
Turenne, General, 168.
Turicum. *See* Zurich.
Turretin, 189.
Tutilo, 20.
"Twing-Uri." *See* Zwing-Uri.
Tyrol, the, 6, 111(3), 164.

Uerikon, 13.
Ufenau, 36, 87.
Ulrich, 79.
Ultramontanism, 243, 259, 263, 266, 269, 283, 287.
Ungeld. *See Ohmgeld*.
Unionists. *See* Centralists.
United States (America), 271, 282.
Universities, 199, 258, 271, 276, 288, 290. *And see* Basle, Berne, etc.
Unterseen, 67.
Unterstrass, 266.
Unterwalden, 34(2), 38, 40, 41, 44, 45, 48, 49(2), 50, 52, 62, 64, 69, 70, 79, 82, 87, 136, 143, 160, 223, 227, 230, 253, 255, 265, 285.
— Nidwalden, 46, 57, 225(2), 285.
— Obwalden, 46, 82(2), 101, 285.
Upper March, the, 85.
Uri, 18, 34(5), 38, 39(3), 40(2), 43, 44 (2), 45, 46, 48-50, 51(4), 52(2), 53, 54(3), 70, 72, 73(2) 79, 81, 82(5), 83(2), 87, 98, 105, 111, 136, 160, 166, 168, 178, 210(2), 221, 223, 227, 239, 253, 255, 265, 285.
— lake of, 50.
— traditions of, 51, 52.
Urseren, 43.
Ursus, the martyr, 10.
Uster, 196, 248, 249(2), 285.
— Day of, 249, 260, 265.
— Memorial of, 249.

Usteri, Martin, 233, 234.
— Paul, 212, 226, 230, 245(2), 247, 254.
Utrecht, Peace of, 185.
Utznach, 85, 86(3), 87, 144, 145, 164, 219, 239.

Vadian. *See* Watt.
Valais (Wallis), 4, 6, 10(2), 15, 17, 19, 28, 38, 74, 80, 82, 117, 145, 156, 159, 160, 213, 222, 236, 239, 240, 242, 262, 265, 266, 269, 270.
— liberation of the, 78, 79.
— Lower, 7, 12, 79, 97, 99, 100, 212, 252(2), 263, 265.
— Upper, 25, 71, 78, 79, 97(2), 99, 212, 252, 255, 262, 263, 265(2).
Val Blegno, 159.
Val de Moutier (Münstertal), canton Berne, 218.
Val Leventina, (Livinen), 81, 82, 105, 106, 209, 210, 239.
Valtelline (Weltlin), the, 81, 114, 116, 142, 164(2), 165(2), 166, 216, 239, 240.
— massacre of, 165.
Varese, 82.
Vaud, the (Waadt), xv, 8, 12, 17, 28, 41(2), 97(3), 100, 149, 151(2), 164, 172, 178, 200, 208-210, 212-214, 216-218, 220(5), 222, 223, 230, 232, 236, 238, 239, 245, 249, 251, 258, 266(2).
— conquest of, 146-148.
Vaz, 80.
— family of, 85.
Venice, 114, 129, 142, 164.
Veragri, the, 4.
Verbigeni, the, 4.
Verdun, Treaty of, 19.
Veto, the, 284, 286.
Victor, the martyr, 10.
Victor Emmanuel, King, 279.
Victorides, the family of, 14.
Vienna, 239.
— Congress of, 239(2), 240, 279, 280.
— university of, 130.
Vilmergen, 84.
— Wars of, 180-191.
Vindonissa. *See* Windisch.
Viol, Hans, 121.
Viret, Peter, 148.
Vischer, Colonel, 256.
Visconti, family of, 105.
Visp, 78.
Vitellius, 6.
Vitudurum. *See* Winterthur.

Vogel, the artist, 243.
Vögelinseck, 76.
Volketswil, 13.
Voltaire, 195, 208.
Vorarlberg, 77, 85.

Wädenswil, 12, 173(2), 174, 178, 200.
— Steffan von, 249.
Wagner, Sebastian, 137.
Waldmann, Hans, xii, 99(2), 100-108, 122, 124, 128, 129, 134, 171, 172(2), 173, 214.
Waldshut, 93(3), 95, 238.
— Peace of, 93, 94.
Wallenstadt, 86.
— lake of, 235.
Wallerau, 87, 224.
Wallgau, 111.
Wart, 42.
— Rudolf von, 45.
Wartau, 185.
Waser (of Zurich), 174, 180, 207.
Watt, Joachim von (Vadian), 137, 154, 156.
Wattenwil, General von, 238.
Wattenwyl, family of, 179, 204.
Wattwil, 250.
Weber, Johannes, 221.
— Veit, 121.
Weggis, 101.
Wehrli, J. J., 235, 236, 258.
— Max, 139.
Weimar, Bernhard, Duke of, 167, 168.
Weinfelden, 247.
Weissenburg, lords of, 58(2).
Wengi, Nicholas, mayor of Soleure, 145, 157.
Wengistein, the, 244.
Werdenberg, 76, 80, 145, 209, 219.
— Count Rudolf von, 76.
Werdmüller, Conrad, 178(2), 181.
— General Rudolf, 181, 190.
Werenfels, Pastor, 180.
Wergeld, 13.
Wermatsweil, 196.
Wernier, 206(2).
Wesen, 67, 68(3), 85(3), 86(2), 144.
— dean of, 130.
— massacre of, 68.
Wessenberg, Baron von, 243.
Westphalia, Peace of, 167, 168.
Wettingen, 200.
— monastery of, 35, 72, 73.
Wettstein, Rudolf, 168, 182(2).
Wetzikon (canton Zurich), 234.
Wieland, 195.
Wigoldingen, 185.
Wil, 75, 186.

Wilchingen, 209.
Wildenstein, Geo. von (Abbot of St. Gall), 75(2).
Wildhaus (in Toggenburg), 130.
Willi (of Horgen), 233(3).
Windegg, 85(2), 86(2).
Windisch (*Vindonissa*), 7(3), 10, 16.
"Wine Land," the, 73.
Winkelried, Arnold, 67.
— fund, 289.
— monument, 289.
Winterthur (*Vitudurum*), 7, 22, 33, 41, 42, 45, 47, 92, 93, 135, 200, 201, 204, 209, 274, 285.
— John of, 46.
Wirth, under-bailiff of Stammheim, 136(2).
Wittenbach, Thos., 123, 128, 130.
Wittenberg, 137.
Wohlenswil, 178, 246.
Wolfenschiess, ——, 53.
Wölflin (Lupulus), 130(2).
Wolhusen, 175, 176.
Wolleb, Heinrich, 111(2).
Worms, 11, 81, 239, 240.
Wormser Joch, the, 114.
Wrangel, General, 168.
Wuilleret, 283.
Wyss, J. Rudolf the younger, 243.
Wytikon, 132.

Yverdon, 27, 200, 235.

Zangger, 285.
Zäringen, Berchtold of, 26.
— — II. of, 26(2).
— Conrad III. of, 27.
— House of, 1, 26, 28, 33(2), 37-38, 42, 43.
— — extinction of, 37, 38.
— — supremacy of, 25-28.
Ziegler, Colonel, 269.
Zingg, Michael, 190.
Zofingen, 83, 244.
Zoller, Matthias, 121.
Zollikon, 73.
Zörnli, ——, 89.
Zschokke, the historian, 234, 244, 245, 254, 290.
Zug, 38, 41, 46, 61-63, 65, 69-70, 72, 82, 104, 136, 143, 144, 160, 186, 187(2), 208, 209, 224, 243, 253, 254, 265, 269.
— church of St. Oswald in, 124.
— enters the League, 59-62.
— lake of, 4.
— the quay in, 289.
Zur Frauen, family of, 50.

Zurich, 5, 6, 10(2), 18, 20, 22, 24, 26, 27, 33, 35, 37, 38, 40(3), 41, 42(5), 44, 45(2), 61, 62, 65, 66, 68(2), 70(3), 72, 73, 77, 84-87, 92-95, 100, 101, 104-106, 116-119, 122, 123, 124, 128, 136-145, 151-158, 162, 164, 165, 167(4), 170-174, 176, 178-181, 184-187, 189, 190, 192, 193, 195-202, 204(2), 205, 207-209, 212, 214(2), 221, 223(2), 227, 228, 230(2), 232, 234, 235, 237, 241(2), 243-245, 247-251, 253-255, 257, 259-264, 266, 267, 283, 285(2).
— abbey of, 34.
— burgomaster of, 68, 106, 114, 174, 180, 258.
— canons of, 49, 91, 122, 127.
— *Carolinum* in, 18, 133, 153.
— *Chorherrenstift* (Institute of Canons) in, 18, 132.
— Compromise of, 150.
— *Constafel* of, 70, 105(2).
— council of, 68, 70, 107, 128, 132(2), 133, 135, 179, 249.
— counts of, 22.
— Diets held at, 22, 238, 240, 256.
— duke of, 26.
— enters the League, 59-62.
— first railway from, 292.
— *Fraumünster* at, 18, 19, 31, 48, 73.
— government of, 214, 219, 283.

Zurich, *Grossmünster* in, 18(2), 36, 73, 133.
— houses in:
    Zum Loch, 18.
    Zur Krone, 201.
    Zur Meise, 201.
— industries in, 151, 199, 235.
— institutions in, 236, 258.
— lake of, 2, 4, 16, 22, 86, 91, 106, 173, 214, 219, 224, 232, 235, 248.
— League of, 71.
— massacre of, 60.
— Old War of, xii, 84, 88-91, 109, 127.
— Polytechnic in, 276, 290.
— *Rathaus* in, 188.
— Reformation in, 130-135, 150.
— sieges of, 61, 62-64, 230.
— university of, 261.
— *Wasserkirche* in, 124, 189.
— *Wellenberg* in, 107.
Zurichgau, the, 17.
Znrlauben, family of, 208.
Zurzach, 7, 123.
Zwier, General, 178.
Zwingli, Bartholomew, 130.
— Ulrich, 130-135, 137(7), 138(2), 139, 140, 141(3), 143(2), 144(3), 153, 154, 164, 181, 187.
— — death of, 143.
— — marriage of, 132.
Zwing-Uri ("Twing-Uri"), 51.

www.ingramcontent.com/pod-product-compliance
Lightning Source LLC
Chambersburg PA
CBHW030004240426
43672CB00007B/822